Read This First

The information in this book is as up to date and accurate as we can make it. But it's important to realize that the law changes frequently, as do fees, forms, and procedures. If you handle your own legal matters, it's up to you to be sure that all information you use—including the information in this book—is accurate. Here are some suggestions to help you:

First, make sure you've got the most recent edition of this book. To learn whether a later edition is available, check the edition number on the book's spine and then go to Nolo's online Law Store at www.nolo.com or call Nolo's Customer Service Department at 800-728-3555.

Next, even if you have a current edition, you need to be sure it's fully up to date. The law can change overnight. At www.nolo.com, we post notices of major legal and practical changes that affect the latest edition of a book. To check for updates, find your book in the Law Store on Nolo's website (you can use the "A to Z Product List" and click the book's title). If you see an "Updates" link on the left side of the page, click it. If you don't see a link, that means we haven't posted any updates. (But check back regularly.)

Finally, we believe accurate and current legal information should help you solve many of your own legal problems on a cost-efficient basis. But this text is not a substitute for personalized advice from a knowledgeable lawyer. If you want the help of a trained professional, consult an attorney licensed to practice in your state.

Nolo's IEP Guide:

Learning Disabilities

by Attorney Lawrence M. Siegel

First Edition	JANUARY 2004
Editor	LISA GUERIN
Illustrations	MARI STEIN
Book Design	TERRI HEARSH
Cover Design	TONI IHARA
Production	MARGARET LIVINGSTON
Index	THÉRÈSE SHERE
Proofreading	JOE SADUSKY
Printing	DELTA PRINTING SOLUTIONS, INC.

Siegel, Lawrence M., 1946-
    Nolo's IPE Guide : learning disabilities / by Lawrence M. Siegel.--1st ed.
        p. cm.
    Includes index.
    ISBN 0-87337-984-5 (alk. paper)
    1. Individualized education programs--Law and legislation--United States--Popular
works. 2. Learning disabled children--Legal status, laws, etc.--United States--Popular
works. I. Title: IPE guide. II. Title.

KF4209.3Z9 S573 2003
371.9--dc22

                                                    2003055786

For information on bulk purchases or corporate premium sales, please contact the Special Sales Department. For academic sales or textbook adoptions, ask for Academic Sales. Call 800-955-4775 or write to Nolo, 950 Parker Street, Berkeley, CA 94710.

Dedication

With love to Nancy, my wonderful sister and a heroine (long-standing) in the classroom—I'm not sure which of these two poses the greatest challenge to you.

Acknowledgments

The author wishes to thank Jim Orrell and John La Londe for providing an example of a comprehensive IEP document.

Thanks to Margaret Livingston, for her meticulous production and design work, to Toni Ihara, for a terrific book cover, and to Joe Sadusky, for his careful proofreading.

Much appreciation to Marcia Stewart for reading the drafts and adding her unique and strong thoughts to the package.

Thanks to Joe Feldman and the Community Alliance for Special Education of San Francisco, for their longstanding commitment to providing passionate and highly skilled, low-cost advocacy to children with learning disabilities.

Thanks to Joan Troppmann, the best RSP in California, for her kind and patient help.

And finally and in particular to Lisa Guerin, for her thorough, patient, highly professional and insightful editing of this book.

Table of Contents

Appendices

Index

1

Introduction to Special Education for Children With Learning Disabilities

The call I received, from the father of a child with a "learning disability," was not unusual. He was confused, overwhelmed, and angry.

"My 12-year-old has always done pretty good at school, is great at sports, and has friends, but the last year or so has been a mess. He's stopped doing his homework and his grades have gone south. He used to be a really outgoing kid, but now he's often quiet and moody. His teacher thinks he's depressed."

The pain and frustration in this father's voice weren't new to me. I've heard this profile from many parents, all of them concerned about their child and unsure what to do next.

"The teacher thinks my son has a learning disability. She said something about auditory memory and a processing problem. He has always been very meticulous, but now that he is in junior high, his homework seems to take all night and then he's even further behind. It sure seemed easier when I was in school, when there wasn't so much homework and kids didn't have to take so many standardized tests."

Homework and the quantification of American education. My opinions about how education has lost sight of its real purpose in the mad rush to show progress through numbers, the frustrations I have shared with my wife too many times, were ready for delivery, but that wasn't going to help this parent or his child.

"I don't know what to do. I don't know how to help him—and he won't listen to me, anyway. He was suspended last month for fighting and he no longer qualifies for the football team. We're no longer thinking of a good college for him—we just want him to make it through high school."

"Is your son in special education?"

"No, but you know, I'd be happy to pay your legal fees just to help with tonight's algebra. This learning disability stuff is so vague, its like a jellyfish. It isn't like a broken arm—we can't take my son to the doctor, get a cast put on him, and know that he'll be fine in a couple of months. How do you fix these auditory memory and processing problems?"

The pain of this father and son is shared by the more than two million children (and their parents) in this country who are dealing with learning disabilities. Late nights, bad report cards, tears, yelling, frustration—this wasn't what we thought school would be like for our kids.

The fundamental purpose of this book is to help these children and their parents or guardians through the maze that is special education—including the special twists and turns that apply to kids with learning disabilities.

A. What Is Special Education?

"Special education" is the broad term used to describe the educational system available for children with disabilities. A learning disability is a specific disability category covered by special education law and addressed by special education programs.

As discussed in greater detail later in this book, learning disabilities can range from minor differences in learning style to serious difficulties processing information. A lot of people, many of them highly intelligent, have learning disabilities. There is no relationship between native intelligence and the existence of a learning disability—indeed, the law defines a learning disability as a substantial gap between a child's intelligence and her actual achievements. But before you can get into the specifics of how to address your child's needs, you will have to understand how the special education system works.

There are three fundamental questions to consider as you begin the special education process:

- Where is your child now? How is your child doing at school and at home?
- Where do you want your child to be? What are your specific goals—for example, do you want your child to read more fluently, to write legibly, or to do his schoolwork more efficiently?
- What does your child need to reach these goals?

The federal law governing the special education system is the Individuals With Disabilities Education Act or IDEA. This law creates a formal process for evaluating children with disabilities (including learning disabilities) and providing specialized programs and services to help them succeed in school. IDEA entitles children with learning disabilities to an "appropriate" education that meets their unique needs. You'll have a better sense of what constitutes an appropriate education as you read this book. Broadly speaking, an appropriate education includes all of the following:

- The specific program or class (called "placement") for your child. Placement is more than just a particular classroom; it can also include characteristics such as location, class size, teacher experience, and peer make-up. For example, a child with Attention Deficit Disorder (ADD) might be placed in a regular classroom with a teacher who has experience working with kids who have ADD.
- The specific support help (called "related services") your child needs, including who will provide it and how often. For example, a child who reads well below grade level might work with a reading specialist for one hour each day.
- Other educational components, such as curricula and teaching methods. These can be particularly important for students with learning disabilities. For example, a child with dysgraphia (handwriting problems) might be allowed to answer test questions orally, rather than in writing.

But how do you figure out what constitutes an appropriate education for your child? Special education law provides a process for evaluating your child and developing her academic plan through an "individualized education program," or IEP. You'll find this term used frequently throughout this book and by your school district, your child's teachers, and others familiar with special education. The acronym IEP refers to several related things:

- the meeting where the school district determines whether or not your child is eligible for special education (referred to in this book as the IEP eligibility meeting)
- the annual meeting where you and school representatives develop your child's educational plan for the coming school year (the IEP program meeting), and
- the detailed written description of your child's educational program, including specific ways in which your child's learning disabilities will be addressed through programs, teaching strategies, and support services.

"Learning Disability" Is a Loaded Term

Webster's *New World Dictionary* defines disability as an illness, injury, or physical handicap that "restricts" or causes "limitations" and "disadvantages." Advocates in the field of special education and disability rights understandably object to the term "disabled," preferring the term "child with disabilities"—this is the term used throughout this book.

More important, all human beings come into this world with a variety of qualities and characteristics, strengths and weaknesses. Having special education needs does not mean that your child should be treated as "different" or denied the care and respect that all children deserve. Because human beings are complex, determining who is "able" and who is "disabled" is an effort in futility. Albert Einstein and Winston Churchill both had learning disabilities, but Dr. Einstein certainly had a way with the universe and, besides being a pretty good Prime Minister, Mr. Churchill was a fairly effective painter.

It is not a cliché to say that we all have some kind of disability, even as we realize that the difference in degree between one disability and another can be significant and life-altering. Terms that define should not be terms that judge.

Special education laws give children with disabilities and their parents important rights not available to children and their parents in regular education. These include the right to:

- have the child assessed
- attend an IEP meeting
- develop a written IEP plan, and
- resolve disputes with the school district through an impartial administrative and legal process.

While children's special education needs may vary—for example, one child with a learning disability may need placement in a private school while another needs a one-to-one aide for full-time participation in a regular class (called mainstreaming)—all parents should master the IEP process to help secure an appropriate and individualized education for their children. Even though the rules governing the IEP process are the same for each parent and child, your child's particular IEP will be entirely individual. The program you and the school district develop must fit your child, not the other way around. What works for other students is irrelevant if it won't work for your child. What may be appropriate for a child with hearing loss, autism, or emotional difficulties may not be appropriate for your child and his learning needs. IDEA does not tell you or the school district specifically how your child will be educated. Rather, IDEA provides rules to govern the process, so the IEP team can decide what is appropriate for your child. IDEA provides the outline; the IEP team—you and the school—fill in the details.

B. Special Education and Learning Disabilities

A child with a learning disability has different educational needs than a child with mobility problems or emotional difficulties. And different learning disabilities require different educational strategies—a child who has reading difficulties, for example, will need different types of assis-tance from a child who has trouble with auditory processing.

Within the world of special education, there are specific laws, rules, and requirements that apply to learning disabilities. A child with a particular learning disability may require specialized classroom techniques, strategies, and methodologies—for example, a child with ADD may need extra help when classroom activities generate lots of activity or noise, or a child with memory problems may benefit from using mnemonics to remember important facts. Later chapters explain what constitutes a learning disability, how it differs from other types of disabilities recognized by IDEA, and how a child becomes eligible for special education based on a learning disability. As you go through the special education process with your child, you will no doubt hear a variety of terms, such as Attention Deficit Hyperactivity Disorder (ADHD); auditory, short, and long-term memory problems; processing, spelling, reading, and math difficulties; and multisensory development. As is often the case, these words may sound intimidating and/or vague. If there had been IEPs in the 1950s, I'm fairly sure I would have qualified as an ADD student, but I'd prefer a term that conveys this a bit differently. I'm restless, my mind often deals with a dozen things at once and sometimes just plain wanders. I like the term "can't-sit-still-ism," but that is not quite precise enough (and anyway, it is long past the time when I would qualify for an IEP).

Regardless of whether we like these terms, they are part of the learning disability world—and you'll need to master them to become the best possible advocate for your child. As you go through this book, you will learn about broad special education rules and processes as well as specific items that relate to learning disabilities. You'll need both types of information to successfully navigate the IEP process. Don't worry about memorizing any of these terms; you'll become familiar and even comfortable with them as you move forward.

C. Being Your Child's Advocate

It isn't hard for most parents to advocate for their children—of course, all of us want the best for our kids. Still, becoming a successful advocate in the world of special education presents some challenges. The IEP process often seems like a maze—it can involve lots of technical information, intimidating professionals, and confusing choices. For some families, it goes smoothly, with no disagreements; for others, it is a terrible encounter in which you and your school district cannot even agree on the time of day. Families of a child with learning disabilities may have to argue with school officials over whether the child's problems amount to a disability; whether, for example, a child's inability to "stay focused" or "listen to instructions" is serious "enough." Your child may be painted as lazy, disruptive, or hard to control, rather than as a child with a learning problem. One teacher may think your child is a slacker, while another may be a saint who stays late and comes in early to give your child extra help.

Don't fall into the trap of thinking that teachers, school administrators, and experts know everything and that you know nothing. Respect their knowledge, experience, and opinions, but don't devalue your own. Right now, you may not have all the information you need and you may not know where to look for it. But the law states that you and your school district are equal decision-makers and that the school district must provide you with a good deal of information along the way.

You do not need to be a special education expert or a lawyer to be an effective advocate for your child. The general strategies for helping a child in the IEP process are not complex. The cliché that knowledge is power is absolutely true in the world of special education.

D. Using This Book

The purpose of this book is to help parents effectively proceed on their own through the IEP process, whether it's their first or fifth time through the maze.

This book will help you:

- understand special education law
- understand eligibility rules and the role of assessments in determining whether your child qualifies for special education because of a learning disability
- gather current information and develop new material about your child—in other words, become an expert about your child and how a learning disability affects him
- develop a far-reaching blueprint describing what would constitute the best possible program for your child
- determine your child's specific goals and educational needs as they relate to his learning disability
- gather current information and develop new material about various school programs, teaching strategies that work for children with learning disabilities, and options outside the school district
- prepare for the IEP meeting
- attend the IEP meeting and develop your child's IEP plan, and
- resolve disputes with the school district on your own or with the help of a lawyer.

Mastering these tasks will require you to be generally organized (but not fanatically so) and willing to ask questions and make use of resources that are widely available. The suggestions and forms in this book will help you stay on track throughout the IEP process.

Detailed appendices provide invaluable information, including:

- copies of key federal special education statutes and regulations
- addresses and websites of federal and state special education agencies

- addresses and websites of national and state advocacy, parent, and disability organizations, including those that provide specific help and information for parents of children with learning disabilities
- a bibliography of other helpful books, and
- two dozen tear-out forms, letters, and checklists to help you through every stage of the IEP process.

Using the Web and Other Resources

Throughout this book, I'll refer you to the Web for information about learning disabilities, support organizations, governmental agencies, and other resources that can provide you with valuable help as you try to learn more about your child's educational needs. If you don't have access to the Web, you should ask your school district administrator and the reference librarian at your local library for written materials on learning disabilities. Other good sources of information include your state department of education and national organizations on learning disabilities, listed in Appendixes 2 and 3.

Some of the material will be very familiar to parents who have been through many IEPs—you may already know the cast of characters and the basic legal requirements all too well. Still, you should review each chapter, even the ones that cover familiar territory. You may find fresh insights or new angles on old problems. Of course, you can skip material clearly not relevant—for example, if your child is already in special education, you don't need to prepare for an eligibility meeting.

If you are new to special education, very little in this book will be familiar to you. You might want to start by taking a quick look at the chapter titles and table of contents to become familiar with key ideas and how they relate to each other before you start reading.

The special education process has a discernible beginning and end. In general, it covers a year. There are similarities and differences between the first IEP year and subsequent years. For example, each year you will gather information and prepare for the yearly IEP meeting. But the first year always includes assessing your child and determining whether she is eligible for special education. In subsequent years, your child may or may not be assessed. Eligibility is not generally addressed after the first year, unless you or the school district feels a change is justified—for example, if your child no longer needs special education or may qualify under a different eligibility category.

What This Book Doesn't Cover

IDEA provides rights and procedures for children between the ages of three and 22. There is another procedure for children under three, but it isn't covered in this book. In addition, certain IDEA issues that involve very complex and detailed procedures—such as transition services to help children over the age of 14 prepare for a job or college and develop independent living skills—are only briefly discussed in this book.

If your child is not found eligible for special education under IDEA, she may still qualify for help under another federal law, Section 504 of the Rehabilitation Act. (Section 504 is briefly discussed in Chapter 7.) Many of the tips and strategies in this book will help you come up with an effective plan to help your child, even if she isn't eligible for an IEP. Because this book focuses on the IEP process, it doesn't cover Section 504 in detail.

E. Icons Used Throughout

The icons listed below appear throughout this book and are intended to help you more easily use the book.

 Books or organizations that give more information about the issue or topic discussed in the text.

 Related topics covered in this book.

 Slow down and consider potential problems.

 You may be able to skip some material that doesn't apply to your situation.

 A practical tip or good idea.

 A tear-out copy of the form discussed in the text is in Appendix 5.

 State law may vary on this issue.

F. Getting Help From Others

Other parents, local groups, and regional or national organizations can be a great help as you wend your way through special education. This is especially true when it comes to learning disabilities. The amount of information these folks have can be amazing. Other parents and parent groups can be your best resource—and certainly a source of support to help you through hard times and help you avoid mistakes or unnecessary tasks Most important, they can be a source of real encouragement. Chapter 15 provides further thoughts on making use of your local special education community.

Note: Reference is made throughout this book to parents, but I intend that term to include foster parents and legal guardians. ■

2

Your Child's Rights Under the IDEA

As mentioned in Chapter 1, a federal law, the Individuals With Disabilities Education Act (IDEA) furnishes a formal process for assessing children with disabilities and providing specialized programs and services to help them succeed in school. Special education is unique because of the central role parents play in determining their child's educational program. Under IDEA, the program and services your child needs will be determined through the individualized education program, or IEP, process. The term IEP is used to refer to a meeting about and a written description of your child's program. Your ability to understand and master the IEP process is central to your child's educational experience. Indeed, the IEP is the centerpiece of IDEA.

Although parts of IDEA refer specifically to learning disabilities, most of the law establishes general rules that apply to all children with disabilities. This chapter provides an overview of your child's legal rights in the special education process. Later chapters discuss each step in the IEP process in more detail—this chapter introduces the key concepts you'll need to know so you can understand how the whole system works.

The actual language of IDEA appears in this book. While this book provides plain-English descriptions of special education law, you can find the actual law as passed by Congress in Appendix 1. IDEA is found in the United States Code starting at 20 U.S.C. § 1400. Key sections of IDEA's regulations (these are in the Code of Federal Regulations at 34 C.F.R. §§ 300.1 to 300.756) are also in Appendix 1. The U.S. Department of Education wrote these regulations to provide guidance on how IDEA should be implemented. This book refers to these regulations frequently—they generally include greater detail than the statutes.

Don't let the word "law" throw you: The actual language of the IDEA—and more important, its underlying purpose—can easily be mastered. The legal concepts in IDEA are logical and sensible.

The IEP is a process and a document. The Individualized Education Program or IEP is the centerpiece of the special education process. IEP refers to two related things: It's a meeting at which you and the school district will develop your child's individual program for special education, *and* a written document that provides the details of your child's program. See Section B, below, for more information about the IEP.

A. What IDEA Requires

The purpose of IDEA is to ensure that children with disabilities receive an appropriate education. To achieve this goal, IDEA imposes a number of legal requirements on school districts.

Keeping Up to Date

IDEA was passed in 1975 and revamped (technically called "reauthorized") in 1997. Like many laws, IDEA is subject to change—in fact, as this book goes to press, IDEA is going through another reauthorization. Some of the anticipated changes could affect how schools discipline students with disabilities, how frequently a child is assessed, and whether attorney's fees will be awarded to parents who prove that a school district violated the law. Be sure to check the resources and links found in Appendix 3 for updates and information on IDEA reauthorization.

1. Eligibility and Assessments

Every school district has the legal duty to identify, locate, and evaluate children who may be in need of special education. This duty extends to children who have no fixed address (such as migrant or homeless children) and children who may be advancing from one grade to the next but nonetheless need special education. (20 U.S.C. § 1412(a)(6)(B)(7); 34 C.F.R. § 300.125; see Appendix 1.) Once a child is identified as possibly needing help, the school district must evaluate him to determine whether he's eligible for special education. The school must provide special education programs and services, but only *after* a child is found eligible.

IDEA has 13 distinct disability categories, each with its own set of detailed requirements. You can find the rules for the learning disability category at 34 C.F.R. § 300.541 ("Criteria for determining the existence of a specific learning disability"). These rules are covered in detail in Chapter 7.

IDEA defines "children with disabilities" as individuals between the ages of three and 22 who have one or more of the following conditions (20 U.S.C. § 1401(3)(26); 34 C.F.R. § 300.7):

- autism
- blindness
- deafness
- emotional disturbance
- hearing impairment
- mental retardation
- multiple disabilities
- orthopedic impairments
- other health impairment (including Attention Deficit Disorder [ADD] and Attention Deficit Hyperactivity Disorder [ADHD])
- specific learning disability (34 C.F.R. § 300.7(c)(10))
- speech or language impairment
- traumatic brain injury
- visual impairment

 You'll notice that Attention Deficit Disorder (ADD) and Attention Deficit Hyperactivity Disorder (ADHD), often thought of as learning disabilities, are listed under the category of "other health impairments" rather than as "specific learning disabilities." Chapter 3 discusses these distinctions.

For your child to qualify for special education under IDEA, he must have one of the 13 listed disabilities *and* the disability must "adversely affect" his educational performance. (See Chapter 7 for more information on eligibility.)

 The IEP must address all of your child's disabilities, including her learning disability. Keep in mind that children with learning disabilities often have other qualifying conditions or characteristics. If you suspect that your child has learning disabilities but he ultimately qualifies for special education in another category, his learning disability needs can still be addressed in the IEP.

Your child has a right to an initial evaluation or assessment to determine whether she has a disability as defined by IDEA, as well as a reassessment at least every three years. If you are not satisfied with the initial evaluation or you feel that your child's disability or special education needs have changed, your child is entitled to more frequent assessments and even independent assessments conducted by someone who isn't affiliated with the school district (20 U.S.C. § 1414; 34 C.F.R. §§ 300.530-543).

 Eligibility for learning disabled children is discussed in detail in Chapter 7. Assessments are described in Chapters 6 and 8.

2. Educational Entitlement

Once your child qualifies for special education under IDEA, she is entitled to a free appropriate public education (FAPE), individually tailored to meet her unique needs (20 U.S.C. § 1401(8)(25)).

 Chapter 5 explains how to develop a blueprint of your child's program and service needs.

IDEA requires the educational program to fit your child, not the other way around. For example, it is not appropriate for a school district to place your child with a learning disability in a class of emotionally disturbed students unless that placement meets your child's unique needs. Without your approval or evidence that such a placement was appropriate, this would not be an individually tailored IEP. The classroom setting, teaching strategies, and services provided for the emotionally disturbed children would not be appropriate for your child. "Appropriateness" is the standard for evaluating every aspect of your child's education—the goals, services, and placement.

Of course, real school programs don't always match legal mandates, so you may have to be vocal and insistent to get what your child needs. Remember, too, that the IEP team must decide together what is appropriate and what constitutes an individually tailored program. One member of the team—be it the parent or the school administrator—can't make that decision alone.

"Appropriate" Doesn't Necessarily Mean "Best"

The law does not require your school district to provide the very best or the optimum education for your child—the school district need only provide an appropriate education. "Appropriate" is an elusive but tremendously important concept. It comes up a lot in IDEA and throughout the IEP process. For one child, an appropriate education may mean a regular class with minor support services, while a hospital placement might be appropriate for another.

Your school district may tell you, in effect, that "we only have to provide a Chevrolet, not a Cadillac." Broadly speaking, the district is right even if the analogy is rough. The devil is in the details: You don't have to accept a car that won't run, but you may have to go without a CD player. Whether a particular placement or service is appropriate will depend on your child's needs—and your ability to prove them. What constitutes an appropriate education will become clearer as you go through this book and develop a stronger sense of the kind of program your child needs.

3. Educational Placement

Decisions about your child's educational placement—the program or class where she will be taught—and related services (covered in Section 4, below) will take center stage in the IEP process.

a. Least Restrictive Environment

IDEA does not tell you or the school what specific program or class your child should be in; that is an IEP team decision. IDEA does require school districts to place disabled children in the "least restrictive environment" (LRE) that meets their individual needs. What is LRE for a particular child, like what constitutes an "appropriate education," will depend on that child's abilities and disabilities. Although Congress expressed a strong preference for "mainstreaming" (placing a child in a regular classroom), it used the term LRE to ensure that individual needs would determine each individual placement decision—and that children who really need a more restricted placement (such as a special school) would have one.

Placement vs. Program

The terms placement and program are often used interchangeably, but there are some differences in meaning. As used in IDEA, placement refers to the various classrooms or schools where a child may be. Program has a broader connotation: It includes not only where the program is located, but also the components of that program, including the services, curricula, teaching methods, class make-up, and so on. Placement and program components should both be addressed in your child's IEP.

IDEA states that a child should be in the regular classroom "unless he cannot achieve satisfactorily even with the use of supplementary aides and services." (20 U.S.C. § 1412(a)(5); 34 C.F.R. § 300.550.) LRE further requires that a child should be educated as close to home as possible and in the class she would attend if nondisabled (20 U.S.C. § 1412(a)(5); 34 C.F.R. §§ 300.550-552). If a child will not participate with nondisabled children in the regular classroom and in other school activities, the IEP team must explain why (20 U.S.C. § 1414(d)(1)(B)(iv)).

Because a learning disability is generally considered less severe than some other special education categories, the LRE for many children with learning disabilities will and should be a regular classroom. There is a much greater burden on school districts to prove that a child with learning disabilities should be placed in a more restrictive environment (such as a special class or a special school).

Is Mainstreaming a Legal Right?

Court decisions interpreting the least restrictive environment rule have been as varied as the children in special education. Some court opinions have concluded that mainstreaming is required by IDEA; other judges have ruled that it is "a goal subordinate to the requirement that disabled children receive educational benefit." *Doe v. Arlington*, 882 F.2d 876,878 (4th Cir. 1999).

The goals of mainstreaming and providing an appropriate education may conflict if a child needs very specialized curricula, intense services, specialized staff, or a protected environment. In this type of situation, the child's unique educational needs may go unmet if the child is mainstreamed.

What's clear from these court decisions is that mainstreaming is preferred, but there is no absolute right to either a mainstreamed or an alternative program. Whether the right to be mainstreamed is more powerful than the right to an appropriate education, or vice versa, will depend on the individual facts of each case.

b. Range of Placements

If a regular classroom placement is not appropriate for your child, the school district must provide what is called a "Continuum of Placement options"—a range of alternative placements. That continuum must include:

- regular classes
- regular classes for part of the school day
- special classes in regular schools—for example, a special class for children with learning disabilities
- special public or private schools for children with disabilities
- charter schools (34 C.F.R. § 300.212)
- residential programs

- home instruction, and
- hospital and other institutional placement. (34 C.F.R. § 300.551.)

If a child's unique needs dictate an alternative to a regular classroom, the continuum requirement ensures that the school district will make different placement options available. No matter where children are placed, however, IDEA requires every child to have access to the general curriculum taught in the regular classroom. The IEP must specifically address how this requirement will be met (34 C.F.R. § 300.347).

4. Support or Related Services

Related services, as listed below, are the educational, psychological, therapeutic, cognitive, and other services that will help your child meet his educational goals. These serves can be of paramount importance to children with learning disabilities, who are often placed in a regular classroom.

IDEA requires schools to provide related services for two reasons:

- to help your child benefit from special education, and
- to ensure that your child has the chance to "achieve satisfactorily" in a regular classroom.

Under IDEA, related services include:

- speech-language pathology and audiology services
- psychological services
- physical and occupational therapy (for example, help with fine motor skills, like handwriting and drawing)
- recreation, including therapeutic recreation
- social work services
- counseling services, including rehabilitation counseling
- orientation and mobility services
- medical services for diagnostic and evaluation purposes
- sign language or oral interpreter

- psychotherapy (for example, for anxiety or low self-esteem caused by a learning disability)
- one-to-one instructional aide
- transportation
- art therapy
- technological devices, such as special computers or voice-recognition software, and
- nursing and other similar medical care (20 U.S.C. § 1401(22) and § 1414(d)(1)(A)(iii); 34 C.F.R. § 300.24).

While any of these related services might be appropriate for a child with a learning disability, some common related services used by children with a learning disability include one-on-one work with an aide who can help the child with her particular learning disability (such as reading, mathematical, or comprehension problems), counseling when the learning disability leads to emotional difficulties, speech and language services to assist a child with language processing or speech problems, and occupational or physical therapy for children with small or large motor difficulties.

This is not an exhaustive list. Because everything under IDEA is driven by a child's individual needs, the IEP team has the authority to provide any service your child needs, even if it's not listed in the law.

Is a Medical Service a Related Service?

The question of what constitutes a related service has been debated since IDEA was enacted in 1975. One particularly difficult issue has been whether a medical service constitutes a related service, if it is needed for a child to benefit from special education. In 1999, the U.S. Supreme Court ruled that a medical service is a related service if it is limited to "diagnostic and evaluation purposes" (20 U.S.C. § 1401(a)(17)).

The Court also ruled, however, that other medical services might constitute related services under IDEA if they can be performed by a nonphysician. In the case heard by the Court, the child needed and was granted the services of a nurse to provide, among other things, daily catheterization, suctioning of a tracheotomy, and blood pressure monitoring. *Cedar Rapids Community School District v. Garret F.*, by Charlene F., 119 S. Ct. 992 (1999).

You might be asking—and rightfully so—why does it matter whether a physician or a non-physician provides the service, as long as the child needs it? While there are many reasons, courts are quite reluctant to require school districts to provide and pay for expensive, non-educational services. Traditionally, schools have not been responsible for providing services by doctors and psychiatrists. This raises an interesting and difficult philosophical question: What is the limit of a school's responsibility for meeting all of a child's needs?

5. Assistive Technology

IDEA requires that a child be provided with assistive technology services, defined as any item, piece of equipment, or system acquired, modified, or customized to maintain, increase, or improve the functional capabilities of a child with a disability. These services might include:

- evaluating how the child functions in her customary environment
- leasing or purchasing assistive technology devices
- fitting, maintaining, and replacing assistive technology devices
- using and coordinating other therapies, interventions, or services in conjunction with such technology, and
- training and technical assistance for the child, the child's family, and the educational staff.

An assistive technology device or service might be an augmentative communication system, a computer, computer software, a touch screen, a calculator, a tape recorder, a spell-checker, and books on tape. (See U.S.C. § 1401(1)(2); 34 C.F.R. §§ 300.305,306; and Appendix 1.) This part of the law may be especially helpful to children with learning disabilities—computer programs alone can provide opportunities for tremendous improvement in the educational experiences of these kids.

Section 504 of the Rehabilitation Act of 1973 and the Americans with Disabilities Act

Separate from any rights under IDEA, your child may also qualify for special services under the Rehabilitation Act of 1973 (29 U.S.C. § 794), more commonly known as Section 504, and the Americans with Disabilities Act, 42 U.S.C. § 12101, often referred to as ADA. Both Section 504 and ADA are intended to prevent discrimination against children with disabilities, although the laws impose different procedural requirements. Section 504 is essentially an access law that prohibits a school district from denying your child access to an educational program or educational facilities. Section 504 is covered briefly in Chapter 7; Appendix 1 includes key sections of the law.

6. Transition Services

IDEA requires the IEP team to consider, for a child who is 14 or older, vocational and advanced-placement needs and courses (20 U.S.C. § 1414(d)(1) (A)(vii); 34 C.F.R. §§ 300.29, 300.347(b)). Because some students with learning disabilities have difficulties developing independent living skills and/or pursuing college and employment options, there should be a transition IEP that focuses on your child's progress towards graduation and on those writing, reading, processing, and other skills needed to become an effective adult. For example, if your child's learning disability involves math difficulties, then transition services should focus on developing strategies for dealing with money and balancing a checkbook, consumer skills, and other activities that require calculation.

7. Due Process

In law, "due process" generally refers to the right to a fair procedure for determining individual rights and responsibilities. Under IDEA, and as used and discussed in detail in this book, due process refers to your child's right to be evaluated, receive an appropriate education, be educated in the LRE, have an IEP, and be given notice of any changes in the IEP.

Due process also refers to your right to take any dispute you have with your child's school district—for example, a disagreement about an assessment, eligibility, or any part of the IEP, including the specific placement and related services—to a neutral third party to resolve your dispute. These rights are unique to IDEA; children who are not in special education do not have them (20 U.S.C. § 1415; 34 C.F.R. §§ 300.500-517).

There are two options for resolving disputes through due process: mediation and a due process hearing. Mediation is a process in which you and the school district meet with a neutral third party who tries to help you come to an agreement. The

mediator has the power of persuasion, but no authority to impose a decision on either side.

If you cannot reach an agreement in mediation (or prefer to skip mediation altogether), you can request a fair hearing, in which you and the school district present written and oral testimony about the disputed issues before a neutral administrative judge, who will decide who is right and issue an order imposing a decision on all parties. Both you and the school district have the right to appeal the decision to a federal or state court, all the way to the U.S. Supreme Court. But before you conjure up images of walking up the marble stairs to the highest court in the land, you should know that most disputes with school districts are resolved before a hearing (and certainly before you find yourself in a courtroom).

Chapter 12 discusses in detail how to resolve disputes through mediation or a fair hearing.

If you believe that your school has violated a legal rule—for example, by failing to hold an IEP meeting—you should file a complaint. The complaint process is quite different from due process. A due process matter involves a factual dispute between you and the school district. A complaint alleges that the district failed to follow the legal requirements of IDEA. (See Chapter 13 for a more detailed discussion of complaints and how they differ from due process proceedings).

8. Suspension and Expulsion

Some children with learning disabilities have trouble behaving themselves in school. Like all other kids, children with learning disabilities sometimes act out, try to get attention in the wrong ways, or are more interested in their friends than their schoolwork. But, sometimes, children with learning disabilities have behavioral problems that are directly related to their disabilities. A child with ADD who can't pay attention in class, a child whose reading difficulties lead to immense frustration, or a child whose processing problems make it hard to follow a teacher's instructions can create disciplinary problems. A child who has secondary emotional difficulties because of a learning disability may be disruptive or even get into fights as a result of her learning disability. How can schools balance their responsibility to maintain order with their duty to provide an appropriate education for children with disabilities?

Most states have laws and procedures about disciplinary action—including suspension and expulsion—quite separate from the special education laws and procedures. These disciplinary rules apply to all students within a school district. For special education students, however, these rules must be applied in conjunction with the laws and procedures of IDEA, including specific protections that apply when a child with a learning disability is subject to suspension or expulsion. Like all children in school, your child must follow the rules; if she does not, she may be suspended or expelled. Before the school district can take this type of action, however, IDEA requires a very careful analysis of whether her disability played a role in her behavior and, if so, whether suspension or expulsion is really justified.

When IDEA was reauthorized in 1997, Congress included many new rules regarding the suspension and expulsion of special education students. Although these rules provide specific rights and procedures for children in special education who are subject to discipline, Congress clearly intended to allow school districts to remove students who misbehave or are dangerous.

The IDEA rules and procedures applicable to suspensions and expulsions are pretty complicated—and the stakes for your child in these situations are potentially very high. This section provides an overview of this area of the law, but you'll probably want to contact a parent support group or special education lawyer if your child faces serious disciplinary action. This is one situation in which you shouldn't try to go it alone.

a. IDEA and Disciplinary Action

IDEA provides that a student with an IEP cannot have his program, placement, or services changed unless the school district and the child's parents agree to the change. Absent such an agreement, the child is entitled to remain or "stay put" in his current program until either a new IEP is signed or a hearing officer decides that the child's program can be changed. (20 U.S.C. § 1415(j); 34 C.F.R. § 300.514.) The school district cannot remove your child or unilaterally change your child's program—if it tries to do so, you can assert your child's "stay put" right to maintain his current placement until a new IEP is in place or a hearing officer approves the change. This very broad rule is intended to prevent a school from moving a child without parental approval.

A proposed suspension or expulsion clearly constitutes a change in placement, and this is where state laws on suspension and expulsion run directly into IDEA requirements. Can a school district suspend or expel (remove the child from school) without violating the "stay put" rule? The answer is, as you probably expected, yes and no. The law clearly states that a child with disabilities can be suspended or expelled, but the suspension or expulsion cannot take place unless certain IDEA procedures are followed. (20 U.S.C. § 1415(j)(k); 34 C.F.R. §§ 300.520-529.)

Congress created different rules depending on the length of the suspension or expulsion. This part of IDEA is fairly complex, but, generally, children who are facing more than ten days out of school have more procedural protections under the law.

b. Suspensions or Expulsions for Up to Ten Days

Any special education child removed from school for *up to ten consecutive days* is not entitled to the IDEA procedures and protections. Because such a removal does not constitute a "change in placement," the child cannot claim her "stay put" right. Since many suspensions are for fewer than ten consecutive days, most special education students who are suspended do not have the right to contest that removal based either on IDEA's "stay put" rule or on IDEA's specific disciplinary procedures. In short, a child with disabilities can be suspended from school for up to 10 days just like any other student.

c. Suspensions and Expulsions Exceeding Ten Days

If a school district intends to suspend or expel a special education student for more than ten consecutive days, that *might* constitute a "change in placement." In these situations, additional IDEA procedures kick in before the child can be removed. These procedures might also apply to a child who is removed from school for more than ten nonconsecutive days, if the removal represents a "pattern." What is meant by a "pattern?" The law isn't very clear, but essentially you have to look at whether the frequency and length of the removals—and the total time the child is out of school—create a change in placement similar to that caused by a removal for more than ten consecutive days. Courts have begun to issue some decisions on what constitutes a "pattern," but this is still a vague and uncertain part of the disciplinary process—and one good reason why you will probably want to talk to an expert and/or attorney if your child is in this situation.

Once a special education student is to be removed for more than 10 days (whether consecutively or over a longer period of time), specific IDEA procedures kick in to protect the child. Before the removal takes place, an IEP team must hold a "manifestation" review to decide whether the student's behavior was a manifestation of his disability. If the IEP team determines that the behavior was a manifestation of the child's disability, then the student's placement cannot be

changed except through an agreed-to IEP (signed by the school district and the parents) or a fair hearing decision. The child can remain in his current placement and assert his "stay put" right (no change without an IEP agreement or fair hearing decision). The student cannot be suspended (for more than 10 days) or expelled unless the school follows IDEA procedures for a change in placement.

If the IEP team determines that the behavior was not a manifestation of the disability, the child has no "stay put" rights and can be removed. To reach this conclusion, however, the team must decide that all three of the following statements are true:

- In relationship to the behavior that led to the disciplinary action, the IEP placement and services were appropriate and behavior intervention strategies were provided consistent with the IEP.
- The child's disability did not impair his ability to understand the impact and consequences of the behavior.
- The child's disability did not impair her ability to control the behavior subject to the disciplinary action.

(34 C.F.R. § 300.523.)

d. Dangerous Behavior

IDEA makes an exception to the ten-day rule for disciplinary problems involving weapons or drugs. If a special education student brings a weapon to school or possesses, uses, sells, or solicits the sale of drugs at school or during a school function, she can be removed for up to 45 days without parental agreement. This means the student cannot assert her "stay put" right and argue that she is entitled to remain in her current placement pending the conclusion of the required IDEA disciplinary procedures. The student is entitled, however, to an "interim alternative placement" as determined by the IEP team.

e. Related Requirements

As a general rule, IDEA requires the IEP team to develop a "behavioral intervention" plan for those students whose behavior "impedes his or her learning or that of others." (34 C.F.R. § 300.346(a)(2)(i).) It would not be surprising if a special education student facing suspension or expulsion had such a plan in his IEP. If a student is removed for more than ten days, IDEA also requires the IEP team to do a "functional behavioral assessment" and implement a "behavioral intervention plan" if one is not already in place.

For a child with a learning disability whose condition impairs his ability to relate to others or behave appropriately, the plan should address those needs and provide strategies for helping that student improve his peer relationships and/or his school behavior. For example, a child who takes out the frustration of her learning disability by lashing out at other students might be taught alternative methods to express her frustration, such as talking to a counselor, taking a "time out," or expressing her anger more constructively ("I don't like it when you interrupt me when I'm speaking in class").

For lots of great ideas on dealing with disciplinary and behavior problems, as well as detailed information on drafting behavioral intervention plans, check out the website of the Center for Effective Collaboration and Practice (a group dedicated to helping students, teachers, and parents address emotional and behavioral concerns) at http://cecp.air.org.

9. Additional IDEA Rights

IDEA also gives children the following rights.

a. Summer School

IDEA requires the school district to provide your child with summer school (called an "extended school year") if necessary to meet his needs or if, without summer school, his skills will decline because of the pause in program and services. (See 20 U.S.C. § 1412 (a)(1); 34 C.F.R. § 300.309; and Appendix 1.)

b. Private School

IDEA gives your child the right to be placed in a nonprofit or private (including parochial) school if your school district cannot provide an appropriate program. (34 C.F.R. §§ 300.302, 349, 403, 450-462.) IDEA does not give your child an automatic right to attend a private school (often referred to as a NPS), however, and it is generally difficult to get a private placement—particularly for kids with learning disabilities, whose needs may not be severe enough to warrant a NPS. Under IDEA, school districts are required to show that they cannot serve a child before they are allowed to place and pay for a child in a private school.

Although there are impediments to securing a NPS, it is certainly possible. Your child's needs and the nature of the available public programs will largely determine whether a NPS is appropriate and feasible. If you feel that your child needs a private placement, you should certainly pursue it through the IEP process. (See Chapter 12 for more information.)

There must be either an IEP agreement or a due process or court ruling that the private school is appropriate before the school district is required to pay for a private school placement. If you place your child in a private school on your own, your school district is not required to pay. See "IDEA Notice Requirements and Private School Placements," below.

IDEA does require, however, that school districts offer special education and related services in a public program to a child whose parents have placed him in a private school. The rules on this are fairly complicated. While IDEA allows the school district to provide those special education services at a private (including a parochial) school if it so chooses, the law also limits how much money the district can spend on such special education and services (20 U.S.C. § 1412(a)(10).) Most courts have ruled that while a district must make related services available to a child placed in private school by her parents, the services need not be provided *at* the private school, but at an appropriate public school site. The regulations differ for school-placed and parent-placed private school children. (34 C.F.R. §§ 400.400-403, 450-462.) Because private school placement can get complicated, you should contact a special education attorney or one of the support groups listed in Appendix 3 if your child is in this situation.

IDEA Notice Requirements and Private School Placements

If you plan to remove your child to a private program, you must notify the school district of your intent either:

- at the most recent IEP meeting you attended prior to removing your child from public school, or
- at least ten business days before the actual removal.

(20 U.S.C. § 1412 (a) (10) (C).)

If you don't provide this notice, your request for the school district to reimburse you for the cost of your child's placement in a private school may be denied, or you may receive only partial repayment.

---

c. Special Education in Prison

Imprisoned children between the ages of 18 and 21 who were identified and had an IEP prior to incarceration are also entitled to a free appropriate public education. (34 C.F.R. § 300.311.)

B. Individualized Education Program

The IEP may seem complicated—after all, the term refers to a meeting, a document, and a description of your child's entire educational program. While the IEP is discussed in detail in Chapters 10 and 11, here are a few introductory concepts to help you get started:

- By law, you are an equal partner in the IEP process. As a general rule, no part of the IEP can be implemented without your approval or that of the school district.
- Your child's entry into special education will follow an initial eligibility IEP. Thereafter, IEP meetings will be held yearly, focusing on your child's current educational program and what next year's IEP will look like.

While the procedures for these two kinds of IEPs (referred to as eligibility and program IEPs) are the same, there are some important differences—see Chapters 7, 10, and 11.

- You and the school district must agree to and sign a written IEP document before your child either begins special education or begins a new school year.
- Whenever you or your child's school district wants to change your child's current IEP, the district must schedule a new IEP meeting and develop a new written IEP.
- You are entitled to an IEP meeting whenever you feel one is needed—for example, if you have concerns about your child's progress, there are classroom problems, or the related services or placement are not working.
- Once signed by you and the school district, the IEP is binding; the school district must provide everything included in that IEP.

 The written IEP and IEP meeting are discussed in detail in Chapters 9, 10, and 11. Appendix 4 includes a sample IEP form.

This section provides details about the written IEP. Although forms will vary, every IEP, in every school district in every state, must include the same IEP information.

1. Current Educational Status

The IEP must include a description of your child's current status in school, including cognitive skills, linguistic ability, emotional behavior, social skills and behavior, and physical ability. (20 U.S.C. § 1414(d)(1)(A)(i)(I); 34 C.F.R. § 300.347(a)(2); 34 C.F.R. § 300.347(a)(1).) Current functioning may be reflected in testing data, grades, reports, or anecdotal information, such as teacher observations. IDEA calls this the "present level of educational performance." This part of the IEP must describe how your child's disability affects her involvement and progress in the general curriculum.

Formal testing or assessments of your child will provide a good deal of the information necessary to describe your child's current educational status. Chapters 6 and 8 cover assessments and other information-gathering tools you can use to develop useful evidence of your child's needs.

2. Goals and Objectives

Goals and objectives are the nuts and bolts of your child's daily program as detailed in the IEP. They generally include academic, linguistic, and other cognitive activities.

> Example:
> **Goal:** John will increase his reading comprehension.
> **Objective:** John will read a three-paragraph story and answer eight out of ten questions about the story correctly.

While goals and objectives are usually academic and cognitive in nature, there are few rules about what constitutes a proper goal or objective. IDEA refers to them as "measurable annual goals, including benchmarks or short-term objectives" related to your child's specific educational needs and involvement in the general curriculum, if appropriate. (20 U.S.C. § 1414(d)(1)(A)(ii); 34 C.F.R. § 300.347(a)(2); 34 C.F.R. § 300.347 (a)(1).) They should reflect whatever the IEP team determines is important to your child's education. Goals and objectives can relate to specific subject areas—reading, spelling, math, or history—as well as physical education, how your child socializes with peers, emotional needs, and even how your child will move about the school.

Whether or not your child is receiving a "free appropriate public education" (FAPE) may depend on whether the program offered by the school district can help her achieve her goals and objectives. If you and the school district disagree about whether a specific placement or service is necessary, a key issue will be whether your child's goals and objectives can be met without that placement or service.

Because writing goals and objectives is so important, all of Chapter 9 is devoted to the topic. That chapter shows you how to write goals and objectives that address your child's learning disabilities and support his placement and service needs.

3. Instructional Setting or Placement

The IEP must include information about the appropriate instructional setting or placement for your child. Section A3a, above, discusses LRE and various placement options; here are a few examples of IEP placements:

- A child with significant learning disabilities might be placed in a regular classroom with support services, such as assistance from a one-on-one aide.
- A child with significant language and cognitive delays might be placed in a special class.
- A child who is terrified of large spaces and crowds could be placed in a small, protected nonregular school.
- A child with serious emotional difficulties might be placed in a residential program.

A child with learning disabilities can be placed in any of these classes or programs, depending on the severity of need, although children with learning disabilities are less likely to be placed in the more restrictive placements, such as separate schools or residential programs. Many children with learning disabilities are placed in regular classrooms; however, those placements may require some fine-tuning to meet your child's needs. For example, your child may need a seat near the front of the class, a note taker, more time to take tests or complete homework, specialized curricula, or the opportunity to use a computer for writing assignments.

4. Related Services

As mentioned in Section A, above, related services are developmental, corrective, and other supportive services necessary to facilitate your child's placement in a regular class or to allow your child to benefit from special education. These must be specifically included in the IEP.

Once the IEP team determines the appropriate related support services, the team should give details about each service, including:

- when it begins
- the amount (such as all day, once a day, twice a week, once a week, or once a month)
- the duration (such as 15, 30, 45, or 60 minutes per session)
- the ratio of pupils to related service providers, and
- the qualifications of the service provider.

5. Other Required IEP Components

As part of the 1997 reauthorization of IDEA (20 U.S.C. § 1414(d)(3)(B)(i)-(v); 34 C.F.R. § 300.347), the IEP must specifically address:

- how your child's disability affects her involvement and progress in the general curriculum used in the regular classroom
- how your child's need to be involved in the general curriculum will be met
- how special education and related services will help your child attain annual goals; be involved in the general curriculum, extra-curricular and nonacademic activities; and participate with children with and without disabilities
- how parents will be regularly informed of their child's progress
- how your child will participate in any district or statewide assessment of student achievement used for the general student body, and whether he needs any modifica-

tions or accommodations in order to take the assessment

- how your child's transition services will be provided, and
- how your child's need for assistive technology will be met.

For blind and visually impaired students, the IEP team must provide for instruction in Braille and the use of Braille, unless the IEP determines that Braille is not appropriate (20 U.S.C. § 1414 (d)(3)(B)(iii); 34 C.F.R. § 300.346(a)(2)(i)).

In addition, IDEA requires the IEP team to "consider" the following:

- strategies, including positive behavioral interventions, to address the needs of children with behavior difficulties (20 U.S.C. § 1414(d)(3)(B)(i))
- the language needs of children with limited English proficiency (20 U.S.C. § 1414(d) (3)(B)(ii)), and
- the communication needs of deaf and hard of hearing children, including opportunities for direct communication with peers and staff and instruction in the child's language and communication mode (20 U.S.C. § 1414 (d)(3)(B)(iv); 34 C.F.R. § 300.356(a)(2)(i)).

For more details, contact your school district, your state department of education (Appendix 2), or a disability group (Appendix 3). See Appendix 4 for a sample IEP.

6. Optional Components

The IEP may include other components, such as specific teaching methods, particular class subjects, or anything else the IEP team agrees should be included (20 U.S.C. § 1414(d)(1)(A)).

Examples:

- a specific methodology or teaching strategy designed to help your learning disabled child, such as a multisensory approach (see Chapter 5)

- pull-out services with a resource specialist to work on specific areas of need, like reading, math, or handwriting
- visual aids for a visually impaired child

C. State Special Education Laws

IDEA is a federal law, binding on all states. The federal government provides financial assistance to the states for special education; to receive this money, states must adopt laws that implement IDEA.

State laws generally parallel IDEA and often use identical language. State laws cannot provide a child with fewer protections than IDEA does—but they can provide additional rights (and some do). IDEA is always your starting point, but you should check to see what your state law says about special education—it may give your child more rights and options.

States Use Different Definitions of Learning Disability

State laws vary considerably in the way learning disabilities are defined; some states use the federal definition of learning disabilities, other states use different language. Your child's eligibility for special education may well depend on how your state defines learning disabilities—so make sure you know your state's rules. Eligibility is covered in detail in Chapter 7.

Each state's educational agency is responsible for making sure that local school districts comply with the federal law. While federal support for special education has been in the $5 to $8 billion range, states are under a lot of pressure to come up with special education funding, particularly given competing interests for education dollars.

When IDEA was enacted, Congress promised to pay approximately 40% of special education costs. Only 8% to 13% of those costs have actually been provided, however, which has created significant shortfalls for states and local school districts.

The special education funding process varies from state to state, but it is often complex. No matter how your state funds special education, remember this rule: Even though money (and how it gets from Washington to your state to your district to your child) should not determine the contents of your child's IEP, financial constraints affect almost all school districts. This is especially so today, when budget cuts and shortfalls have had a devastating impact on educational funding. As greater legal mandates and responsibilities are placed on schools and teachers, there appears to be no corresponding increase in the necessary dollars. Although politicians often complain that the federal government shouldn't just "throw money" at social problems, special education and education in general could certainly stand to have some money thrown their way.

More Information on State Special Education Laws

State special education laws (statutes) are normally found in the education code of each state. State departments of education often have their own regulations implementing the law.

Appendix 2 includes addresses, phone numbers and websites of state departments of education. When you contact your state's department, ask for a copy of your state laws and any publications explaining your legal rights (many are available online). Ask about the state special education advisory commission—IDEA requires each state to have one, composed of educators and parents.

Because laws and policies change, it is important to keep up to date, especially if you are involved in a dispute with your school. For more information on legal research, see Chapter 14.

D. Working With Your School District

Most, if not all, of your dealings will be with your local public school district, which has the legal responsibility for your child's IEP. Sometimes, however, special education programs are the responsibility of a larger educational unit, such as a county office of education. This is often the case when a school district is small or there are not enough children to establish a special education class. Always start with the school district where you reside. It has the ultimate responsibility for your child, even if there is a larger, area-wide agency involved. As used in this book, the term "local school district" refers to the responsible educational unit.

1. Key Players in the IEP Process

The key participants in the IEP process are:

- You.
- Your child (if appropriate).
- Your child's teacher—potentially your best ally or worst enemy in the IEP process. Because many children with learning disabilities will be in regular classrooms, this will often be the regular teacher or a resource specialist, because many children with learning disabilities may be pulled out of their regular class to work with a specialist on particular areas of need. (Older children, particularly those in junior or senior high school, may have a separate teacher for each academic class.)
- A school administrator with responsibility for special education—a site principal or special education administrator.
- Specialists, such as a school psychologist, speech or occupational therapist, communications specialist, resource specialist, or adaptive physical education instructor.
- Anyone else you or the school wants to attend, such as your child's physician, your

lawyer, the school's assessor, or an outside independent assessor you selected.

 Chapter 10 covers the IEP participants in detail, including their roles, who has authority, and who should attend the IEP meetings. It also explains how to prepare for the IEP meeting.

2. The Realities of Schools and Special Education

School districts and their special education administrators are as varied as parents. Their programs, services, and budgets will differ, as will their personalities. All of these factors influence what programs school districts have to offer and how they deal with children and parents. Depending on the population breakdown in the district, there may be many special education programs or only a few. Philosophical or pedagogical differences may have an impact on programs and services. Some administrators believe very firmly that most, if not all, children with disabilities should be mainstreamed or in regular education. Some administrators believe with equal vigor that special programs are important and that children with disabilities, more often than not, belong in special classes.

More Information on Special Education and Local Schools

Your school district is required by IDEA to provide you with a copy of federal and state statutes and regulations and any relevant policies. Be sure to request this information, along with the school's IEP form. Most school districts have some kind of parent guide, as do most states. Contact your school district for a copy.

Finding out what programs are available in your district, and what personalities and philosophies dominate, is important. Ask around. Talk to your child's teacher and other parents; go to a PTA meeting. Many school districts have a community advisory committee for special education; the parents involved in that group will likely know the specific programs, players, and philosophies in your school district. (See Chapter 15 for more information on parent organizations.)

It is not uncommon for parents to view school administrators and other staff as impediments rather than as partners in the special education process. Sometimes school personnel view parents as unreasonable and difficult.

While there are times when these viewpoints are justified, remember that a majority of educators are passionate, hard-working, and caring individuals. They teach in a complicated environment in which there is too much paperwork, too many requirements, and not enough support or pay. It's not fair or justified to demonize them—and it won't help you secure the best possible education for your child.

 Chapter 8 provides detailed advice on how to explore available school programs. Chapter 15 discusses parent groups.

No Child Left Behind

In 2001, Congress passed legislation called "No Child Left Behind" (NCLB). Because this law applies to all children, it will certainly affect how your child is educated. Since NCLB is not directly related to IDEA, however, it's not yet clear how it will impact special education.

NCLB's stated purpose is to increase "accountability" for schools by requiring rigorous state educational standards in reading and math and by mandating state testing to determine whether children are meeting those standards. Test results must be broken out by race, ethnicity, income, English proficiency, and disability. School districts that do not show yearly progress, as reflected in standards and testing, will be subject to corrective action and possibly even forced restructuring. Children who attend schools that are not making yearly progress will have the opportunity to transfer to other schools, including charter schools, and to obtain supplemental services.

Because NCLB is so new, nobody knows exactly how it will affect kids in special education. On the one hand, NCLB is not a special education law, and the programs and services available under NCLB are entirely separate from programs and services available through IDEA. On the other hand, certain parts of NCLB deal with topics of special importance to children with learning disabilities.

For example, one of NCLB's stated goals is to ensure that all children can read by the end of the third grade. To achieve this goal, the law increases funding for scientifically based reading instruction programs and provides grants for school districts to assess students in the K-3 grades to determine which ones are at risk for reading failure. Because developing reading skills is so important—and often so difficult— for children with learning disabilities, how your school district implements this part of NCLB could really affect your child's program.

Many educational advocates worry that NCLB imposes detailed accountability requirements, but insufficient funding to meet them— which could result in fewer dollars available for all educational programs, including special education.

The impact of NCLB on your child's program will depend on how your school district implements the law. Contact your district and your state department of education to find out how the law will be administered locally.

3

What Is a Learning Disability?

The term "learning disability" means different things to different people. In the most basic sense, a learning disability is a problem taking in, processing, understanding, or expressing thoughts and information, as reflected in difficulties with reading, calculating, spelling, writing, understanding or expressing language, coordination, self-control, and/or social skills development.

Beyond this basic definition, people use different terms to describe learning disabilities, depending on their area of expertise. The way a parent might explain a child's learning difficulties is often quite different from the labels a neurologist, psychologist, or educational specialist might use. And, as always, lawyers have their own set of technical definitions.

Mastering this terminology can be a challenge; you might wish you'd gotten a double major in law and neurology, with a minor in Latin. But don't worry—while you need to learn the basic terms specialists use for various kinds of learning problems, you don't need to become an expert in complicated jargon. While this chapter will help you understand the terminology various experts might use to "diagnose" your child, always keep your eye on the ultimate goal: to use these various definitions to make sure your child receives the individual help she needs to succeed in school.

Section A, below, covers the legal definitions of learning disability that are used in IDEA. These terms are vitally important for one reason: Your child must meet these requirements to qualify for special education. Section B, below, explains some of the technical terms used to describe and diagnose learning disabilities and the basic learning deficiencies and problems these terms cover. Section C, below, describes the first hints, signs and indications that your child might be struggling with a learning problem.

A. Legal Definitions

Your child will be eligible for special education only if his condition falls within the IDEA's definition of a learning disability. IDEA actually uses the term "specific learning disabilities" (see Section 1, below) to refer to most learning disabilities. IDEA does not classify Attention Deficit Disorder (ADD) and Attention Deficit Hyperactivity Disorder (ADHD) as "specific learning disabilities"—these conditions are addressed in a different section of IDEA. ADD and ADHD are covered in Section 2, below.

1. Specific Learning Disability

IDEA defines a specific learning disability as a "disorder in one or more of the basic psychological processes involved in understanding or in using language, spoken or written, that may manifest itself in an imperfect ability to listen, think, speak, read, write, spell, or to do mathematical calculations, including conditions such as perceptual disabilities, brain injury, minimal brain dysfunction, dyslexia, and developmental aphasia" (20 U.S.C. § 1401(26); 34 C.F.R. § 300.7).

In order for a child to be eligible for special education based on a learning disability, the IEP team must agree that he (1) "does not achieve commensurate with his or her age and ability levels" and (2) has a "severe discrepancy between ability and achievement" in one of the following areas:

- oral expression
- listening comprehension
- written expression
- basic reading skill
- reading comprehension
- mathematics calculation, or
- mathematics reasoning (34 C.F.R. § 300.541).

In other words, there must be a significant gap between what your child should be able to achieve in school, based on her age and general intelligence, and what she is actually able to accomplish in school, based on her grades, test scores, classroom work, homework assignments, and so on. Chapter 7 covers these criteria in detail, including various ways to show that your child has a severe discrepancy.

2. ADD/ADHD

Although many advocacy organizations designate Attention Deficit Disorder (ADD) and Attention Deficit Hyperactivity Disorder (ADHD) as kinds of learning disabilities, IDEA does not. Instead, IDEA classifies ADD and ADHD as part of a category it calls "other health impairment."

The "other health impairment" category lists ADD and ADHD as examples of conditions that result in limited strength, vitality, or alertness, "including a heightened alertness to environmental stimuli, that results in limited alertness with respect to the educational environment," due to a chronic or acute health problem. (34 C.F.R. § 300.7(c)(9).)

Of course, a child with ADD or ADHD might also have symptoms or difficulties that fall within the description of a specific learning disability. In these circumstances, the child might qualify for special education under either category. The important issue is not the name or label ascribed to your child, but how her condition affects her ability to learn. Once your child is found eligible for special education—under any of the listed categories—her IEP must address all of her educational needs, whether they are created by ADD, ADHD, or a specific learning disability.

B. Scientific and Professional Definitions

Beyond these legal definitions, scientists, educators, and other experts have their own ways of explaining and defining learning disabilities. You may run across these terms and ideas as you start trying to understand your child's problems (and what can be done to address them).

1. Organizational Definitions

Organizations and groups that specialize in learning disability education and advocacy use a variety of definitions to describe learning disabilities. The Learning Disabilities Association (LDA), for example, defines a learning disability as a "severe difficulty in some aspect of learning, speaking, reading, writing, or spelling." The National Center for Learning Disabilities defines learning disabilities as "neurological disorders that interfere with a person's ability to store, process, or produce information and create a 'gap' between one's ability and performance …. [and] can affect one's ability to read, write, speak, or compute math, and can impede social skills."

The Child Development Institute (CDI) acknowledges that there is "no clear and widely accepted definition" and notes at least 12 different definitions in professional literature. The CDI looks to factors that indicate a learning disability, stressing "difficulties with academic achievement and progress … an uneven pattern of development (language, physical, academic, and/or perceptual.)"

The University of Arizona SALT Center states that a learning disability "affects the manner in which individuals take in information, retain it, and express the knowledge and understanding they possess" as reflected in "deficits in reading comprehension, spelling, mechanics of writing, math computation, and/or problem solving."

2. Specific Learning Disabilities

In addition to the broad definitions of a learning disability found in IDEA and recognized by experts, there are specific learning disabilities whose names may be familiar to you. Some of the more well-known are:

- **Dyslexia:** problems with reading, spelling, and writing (including transposing letters and pronunciation difficulties).

- **Aphasia:** difficulties in processing information; more specifically, a limited ability to use or comprehend words, often as the result of a brain injury or a stroke. Someone with mild aphasia might have difficulty remembering the names of people or objects; more severe aphasia might impair a person's ability to speak or understand language at all.
- **Dyscalculia:** difficulties in calculating numbers or grasping mathematical concepts, such as algebra or geometric equations.
- **Dysgraphia:** difficulties with handwriting (including illegible writing, inappropriately sized or spaced letters, or spelling problems).
- **Dyspraxia:** difficulties with motor tasks, such as large movements (walking) or small movements (picking up a pencil or drawing).
- **Auditory processing disorder:** difficulties in understanding (processing) sounds; a child physically hears the word but can't understand its meaning or usage. A child with this problem might have trouble understanding spoken directions or following a conversation, or be easily distracted by noise.
- **Visual processing problems:** difficulties in understanding visual input; a child has no sight impairment but has difficulties in understanding and using visual information. A child with this problem might have trouble judging physical distance (including appropriate social distances—for example, the child might physically crowd others), differentiating between similar letters or objects, or understanding spatial relationships.
- **Short- and long-term memory problems:** difficulties in creating or retrieving memories (for example, trouble remembering facts, phone numbers, or assignments, difficulty following instructions).

Find Out Much More on the Web

You can find lots of helpful information about specific learning disabilities on the Internet. In addition to the many websites and organizations referred to throughout this book and in Appendix 3, you will find websites for many of the definitions and terms used in this chapter. If you go to your search engine and type in ADD or ADHD, aphasia, dyslexia, or any of the many other terms used here, you will find a number of useful sites. Just a few are www.add.org for the Attention Deficit Disorder Association, www.add-adhd-teen-help.com for Teen Help/ADD/ADHD, and www.aphasia.org for the National Aphasia Association. You can also go to www.ldaamerica.org (the Learning Disabilities Association of America), which provides a good deal of information about many different types of learning disability.

---

3. ADD and ADHD

ADD and ADHD are common behavior disorders characterized by a number of symptoms that often appear in early childhood and can continue into adulthood. The terms ADD and ADHD are often used interchangeably and the characteristics of each are often quite similar (if not identical). Some consider ADHD a subcategory of ADD.

ADD/ADHD is a syndrome or disorder often characterized by:

- inattention or inability to stay focused over a period of time
- impulsivity—a tendency to act without thinking, and
- hyperactivity—an inability to sit still and focus.

A child with ADD/ADHD may be easily distracted or squirmy, quickly shift from one activity to another, talk excessively and interrupt, have difficulty following instructions, be unable to wait her turn, engage in dangerous behavior, or lose things.

Treatment for ADD/ADHD

There is no "cure" for ADD/ADHD. Among the more common treatments for ADD/ADHD are medication—Ritalin is frequently used—as well as behavior modification or management training, socialization training, counseling, self-verbalization, and self-reinforcement.

Some children with ADD/ADHD can achieve significant improvement by taking medication. For other children, medication doesn't help—or leads to new problems. Medicating a child is, of course, a very serious matter. You don't want to go that route until you are absolutely sure it is appropriate as explained by your child's medical doctor. *Your child cannot be forced to take medication without your express permission.*

Children With Learning Disabilities May Have Other Special Education Needs

Like any other child, a child with learning disabilities can have other special education conditions or needs. A child with learning disabilities can be gifted, have emotional or behavioral problems, or have a hearing loss, limited vision, or physical disabilities.

A learning disability directly affects how a child does in school, including how she relates to peers. If the disability goes unnoticed or untreated, there can be emotional and behavioral consequences. A child may withdraw, have sleeping problems, or show signs of anxiety or fear. He may develop behavioral problems. You should watch your child for signs of secondary emotional and behavioral reactions—and share what you see with your school. If your child is found eligible for special education, the IEP must address all of her needs and conditions, not just her learning disability.

4. What Causes Learning Disabilities?

A learning disability can be the result of genetics, a brain injury, neurological problems, biochemical reaction, and perhaps even psychological issues. Current theories on ADD/ADHD, for example, indicate that it may be caused by chemical imbalance in the brain, genetics, brain trauma or damage, allergies, or neurological factors. The truth is that no one really knows what causes learning disabilities generally, although your physician might be able to pinpoint some of the reasons why your child has a learning disability and the effects of that disability, so you can get the support and develop educational strategies, programs, and resources your child needs to succeed. For more information on what causes learning disabilities, check the online and other resources in Appendix 3.

It's important not to get so focused on what "caused" your child's learning disability that you lose sight of the goal at hand: to get your child the help he needs. Your child will be best served by moving forward, not by looking backwards. We all come into this world with a set of characteristics, inclinations, conditions, and, yes, difficulties. Granted, some are more serious than others. A learning disability is not a neutral characteristic like hair color or height, but it is an understandable and common condition that does not mark your child for failure or you for blame. By following the procedures and strategies in this book, you can help your child deal with his learning disability in a successful way.

C. Does Your Child Have a Learning Disability?

Many parents have a strong sense, very early on, that their child has problems with learning, while others are surprised to hear from their child's doctor, teacher, or psychologist that the child may have a learning disability. Of course, learning disabilities might manifest in countless ways, depending on the type and severity of the disability, your child's personality, how your child is educated, and other factors.

1. When Will a Learning Disability Become Apparent?

Generally, the more severe the learning disability, the more likely it will be apparent at an early age. The difficulty for parents is to isolate what's going wrong and why.

As any parent knows, children develop at different paces. This means parents have to walk a fine line between missing a sign of a learning disability and overreacting to a delay that is simply part of your child's normal developmental timeline. Because school work becomes more complicated each year, some learning difficulties may not be evident in the earlier grades. For example, problems understanding abstract concepts may only become apparent when a child begins studying historical movements, scientific theories, or mathematical equations.

The earlier you find out about a learning disability, the better chance your child will have to develop strategies to minimize the disability's effect on his educational and social growth. While there is no hard and fast rule, it becomes exponentially more difficult for a child to catch up if his learning disability is identified only in the 4th or 5th grade rather than the 1st. The longer you wait, the more complicated and demanding school becomes—and the greater the impact of the learning disability on your child. If your child doesn't receive help, self-esteem, emotional, behavioral, and even physical problems may develop over time.

Learning Disabilities for Older and Younger Children

The earlier a learning disability is identified and assessed, the better. But, sometimes, a learning disability may go unnoticed until a child is older. The signs you'll see in a younger and an older child may be different. For example, a younger child will demonstrate problems in more basic processes, such as pre-reading, speech, listening, simple calculations, and early socialization (sharing, group play, or taking turns, for example). For an older child, the signs may be more complex and even more upsetting. There may have been a slow erosion of confidence, a year-by-year drop in grades and schoolwork.

Peer pressure and self-awareness is much more intense for a 14-year-old than for a six-year-old; the older child will probably be dealing with both the learning disability and the anger, fear, and embarrassment it generates. Older children with a learning disability may be much more self-conscious, more reluctant to face up to the difficulties they experience, and less willing to share those difficulties with you.

The needs of younger and older children with learning disabilities are also quite different. Younger children will be in one school environment all day, while older children will be going from class to class and perhaps receiving pull-out help for their learning disabilities. And for the older child with a learning disability, particularly in junior and senior high school, it will be important to consider his graduation plans, how he will take required exit and state exams, and his college and/or work plans.

2. Signs of a Learning Disability

You want to be aware of basic developmental stages and benchmarks so you can identify difficulties as early as possible.

a. Developmental Milestones and Benchmarks

Early signs of a learning disability include difficulty with spoken instructions, initial reading problems, handwriting difficulties, and spatial confusion. What's important is whether your child is significantly delayed in reaching important milestones, compared to other children of the same age. Here are a few benchmarks most pediatricians agree upon:

- A one-year-old should be able to reach for objects, roll over, stand with some support, follow objects, laugh, respond to "no," and use a crayon.
- By the age of two, a child should respond to other children, walk, use some words, recognize familiar persons, point, and understand some simple shapes
- A three-year-old should be able to move easily and go up stairs, be understood when speaking, use scissors, and draw pictures.
- By age four, a child should be able to catch a ball, copy shapes, count, identify some colors, dress herself, and play appropriately with peers.

Remember, children who are not learning disabled may meet certain milestones but not others, or may meet some more fully than others. No one milestone—met or missed—should either make you despondent or encourage you to fill out a Mensa application for your child. Try to keep a balance between being aware of important milestones (emphasis on the plural) and assuming the worst because your three-year-old's drawing of a dog looks more like a cow.

b. Signs of a Learning Disability for Children in School

If your child is already in school, there are some additional signs to watch out for, including:

- educational manifestations—difficulties in reading, writing, spelling, mathematics
- difficulties in processing, understanding, and expressing information through language
- neurological or memory problems, including trouble with auditory memory (remembering what is spoken), encoding information, and attending to stimuli, or limited ability to integrate, store, and retrieve information
- delays or difficulties in language or fine motor skills or understanding simple instructions
- social or emotional problems, such as trouble sleeping, eating, or getting along with the family
- difficulties paying attention or staying focused, including inappropriate or hyperactive behavior, or
- physical delays or difficulties, such as hearing loss, sight problems, or mobility or handwriting problems.

Misdiagnosis of ADD/ADHD

Sometimes, school representatives misconstrue signs of ADD/ADHD behaviors—including impulsivity, inattention, hyperactivity—as merely "bad behavior." Other times, children (especially boys) who are simply energetic and physical are presumed to have ADD/ADHD, without any further assessment. Either situation can be detrimental to your child. Armed with information about ADD/ADHD and your child's specific needs, you should be prepared to discuss with your school district why some of the more frequently misdiagnosed or missed ADD/ADHD behaviors are signs of a disability, not of laziness or poor behavior. If you think that the school district has mistakenly tagged your child with the ADD/ADHD "label," you should insist on an assessment as soon as possible (see Chapter 6).

3. Keeping Track of Your Child and Securing Professional Assistance

It can be very difficult for parents to figure out whether their child has a learning disability—and, if so, the type and severity of that disability. Your child is having difficulty in school or paying attention at home—what should you make of that? Is it a disability or is it just her unique way of doing things? Is he having trouble reading because of a learning disability or because his early reading program was inappropriate? What is the difference between a disability and the individual characteristics that may make your child a little less skilled in reading, but also make her a remarkable artist?

You should track your concerns about your child's progress, then consult a professional (in or out of school) to get some feedback. Here are some tips that will help you organize your thoughts:

- Keep a record of important benchmarks and milestones—including those listed above and others provided by your pediatrician—and note any areas where your child seems to be lagging significantly.
- Keep track of comments by others about your child's progress, including information provided to you by neighbors, teachers, doctors, or family members.
- Keep copies of all written information about your child, such as reports, report cards, and the statements of teachers and other professionals.
- Find out (from books, articles, and Web resources on learning disabilities) what your child's general skill level should be, and compare that to how he is actually doing.
- Ask your doctor, your child's teacher, and others whom you trust whether they think your child might have a learning disability.

As you begin this process, let me offer some advice: Stay vigilant, watch for signs, try to be objective, think things over before you panic, and be sure to talk to others, particularly professionals, *before* you jump to any conclusions.

How Serious Is Your Child's Learning Disability?

After finding out that their child has a learning disability, most parents want to know how "bad" it is. Of course, the answer depends on what type of learning disability your child has. Certainly, some learning disabilities are more serious than others. If a child has other disabling conditions, the learning disability can have a more complicated impact and be more difficult to address.

Even though your child's learning disability might make school difficult, it may not be as traumatic, ultimately, as many other disabilities. A learning disability is not the same as an emotional disturbance and probably not as life-affecting as the loss of one's mobility, hearing, or vision, for example.

With early intervention and help, your child can overcome her disability and become an effective, successful human being. Your child can go to college, play sports, be the school vice president, flourish academically, and have friends despite her learning disability. It may be harder for her than for some other students, but she can go as far as her talents and energies take her, if she receives the help she needs.

D. Learning Disabilities and the IEP Process

As noted in Chapter 2, the rights and procedures provided by IDEA apply to children with all kinds of disabilities. They provide a general structure within which each child's unique needs can be evaluated and addressed. Certain parts of the IEP process are especially important to children with learning disabilities, however. Each of these topics is covered in detail in later chapters of this book. For now, keep in mind that you'll want to pay special attention to:

- **Assessments.** Assessments are the tests and evaluations performed on your child to determine whether he has a learning disability—and, if so, what strategies will help him in school. They provide the evidence of a learning disability necessary to qualify your child for special education. Unlike physical disabilities, which are often obvious, learning disabilities can be tough to detect on casual observation—which is why assessments are so important. Assessments are covered in Chapter 6.

- **Eligibility.** Proving that your child is eligible for special education based on a specific learning disability can be pretty tough sledding. The basic concept is simple: You must show, through test results and other evaluations, that there is a significant gap between your child's intelligence (as measured by IQ tests) and your child's ability to achieve (as measured by achievement tests, grades, and so on.) However, the mathematical formulas used to measure this gap can be complicated. You'll find more on eligibility rules and formulas in Chapter 7.

- **Placements.** IDEA requires the school to offer a range of appropriate placement options. However, most children with learning disabilities will be placed in a regular classroom or perhaps in a special day class, unless they have additional, serious conditions that make a more restricted placement appropriate. You might be happy to have your child mainstreamed in a regular classroom, but you'll have to make sure that classroom is appropriate for your child. Placements are covered in Chapter 8.

• **Techniques and methodologies.** Kids with learning disabilities need different educational strategies from kids with physical disabilities. Methodologies for helping children with learning disabilities tend to focus on basic learning skills, such as reading, spelling, calculating, memory, and processing. Classroom strategies—such as placing your child's seat away from distractions or arranging for someone to take notes for your child—can also be effective. Methodologies are covered in Chapter 5.   ■

4

Getting Started

Y ou may have noticed very early in your child's life that she was not meeting certain developmental milestones. Or perhaps a teacher, pediatrician, neighbor, or friend pointed something out to you. The recognition may come as a surprise or even a shock. What does this mean for your child's immediate educational experience? What does it mean for the future? Will your child now be labeled as learning disabled? Will the learning disability lead to psychological, behavioral, or other problems? How can you help your child succeed—in school and beyond?

The process you are about to embark on can be hard and frustrating. There may be times when school personnel don't seem sensitive, caring, or knowledgeable about your child. Your child's difficulties may seem to persist—or even get worse. At times, the problems may seem insurmountable. There may be a teacher shortage, insufficient school funds, or ineffective program options. For all your preparation, you may feel like you're getting nowhere. There is no sugar-coating things—the IEP process can be hard.

There may be times when you ask yourself why this happened to your family. But if you plan, organize, and persevere, if you take small, daily steps (rather than try to solve the whole problem in one day), you will help your child. You may not make the school experience perfect, or even always tolerable, but your child will benefit from your efforts.

Whether you, your child's teacher, or another professional first discovers your child's learning problems, your school district has a clear legal responsibility under IDEA to ensure that all children with special education needs are identified, located, and evaluated. (See Chapter 2A.) Usually, this means that your child's teacher, school principal, or school psychologist will contact you, mention areas of initial concern, and perhaps suggest a meeting to discuss these concerns. The school will then likely recommend an assessment by a specialist in your child's disability. And if your district does not take the initiative, this chapter will help you get things started. Having your child assessed is the first major step in the special education process and ultimately the development of an IEP. (Chapter 6 discusses assessments in detail.)

Eligibility of Young Children (Ages Three to Five)

If your child is between the ages of three and five and is not yet enrolled in school, contact your local school district if you believe your child has a learning disability. Your child may be entitled to services under IDEA even though she hasn't yet started school. For example, a child with speech delays may be eligible for special instruction that focuses on language acquisition. To be eligible, your child must be experiencing developmental delays in physical, cognitive, communication, social, emotional, or adaptive development. (20 U.S.C. § 1401(3)(B)(i).) If your child is found eligible, the IDEA rules and IEP procedures outlined in this book will apply.

If your child has already been found eligible for special education or you have had experience with the IEP process, you can skip Section A. Even if you have been through the IEP process, however, be sure to read Sections B, C, and D, which explain how to gather and manage your child's records and keep track of deadlines. Even the most seasoned veterans of the IEP process will find these organizational strategies valuable.

A. First Steps

What's the first thing you should do if you believe your child is eligible for special education? This section provides some suggestions on how to get started. Keep in mind that although most children with learning disabilities experience difficulties at an early age, some do not run into real trouble until they are in junior or even senior high school.

1. Recognize Your Child's Special Learning Needs

It is very common for parents to realize that their child has unique needs but have no idea how those needs can be addressed in the educational process. It may be that your child's problems can be isolated and addressed fairly easily, or the problems may be more serious. But don't assume the worst; let the information you gather determine how serious the problem is and what you should do about it.

As any parent of a child with learning disabilities can tell you, there are lots of different learning disabilities that manifest in a wide variety of ways. Of all the categories of disability recognized by special education law, learning disabilities may be the hardest to define—even though children with learning disabilities make up the largest part of the special education population (in 2001, the U.S. Department of Education found more than 6.0 million children with disabilities in the United States, and 2.8 million with specific learning disabilities). The learning disability category includes lots of apples and oranges—dyslexia, ADD, ADHD, writing or calculating difficulties, memory problems, processing problems, letter or number reversals, spelling mistakes, language difficulties, organizational problems, or behavioral issues.

Instead of trying to diagnose your child's precise disability, focus instead on her needs: Does she have trouble understanding what she's reading? Does he struggle with basic math concepts? Does she have handwriting problems? Does he have difficulty remembering, understanding, and following spoken instructions? Here are some other behaviors or difficulties that might indicate a learning disability (Chapter 3 explains in more detail some of the signs of a possible learning disability):

- delays in developmental areas, such as language or fine motor skills (for example, the child can't use scissors, tie her shoes, or draw accurately)
- difficulties processing or retaining information, such as understanding simple instructions, or problems with short- or long-term memory
- trouble with organization, planning, and being on time (such as missing deadlines or failing to hand in homework)
- social or emotional problems (including trouble making friends or inappropriate emotional responses to events)
- trouble sleeping, eating, or getting along with the family
- sustained difficulties in paying attention or staying focused
- inappropriate or hyperactive behavior, or
- delays in physical milestones or other physiological difficulties, such as hearing or vision loss, poor coordination, difficulties with mobility, or handwriting problems.

Take notes on anything you can remember that might relate to these kinds of behaviors, delays, or difficulties. Don't worry at this stage about what might be "causing" these difficulties or what the proper term for your child's condition might be. Instead, focus on how your child's problems are manifesting themselves in daily life and in the classroom. Look at how your child performs basic tasks, at home and at school.

Don't Let Your Fears Hold You Back

Try to think clearly about your child's problems, even though you may feel some emotional upheaval or fear. You may feel anxious about the future. You may worry that you have done something wrong. These feelings are normal. Almost everyone who has had a child with a learning disability has felt exactly as you do right now.

The trick is to acknowledge your fears without letting them get in your way. No parent wants her child to face extra obstacles in life, but refusing to recognize potential problems won't make them go away. There is only one way to begin to get your child the help he needs to be successful—and that's to recognize which subjects, tasks, and behaviors give him trouble. Once you know where the problems lie, you can then figure out ways to address those problems effectively.

A True Learning Disability or Something Else?

Because learning disabilities can be hard to pin down, the category is sometimes used as a catch-all classification—one in which children are sometimes improperly placed. Many experts believe that the number of children categorized as "learning disabled" would diminish significantly if children were taught to read properly. In California, for example, there was a time when reading was taught using a "whole language" approach rather than a phonics-based system. Many children who later ended up in special education simply never learned to read (and not because of any learning disability). You should therefore talk to your child's teacher to find out whether other children in your child's age group are having similar difficulties, and whether those problems might be due to the way these children were taught rather than the way they learn.

Keep in mind that the above list of "symptoms" is not identical to the more specific and formal list of conditions that may qualify your child for special education (34 C.F.R. § 300.541; see Chapter 7). At this stage, your child may or may not qualify for special education. She may or may not be learning disabled. Right now, you should be less concerned about the specific eligibility category than with identifying those behaviors that raise red flags for you. Certainly some of those behaviors may indicate a learning disability, but further assessment and testing is almost always required to be sure. (See Chapter 6 for more information on assessments.)

A child who is currently having difficulty in school will not automatically qualify for or be placed in special education. There may be interim steps or non-special education solutions for your child. Those steps are discussed in Section A3, below.

As you begin to collect your thoughts, recollections, and observations about your child, you may also want to contact the school principal to request information about special education.

A sample letter requesting information on special education is below; a blank, tear-out copy is in Appendix 5.

Get into the habit of writing. You can always request information about special education by calling the school principal, who is likely to either provide you the information or refer you to the district's special education administrator. But the best approach is to make your request in writing. A letter is more formal, won't be forgotten as easily as a phone call, and creates a record of your contact with the school district.

Request for Information on Special Education

Date: _February 20, 20xx_

To: _Ronald Pearl, Principal_

Mesa Verde Elementary School

123 San Pablo Avenue

San Francisco, CA 94110

Re: _Amber Jones, student in 2nd grade class of Cynthia Rodriguez_

I am writing to you because my child is experiencing difficulties in school. I understand there is a special process for evaluating a child and determining eligibility for special education programs and services. Please send me any written information you have about that process. Please also send me information about how I can contact other parents and local support groups involved in special education.

Thank you very much for your kind assistance. I look forward to talking with you further about special education.

Sincerely,

Mary Jones

Mary Jones

243 Ocean Avenue

San Francisco, CA 94110

Phones: 555-1234 (home); 555-2678 (work)

2. Make a Formal Request to Start the Special Education Process

You can formally ask to begin the process of special education evaluation at any time. To start:

- Call your school and ask for the name and phone number of the special education administrator.
- Call the special education administrator and ask about the eligibility assessment process in the district.
- Follow up your phone call with a written request (and keep a copy for your records).

One letter or many—it's up to you. A sample letter making a formal request to start the special education process and conduct an assessment is below; a blank, tear-out copy is in Appendix 5. Other sample letters in this chapter make other requests. You can combine some or all of these requests into one letter, if you wish.

3. Gather Information

Whether you plan to begin the formal assessment process right away or wait a bit, you should start gathering information on your child and his learning problem. Here are a few good ways to start.

a. Talk to Your Child's Teacher

Find out what your child's teacher(s) thinks is going on and whether she can recommend any possible solutions. Here are a few specific questions to ask:

- What are the teacher's observations? What are the most outstanding and obvious problems and how serious are they? Does your child have a problem with math, reading, or broader cognitive issues (processing information or memory lags)? Does the problem have social or emotional manifestations?

- Does the teacher think that some adjustments in the classroom—such as extra attention from a teacher or aide, after-school tutoring, or measures to address behavioral problems—might help?
- What activities or strategies might be useful at home? Does she think that you need to spend more time on homework, focusing on certain subject matters?
- Has she consulted any other school staff? If so, what are their observations, conclusions, and recommendations?
- Does she believe the difficulties are serious and require more formal, special education involvement? If so, why and what are the next steps?
- Are there any specific signs of a learning disability, such as difficulty processing information, trouble understanding instructions or cues, reversing letters or numbers, inability to concentrate, trouble sitting still, or problems expressing thoughts?

If you and the school agree to go ahead with interim, non-special education steps, be sure to monitor your child's progress closely so you can determine whether they are working. Chapter 8B provides suggestions about tracking your child's progress.

b. Talk to Your Child's Pediatrician

Your child may have an organic or medical problem. While your pediatrician may not be an expert in special education, she can discuss your child's developmental growth (or lack of), other health-related matters that will affect the educational experience, and cognitive, physical, linguistic, and emotional factors that might affect special education eligibility and also suggest solutions. There are pediatricians who specialize in treating children with learning disabilities—if your own doctor doesn't know much about the subject, consider getting a referral to someone who does.

c. Talk With Other Parents

Talk to parents in your area, particularly those whose children have learning disabilities. Find out what experiences they've had and how they determined something was amiss. The local PTA should have information on parents with special education children, and most school districts have advisory committees of parents with children in special education. Call the school principal to find out more.

Chapter 15 explains how to find or start a parents' group. Appendix 3 has information on various national special education support groups.

d. Do Some Research

Look for written materials on special education, particularly for children with learning disabilities. A wealth of information is available online and in print. As you look into these resources, you'll see that they approach learning disabilities from very different perspectives. For example, this book focuses on how to navigate the special education process and develop positive and effective IEPs for your child. Other books focus more exclusively on the reasons for and nature of learning disabilities or provide significant detail on particular educational strategies for children with learning disabilities.

There is an ever-growing number of websites with general and disability-specific information. Enter "learning disabilities" into your favorite search engine and you will find a wide range of resources. Some of my favorite general sites are the National Center for Learning Disabilities at www.ncld.org, the Learning Disabilities Association of America at www.ldaamerica.org, and Resources for Special Children, www.irsc.org. There is also a good number of information-rich sites for specific learning disabilities, such as the Attention Deficit Disorder Association at www.add.org and www.dyslexic.com.

e. Learning Disability Support Organizations

Appendix 3 provides more detail on organizations devoted specifically to learning disabilities. Because learning disabilities are such a large part of the special education world, there are a lot of excellent and helpful groups out there. Call or write the American Learning Disabilities Association or your state learning disabilities group for more information.

B. Obtain Your Child's School Records

As part of your information gathering, you must find out what is in your child's school file and what effect that information will have on the IEP process. You'll need this information to assess the severity of your child's difficulties and the possible need for special education. If your child is found eligible for special education, reviewing the school file will help you determine which services and programs may be appropriate.

Whether you are new at this or have been through many IEPs, whether you anticipate a major change in your child's educational program or no change at all, and even if you're not sure you want your child in special education in the first place, you should secure copies of your child's school file on a yearly basis. New information is usually added each year.

While the contents of your child's file may vary, here are some things you're likely to find:

- report cards and other progress reports
- medical data (immunization records, health reports)
- attendance records
- disciplinary reports
- testing data
- assessments and other testing material
- teacher comments and other observations, and
- pictures of your child (it's fun to see the kindergarten picture, the second grade picture with the missing teeth, and so on).

Request to Begin Special Education Process and Assessment

Date: _February 20, 20xx_

To: _Ronald Pearl, Principal_

Mesa Verde Elementary School

123 San Pablo Avenue

San Francisco, CA 94110

Re: _Amber Jones, student in 2nd grade class of Cynthia Rodriguez_

I am writing to you because my child is experiencing difficulties in school. _As I_
mentioned to you over the phone this morning, she is way behind in reading [or other
specific difficulties your child is exhibiting].

I am formally requesting that the school immediately begin its special education process, including initial assessment for eligibility. I understand that you will send me an assessment plan explaining the tests that may be given to my child. Because I realize the assessment can take some time, I would appreciate receiving the assessment plan within ten days. Once you receive my approval for the assessment, would you let me know when the assessment will be scheduled?

I would also appreciate any other information you have regarding the assessment, how eligibility is determined, and general IEP process.

Thank you very much for your kind assistance. I look forward to working with you and your staff.

Sincerely,

Mary Jones

Mary Jones

243 Ocean Avenue

San Francisco, CA 94110

Phones: 555-1234 (home); 555-2678 (work)

1. Your Right to See Your Child's School File

You have a legal right to inspect and review any education records relating to your child. If your child is already in the special education system, you have this right under IDEA. (20 U.S.C. § 1415(b)(1); 34 C.F.R. §§ 300.501, 560-577.) If your child has not yet been found eligible for special education, you still have a legal right to her file under the Family Educational Rights and Privacy Act (FERPA). (20 U.S.C. § 1232 (g).) State law may also provide a right to your child's file, separate from IDEA or FERPA rights. Call your state department of education or your school district for information on your state's rules—including how you must make the request and how much time the school has to provide you the file.

2. How to Get Copies of Your Child's File

When you ask to see your child's school file, put your request in writing and ask for everything. Send the written request to the administrator in your school district who is responsible for special education. That may be the school principal or a person in your district's central office. The site principal should be able to refer you to the appropriate person.

A sample letter requesting your child's school file is below; a tear-out copy is in Appendix 5.

IDEA requires your child's school to grant your request without unnecessary delay and before any IEP meeting. The school must send you the file within 45 days, although it can and should send it more quickly. (34 C.F.R. § 300.562(a).) FERPA includes the same 45-day deadline.)

If you have any problem getting a copy of your child's school file in a timely manner, you can:

- Call and write the appropriate administrator, indicating that the law requires the school to provide the records without "unnecessary delay."
- If the principal or administrator does not respond to your request, contact the school district superintendent and your state department of education. Failing to give you your child's records is a violation of the law. Chapter 13 covers procedures for handling legal violations by your district.

Your state special education law may give schools a shorter deadline to provide copies of your child's record than the 45-day limit imposed by IDEA. California schools, for example, must provide copies of the record within five days of a parent's request. Get a copy of your state's special education laws from your department of education early on so you know your rights—and cite the law when you request your child's file.

3. Cost of Getting Files

The school is allowed to charge you a fee for copying your child's records, as long as the fee "does not effectively prevent you from exercising your right to inspect and review those records." (34 C.F.R. § 300.566.) This means that you cannot be charged an excessively high fee—or any fee at all, if you can show you cannot afford it. In addition, the school cannot charge a fee for searching and retrieving records.

If your child is not in special education, any fee for records might violate the Rehabilitation Act of 1973 (29 U.S.C. § 794) and the federal Freedom of Information Act. At least one court (*Tallman v. Cheboygan Area School*, 454 N.W. 2d 171 (Mich. Ct. App. 1990)) has said that charging a fee for search and retrieval would violate the Freedom of Information Act.

While some districts can be uncooperative about providing free copies of your child's file,

Request for Child's School File

Date: _____March 3, 20xx_____

To: Ronald Pearl, Principal

Mesa Verde Elementary School

123 San Pablo Avenue

San Francisco, CA 94110

Re: Amber Jones, student in 2nd grade class of Cynthia Rodriguez

I would like a copy of my child's file, including all tests, reports, assessments, grades, notes by teachers or other staff members, memoranda, photographs—in short, *everything* in my child's school file. I understand I have a right to these files under _IDEA, specifically_ _20 U.S.C. § 1415(b)(1) and 34 C.F.R. § 300.562_ [or the Family Educational Rights and Privacy Act (FERPA) (20 U.S.C. § 1232(g)) if your child has not yet been found eligible for special education].

_____.

I would greatly appreciate having these files within the next five days. I would be happy to pick them up. I will call you to discuss how and when I will get the copies.

Thank you for your kind assistance.

Sincerely,

Mary Jones

Mary Jones

243 Ocean Avenue

San Francisco, CA 94110

Phones: 555-1234 (home); 555-2678 (work)

others provide them as a matter of course. If your district charges you for searching and retrieving the file or charges you when you can't afford to pay a fee, write a letter to your administrator, citing to 34 C.F.R. § 300.566.

Request for Reduction or Waiver of Fee Charged for Child's School File

Date: March 20, 20xx

To: Ronald Pearl, Principal
Mesa Verde Elementary School
123 San Pablo Avenue
San Francisco, CA 94110

Re: Amber Jones, student in 2nd grade class of Cynthia Rodriguez

On March 3, 20xx, I requested copies of everything in my child's school file. Your secretary called me on March 19, 20xx, and stated that there would be a fee for the copies [or an excessive fee or a fee for searching and retrieving]. IDEA (34 C.F.R. § 300.566) specifically states that you cannot charge a fee if it prevents me from exercising my right to inspect and review my child's file. I am on a fixed income and I cannot afford the fee you are charging.

[or: IDEA prohibits you from charging such a high fee. A fee of 15¢ a copy seems fair, not $1 a copy]

[or: IDEA specifically prohibits you from charging a fee for searching for and retrieving the files]

Therefore, I would appreciate it if you would send me copies, at no cost, at once. Thank you for your kind attention to this matter.

Mary Jones
Mary Jones
243 Ocean Avenue
San Francisco, CA 94110
Phones: 555-1234 (home); 555-2678 (work)

Always Get Copies

IDEA allows you to review your child's school file *and* receive copies. (34 C.F.R. § 300.562.) These are two different rights—and you should exercise them both. You should always secure actual copies of your child's file. If you can, you should also go to the school and review the original file, just to make sure the school district gave you everything.

4. What to Look for in Your Child's School File

Items that you are likely to find in your child's file are listed at the beginning of this section. As you review those documents, look for any information about your child's performance and needs, as well as the opinions of his teacher and other professionals. Make sure you ask for everything, even if some items seem unimportant—you never know what you'll find buried in the file.

5. Amending Your Child's File

You have the right to request that any false, inaccurate, or misleading information, or information that violates the privacy or other rights of your child, be amended or removed from your child's school file. (34 C.F.R. § 300.567.) You also have the right to an explanation of the records. (34 C.F.R. § 300.562(b)(1).)

If the school refuses to amend or remove the information, you have the right to a due process hearing on the issue. (See Chapter 12.)

A sample request to amend the child's school file is below; a blank, tear-out copy is in Appendix 5.

Request to Amend Child's School File

Date: _April 1, 20xx_

To: _Ronald Pearl, Principal_

Mesa Verde Elementary School

123 San Pablo Avenue

San Francisco, CA 94110

Re: _Amber Jones, student in 2nd grade class of Cynthia Rodriguez_

I recently reviewed a copy of my child's file and would like to have a portion of the file amended, specifically:

The assessment/memorandum from the school psychologist, Ms. Taylor, stating that

my child had severe emotional problems, is inaccurate and inappropriate because

Ms. Taylor did no testing and only observed my child briefly. This is insufficient to sup-

port the conclusion she reached.

IDEA provides that I have the right to request that all information that is "inaccurate or misleading, or violates the privacy of [my] child" be amended. (34 C.F.R. § 300.567.) I feel that this is just such a case. Therefore, I request that you immediately rectify the situation.

Please notify me in writing as soon as possible of your decision regarding this matter. Thank you.

Sincerely,

Mary Jones

Mary Jones

243 Ocean Avenue

San Francisco, CA 94110

Phones: 555-1234 (home); 555-2678 (work)

C. Start an IEP Binder

Many parents have found a simple three-ring binder with clearly labeled sections to be an invaluable organizing tool. A binder allows you to keep everything in one convenient location—from report cards to test results to IEP forms.

Include every important item in your IEP binder. What's an important item? Anything that contains substantive information about your child or procedural information concerning how and when things happen in the IEP process. While certain items can probably go into a file drawer labeled "not relevant," if you have any doubt, add them to your binder.

Use the Forms in This Book

Nearly two dozen sample forms, checklists, and letters appear throughout this book, with tear-out copies in Appendix 5. You can simply photocopy (make as many copies as necessary) and insert the relevant forms into your IEP binder—either as a separate section or folded into one of the major sections we list below. The IEP Blueprint (discussed in Chapter 5) is one key document you should include as a separate section in your binder. Another is the IEP Material Organizer form (discussed in Chapter 10), which you'll use to highlight key information in your binder and easily access your materials during the IEP meeting. These and other forms have space for far more information than you'll be ready to provide right now. That's okay. You're just getting started. It's perfectly fine to leave many of the form sections blank. You can fill them in later, as you read through this book and get into the IEP process.

Listed below are some of the most important materials for your binder. Make as many sections as necessary to help you easily locate the information you'll need throughout the IEP process.

1. Your Child's File and Relevant School Materials

Your child's school records will play a key role in the IEP meeting, in developing the IEP itself, and possibly at any due process mediation or hearing. When you get copies of your child's file (including report cards, attendance and disciplinary records, assessments and testing data, and teacher comments), review the documents carefully and put important items in your binder.

You can put everything in one large section of your binder labeled "school records," or you can divide the material into several sections. You'll probably have an easier time locating the information if you break it down into categories.

In addition to your child's file, your binder should contain other relevant school materials, such as:

- assessments completed by the school
- samples of your child's work
- notes from your child's teacher and other staff members
- correspondence to and from the school
- past IEPs
- your notes and information on available programs and services, including the qualifications of particular teachers or service providers within the school district (Chapter 8 discusses how to develop information on available school options), and
- forms and informational materials sent to you by the school district, such as the school's IEP form and copies of key statutes and regulations on special education. (As mentioned earlier, the school is required by IDEA to provide you with a copy of federal and state statutes and regulations.)

It's never too early to secure a copy of your school's IEP. If you're new to the IEP process, be sure to get a copy of the local form (this varies from district to district) and any school guidelines on the IEP process. Keep the form and related materials in your binder.

Binder Versus File Drawer

As your child progresses in school, your binder could quickly become unwieldy. Consider developing a new one each year. You can keep a file drawer or box of dated material—for example, "1996 assessment" or "1998 report cards." In your binder, you should keep only materials that are relevant to the current IEP year.

---

2. Your Child's Health and Medical Records

Your child's school file will probably include some medical information, such as the results of hearing or vision tests done at school. Be sure your binder includes these documents, as well as medical records and important letters from your child's pediatrician and other health professionals.

3. Independent Assessments

As explained in Chapter 8, an independent assessment or evaluation may be the most important document supporting what you want for your child. You'll definitely want to keep a copy of all independent assessments in your binder.

4. Information on Programs and Services Outside the School District

If you're exploring private programs or service options, such as a specialized school for children with learning disabilities, be sure to keep the details in your binder, including suggestions made by other parents, school brochures, and notes of your conversations and visits. (Chapter 8 explains how to develop information on programs and services outside of your school district.)

5. Special Education Contacts

You'll want to have a list of the names, mailing addresses, phone and fax numbers, and e-mail addresses of people you deal with on a regular basis, such as your child's teacher, the district's special education administrator, your child's physician, the school nurse, staff members who provide related services, parents or parent groups, and the like.

Keep this list of contacts in a prominent place in front of your binder. Also, keep a copy with you, in case you need to phone or write any of your contacts when you're away from home.

A sample Special Education Contacts form is below; a blank, tear-out copy is in Appendix 5. Make as many copies as you need.

6. Articles and Other Information on Your Child's Learning Disability

Your binder should include copies of articles or other printed materials about your child's disability. There's no need to keep everything you find; just make copies of the most informative and helpful materials. That way, you'll have an authoritative reference on hand if a school representative questions what you want for your child ("According to an article I read, multisensory approaches can be very effective for children with dyslexia; I have a copy right here, if you'd like to take a look"). The articles will also remind you of good ideas for the blueprint and IEP.

7. IEP Journal

The importance of keeping a record of all conversations, visits, and information-gathering activities, whether on the phone or in person, cannot be over-emphasized. To help you remember who said what (and when), start an IEP journal. For every important conversation or incident, make a note of:

Special Education Contacts

Name, Address, Phone and Fax Numbers and Email Address

School Staff

School: Lewis Elementary, 123 Rose St., Chicago, 60611; 555-1234 (main phone), 555-5678 (fax)

David Werner, Principal, 555-9876, DWE@aol.com

Charlene Hanson, District Special Ed. Administrator, 4444 Main, Chicago, 60611, 555-4201 (phone), 555-7451 (fax), chsed @dusd.edu

Thayer Walker, Carrie's teacher, 567 Elm Ave., Chicago, 60611 (home), 555-0111 (classroom), 555-0114 (home)

Dr. Judy Goffy, school psychologist, 555-4333 (phone), 555-7455 (fax), drjg@aol.com

Outside Professionals

Dr. Hugh Maloney, independent assessor, 780 Spruce Lane, Chicago, 60612, 555-5169 (phone), 555-5170 (fax), drhm @compuserv.com

Martha Brown, tutor, 2229 Franklin, Chicago, 60612, 555-1490

Other Parents

Kevin Jones (son Robert in Carrie's class), 7 Plainview Dr., Chicago, 60614, 555-5115, kj@aol.com

Melaney Harper, District Community Advisory Chair, 764 Rockly, Chicago, 60610, 555-7777 (phone), 555-9299 (fax)

Support Groups

Chicago Learning Disabilities Association (contact: Mark Kelso), 775 Kelly Rd., Chicago, 60610, 555-6226 (phone), 555-7890 (fax), chldas@aol.com

State Department of Education

Special Ed. Office (contact: Dr. Hillary Casper), State Department of Education, 88 Capitol Row, Springfield, 61614, 217-555-8888 (phone), 217-555-9999 (fax), ilsped@worldnet.att.net

Other

Dr. Joan Landman, Carrie's pediatrician, 32 Ashford Rd., Chicago, 60611, 555-2222 (phone), 555-0987 (fax)

Illinois Special Ed. Advocates (Steve Miller, Esq.), 642 Miller Dr., Chicago, 60611, 555-4511(phone), 555-8709 (fax), spedatt@netcom.com

- the date and time of the conversation or meeting
- the names and positions of everyone who participated in the discussion, such as your child's teacher, other school staff, the special education administrator, your pediatrician, or another parent
- what was said by whom (this is really important), and
- any necessary follow-up actions (for example, a person to call or documents to provide to the school or assessor).

You'll want to fill in your IEP journal just as soon as possible after a conversation or meeting has ended. The longer you wait, the more likely you are to forget important details or confuse dates, times, and statements or promises made. Don't be shy about taking notes when you meet or talk with someone. To establish written verification of what you've been told, send a confirming letter soon after your conversation. Confirming letters are covered in Section C8, below.

A sample IEP Journal page is below; a tear-out copy is in Appendix 5. Make several copies and keep a few with you—for example, if you make phone calls from work. You can use the Class Visitation Checklist in Chapter 8C to keep detailed notes on your visits to school programs.

8. Confirming Letters

Confirming what someone has said to you provides some proof of that conversation. A confirming letter can provide useful evidence—of what was said, by whom, and when—for an IEP meeting or a due process hearing.

To be sure the school district receives confirming letters, send them certified mail, return receipt requested.

Example:

Your son needs a good deal of one-to-one help. You want a qualified aide to work with him on reading, math, and spelling at least half of the school day. Your child's teacher tells you during a classroom visit that he agrees that your son needs one-to-one help for much of the day. In addition, the special education administrator admits to you that the amount of aide time your son is currently receiving is not enough. You note both of these conversations in your IEP Journal and send the administrator a confirming letter. Later, at the IEP meeting, the administrator balks at providing your son with more aide time. Your confirming letter will be quite helpful in establishing that both your son's teacher and the school administrator told you your son needs more aide time.

Sample Confirming Letter

Date: May 14, 20xx

To: Salvador Hale, Special Education
Administrator
Coconut County School District
1003 South Dogwood Drive
Oshkosh, WI 50000
Re: Rodney Brown,
4th grader at Woodrow Wilson School

I appreciated the chance to speak with you yesterday regarding Rodney's current problems with reading comprehension. I agree with your comment that he will need at least half of the day with a one-on-one aide. I look forward to our IEP meeting next week and resolving Rodney's current difficulties in school.

Sincerely,

Martin Brown

Martin Brown
145 Splitleaf Lane
Oshkosh, WI 50000
Phones: 555-4545 (home); 555-2500 (work)

IEP Journal

Date: _____11/3/02_____   Time: _____4:30_____ ~~a.m.~~/p.m.

Action: ☒ Phone Call ___201-555-0105___   ☐ Meeting _____

☐ Other: _____

Person(s) Contacted: _____Dr. P. Brin (Sp. Ed. Administrator)_____

Notes: ___I explained that Steve is having problems in reading, comp., and spelling, plus some___

social difficulties.

I said Steve needs an aide.

Dr. B: "We can't do that now; wait until the IEP."

I said we need IEP at once.

Dr. B: "We just had one; can't schedule another for at least _two_ months."

---

9. Calendars

Section D, below, describes the typical tasks and events during the yearly IEP process, and explains how to keep track of these tasks and events on a monthly calendar. To stay organized, keep a copy of your calendar in your binder.

D. Keep Track of Deadlines

A large part of your organizational chores will involve tracking and meeting the various deadlines in the IEP process. This section explains the yearly IEP cycle and shows you how to stay on top of your deadlines.

1. The Yearly IEP Cycle

To really get organized, you'll need to know when things happen in the IEP cycle. Once your

child is assessed and found eligible for special education, the yearly IEP process will involve three broad considerations:

- Review—how are things currently going?
- Reassess—what additional information is needed?
- Rebuild—will the program be the same next year or should it be changed?

IDEA requires that an IEP be in place before your child begins the school year. (34 C.F.R. § 300.342.) To develop a complete IEP, you'll need to gather information, deal with assessments, prove that your child is eligible for special education, prepare for the IEP meeting, attend the IEP meeting, and work out any disagreements you might have with the school. This means you'll have to start planning well in advance to make sure everything gets done in time.

The best way to think about the IEP cycle is to start from your final goal—an IEP in place by the start of the school year—and work backwards.

a. Finish Before Summer

To make sure that all special education issues are resolved before the new school year begins, you will want an IEP meeting in the spring of the previous year. This will give you time to resolve any disputes before the next school year starts. Because school personnel are usually gone during the summer, plan for the IEP meeting in May—or better yet, April—in case there is a dispute that has to be resolved through due process.

b. Request Your Meeting During the Winter

To ensure that your child's IEP meeting takes place in the spring, put the school district on notice by submitting a written request in February or March stating that you want the annual IEP meeting in April or May.

c. Begin Planning in the Fall

You'll need to be well-prepared for the spring IEP meeting. Don't start collecting information a few weeks or even a month or two in advance. You'll need much more time than that. Start in the fall or early winter of the preceding year.

Keep in touch with your child's teacher. It's crucial to monitor your child's progress throughout the school year. Talk regularly with your child's teacher, and spend some time in the classroom, if possible. By keeping in touch with the school, you'll be able to assess how your child's reading, writing, and other goals are being met. This will also give you the opportunity to identify problems early on that might require an immediate IEP. Chapter 8B gives advice on keeping tabs on your child's progress.

d. The Cycle Isn't Set in Stone

Let's say you've just discovered that your child's problems in school make her a candidate for special education. It's October. You didn't participate in the IEP cycle the previous year because it wasn't an issue. You'd prefer not to wait until the spring to have an IEP meeting to develop a plan for the following year, because your child would lose almost a whole year of school. Or, you went through the IEP cycle the previous year, but the current program is not working. It's November, and you don't want to wait until spring for a new program. What do you do?

Don't wait until spring to raise issues that need immediate attention. Start gathering information, and request an assessment and IEP meeting ASAP. The IEP cycle is an ideal, but any time you need an immediate IEP meeting, you should request one.

Midyear IEP meetings aren't a good idea. Many students' IEP meetings take place in December or January. While you can request an IEP meeting at any time, and should when there is an immediate concern, it is generally a good idea to have your yearly IEP well before school starts. Otherwise, you'll be making decisions after your child is already in a program. The easiest way to get back on schedule is to indicate at the midyear IEP meeting that you want another one at the end of the school year, preferably in April or May. Follow up your request with a confirming letter.

2. A Sample Year in the Life of Your Child's IEP

Let us assume you are planning for the school year that begins in the fall of 2005. Ideally, by starting your preparation a year ahead of time, in the fall of 2004, you will have enough time without rushing or facing last-minute problems.

a. Information Gathering: Fall 2004

No matter how many times you have been through the special education process, you should take some time in the fall to gather information and develop a sense of what your child's program should be. Here are some tasks you'll want to accomplish:

- talk to teachers, school staff, and other parents
- request copies of your child's school records
- request an assessment of your child as needed (see Chapter 6)
- begin drafting your child's blueprint (see Chapter 5)
- schedule visits to your child's class or other programs you think might be viable (see Chapter 8C), and
- gather other information such as letters from your pediatrician and your child's tutor (see Chapter 8F).

b. Evaluation: Winter 2005

After the first few months of school, the key issues for your child should begin to crystallize for you. You will know either that your child needs to be in special education or, if she is already eligible for special education, which programmatic components make sense. Now is the time to assess the information you have or need to make a strong case for eligibility and/or the program and services you want for your child. Here are some steps to take:

- Assess the current information in your child's record and decide whether it supports your IEP goals for your child.
- Monitor the progress your child is making under the current program.
- Complete additional assessments, if you need more supporting information (discussed in Chapters 6 and 8). Depending on

who will be doing any additional assessments and how busy their calendars are, you may need to plan for those assessments earlier in the year.

- Continue developing your child's IEP blueprint (see Chapter 5).

c. IEP Preparation and IEP Meeting: Spring 2005

Spring is the time to work toward getting an IEP program in place for your child. This may be the most labor intensive time of the whole cycle. Some of the things you'll need to do are:

- finalize your child's IEP blueprint of program and service needs (see Chapter 5)
- draft your goals and objectives for your child's IEP program (see Chapter 9)
- prepare for the IEP meeting and invite participants who will speak on your child's behalf (see Chapter 10), and
- attend the IEP meeting (see Chapter 11).

d. Dispute Resolution: Spring-Summer 2005

If you did not reach an agreement with the school administrators on your child's IEP program, then you can go to a due process mediation or hearing. (See Chapter 12.) It is important to complete this process before the beginning of the new year.

e. School Begins: Fall 2005

You've been through your first (or another) IEP cycle. You'll want to monitor your child's progress in school and see if the IEP program is working. Remember: If it's not, you can request another IEP meeting and try to come up with some changes that make sense.

3. Keep a Monthly Calendar

It is vitally important to keep a written calendar that includes the details of IEP tasks (such as drafting goals and objectives) and events (such as assessments, school visits, and the IEP meeting).

Write down these details on some type of month-at-a-glance calendar (your own or the form we provide here), including dates on which:

- you were told things would happen—for example, "Scott's school file should be mailed today"

- you need to schedule a meeting—for example, "Request IEP meeting no later than today"
- you need to call or meet with someone, such as a teacher, a pediatrician, or another parent, or
- you need to start or complete a particular task, such as develop an IEP blueprint.

A sample Monthly IEP Calendar is below; a blank, tear-out copy is in Appendix 5. Make 12 copies of this for each month of the year.

Monthly IEP Calendar

Month and Year: _____ Oct 03

1	2	3	4	5	6	7
			call teacher re: math probs			
8	9	10	11	12	13	14
		written req. for access			meet w/sp. ed. spt gp	
15	16	17	18	19	20	21
				call Am Lrg. Disab. Assoc. #: math resources		
22	23	24	25	26	27	28
		visit class 10:30	meet w/ Mary S., son in same class		follow up phone call re: assess rqst	
29	30	31				

5

Developing Your Child's IEP Blueprint

The whole purpose of the special education process is to develop a positive and comprehensive program for your child. In order to do that, you must first have a clear idea of what you want for your child. I call this description a blueprint: a specific list of the educational components, including placement, teaching methodologies, and support services, that you want for your child.

Why create a blueprint? To convince others that your child requires particular services or assistance, you must first be able to state, clearly, exactly what you want—and why it's appropriate. Parents often have a broad sense of which tasks give their child trouble, but are less able to describe in detail what their child needs and why.

Creating a blueprint will help you succeed in the IEP process for a number of reasons:

- It forces you to be specific. For example, stating that your child needs help in reading is not as effective as saying that your child needs to work one-on-one with a reading specialist for one hour per day, four days per week.

- You'll know what documentation or evidence you will need to develop before the IEP meeting. For example, if your blueprint includes a one-on-one reading specialist one hour per day, four days per week, you'll need information from your child's school record and other supporting material—and perhaps people to speak at the IEP meeting—to justify this type of help.

- IDEA requires that the program fit the child, not the other way around. Just because your school district offers a particular class or program doesn't necessarily mean it's an appropriate placement for your child. For example, if your school has a special education class geared towards students who are developmentally disabled, that might not work for your child who has handwriting problems. A blueprint can help you determine what may be missing from the school's proposal.

- The blueprint serves as a standard against which you can evaluate your child's existing program and the options currently available to you.

- The blueprint provides you with a continual reference point as you talk with others about your child's needs and move toward the IEP meeting.

- The needs of a child with a learning disability can sometimes be hard to pin down. Making a blueprint will help you, your child, and her teachers and aides hone in on those needs and the educational strategies that will meet them most effectively.

The blueprint represents your ideal IEP program. It is your starting point—a sort of "druthers" test. If you could be the special education administrator for your school district for one day, this is the IEP program you would design for your child.

You may think it's too early to draft a blueprint. Perhaps your child was just assessed and found eligible for special education, but hasn't been in special education yet. Or maybe your child has been in special education for some time, but is scheduled for a new assessment in another month. It's possible a new special education administrator will take over in the spring, with promises of new program options about which you know little. In any of these situations, you may think you don't have enough information to do a good job—and, in truth, there are always more facts you can gather. But you have to start sometime, and now is as good as any. Don't worry if your blueprint is skeletal or incomplete at first.

Even parents new to special education usually have some intuitive sense of what their children need—for example, help organizing their homework and assignments, extra work on handwriting or spelling, or strategies to control impulsive behavior. Take a moment to think about it; by the time you finish this chapter, you'll have the beginnings of a useful blueprint, not just vague notions of what might help (or what's going wrong). And as you use this book and gather more information on your child's needs, you'll be able to develop a more complete blueprint.

A. Begin at the End: Define Your Child's Needs

It's the first day of school in the upcoming school year. Close your eyes and picture what your child's classroom will look like. Is it a regular classroom, a special classroom for children with learning disabilities, or even a private school? Don't limit yourself—after all, you're imagining the best plan for your child. Is there an aide that helps your child? What subjects do they work on? How often does the aide work with your child and in what kind of setting—alone or with other children? How many students are in the class? Do they also have learning difficulties? Does your child have access to voice-recognition software, books on tape, a calculator, or other technological assistance? What classroom strategies do you want for your child—does she need written instructions for assignments, rewards for good behavior, or opportunities to work with other children in a small group?

Sit down with a pad of paper and pen (or in front of your computer) and start to write out the ideal program and services for your child. Remember that your blueprint is your wish list for your ideal IEP. Don't dwell on the fact that you fought over the IEP last year or you're expecting a fight again. Don't draft your blueprint to follow the school district's program if you think it's not sufficient. This is your (first) chance to detail exactly what you want for your child. Be creative.

B. Preparing an IEP Blueprint

This section covers the seven key components of a blueprint, the items you want included in your child's IEP. You can use the blueprint to develop your IEP form, although the two documents won't be identical. (Chapter 11C explains how to do this.)

Some components are quite general, such as ideal classroom setting; others are very specific, such as a particular class or teaching method.

Some of these components may not be relevant to your child's situation—feel free to skip any sections that don't apply. You may not have enough information to complete the entire blueprint now, especially if you've only just realized that your child is having trouble. As you learn more, you'll fill in the gaps.

As you develop your child's blueprint, be sure to make it as specific to his learning disability needs as possible. The fact that a specific item is not referred to in IDEA or is not "common" does not mean it cannot be in your blueprint and ultimately in your child's IEP. For example, IDEA does not refer to or require that a child with learning disabilities be provided the Lindamood-Bell program (a multisensory program that helps children understand phonics; see Section B3, below), but if your child needs that program, it should be on the blueprint.

One of my first clients was a deaf child whose parents could not communicate in sign language. We asked for and eventually got sign language classes for the parents as part of the child's IEP, even though IDEA does not mention sign language classes for parents of deaf children. Remember, IDEA does not list every conceivable IEP item, because it recognizes that the IEP team needs the flexibility to include those items that meet the individual child's unique needs.

A sample IEP Blueprint is below; Appendix 5 includes a blank, tear-out copy. Be sure to put your blueprint draft into your binder, along with supporting information and documents. (See Chapter 4.)

IEP Blueprint

The IEP Blueprint represents the ideal IEP for your child. Use it as a guide to make and record the educational desires you have for your child.

Areas of the IEP	Preferred Situation for Your Child
1. Classroom Setting and Peer Needs—issues to consider:	
☐ regular versus special education class	
☐ partially or fully mainstreamed	
☐ type of special education class	
☒ number of children in the classroom	A class of no more than 10 students
☒ ages and cognitive ranges of children in class	Age range 9-10; same cognitive range as Mark
☒ kinds of students and behaviors that might or might not be appropriate for your child, and	No behaviorally troubled students No mixed "disability" class
☐ language similarities.	
2. Teacher and Staff Needs—issues to consider:	
☒ number of teachers and aides	1 teacher; 1 full-time aide or 2 half-time aides
☒ teacher-pupil ratio	10:1 pupil-teacher ratio
☒ experience, training, and expertise of the teacher, and	Teacher with specific learning disability training, experience, credentials
☒ training and expertise of aides.	Aide: previous experience working with L-D students
3. Curricula and Teaching Methodology—be specific. If you don't know what you *do* want, specify what you *don't* want.	Slingerland method Large print material Teaching strategies that include significant repetition

Areas of the IEP	Ideal Situation for Your Child
4. Related Services—issues to consider: ☒ specific needed services	1:1 aide two hours per day
☒ type of services	Speech and lang. therapy three times/week, 40 min. per session, 1:1
☒ frequency of services, and ☒ length of services.	30 minutes of psych. counseling once a week with psychologist experienced with children with learning disabilities and emotional overlay
5. Identified Programs—specify known programs that you think would work for your child and the school that offers them.	Special day class (5th grade) for learning disabled at Washington School (Ms. Flanagan)
6. Goals and Objectives—goals are long range in nature, while objectives are more short term.	Improve reading fluency and comprehension: Read three-paragraph story with 80% comprehension; complete reading within 10 minutes Improve peer relationships: Initiate five positive peer interactions/week
7. Classroom Environment and Other Features—issues to consider: ☒ distance from home	No more than five miles and less than 30-minute bus ride to neighborhood school
☐ transition plans for mainstreaming	
☐ vocational needs	
☒ extracurricular and social needs, and	Involvement in afterschool recreation and lunch-time sports activities
☒ environmental needs.	Small school (no more than 250 students); quiet classroom; protective environment (school procedures to ensure students do not wander); acoustically treated classroom

1. Classroom Setting and Peer Needs

In this section, specify the type of classroom you'd like for your child, including the kinds of peers she should be with. You may not have a good sense of all of these details right now. Start by putting general information in the blueprint (for example, that you want your child to be in a small, mainstreamed class, without any children who have serious behavioral problems). You'll fill in the details as you get more fully immersed in the process.

Specific items to address (when relevant) include:

- regular versus special education class
- partially or fully mainstreamed
- type of special education class (for example, for learning disabled students or students with language delays)
- number of children in the classroom
- ages and cognitive ranges of children in class
- kinds of students (with similar or dissimilar learning disabilities) and behaviors that might or might not be appropriate for your child—for example, a child with attention deficit disorder may need a classroom where other children do not act out, and
- language needs—for example, if your child has language processing problems or a delay, he may need to model children with higher language abilities.

One of the more complex issues for some parents of children with learning disabilities is how to balance the need for a program that will serve your child's unique needs against the importance of placement in a regular classroom. In many cases, your child's needs can be met in a regular classroom, but there are circumstances in which you may feel you have to choose one over the other.

Sometimes, IDEA's goal of placing disabled children in a regular classroom (sometimes called mainstreaming or inclusion) must give way if a child needs to be placed in a more specialized program. There are plusses and minuses to each type of placement. A regular classroom placement offers your child the chance to be in a regular environment with children who don't have disabilities, to model their behaviors, to work on standard curriculum and subject matters, to participate in sports and other extracurricular activities, and to gain from all that a regular school environment provides, including the chance to be inspired by the challenges it poses. Conversely, a regular classroom may prove too difficult for some children with learning disabilities. The child may not be ready for the subject matter, may not have developed sufficient basic skills to be able to keep up, or may simply be overwhelmed by the size, activity, and amount of work in a regular classroom.

Placement in a special classroom may allow a child with learning disabilities to develop basic learning skills more efficiently and effectively, reduce the pressure on that child, allow a child to be with other children at the same level of development, and give the child a chance to work with staff that specialize in learning disabilities. Conversely, a special classroom may include too many different types of students and behaviors, may feel stigmatizing to the child (this issue may be particularly important to older children), and generally will not expose the child to all the characteristics and options of a regular classroom.

As you develop the classroom section of your blueprint, analyze the plusses and minuses of a regular or special day class and develop the blueprint accordingly.

2. Teacher and Staff Needs

Use this section to identify your child's needs concerning teachers and other classroom staff, such as:

- number of teachers and aides
- teacher-pupil ratio—for example, your child may require a ratio of no more than four students to one teacher (while this may be

possible in a special day class, it won't be available in a regular class)

- experience, training, and expertise of the teacher—regular education teachers may not always have special education experience or training in teaching children with learning disabilities, and

- training and expertise of classroom aides—resource specialists are often used in class or for pull-out sessions to remediate learning disabilities; you want specialists who are experienced in dealing with your child's disability and the particular learning disability strategies and methodologies your child needs.

3. Curricula and Teaching Methodology

In this section, identify the curricula and teaching method or methods you feel are appropriate for your child. These might include both formal and informal methods for helping your child work on her areas of difficulty. Teaching strategies and methodologies may range from simple exercises, day-to-day tactics, and plans used at school or home to improve reading, spelling, math, and language skills, to specific, named teaching programs and approaches. Strategies and methodologies don't only address academic subjects: they might also include helping a learning disabled student organize his desk or showing a student with social anxiety how to take a time out, count to ten, or take a deep breath when faced with a difficult situation.

a. Multisensory Methodology

You may have already heard about multisensory methodology, a common approach to teaching children with learning disabilities. A multisensory approach uses a child's visual, auditory, and tactile-kinesthetic skills (that is, the child's sense of sight, hearing, and touch) to develop reading, language,

spelling, and math skills. These methodologies often break learning tasks down into sequential steps, so the child can develop basic learning skills from the ground floor up. Multisensory approaches are often used for children with learning disabilities because they develop and encourage language acquisition and reading development.

Some well-known multisensory methodologies include:

- Lindamood-Bell: a sequencing program that helps children develop phonemic awareness and understand how sounds are developed—and, therefore, improve their reading, speech, and spelling skills

- Slingerland: this methodology uses multisensory skills simultaneously to teach the rules and structure of the English language. Students build from the most simple level of language—the letter—to spelling, reading, writing, and oral language skills.

- Wilson Reading System: teaches word structure by focusing on spelling and decoding for students with language and reading difficulties.

- The Spalding Method: like Slingerland, Spalding uses an integrated, multisensory, and simultaneous approach to help students develop reading, writing, spelling, and oral language skills.

- Orton-Gillingham: using this simultaneous, sequential, and multisensory approach, students start by learning how letters look, sound, and feel, then move on to forming words and understanding written language.

You can find out a good deal more about particular teaching methodologies on the Internet. Start by searching the websites of the organizations listed in Appendix 3, particularly www.ldonline.org. Also, check out the website of the Child Development Institute at www.childdevelopmentinfo.com, which has lots of helpful information on strategies for students with learning disabilities. Or, go to your favorite search engine and plug in the name of a particular methodology, such as Slingerland or Lindamood-Bell.

You can also buy programs which will help your child spell, multiply, or read more easily. While these programs are usually not part of the IEP, you can use them to give your child some extra help. These programs might include books, tapes, and software about reading through phonics, developing better memory, mastering spelling, and so on. As with any item you purchase, check the websites listed above as well as national organizations such as the Learning Disabilities Association of America, at www.ldaamerica.org.

b. Strategies and Methodologies for Specific Learning Disabilities

In addition to the above-named teaching methodologies, there are teaching strategies, methods, and materials that educators often use to help children with a particular learning disability, such as dyslexia or auditory processing disorder. Some common ideas are listed here; you can find lots more on the Web, as noted above.

- **ADD/ADHD:** a structured classroom and regular schedule; help with transitions during the school day (such as returning from recess or changing classrooms); help organizing thoughts and ideas for projects; rewards for positive behavior; breaks during the day for physical activity.
- **Dyscalculia:** allowing the student to use a calculator; using games to teach mathematical concepts; asking the student to explain a mathematical process orally; using concrete examples before moving to abstract ideas; asking the student to estimate an answer before beginning to solve a math problem.
- **Dysgraphia:** providing alternatives to writing (such as using a computer or giving oral presentations); giving extra time for writing assignments; allowing a student to use a spell-checker; varied writing assignments (for example, writing letters, a journal, lists, or reports on a topic of special interest to the student); written handouts that allow the student space to write (for example, an outline of a lecture with space for notes or a worksheet with math problems and space to calculate the answers); allowing the student to use graph paper or heavily-lined writing paper.
- **Dyslexia:** books on tape; assigning varied reading materials (such as magazines, newspapers, comics, and advertisements); allowing more time for homework and other assignments; phonics-based instruction and multisensory approaches.
- **Auditory Processing Disorder:** seating the child near the teacher; teaching that combines oral instruction with visual aids; asking the student to repeat information and instructions back to the teacher or aide before beginning an assignment; rhyming games; giving the student a note-taker; speech-language therapy.
- **Visual Processing Disorder:** large-print books, written materials, and other adaptations (such as enlarged projected materials); teaching that combines writing (on the blackboard or charts) with oral information; allowing the student to explain test answers orally; puzzles and other games that emphasize spatial relationships; allowing the student to use a ruler, highlighters, and graph paper.

Does Your Child Have a Right to a Specific Methodology?

While IDEA does not require that a particular methodology or curriculum be included in the IEP and provided to your child, there is no prohibition against it. If a child needs a specific methodology to benefit from special education, then it is required; if he does not need it (or you cannot prove that he needs it), the school district does not have to provide it.

Ultimately, your child's goals and objectives are the key learning strategies in your child's IEP. They describe how your child will accomplish specific educational tasks. They may not be called strategies or methodologies, but they do set forth the detailed, day-to-day activities that will help your child with her learning disability. If you can't get a particular methodology into the IEP, make sure that your child's goals and objectives describe how you want her to be taught.

4. Related Services

Include in your blueprint a detailed list of necessary services, specifying the type and amount to be provided (for example, how many sessions per week and how long each session will last). The law does not limit the kinds of related services that must be provided to a child with learning disabilities. Generally, a school district must provide a related service if it is necessary to ensure that your child benefits from her education or if she needs such services to be in a regular classroom. Related services for a learning disabled child might include a one-on-one aide, speech therapy, physical therapy, transportation, and/or psychological services. (See Chapters 2 and 8 for a more detailed discussion of related services.)

5. Identified Programs

In Section 1 of the blueprint, you may have stated whether you want your child in a regular or special education classroom. If you know about a program in a particular school that you think would work best for your child, be it a regular classroom or a special education classroom, public or private, identify that program here.

6. Goals and Objectives

As discussed in Chapter 9, goals are long range in nature, while objectives are more short term.

Examples of *goals* for students with learning disabilities include:

- improve reading comprehension or other academic skills, such as math, spelling, or writing
- improve social skills
- resolve a serious emotional difficulty that impedes school work
- improve fine or large motor skills
- develop greater language and speech skills
- develop independent living skills, or
- improve auditory or visual memory.

Objectives tie in specifically to the goals identified above. For example, if your goal is to improve your child's reading skills, then a specific objective may be to improve reading comprehension from the 3rd to the 4th grade level or to master specific speech sounds.

Chapter 9 discusses goals and objectives in detail, and explains how to write effective goals and objectives for children with learning disabilities.

7. Classroom Environment and Other Features

Use your blueprint to identify any other features of the program you want for your child, such as:

- distance from home
- transition plans for mainstreaming
- vocational needs
- extracurricular and social needs
- environmental needs—protective environment, small class, small campus, acoustically treated classroom, or the like
- technological, computer programs and services that can help your child, and
- any plans you have for addressing your child's needs outside of school—for example, tutoring, helping your child with homework, helping organize assignments and school materials, or after-school activities to build coordination or social skills.

C. Other Sources of Information for the Blueprint

Your blueprint will be a work in progress. As you learn more about your child's needs (from professionals and others) and find out what services and programs are available, you can add to or change the information on your blueprint.

People who are trustworthy and know your child—such as other parents, your pediatrician, the classroom teacher, or a tutor—are excellent sources of information for your blueprint. Pose your question like this: "Terry is having some problems with reading (math, cognitive growth, language development, social issues, emotional conflicts, mobility, fine or gross motor activities, or whatever) and I'm wondering if I should look for a new program (or different related services). Do you have any suggestions of people I might talk to or programs or services I might consider?"

Chapter 8 contains important information about gathering facts, visiting school programs, and developing supportive material, such as an independent assessment. This information will help you with your blueprint.

D. What's Next?

If you are new to special education, your next step is to learn about the assessment and eligibility processes—how your child is evaluated for special education and how he becomes eligible for special education. Review Chapters 6 and 7 carefully.

If you are not new to special education, your next step will depend on your child's situation. Your child may need an assessment before the IEP meeting—if so, be sure to read Chapter 6. If your child does not need an immediate assessment and has already been found eligible for special education, move on to Chapter 8. ■

6

Assessments

Assessments are important tools that help you and the school district determine what your child's needs are and how they can be met. The school district will rely very heavily on the results of the assessment in determining whether your child is eligible for special education and, if so, what her IEP will include.

💡 **Evaluations are assessments.** IDEA uses the terms "assessment" and "evaluation" interchangeably. Both terms refer to the tests and other information-gathering methods used to determine your child's eligibility for special education. Your school district might also use these terms interchangeably.

Assessments are observations, reports, and tests that provide specific information about your child's cognitive, academic, linguistic, social, and emotional status. Assessments describe your child's current developmental levels—how he reads, perceives information, processes information, calculates, remembers things, performs physical tasks, relates to other children, and takes in, expresses, and understands language.

Special Education Assessments vs. General Assessments

Most (if not all) states require schools to administer a variety of tests to measure how children are doing in school and whether they are meeting certain state standards. These tests—often called general assessments—measure a child's mastery of specific subject matter, such as American history or algebra. Most children also take tests to graduate from high school and qualify for college. While special education assessments often measure similar abilities or aptitudes, they are intended to be used for a different purpose: to determine whether a child is eligible for special education and which special education services will be helpful to a particular child.

Since 1997, IDEA has required that children in special education be included in state- and district-wide assessments, with appropriate accommodations for the child's unique needs. (20 U.S.C. § 1412(a)(17)(A); 34 C.F.R. § 300.300.138.) Not all of these tests are sensitive to special education test-takers, however. For example, California requires high school seniors to pass an "exit exam" before they graduate—but the State Board of Education has generally ignored the needs of special education students and failed to make appropriate exit exam accommodations or modifications. The state was recently sued for this inexcusable oversight. You should carefully review any state or district tests in which your child participates to make sure that the test is appropriate and that your child receives the accommodations necessary to take the test.

Because assessments will determine your child's eligibility for special education and provide information on which programs and strategies might be helpful to your child, they should be completed before any educational decisions are made. Ideally, the assessment report will support what you want included in the IEP, as set out in your blueprint. (See Chapter 5.) For example, if you feel your child should be placed in a regular classroom where distractions are minimized (in a seat near the front of the class, for example), or if your child has difficulties with handwriting and needs to take oral rather than written tests, your chances of getting these accommodations are increased if the assessment report addresses those particular issues.

The Assessment Process, Step by Step

Here is how an assessment typically proceeds:

1. You request an assessment or the school identifies your child as possibly needing special education. (See Chapters 2 and 4.)

2. The school presents you with a written assessment plan listing all testing to be done on your child. This plan should focus on identifying your child's strengths and weaknesses and pinpointing possible learning and other disabilities.

3. You approve the assessment plan (or ask that certain tests or evaluation tools be added and/or others eliminated).

4. You meet with the assessor to discuss areas where your child seems to be having problems, based on your personal observations, physician reports, and the like. You can also discuss any concerns you have about the assessment. IDEA does not require this meeting, but I recommend it.

5. The school assesses your child.

6. You receive a copy of the school's assessment.

7. You schedule independent assessments if necessary. (See Chapter 8.)

8. You attend the IEP eligibility meeting or, if your child is already in special education, the yearly IEP meeting (see Chapter 11), where the assessment results are discussed.

This chapter explains when assessments are done (Section A); how an assessment plan is developed (Section B); how to evaluate assessment tests, including the tests often used for children with suspected learning disabilities (Section C); and how to review, change, or challenge an assessment (Sections D and E).

Should Your Child Be Assessed At All?

Some parents resist having their children assessed because they do not want their child in special education, they believe that testing will categorize their child in ways that are harmful, or they think that their child will be set apart from the rest of the school or from regular education. While these are understandable positions, you must weigh them against the importance of finding out as much as you can about your child's needs and how they can be addressed. Because parents can exercise a lot of control over the assessment process, the opportunity to learn more about your child should outweigh your emotional reluctance.

A. When Assessments Are Done

There are two kinds of assessments: an initial assessment to determine whether your child qualifies for special education services and subsequent or follow-up assessments to get up-to-date information on your child's status and progress. While assessments can generally be done at almost any time in your child's school year or even school career, the initial assessment must be done *before* your child can be found eligible for special education services.

While the school district has a proactive duty to identify and evaluate all children who may be in need of special education (referred to as the district's "child find" responsibility) (20 U.S.C. § 1412(a)(3); 34 C.F.R. § 300.125), you don't have to wait for your school district to act. If you suspect your child needs help, contact your school right away to request an assessment.

📄 You can find a sample Request to Begin Special Education Process and Assessment in Chapter 4, Section A2; a tear-out copy is in Appendix 5.

Once your child is found eligible for special education, he must be re-assessed at least every three years, or more frequently if requested by a parent or teacher (20 U.S.C. § 1414(a)(2); 34 C.F.R. § 300.321).

Your Child May Have Other Needs

When your child is "suspected" of having a learning disability, the assessment process must necessarily focus on that concern, but not to the exclusion of other possible problems. A child with a specific learning disability may have other needs and therefore other potential areas of eligibility for programs and services. Remember that your child can and must be assessed in all areas of suspected disability or need. See Chapter 7, particularly Section B, regarding IDEA's criteria for determining whether a child has a specific learning disability. (34 C.F.R. § 300.541.)

IDEA does not require your school district to submit an assessment plan to you or to complete the assessment within a specific time limit; it requires only that the school district complete the assessment within a reasonable time after it receives your request or consent to the assessment. Your state, however, may impose its own assessment deadlines. For example, California requires the school to give you an assessment plan within 15 days after you request an assessment, and to develop an IEP program within 50 days of your request. This is one of those areas in which you can really benefit from knowing your state's special education law (remember, if the state special education law provides more protection for your child, you can and should use it). Contact your state department of education to see if your state imposes more specific timelines than IDEA. Your school district is also required to provide you with an explanation of all applicable special education laws (federal or state), including any state time limits relating to the assessment process.

⚠️ **Don't take no for an answer.** Not all teachers are experienced at recognizing learning disabilities. If you suspect that your child has a learning disability, insist on an assessment, even if the school is resistant. School representatives may try to convince you that your child is just having a normal developmental delay, or that an "informal assessment"—usually just the teacher's impressions of your child—doesn't point to a learning disability. This may be the case, but the only way to know for sure is to have your child assessed.

B. The Assessment Plan

Before an assessment can begin, the school district must give you a written assessment plan listing all testing procedures that will be used to evaluate your child (including the specific tests that will be administered).

Assessments will test for intellectual, cognitive, academic, linguistic, social, and emotional status, including how your child reads, perceives information, processes information, calculates, remembers things, performs physical tasks, relates to other children, and takes in, expresses, and understands language.

Assessment plans will vary from child to child and from learning disability to learning disability.

1. Developing the Assessment Plan

Assessment plans can be drawn up by a group of people, usually including the parents, the child (if appropriate), a regular education teacher, a representative of the school district, someone who can interpret the instructional implications of the evaluation results, and, at the discretion of the school or parents, other individuals who have knowledge or special expertise regarding the child. (20 U.S.C. § 1414 (c)(1)(2), and (3); 34 C.F.R. § 300.533.) In reality, however, assessment plans are usually developed by the school district and then given to you.

This group is not legally required to meet. If it does decide to meet, it must:

- review any existing data, including evaluations and information you provide
- review current classroom-based assessments and observations (by teachers and related services providers), and
- based on these materials and input from the child's parents, identify any additional information necessary to determine whether the child has a qualifying disability (or in the case of a re-evaluation, whether the child continues to require special education); the child's present levels of performance and educational needs; and whether any changes should be made to the child's current educational program and services. (20 U.S.C. § 1414 (c)(1)(2), and (3); 34 C.F.R. § 300.533.)

Can a School District Force Your Child to Be Assessed?

Believe it or not, a school district can assess your child against your wishes. You are entitled to receive an assessment plan, to approve or object to that plan, or to say that you don't want your child assessed at all. The district can override your objections by going to a due process hearing to secure an order requiring an assessment. ((34 C.F.R. §300.505(b); for more on due process, see Chapter 12.) Of course, you have the right to oppose the district, to submit evidence and arguments showing that an assessment is not required, and to appeal any due process decision compelling your child to be assessed against your wishes.

There have been a number of cases in which a due process hearing judge ordered a child to be assessed over the objection of a parent. In making this decision, the hearing judge considers evidence as to why the assessments should or should not proceed, including whether there is already enough information to determine your child's eligibility and whether the assessment might harm your child.

This planning process is your first chance to make sure that the assessment is broad enough to give the assessor a complete picture of your child's strengths and weaknesses. The best way to ensure that you are included from the beginning of the assessment planning process is to call and write your special education administrator to formally request that you be involved in any assessment planning per 34 C.F.R. § 300.533 (keep a copy of your letter for your records). Be sure to give yourself a reminder by including this step on your planning calendar. (See Chapter 4.)

The Relationship Between Assessments and Eligibility for Special Education

Your child's initial assessment will determine whether she is eligible for special education. Of course, you will want an assessment that is thorough, fair, and informative about your child's ability and needs. And if you believe that your child needs special education services, you will also want the assessment results to clearly demonstrate your child's eligibility.

As discussed in Chapter 7, your child is eligible for special education based on a specific learning disability if she has a disorder that results in (1) a failure to achieve commensurate to her age and ability level, and (2) a severe discrepancy between her intellectual ability and her achievement in one of the following areas: listening, thinking, expressing and understanding language, reading, writing, spelling, or math. As you go through the assessment process, remember that your child will have to meet this definition in order to qualify for special education.

Ignoring these eligibility requirements until the assessment process is underway—or completed—may doom your plan to secure services for your child. You do not want to proceed with the assessments until you know which assessment findings will support eligibility (and which will not). Armed with this information, you can maximize the chances of the assessor finding your child eligible.

Legal Requirements for Assessments

IDEA guarantees every child certain rights in the assessment process. An assessment must:

- use a variety of tests, tools, and strategies to gather information about your child
- not be racially or culturally discriminatory
- be given in your child's native language or communication mode (such as sign language if your child is deaf or hard of hearing)
- validly determine your child's status—that is, it must include the right test(s) for your child's suspected areas of disability
- be administered by trained and knowledgeable personnel, in accordance with the instructions provided by the producer of the tests
- not be used only to determine intelligence
- if your child has impaired speaking or sensory skills, accurately reflect your child's aptitude or achievement level—not just your child's impairment
- assess your child in "all areas of suspected disability," including health, vision, hearing, social and emotional status, general intelligence, academic performance, communicative status, motor abilities, behavior, and cognitive, physical, and developmental abilities, and
- provide relevant information that will help determine your child's educational needs. (20 U.S.C. § 1414(a)(6)(B); 34 C.F.R. § 300.532.)

In addition, the assessment process must include other material about your child, such as information you provide (a doctor's letter or a statement of your observations, for example), current classroom assessments and observations (such as objective tests or subjective teacher reports), and observations by other professionals. (20 U.S.C. § 1414(c)(1,2,4); 34 C.F.R. § 300.353.)

2. The Assessment Plan Document

At the end of this planning process, your district will come up with a written document listing the formal tests and other tools that will be used to assess your child, including observation, interviews, and careful analysis of how your child functions.

While school districts use different assessment plan forms or templates, the assessment plan document must include:

- named tests and other assessment tools (such as observations, interviews, or evaluations)
- a section where you can request additional tests or other methods of evaluation, and
- a place for you to indicate your approval or disapproval, and space for you to sign and date the plan.

See Section D, below, for information on how to evaluate the plan, including a list of items you might want added to the assessment.

C. Evaluating the Assessment Tests

Usually, a person who is associated with your school district and who knows something about learning disabilities will determine which tests are to be given to your child. There's a very good chance that this person will also administer or supervise the assessments. How will you know if the proposed tests are appropriate for your child?

You'll need to do some homework to find out what the tests measure, how their results are reported, and, most important, whether they're appropriate for your child. The information in this section will help you get started.

1. Gathering Information

Your best sources of information are people familiar with special education testing generally and the specific tests proposed for your child.

These might include your child's teacher, the district's assessor, other parents, and your pediatrician. You might also talk to independent special education assessors you've worked with, school special education personnel you trust, or a private learning disability consultant (more likely to be available in more heavily populated areas). Get in touch with organizations that specialize in your child's learning disability, such as the Council for Exceptional Children or a state association for learning disabilities. You will note specific references throughout this chapter to various organizations and websites that can provide lots of valuable assessment information and help you locate a learning disability expert.

Chapter 8 discusses independent assessments. Appendix 3 provides a list of advocacy, parent, and disability organizations you might consider contacting for information on different types of assessments and learning disability consultants. Appendix 3 also references books on testing and assessments.

Here's what you want to find out:

- whether the proposed tests are appropriate to assess your child's suspected learning disabilities
- what the tests generally measure, such as general cognitive skills, language abilities, memory, math, or reading
- whether the results of the tests are expressed in numeric scores, descriptive statements about your child's performance, or both
- how the results are evaluated—for example, will your child score in a certain percentile ("Mary is in the 88th percentile," meaning she scored better than 87% of the children taking the test) or will your child be given a different result ("Mary scored at the second grade level").
- whether the test results will provide a solid basis for specific recommendations about classroom strategies, teaching methods, and services and programs for your child

- how the tests are administered—for example, are they timed, are they oral or written, and

- who will do the assessment and what specific expertise, training, and experience the assessor has in administering these particular tests.

2. Tests for Identifying and Assessing Learning Disabilities

To make sure your child's assessment will be effective and appropriate, you'll need to know about the specific tests used to identify learning disabilities. Tests for learning disabilities tend to be more objective in nature than tests for other types of disabilities—the assessment results will usually be expressed in terms of a percentile, grade level, or other numerical scale. In contrast, assessments used for children with emotional difficulties, for example, often involve evaluating behavior, mood, and relationships, and the results cannot always be reduced to "numbers." (As discussed in more detail in Chapter 7 on eligibility, reliance on tests with numeric results has its benefits and drawbacks.) The sections that follow divide specific assessment tools into categories based on what they test (intelligence, perception, language, and so on). You'll note that some of the tests cover a wide variety of areas.

The Ever-Changing World of Learning Disability Assessments

Testing, particularly testing for learning disabilities, is complicated and, at times, controversial. While we want and need objective information, we don't want to lose sight of our children as individuals rather than numbers. Educators and even legislators are constantly rethinking how testing should be used to evaluate eligibility for special education. Some argue that we should move away from traditional assessments for learning disabilities because they are designed to measure discrepancies between ability and achievement—which can happen only after the child has failed. There will likely be continued focus on alternative methods to identify children with learning disabilities at an earlier age, so they can receive assistance before they fall behind. While IDEA doesn't currently include any significant alternatives to the existing assessment and eligibility processes for kids with learning disabilities, this could change in the future. Stay tuned.

The sections that follow do not include every test for learning disabilities; there are a variety of assessment tools out there. Don't be surprised if the tests seem to melt into a detailed and somewhat confusing muddle of numbers and phrases, or if you find it difficult to compare the areas covered by these tests—IQ, perception, language and so on—with the language in IDEA that defines learning disabilities. You will learn more about the tests as you read this chapter, do research, and talk to education specialists.

Even experts in learning disabilities—who often have years of experience with these tests—sometimes get bogged down in the numbers and technical language. If you get confused or discouraged, remember these tips:

- Whether anyone else will admit it, a lot of people—even those who work in the field of education—are confused by the multitude of assessment tests. Don't be intimidated by test terminology; if you're confused, chances are good that you're not alone.

- Ask what the test is called, why it is being given, and what all the numbers and phrases mean. If the answer isn't clear, ask again. When the assessor or school administrator uses a term like "short-term auditory memory," "abstract thinking," or "aphasia," ask him or her to explain the concept in language that you (and the other 99% of the population) can understand. I know I have to think for a moment (or longer) to remember what "sequential processing," "simultaneous processing," "spatial memory," and "gestalt closure" are.

- Find out how the test results are recorded—for example, as a percentage score, a "stanine" score (a rating on a scale of 1 through 9), or a chronological score.

- If a number of tests will be given that seem to assess similar skills or functions, find out why. What are the differences between the tests, if any? Is there a reason for giving multiple tests? How does one judge the results of these tests, particularly if they reach different conclusions about the same learning abilities?

Finding Out More About Tests for Learning Disabilities

You can find lots of resources on the many tests for learning disabilities on the Internet; just type the test name into your favorite search engine. Here are some websites you might find especially useful:

- www.parentpals.com (check out their "Special Education Evaluation and Assessment" page)
- www.ldonline.org (the website of Learning Disabilities Online; see the article "Assessments for Young Children" in the "LD In Depth" section), and
- www.nichcy.org/pubs (publications available from the National Information Center for Children and Youth With Disabilities).

If you don't have Web access, your local library should have a number of useful books on learning disabilities and learning disability assessment. Also ask your school district special education administrator for written information on the subject.

Ask the school assessor, other parents, and your pediatrician about tests for learning disabilities. You might also want to check the websites for your state's department of education. For example, the Maryland State Department of Education has a new website for "Identifying Specific Learning Disabilities." These sites often provide other information about learning disabilities, including links to resources within the state department of education. See Appendix 3 for a list of organizations that can provide information about the many tests used in special education.

a. Intelligence Tests

Intelligence tests or IQ tests provide an overall sense of your child's intellectual capabilities and cognitive development. Your child's score will be used, along with other information, to determine whether your child is eligible for special education based on a learning disability. (See Chapter 7 for more on eligibility.) Each of these tests has a number of subtests that assess more specific areas, such as short-term memory and vocabulary.

Here are some IQ tests commonly used for children with learning disabilities:

- Stanford Benet: for individuals from age 2 to adult, this test measures short-term memory and various areas of quantitative, visual, and abstract reasoning.
- Kaufman Assessment Battery for Children (KABC): for children age 2 to 12, the KABC tests both achievement and intelligence (problem–solving rather than factual knowledge); a good test of a child's memory.
- Wechsler Intelligence Scales for Children, 3rd Edition (often referred WISC-III): the WISC-III is often the preferred IQ test. It is used to measure intellectual development and giftedness, and to uncover learning disabilities and developmental delays. The test is divided into Verbal and Performance scales, which measure a child's arithmetic, vocabulary, short-term memory, factual information, comprehension, attention to visual details, and abstract and concrete reasoning skills. The Wechsler scores tend to be in the 60-130 standard score, with a percentile finding ranging from "very superior" to "mentally impaired."

Other important tests, particularly for measuring cognitive development—memory, understanding of concepts, problem-solving and general knowledge—are:

- Battelle Developmental Inventory (assesses motor ability, cognitive levels, and social behavior)
- Bayley Scales of Infant Development (evaluates infant behavior and motor skills), and
- McCarthy Scales of Children's Abilities (tests general verbal, perceptual, and memory IQ).

These three tests are generally used for younger children.

IQ Tests Are Controversial

The use of intelligence or other standardized tests to measure a child's ability is controversial. Compelling arguments have been made that IQ tests do not fully measure native intelligence, but instead reflect certain biases as well as environmental influences on a child. Many tests have been criticized for failing to account for cultural and linguistic differences. For example, the cultural differences between some white and African-American children are not reflected in certain tests, while others do not consider the important linguistic differences between children—some are not appropriate for deaf children (especially those who use American Sign Language) or for children who speak English as a second language.

Some tests have been the subject of pitched court battles. In one federal case, *Larry P. v. Riles*, 793 F.2d 969 (9th Cir. 1984), the court found that IQ tests discriminate against African-Americans. Other tests identify a disproportionate number of racial minorities as needing special education.

At a broader level, many educators and advocates have raised concerns about how heavily schools rely on testing and have questioned whether standardized tests accurately measure ability or achievement. As more and more states require students to take a variety of tests before they can graduate, these questions become increasingly more important.

For what it's worth, statisticians tell us that the "average" range of intelligence, as measured by IQ test scores, is 90-109. One can only wonder how Beethoven, Woody Guthrie, or Rosa Parks might have scored on IQ tests. I wouldn't be surprised if their scores were quite high, but if not, would we question their native intelligence? IQ tests play an important role in the IEP process for kids with learning disabilities, but your child's abilities and potential cannot—and should not—be reduced to a test score.

Test Scatter

IQ tests generally have subtests, and there may be a marked difference—called "scatter"—in your child's subtest scores. For example, a child may score very high on a subtest that evaluates reading comprehension, but very low on a subtest that looks at his understanding of spatial relationships. Your child's IQ score will be an average of these different subtest scores, which may not reflect his true potential and problems. A wide scatter indicates that your child has marked areas of strength and weakness. This is why it's very important to find out how your child scored on the subtests.

b. Assessments for ADD/ADHD

Testing for ADD/ADHD is less technical and formulaic than most tests used for learning disabilities. If you suspect your child has ADD/ADHD, you should have his pediatrician do a thorough medical exam. Observational checklists and teacher and parent rating scales are also often used to determine whether there is ADD/ADHD. These tests are exactly what they sound like—the teacher or parent observes the child and notes whether particular behaviors are present. The Conners' Parent Rating Scales, the Conners' Teacher Rating Scales, and the Child Behavior Checklist are several observational assessment tools that are frequently used for ADD/ADHD.

c. Tests for Perception Abilities

Children with learning disabilities may have difficulties (or strengths) in auditory (listening) or visual (seeing) perception. As part of any evaluation of perception, your child should have his hearing and vision tested to find out whether hearing loss or poor eyesight is part of the problem.

Some tests used to determine whether a student has difficulties processing language (as opposed to a hearing loss) are the Tests of Auditory Perceptual Skills, which assesses auditory memory for numbers, words, and sentences, and the Goldman-Fristoe-Woodcock Test of Auditory Discrimination, which assesses the child's ability to distinguish sounds.

Two tests sometimes used to assess visual perception problems are the Bender Visual Motor Gestalt Test and the Development Test of Visual Motor Integration (in which, among other things, the child is shown designs on a card and is asked to reproduce those shapes).

d. Academic/Psychoeducational tests

These tests measure your child's skill level in specific classroom areas, such as reading, math, writing, and spelling:

- Kaufman Test of Educational Achievement, which assesses decoding skills as well as spelling, reading comprehension, and math skills.
- Wechsler Individual Achievement Test, which assesses some of the same areas as the Kaufman and also oral and written expression and listening comprehension.
- Woodcock-Johnson Psychoeducational Battery, Peabody Individual Achievement Test, which assesses science and social studies comprehension, as well as reading and math skills.
- Test of Written Language (TOWL), which measures writing ability, including capitalization, punctuation, spelling, vocabulary, syntax, grammar, and story composition.

e. Language

Language assessment involves many different areas, including a child's ability to produce and express language through sound, and to receive, understand, and express information.

Some of the more well-known language tests are the Test of Early Language Development (TELD), the Peabody Picture Vocabulary Test (PPVT-R), the Test for Auditory Comprehension of Language (TACL-R), and the Sequenced Inventory for Communication Development—Revised (SICD). The Clinical Evaluation of Language Functioning (CELF) is also a highly respected assessment tool for language. These tests measure, among other things, whether a child understands the words spoken (auditory processing), how to speak, and how to use words in sentences that convey the child's intended meaning.

Make sure you have the right test edition. There are a wide variety of tests used to determine whether a child has a learning disability. Many of these tests have been revised over the years, and now exist in several different version. Make sure that the tests given to your child are the most recent editions. Some tests designate the edition or revision in the title (for example, the WISC-III is the 3rd edition of the Weschler).

D. Approving, Rejecting, or Changing the Assessment Plan

If you have concerns about the assessment plan submitted to you, you have every right to ask for changes. IDEA specifies that the assessment process should include evaluations and information provided by the parents. (34 C.F.R. § 300.533(a)(1)(i).) You can ask that specific tests be administered to your child or that certain information be used to evaluate your child and included as part of the assessment report. This information might include a formal interview with you, a review of your child's school work, a teacher's observations, or a pediatrician's report. Be as specific as possible in your request. For example, if your child has limited fine motor skills and problems with handwriting, ask that the assessor analyze his handwriting samples.

Now is the time to make sure that the plan is appropriate and complete. Before you approve the plan, consider whether the assessment should include any of the following:

- teacher and parent reports
- information from experts specializing in your child's learning disability
- specific tests you want included
- interviews with you and others who know your child well
- letters from a family doctor or counselor
- daily or weekly school reports or diaries, and
- other evidence of school performance, including work samples.

Include a Parent Interview in the Assessment

It is very important to include a parent interview in the assessment. The interview gives the assessor valuable information about your child, much of which may not be available through formal tests—your observations and understanding from living with your child represents a wealth of information for the assessor. A parent interview also gives you a chance to meet with the assessor and make sure that she understands your concerns (and includes them in her report).

How do you know what "other information" should be included in the assessment plan? By this time, you have probably gathered information about your child—secured his school file and talked to his teacher, other parents, or experts—and developed some sense of the key issues. You should also have some ideas about your child's learning difficulties and, therefore, what the assessments should be testing. Be sure to take a look at your blueprint, no matter how incomplete it may be. Also look at Chapter 7, particularly its discussion of IDEA's criteria for determining the existence of a specific learning disability. (34 C.F.R. § 300.541.)

1. Approving or Rejecting the Assessment Plan

If you want changes in the assessment plan, call and write your school district. Explain that you are exercising your right under IDEA (34 C.F.R. § 300.533(a)(1)(i)) to request that additional materials be added to your child's assessment plan and/or items be taken out.

Ultimately, you must sign the assessment plan and indicate whether you accept or reject it. Signing the assessment plan need not be an all or nothing proposition. You can:

- accept the plan
- accept the plan on condition, or
- reject the plan.

a. Accepting the Plan

If you accept the plan as submitted to you, mark the appropriate box—most assessment plans have approval and disapproval boxes—sign and date the plan, and return it to the school district. If there is no acceptance box, write "plan accepted," sign and date the plan, and return it. Be sure to make a photocopy of the assessment plan and add it to your IEP binder.

b. Accepting the Plan on Condition

There are two reasons why you might accept the plan with a condition. First, you might accept the tests proposed, but want additional tests administered or additional information considered. Second, you might not want certain proposed tests administered to your child—perhaps you believe that they aren't reliable or that they test for a problem that your child doesn't have.

Whatever the reason, indicate your partial acceptance of the plan on the form as follows:

> I approve only of the following tests:
> Wrat, Kaufman
> and/or want the following included as part of my child's assessment plan:
> an interview with my child's
> pediatrician and my child's tutor.
> Date: March 1, 20xx
> Signature: Jan Stevens

c. Rejecting the Plan

You have every right to reject the assessment plan and force the assessor or school district to work with you to come up with an acceptable plan. Your reasons for rejecting the plan will usually fall into one or more of the following categories:

- the tests are not appropriate
- you want additional tests and materials as part of the evaluation, or
- the assessor is not qualified.

Assessing the Assessor

Your child's assessment must be "administered by trained and knowledgeable personnel in accordance with any instructions provided by the producer of the tests." (34 C.F.R. § 300.532(c)(ii).) How can you judge the qualifications of the assessor? Here are some guidelines:

- Make sure the assessor has specific knowledge about, and expertise in, learning disability assessments.
- Ask the special education administrator for the credentials of the assessor. If the administrator refuses, assert your right to know under IDEA.
- Ask other parents and your child's teacher what they know about the assessor.
- If you are working with an independent assessor (see Chapter 8), ask her if she knows the school's assessor.
- If possible, meet with the assessor prior to the testing. (See Section D2, below.)

To reject the assessment plan, check off the disapproval box, sign and date the form, and return it to the school district. If there is no box, write "assessment plan rejected," sign and date the form, and return it. Keep a copy.

If the assessment plan is not clear or does not give you enough room for your objections, you should attach a letter to the assessment plan. A sample letter is below. Use this as a model and adjust it depending on your specific situation.

After you submit your rejection (partial or complete) of the assessment plan, the assessor or school district will probably attempt to come up with a plan that meets your approval. If the district feels the original assessment plan was appropriate, it has the right to proceed to mediation or a due process hearing to force the issue, although this is not frequently done. (See Chapter 12.) If the school district does not agree to your changes, you have the right to refuse your consent and/or go to due process yourself for a ruling on your requested changes.

2. Meet With the Assessor

Once you accept the assessment plan proposed by the school district, the assessor will contact you to schedule your child's testing. Now is the time to think ahead. In a few months, when you are at the IEP meeting planning your child's IEP program, the school district will likely pay the most attention to the evaluation done by its own assessor. Therefore, you will want to take some time to establish a positive relationship with the assessor before testing begins.

A good relationship is one in which the parties don't have preconceived ideas about each other or view each other with hostility. Try to put aside any negative comments you might have heard about the assessor from other people (or any bad experiences you've had with the assessor in the past). Start with the assumption (or new attitude) that the assessor is there to help your child get an appropriate education. Of course, this may not be as simple as it seems. The assessor may not be easy to talk to or may be put off by parents who want to play an active role in the assessment process. No matter what attitude the assessor adopts, try to remain rational and pleasant.

Sample Letter Rejecting Assessment Plan

Date: December 14, 20xx

To: Carolyn Ames, Administrator, Special Education
        Central Valley School District
        456 Main Street
        Centerville, MI 47000

Re: Assessment Plan for Michael Kreeskind

I am in receipt of the November 21, 20xx assessment plan for my son Michael. I give my permission for you to administer the Vineland, PPVT-III, and Wechsler (WISC-III) tests, but not the rest of the ones on your list. I have investigated them and feel they are too unreliable.

In addition, I am formally requesting, pursuant to 34 C.F.R. § 300.533, that the assessment plan reflect the following:

- that the assessor will meet with me and my husband to review Michael's entire history and will include the issues raised during that meeting in the assessment report, and

- that the assessor will evaluate samples of Michael's work and letters from professionals who have observed Michael.

I have one final concern. I have reviewed the credentials of Brett Forrest, the assessor selected by the district to evaluate Michael. I am concerned that Mr. Forrest has no prior experience evaluating children with specific or suspected learning disabilities. Specifically, I do not believe he is trained or knowledgeable about the specific tests to be administered, as required under IDEA, 34 C.F.R. § 300.532(c)(ii). Therefore, I do not approve of the assigned assessor, Brett Forrest, and request that an appropriate one be assigned, and that we be given proof of the assessor's qualifications.

Thank you very much.

Michelle Kreeskind

Michelle Kreeskind
8 Rock Road
Centerville, MI 47000
Phones: 555-9876 (home); 555-5450 (work)

Reality Check: The Assessor Works for the School District

While you should assume that the assessor wants to develop a good and appropriate educational plan for your child, don't lose sight of the fact that the assessor is an employee of the school district. Some assessors know exactly what a school district can provide and will tailor their assessment reports accordingly, rather than prepare a report based on what a child truly needs.

On the other hand, just because the assessor's report doesn't support what you want, it doesn't necessarily follow that the assessor is acting against your child's best interests. Her conclusions may be well reasoned and supported by the data. Be objective. Are her recommendations consistent with or contrary to what you know about your child? If you conclude that the assessor is biased against you, request a new one. Remember, you always have the right to an outside or independent assessment. (See Chapter 8.)

Your job is to educate the assessor about your child. She'll have test results to evaluate and reports to read. But she doesn't live with your child. To the extent possible, help the assessor see your child from your perspective, particularly as it relates to the academic programs and services you feel are necessary for your child. Ideally, you want the assessment report completed by the assessor to recommend eligibility and the program and services you want for your child as articulated in your blueprint (in Chapter 5).

So how do you get your points across to the assessor? If possible, meet with the assessor before the testing is done (another reason why including a parental interview in the assessment plan is so important). The law doesn't require an assessor to meet with you (unless that's part of the assessment plan), but the law does not prohibit it, either. Call up and ask for an appointment. Say that you'd appreciate the chance to talk, are not familiar with all the tests, would like to find out how they are used, and would just feel a lot better if you could meet for 10 or 15 minutes. If the assessor cannot meet with you, ask for a brief phone consultation or send a letter expressing your concerns.

Whether you meet in person, talk on the phone, or state your concerns in a letter, you'll want to be clear and objective about:

- **Eligibility assessment.** Let the assessor know the specific problems your child is having in school, the material you have documenting those problems, and why you believe those problems qualify your child for special education.

Example:

"Carl has had a terrible time with reading. He's only in the second grade, but he is way behind. His teacher agrees—I have some notes of my conversation with her from last October. I could provide you with a copy of them if that would help. I'd greatly appreciate it if you could focus on Carl's reading problem in your assessment."

- **IEP program assessment.** If your child is already in special education or is likely to be found eligible, let the assessor know of the IEP program components you believe are important.

Examples:

"Billy needs a small, highly structured class with minimal distractions.

"Howard needs a lot of work with reading, reading comprehension, and language skills. I would like you to evaluate the reports done by his doctor, his teacher, and the classroom aide, and address their suggestions in your recommendations section."

Be careful about how specific you get. The assessor may think you're trying to do his job and might not appreciate being told exactly what to include in the assessment report. For example, coming right out with "Please recommend that Mary have a full-time, one-on-one aide" or "Please write that Tom should be placed in the learning disability program at Center School" may be a little too direct. You may need to be a bit less specific, such as "The teacher wrote that Mary can't learn to read without constant one-on-one attention. Would you please address that need in your report." Remember, your blueprint is a good guide here.

Don't be disappointed if the assessor doesn't fully or even partially agree with what you are requesting. The best you can do is to be clear about your child's problem, what you feel your child needs, and what materials support your conclusions. The rest is up to the assessor. Ultimately, if the assessor does not address your concerns and you have good evidence to support them, the value of the school's assessment may be diminished.

E. Reviewing the Assessment Report

After your child is evaluated, the assessor will issue his report. Some assessors issue their reports in two stages: a draft report and a final report. Ask the assessor how and when he plans to issue his report. Ideally, the assessor will write a draft report that you can review before he submits his final report prior to the IEP meeting. Ask to see a draft report, but don't be surprised if your request is rejected. IDEA does not require your school district to show you a draft of the assessment report.

Even if the assessor will issue only one version of the report, it is imperative that you see it before the IEP meeting. IDEA requires the school district to give you a copy of the evaluation report and information documenting eligibility. (34 C.F.R. § 300.534(a)(2).)

If the district is unwilling to show you the assessment report before the meeting, simply indicate (in writing) that you won't agree to an IEP meeting date until you receive the report. Of course, the district might not care too much about postponing the IEP meeting, so you might also say that holding the IEP meeting before you have the chance to see the report will require additional meetings and use up more district resources.

By asking to see the report (preferably a draft of the report) ahead of time, you let the school district know that you plan to carefully review the assessor's work. This will help you keep a sense of control over the assessment process and prepare for the IEP meeting. It will also keep you from wasting valuable time poring over the report at the IEP meeting.

A sample letter requesting the assessment report is included here; a blank, tear-out copy is in Appendix 5.

If the assessor shows you a draft of the report and you disagree with anything in it or feel something is missing, ask the assessor to make a change or add the missing information. Be prepared to point to material outside the assessment report that supports your point of view.

If the assessor won't make the changes—or sends you only the final version—what can you do if you disagree with the final assessment report? You can reject it. While you can express your disagreement before the IEP, it might be a better strategy to wait for the meeting and prepare your counter-arguments with the evidence you have, including existing material and your independent assessment (if any).

Don't forget independent assessments. Remember that you have the right to have your child assessed by someone outside of the school district, often referred to as a private or independent assessment. As discussed in Chapter 8, such independent assessments are tremendously valuable when you disagree with the school district's assessment. The independent assessor can analyze the district's assessment in detail and point out any shortcomings.

Letter Requesting Assessment Report

Date: _____ November 3, 20xx

To: Harvey Smith, Assessment Team

Pine Hills Elementary School

234 Lincoln Road

Boston, MA 02000

Re: Robin Griffin, student in Sean Jordan's 1st grade class

I appreciate your involvement in my child's assessment and look forward to your report. Would you please:

1. Send me a copy of a draft of your report before you finalize it. As you can imagine, the process can be overwhelming for parents. It would be most helpful to me to see your report, because the proposed tests are complicated and I need time to evaluate the results.

2. Send me your final report at least four weeks before the IEP meeting.

Again, thank you for your kind assistance.

Sincerely,

Lee Griffin

Lee Griffin

23 Hillcrest Road

Boston, MA 02000

Phones: 555-4321 (home); 555-9876 (work)

7

Eligibility

etermining your child's eligibility for special education is a two-step procedure. First, your child is assessed. Next, the IEP team meets to determine whether he qualifies for special education. This IEP meeting is different from the IEP meeting where your child's annual academic program is developed, although they may be combined. (See Section E, below.)

Eligibility, like assessments, IEP meetings, and other aspects of the special education process, is bound by the requirements of IDEA. And like those other procedures, it can be a source of disagreement between parents and a school district (and therefore subject to due process—see Chapter 12).

If your child has already been found eligible for special education, skip ahead to Chapter 8. If your child hasn't yet been found eligible and you haven't read the chapter on assessments, read Chapter 6 before reading this chapter. Your child will be found eligible for special education only if the assessment demonstrates that she meets the criteria explained in this chapter. Therefore, you must keep the eligibility requirements in mind as you prepare for the assessment. Similarly, you must consider what types of tests and analyses might demonstrate a qualifying condition as you learn about eligibility requirements.

Your child may be found eligible for special education based on any of a number of disabling conditions listed in IDEA. To qualify on the basis of a learning disability, your child must meet very specific eligibility requirements. These requirements are fairly technical; if you find yourself in a muddle, remember these tips:

- Take it slowly. Some of the qualifying conditions have multi-layered definitions. Don't try to take it in all at once. Breaking a definition down into manageable parts will help you figure out what evidence you need to show that your child meets all of the eligibility requirements.

- **You're not a specialist in learning disabilities and you don't have to become one.** Don't be put off by some of the complicated terminology. For now, you need a basic understanding of your child's condition and how it affects his or her educational experience. Ask your pediatrician, the school nurse, or the assessor. Contact other parents and local or national learning disability support or advocacy organizations, (Chapter 15 discusses parent organizations, and Appendix 3 lists useful resources.)

- **Focus on key portions of each definition.** Pay attention to words such as "severe" or "significant." These are clues that a minor disability may not qualify your child for special education. If your child doesn't fall under one of the delineated conditions, take a look at the catchall category, "other health impairment." If your child does not ultimately qualify as learning disabled, she may be eligible under other special education categories. (34 C.F.R. § 300.7.)

- **The IEP team has flexibility in finding eligibility.** The IEP team has the authority to find a child eligible under the learning disability category (and other categories) even if that child doesn't meet the formula set forth in the IDEA. As explained in Section B2 of this chapter, below, there are alternative tests for eligibility based on a learning disability, which don't rely on mathematical formulae.

Eligibility Is Not an Annual Event

Once your child is found eligible for special education, he won't need to requalify each year. There are only three situations in which your child's eligibility might have to be determined again:

- Your child dropped out of special education and wants to reenter.
- You or school district representatives propose a change from one eligibility category to another (for example, if it becomes apparent that your child's difficulties in school are related to ADD/ADHD rather than a specific learning disability as defined by IDEA).
- There is evidence that your child no longer qualifies for special education (for example, your older child's reading disability has been remediated to the point where he is reading at grade level and doing well in school).

This chapter covers eligibility, from start to finish. Section A explains the general requirements your child must meet to be eligible for special education. Section B discusses the more detailed (and often more confusing) criteria used to determine special education eligibility based on a learning disability. Sections C, D, and E describe the IEP eligibility meeting: the meeting where the IEP team decides whether your child qualifies for special education. And Section F explains your options if your child is not found eligible.

A. Eligibility Definitions

In order to qualify for special education, your child must meet two eligibility requirements: (1) She must have a disabling condition, as defined in IDEA, and (2) that condition must have an adverse impact on her education. In other words, it is not enough to show that your child has a disability—you must also show that your child's disability is causing enough problems to warrant special education help.

This section covers these requirements. In Section B, below, we discuss the special rules that apply to children with learning disabilities.

1. Disabling Condition

IDEA provides a list of disabling conditions that qualify a child between the ages of three and 22 for special education, including:

- hearing impairments, including deafness
- speech or language impairments, such as stuttering or other speech production difficulties
- visual impairments, including blindness
- multiple disabilities, such as deaf-blindness
- orthopedic impairments caused by congenital anomalies, such as a club foot
- orthopedic impairments caused by diseases such as polio
- orthopedic impairments caused by other conditions such as cerebral palsy
- learning disabilities
- emotional disturbance (see "Emotional Disturbance as a Disabling Condition," below)
- autism
- traumatic brain injury
- mental retardation, and
- other health impairments that affect a child's strength, vitality, or alertness, such as a heart condition, tuberculosis, rheumatic fever, nephritis, asthma, sickle cell anemia, hemophilia, epilepsy, lead poisoning, leukemia, diabetes, Attention Deficit Disorder (ADD), and Attention Deficit Hyperactivity Disorder (ADHD).

A Word About Labels

This list of disability categories asks you to define your child as "this" or "that." Labeling is one of the difficult and unpleasant parts of the IEP process. Many people feel that labels are unnecessary, even harmful—and from a psychological perspective, they may be right. From a legal perspective, however, your child will be eligible for special education only if he fits into one of these categories. If you can, focus on the specifics of your child's condition rather than the label. Remember, your goal is to secure an appropriate education for your child; proving that your child qualifies for special education under one of the eligibility categories is part of the process.

There's a fine line, however, between acknowledging the label for the purpose of meeting the eligibility criteria and making sure your child does not become defined by that label. For example, Bill has dyslexia, which causes him some significant problems in school and qualifies him for special education. But Bill is also a terrific center on the basketball team, he hates to clean up his room, at times he frustrates you and certainly worries you, he has a good heart, and, most important, he is quite determined to make his way in the world. These are the qualities that label him.

You can find the legal definition of each of these disabling conditions at 20 U.S.C. § 1401(3) and 34 C.F.R. § 300.7. (See Appendix 1.) You'll see that the eligibility criteria for each of the listed disabilities are slightly different.

2. Adverse Impact

It is not enough to show that your child has a disabling condition; you must also demonstrate that your child's disability has an adverse impact on her educational performance. Proving this adverse impact will be the crux of your eligibility work.

IDEA does not say how "adverse impact" is measured, but your child's grades, test scores, and classroom or other behavior will provide important evidence of adverse impact. While grades can most directly show whether a disabling condition is adversely affecting educational performance or achievement, they don't tell the whole eligibility story. A parent can (and should) argue that a child who receives As, Bs, or Cs but cannot read at age level, has trouble processing language, or has great difficulty with spelling is not benefiting from her education, and that her disability is therefore directly affecting her educational performance and experience, regardless of her grades.

If your child is getting passing grades, you will need to make the connection between your child's disability and school performance in some other way. Factors to consider (other than grades) include:

- limited progress—for example, little or no improvement in reading, math, or spelling even though the teacher does not fail your child; high school students might have significant difficulty in social studies, algebra, or English
- difficulties in cognitive areas, such as mastering basic concepts, memory, or language skills—forgetting to turn in homework, trouble with reading comprehension, or difficulty grasping abstract concepts in math or history might demonstrate these problems
- discrepancy between performance and ability—for example, the child is developmentally and chronologically ten years old, but reads at a six-year-old's level; your 8th grader has an above-average IQ but is performing at the 6th grade level on math and spelling tests

Emotional Disturbance as a Disabling Condition

A child who has an "emotional disturbance" (this is the term used by IDEA) qualifies for special education. Although this term can conjure up images of bizarre behavior and institutionalization, children with a wide range of emotional difficulties can qualify for special education in this category. When you look at the actual defining language in IDEA, you'll see that it encompasses issues that might affect most human beings at some point in their lives, and certainly could arise for children who might have a learning disability. Some children with learning disabilities, especially those who do not receive support and services, may have difficulties with peers and/or teachers, have trouble sleeping and eating, or experience fears and anxieties as a result of the consequences of the learning disability. For example, it would not be surprising if a child with a learning disability does not want to go to school and seems to feel sick a lot of the time.

IDEA defines an emotional disturbance as a condition that has existed over a long period of time and adversely affects your child's educational performance (20 U.S.C. § 1401(3)(A)(i); 34 C.F.R. § 300.7(c)(4)), resulting in:

- inability to learn that is not explained by intellectual, sensory, or health factors
- inability to build or maintain satisfactory interpersonal relationships with peers and teachers
- inappropriate behaviors or feelings under normal circumstances (for example, extreme frustration, anger, or aggression over minor setbacks or disagreements)
- general pervasive mood of unhappiness or depression, or
- tendency to develop physical symptoms or fears associated with personal or school problems (for example, a child might get a stomach ache before tests or oral reports).

A child who is only socially maladjusted will not qualify for special education, although a child who is emotionally disturbed under IDEA can, of course, be socially maladjusted. A child with a learning disability may also have some of the characteristics listed above but not qualify as having an "emotional disturbance" under IDEA. The IEP team still can (and should) address those emotional difficulties in the IEP by developing goals and objectives and providing services to meet those emotional needs. In this situation, you want to treat the emotional difficulties as part of the learning disability. Rather than label the behaviors as an "emotional disturbance," simply have the IEP team address them as one of many aspects of your child's learning disability. For example, the IEP might describe how the teacher, teacher's aide, school counselor, and written goals and objectives might address your child's fears about taking written tests, or how your child might deal in a concrete and helpful way with peers who tease him because of his difficulties in class.

- evidence of emotional, behavioral, or social difficulties, or
- physical difficulties, such as handwriting or hearing problems.

The IEP team has a lot of discretion in determining whether your child is eligible for special education. If your child has passing grades, the team may have to exercise that discretion to find that her disability has adversely affected her educational performance in other ways. You'll find more on adverse impact in Section B2, below.

B. Eligibility Standards for Children With Learning Disabilities

IDEA refers to learning disabilities in two different places. A general definition of learning disabilities appears in the list of eligibility conditions (34 C.F.R. § 300.7); this definition is covered in Section 1, below. The regulations also provide detailed criteria explaining how a child qualifies for special education based on a learning disability (34 C.F.R. § 541). These rules are discussed in Section 2, below.

1. Learning Disabilities Defined

IDEA defines a learning disability as a "disorder in one or more of the basic psychological processes involved in understanding or in using language, spoken or written, that may manifest itself in an imperfect ability to listen, think, speak, read, write, spell, or to do mathematical calculations." This definition includes such conditions as "perceptual disabilities, brain injury, minimal brain dysfunction, dyslexia, and developmental aphasia." (20 U.S.C. § 1401(26); 34 C.F.R. § 300.7.)

State and Federal Definitions of Learning Disabilities

Many states have their own definitions of learning disabilities. For example, West Virginia law defines learning disabilities as "a heterogeneous group of disorders manifested by significant deficits in the acquisition and use of listening, speaking, reading, writing, reasoning, or mathematical abilities." Minnesota defines a learning disability more simply as a "severe underachievement."

As discussed in Chapter 2, states are allowed to enact special education laws that give children more protections and rights than the IDEA. State law, however, cannot take away rights the IDEA provides—no matter what your state law says, your child is always entitled to the protections and requirements of the IDEA.

As a general rule, state laws defining a learning disability tend to be more complicated and detailed than the IDEA. School districts often use state law definitions, but you can rely on IDEA if your state's law is too confusing or complicated. If you think your state law on learning disability eligibility violates IDEA (that is, it is more restrictive or less protective of your child), you should contact your state department of education and the U.S. Department of Education and Office of Civil Rights. (See Appendix 2.)

2. Criteria for Eligibility Based on a Learning Disability

In order for a child to be eligible based on a learning disability, the IEP team must agree that he (1) "does not achieve commensurate with his or her age and ability levels" and (2) has a "severe discrepancy between ability and achievement" in one of the following areas:

- oral expression
- listening comprehension
- written expression
- basic reading skill
- reading comprehension
- mathematics calculation, or
- mathematics reasoning. (34 C.F.R. § 300.541.)

These two requirements are the key to the IEP eligibility maze for children with learning disabilities—we discuss them in Subsections a and b, below.

Conditions That Don't Qualify as Learning Disabilities

Certain conditions do not qualify as learning disabilities, even if they create a gap between ability and achievement. Your child will not be eligible if a discrepancy is primarily the result of:

- a visual, hearing, or motor impairment
- mental retardation
- emotional disturbance, or
- environmental, cultural, or economic disadvantage.

Of course, your child might qualify for special education based on a visual, hearing, or motor disability; mental retardation; or an emotional disability, even if these problems do not qualify your child as learning disabled. (See 34 C.F.R. § 300.7 (c)(4), (5), (6), (8), and (13).)

Your child also cannot be found eligible based on "lack of instruction in reading or math or limited English proficiency." (34 C.F.R. § 300.534.) In other words, if your child's problems can be chalked up to lack of schooling or lack of fluency in the English language, he will not qualify as learning disabled.

As you read the following sections, you will find some fairly complicated processes for determining eligibility, including statistical terminology and mathematical formulas. Remember, however, that most states also have regulations that provide some kind of alternative way to determine learning disability eligibility. Even though you should try to master the math, remember that your state law may provide alternatives that are a bit easier to navigate.

a. Commensurate Achievement

The first requirement for eligibility based on a learning disability is that your child does not achieve "commensurate" with his age and ability levels. (34 C.F.R. § 300.541(a)(1).) This means that your child's educational achievement is not keeping up with his age and ability in at least one of the listed areas (oral expression, listening comprehension, written expression, and so on). Note that you don't have to show that your child cannot keep up in all seven listed areas, just that his achievement lags behind in at least one of them.

Generally, if your child's grades, test scores, or classroom performance are lower than they should be, based on her age and ability (as measured by IQ tests), she is not "achieving commensurate" and meets this part of the test. For example, if your child's reading skills or math grades are below her age and IQ level, she is not "achieving commensurate." What constitutes a big enough gap between IQ/age and school performance to meet this part of the requirement? There is no specific formula, but an achievement difference of one year or more is common for a child with learning disabilities (for example, the child is ten years old and has an average IQ, but reads at an eight-year-old level or has the language development of a 1st or 2nd grader).

b. Severe Discrepancy

The second requirement is proof of a "severe discrepancy" between your child's achievement and intellectual ability in at least one of the seven areas listed at the beginning of this section. This rule is probably the most confusing part of the entire IEP process. The concept is easy enough to grasp: There must be a significant gap between your child's intelligence and her ability to achieve academically. However, the formulae many states use to determine whether this gap is "severe" are so complicated, you might think it's time to take out your slide rule and sharpen some No. 2 pencils. I will walk you through some common state law requirements below.

As you read through the information that follows, remember that IDEA does *not* include a mathematical formula to prove "severe discrepancy," and many states provide an alternative, nonmathematical method for learning disability eligibility (usually based on other evidence of your child's achievement, such as work samples, grades, or classroom performance).

i.   How States Define Severe Discrepancy

States have adopted many different ways to demonstrate a severe discrepancy. Although these requirements differ, they have at least one thing in common: They can confuse the heck out of anybody. Here are two examples:

- Under West Virginia law (Policy 2419), a severe discrepancy is determined by comparing age-based standard scores of ability and achievement. A regression formula is used to determine the severity of the discrepancy. A severe discrepancy is defined as "a minimum of 1.75 standard deviations difference, taking regression and 1.0 standard error of measurement into account."

- Under California law (5 Cal. Code of Regulations § 3030(j)(4)(A)), a severe discrepancy "is demonstrated by: first, converting into common standard scores, using a mean of 100 and standard deviation of 15, the achievement test score and the ability test score to be compared; second, computing the difference between these common standard scores; and third, comparing this computed difference to the standard criterion which is the product of 1.5 multiplied by

the standard deviation of the distribution of computed differences of students taking these achievement and ability tests. A computed difference which equals or exceeds this standard criterion, adjusted by one standard error of measurement, the adjustment not to exceed 4 common standard score points, indicates a severe discrepancy when such discrepancy is corroborated by other assessment data which may include other tests, scales, instruments, observations, and work samples, as appropriate."

At this point, you probably think you'll have to hire a team of mathematicians to get your child into special education, but these equations aren't as complicated as they seem. Generally, these state rules all boil down to the same thing: figuring out whether the difference between your child's ability and achievement (as expressed in numerical test scores) is large enough to show a severe discrepancy. This process involves three steps:

1. **Measuring** your child's intellectual ability using an IQ test (commonly used IQ tests include the Kaufman Assessment Battery, Wechsler and Stanford-Benet).

2. **Measuring** your child's achievement in areas where learning disabilities are suspected (common achievement tests include the TOWL, Woodcock Johnson, and Peabody Picture Vocabulary; see Chapter 6 for more information on achievement and IQ tests).

3. **Comparing** your child's ability score with his achievement score to determine whether the difference meets the numeric "gap" that your state uses to define a severe discrepancy.

How many tests must show this "severe discrepancy"? States, school districts, and even schools can differ on this question. Because IDEA says that eligibility cannot be based on the results of one test (34 C.F.R. § 300.532), you should assume that your child will have to show a severe discrepancy on several tests to be eligible.

ii.   State Formulas: Defining the Terms

Most state formulas for determining whether a child has a severe discrepancy use statistical terms like "mean score," "standard deviation," and "standard error." What do they mean? A mean score (sometimes called an average score) is the standard score an average child in the appropriate age group will achieve on a test. For example, California refers to tests that have an average standard score of 100—this means that the average child will score 100 on that test.

The term "standard deviation" is a range (plus or minus) of numbers above or below the average, intended to reflect the fact that even average students do not get exactly the same scores on every test. Look at it this way: If a large number of average students took a test with an average score of 100, they would not all score exactly 100 points on the test. Instead, their scores would fall in a range from somewhere slightly above to somewhere slightly below the 100 average. This means the discrepancy in their test scores—the difference between their ability test score and achievement test score—would also fall into a measurable range.

The standard deviation puts a number on that range of average scores. If the discrepancy in a student's test scores fall outside of that range—in other words, if there is a greater-than-average gap between the student's test scores—then the child is outside of the "standard deviation."

States use the concept of standard deviation in a couple of ways. Some states simply assign a number to the standard deviation. In California, for example, the standard deviation is 15. This means that on tests with a mean score of 100, a discrepancy of up to 15 points would still fall within the realm of average (rather than severe) and therefore would not demonstrate that the student has a learning disability.

Other states don't assign a fixed number to the standard deviation, but instead calculate it based on the actual spread in scores on particular tests. A child whose discrepancy is at least a certain number of standard deviations beyond the average will qualify on the basis of a learning disability. For example, in West Virginia, a child must score 1.75 standard deviations off the average to show a severe discrepancy. There is no universal standard deviation—each test will have its own number.

Feeling Confused?

Well, you're not alone. These formulas can be complicated. But the concept behind them is fairly straightforward. They are all ways of measuring how far off the average the discrepancy in a child's test scores must be before the state will attribute the difference to a learning disability.

Trying to figure out all of this math can drive parents a bit crazy. We have to rely on objective standards to prove a learning disability, but the language of these laws shows how easy it is to lose sight of the big picture when we reduce everything to numbers. Although your child's eligibility for special education may depend, in some part, on numbers, your child's life won't be defined by them. As you try to understand and use this process to get your child the help she needs, don't give these tests and numbers more power than they deserve.

The term "standard error" accounts for the inherent imperfections in any test. It means that for any child taking a test, the score could be "off" by a certain number of points because of the inherent inaccuracy of the test as a tool for measuring ability or achievement. California uses a standard error number of 4, which means that the child's actual score could be off by up to 4 points in either direction, based on the inherent flaws of the test. Standard error varies from test to test—there is no universal number.

iii. State Formulas Applied: A Sample Calculation

Now that you're familiar with some of the terminology, you're ready to tackle your state's formula. Let's take California as an example. That formula requires you to compare the discrepancy between your child's achievement and ability test scores (using a mean of 100 and standard deviation of 15) to "the standard criterion which is the product of 1.5 multiplied by the standard deviation of the distribution of computed differences of students taking these achievement and ability tests. A computed difference which equals or exceeds this standard criterion, adjusted by one standard error of measurement, the adjustment not to exceed 4 common standard score points, indicates a severe discrepancy."

Despite the complicated verbiage, the key numbers are 100 (mean score), 15 (standard deviation), 1.5 (multiplier), and 4 (standard error). To find out how large the discrepancy between your child's test scores must be, multiply the standard deviation (15) by the multiplier (1.5), for a total of 22.5 points. Then, add the standard error points (4) for a total of 26.5. This is the number that represents a severe discrepancy between a child's ability and achievement. If your child's ability test scores are at least 26.5 points higher than her achievement test scores, she will be eligible for special education.

Note to California parents: There is some debate about California's eligibility formula. Some school districts do not add the 4 "error" points, which means that the gap must be at least 22.5 (1.5 times 15 standard deviation points). Because this is a lower "discrepancy" number, more children will qualify for special education using this test. You should also know that some school districts in California simply don't use this complicated formula—instead, they look at classroom performance to determine whether there is a severe discrepancy.

Using the 26.5 severe discrepancy number, if your child's ability (IQ) test score is 110 and her achievement score is 96, she won't qualify—the difference of 14 points is not "severe" enough. On the other hand, if her IQ score is 125, she would qualify: The point differential of 29 exceeds the state standard of 26.5. If her ability score is 110 and her achievement score is 81, she would also qualify, because the difference is again 29. As you can see, the key is not how high or low either score is, but the difference between them.

iv. Alternative Tests for Proving a Severe Discrepancy

As noted, there are often alternatives to these complicated mathematical formulas. Many states have what is sometimes referred to as "bailout" language: provisions that set forth other ways to prove a severe discrepancy. Usually, you can find this language in or near the statutory section that includes your state's formulas for learning disability eligibility. For example, California law provides that if the standardized tests are not valid for a particular student, the discrepancy shall be measured "by alternative means as specified in the assessment plan." These alternative means might include other standardized assessment instruments, information from the child's parent or teacher, the student's classroom performance (including work samples and observations) and any other relevant information. (5 Cal. Code of Regulations § 3030 (j)(4)(B) and (C).)

These alternative provisions stem from IDEA's requirement that the specific tests administered to your child must be valid for testing the areas of suspected disability. (34 C.F.R. § 300.532.) If your state does not offer an alternative way to show severe discrepancy and you believe that the proposed tests aren't valid for your child or your child's disability, you can rely on IDEA and ask the IEP team to determine your child's eligibility based on federal law.

How to Argue Against a Mathematical Formula

If your state has a mathematical process for determining "severe discrepancy," how do you argue that it should not be used? The first step is to make sure you have a copy of any state law that provides for an alternative method of proving eligibility (contact your state department of education to get a copy; see Appendix 2). If there is no state "alternative," you can rely on IDEA. Argue that the federal law gives your child rights that state law can't diminish—if your state law is making it more difficult for your child to be served, it violates IDEA.

The eligibility section of the IDEA regulations provide that each school district must "draw upon information from a *variety of sources*, including aptitude and achievement tests, *parent input, teacher recommendations* …" when determining eligibility. (34 C.F.R. § 300.535(a)(1).) The IEP team must also review all "existing evaluation data" including "evaluations and information provided by the parents," classroom and other "observations." (34 C.F.R. § 300.533(a)(1).) This clearly requires the IEP

team to look to input other than tests to determine eligibility. IDEA also prohibits school districts from relying on any "single procedure" as the sole criterion for determining whether a child has a disability and requires the school district to use "assessment tools and strategies that provide relevant information that directly assists persons in determining the educational needs of the child." (34 C.F.R. § 300.532.)

You can also argue that the standardized tests are not valid—for example, that they do not test for your child's specific disabling conditions, that they were given by someone who lacked the necessary training, or that too few tests were administered, any of which violate 34 C.F.R. § 300.532(c)(1)(i)(ii). Taken together, these parts of IDEA clearly underscore the importance of alternative means of assessing a child. You should cite them when you argue that the state mathematical formula is not the only way to prove that your child is eligible under the learning disability category.

You will have to prove eligibility through the alternative methods—for example, by showing that grades, classroom behavior, performance, and work samples reveal the necessary discrepancy. Ask the classroom teacher whether your child's work reflects a gap between her ability and her actual achievement. Compare old and current work samples, grades, and other indicators showing that your child has not progressed at a pace consistent with her abilities. Show the IEP team writing, spelling, or math samples that reveal the struggle your child is having. Tell the team, directly and unequivocally, that these samples reveal a severe discrepancy every bit as valid as any specific testing results.

Some States Don't Require You to Do the Math

Not every state has adopted a complicated mathematical formula for measuring severe discrepancy. For example, Alaska provides that a child will be eligible based on a learning disability if she "exhibits a specific learning disability as defined in 34 C.F.R. 300.7(c)(10) and 34 C.F.R. 300.541." That's it—no standard deviations, no means, and no multipliers. If your state doesn't have a numerical requirement, the severe discrepancy determination will be based on work samples, classroom observations, tests, and other assessment tools, as discussed in this section.

---

v.   How to Find Out About Your State's Severe Discrepancy Law

As you can see, the way your state defines and measures a severe discrepancy is a crucial piece of the eligibility puzzle. To find out more about your state's rules, start by asking your school district these questions:

- Which state law or regulation defines "learning disability" and "severe discrep-

ancy"? (Be sure to ask for a copy—the school district is required to give you one.)
- What tests are used to measure the severity of the discrepancy?
- What scores are used to measure the discrepancy? Some schools use the overall score for a test, while others use only parts or subtests.
- Do the tests used measure the impact of learning disabilities, particularly the skills and abilities listed in IDEA (reading comprehension, oral expression, mathematics calculation, and so on)?
- Are there mean or average test scores? If so, what are they?
- What is the standard deviation?
- Are there other components of the "severe discrepancy" formula, such as standard error?

Once you get this information, ask your school district, child's teacher, special education administrator, or assessor to go through the specific language and meaning of the "severe discrepancy" requirements with you. Ask whether they have any materials that will help you understand these concepts. The assessor should be especially equipped to explain the "severe discrepancy" language and numbers to you. If you are working with an independent assessor or another learning disability specialist, she will also be able to explain how the formula works.

Don't be afraid to ask follow-up questions until you truly understand the eligibility rules. Remember, this language and how it is applied in your school district could determine whether your child qualifies for special education. It's worth taking some extra time to make sure that you understand the state's criteria.

Get a copy of your state's requirements at your state department of education's website (see Appendix 2) or call the department and ask them to send you a copy of the specific eligibility requirements for children with learning disabilities, including statutes, regulations, policies, and any explanatory materials. You can also get state eligibility laws from other websites, such as Megalaw.Com (www.megalaw.com/top /education/php).

C. Preparing for the IEP Eligibility Meeting

After your child is assessed, the school district will schedule an IEP meeting to discuss your child's eligibility for special education. The IEP program meeting—when you and the school district hammer out the components of your child's IEP— must be held within 30 days after your child is found eligible for special education. (34 C.F.R. § 300.343 (b)(2).) Depending on the circumstances of your case, your school district may hold off scheduling the IEP program meeting until after your child is found eligible. But if it seems likely that your child will be found eligible, the school district may schedule the IEP program meeting to immediately follow the eligibility meeting.

The strategies for a successful IEP eligibility meeting and a successful IEP program meeting are the same. To prepare for the IEP eligibility meeting—or the possibility of a joint IEP eligibility and program meeting—review Chapters 10 and 11.

To prepare for the eligibility meeting, follow these tips:

- **Get a copy of your child's school file.** If you don't already have a copy, see Chapter 4.
- **Get copies of all school assessments.** Assessments are covered in Chapter 6. Section E includes a sample letter requesting the assessment report.
- **Find out the school district's position.** If the assessment report recommends eligibility, call the special education administrator and ask if the district will agree with that recom-

mendation. If the answer is yes, ask whether the IEP program meeting will be held right after the eligibility meeting. If the assessment report is not clear about eligibility, call the administrator and ask what the district's position is on your child's eligibility. If the assessment recommends against eligibility, be prepared to show that your child is eligible. Here are a few suggestions:

- ▲ *Review the school file and assessment report.* Cull out information that supports your child's eligibility, such as test results, grades, and teacher comments.
- ▲ *Organize all other reports and written material that support your position on eligibility.* Observations from teachers and teachers' aides are especially important. Ask anyone who has observed your child and agrees that he should be in special education to attend the IEP eligibility meeting. If a key person cannot attend, ask for a letter or written observation report.
- ▲ *Consider having your child assessed by an independent assessor.* An independent assessment may be necessary if the school district's report concludes that your child is not eligible for special education. Even if your child is found eligible, you may disagree with the school's recommendations regarding services and programs—many times these are spelled out in the school district's assessment report. The independent assessor is often your strongest and most qualified supporter for eligibility and the components of the IEP. See Chapter 8G for more on independent assessments.
- **Get organized.** Organize all of your documentation before the eligibility meeting, so you can find what you need right away.
- **Do your homework.** Be prepared to discuss your state's criteria for eligibility based on a learning disability. Plan how you will show

that your child has a severe discrepancy, either through the state's mathematical formula or by alternative means.

Chapter 8 provides tips that will help you organize existing material—and develop new information—to make your case at an IEP eligibility or program meeting. Chapter 8 also discusses how to use an independent assessor.

D. Attending the Eligibility Meeting

Many of the procedures and strategies used at the IEP eligibility meeting are similar to those used at an IEP program meeting. Chapters 10 and 11 explain how to prepare for, and make your points at, an IEP meeting. This section highlights some issues that are particularly important for eligibility meetings.

1. Who Should Attend?

For a child with a learning disability, the IEP team must include the parent, the child's regular teacher (or a regular classroom teacher qualified to teach a child of that age, if the child has no regular teacher or has not yet reached school age), and at least one person qualified to conduct individual diagnostic examinations of children, such as a school psychologist, speech-language pathologist, or remedial reading teacher. (34 C.F.R. § 540.)

You may want to ask others to attend, however, especially if you anticipate a fight over eligibility or don't know the district's position. (If your school district appears ready to find your child eligible for special education, you won't likely need anyone else at the meeting.) Such people might include:

- an independent assessor
- teachers who have worked with your child
- other professionals who know your child, and

- an expert who can explain assessments and how your child meets your state's eligibility requirements, particularly the "severe discrepancy" portion of the rule.

Whether you decide to ask any of these people to attend the IEP eligibility meeting may depend on their availability, the strength of their point of view, and cost. Sometimes, a letter from your pediatrician or another professional might be just as effective (and certainly less expensive) than paying your pediatrician to attend in person. As a general rule, do not pay someone to attend the IEP eligibility meeting unless you are certain that there will be a disagreement and you'll need that person to argue your side. In most eligibility disputes, an independent assessor will be your most effective witness.

2. Preparing Your Participants

Make sure your participants are prepared to:
- describe who they are, their training, and how they know your child
- discuss their conclusions about your child's eligibility for special education and the basis for those conclusions—such as observation, long-term knowledge of your child, or testing
- contradict any material concluding that your child is not eligible for special education, and
- prove that your child has a "severe discrepancy" as defined by your state's rules.

3. Submitting Your Eligibility Material

As you prepare for the IEP eligibility meeting and gather material that supports your child's eligibility (such as an independent assessment), you will have to decide whether to show your material to the school district before the meeting. IDEA does not require you to do so, but consider the kind of relationship you want to have with the school district. If you ask for the school district's assessment in advance, it's only fair to offer the district a copy of yours. Granted, you will give the school a chance to prepare a rebuttal. On the other hand, if you submit an independent assessment or other material at the IEP meeting, the school may ask to reschedule the meeting in order to review your material. In the long run, your best bet is to treat the school district as you want to be treated. If you have favorable material that the school district hasn't seen, submit it in advance or at least call the administrator and ask if he wants your information ahead of time.

4. Meeting Procedures

An IEP eligibility meeting generally proceeds as follows:
- general introductions
- review of school material
- review of any material you want to introduce, and
- discussion of whether and on what basis your child qualifies for special education.

In deciding whether your child is eligible, the team must draw upon a variety of sources, including aptitude and achievement tests, parent input, teacher recommendations, physical conditions, social or cultural background, and adaptive behavior. The group's evaluation must also include observation of the child's academic performance in a regular classroom setting (or, for children who are not in school, in an appropriate environment for a child of that age). The team is required to carefully consider and document all of this information. (34 C.F.R. §§ 300.535, 300.542.)

The team also has to document its eligibility findings in a written report, which must include the following information:
- whether the child has a specific learning disability
- the basis for making the determination
- relevant behavior noted during observation of the child
- the relationship of that behavior to the child's academic functioning

- any educationally relevant medical findings
- whether there is a severe discrepancy between achievement and ability that is not correctable without special education and related services, and
- the effects of environmental, cultural, or economic disadvantage.

Each team member must state, in writing, whether the report reflects his or her conclusions. If it does not, the team member must submit a separate statement of his or her conclusions. (34 C.F.R. §§ 300.542-543.) You are entitled to copies of all evaluation reports and documentation of any recommendations regarding eligibility. (34 C.F.R. § 300.534.)

5. Outcome of Meeting

If the school district determines that your child is eligible for special education, then it will prepare for the IEP program meeting—to happen immediately after the eligibility meeting (see Section E, below) or at some later date. If the school district finds that your child is not eligible for special education, see Section F, below.

E. Joint IEP Eligibility/Program Meeting

The school district may combine the IEP eligibility and program meetings into one. In such a situation, your child is found eligible for special education, then the IEP team shifts gears and immediately begins to develop the IEP program: goals and objectives, program, placement, services, and the like. Holding one meeting may save you time and scheduling headaches, but it also requires you to do a lot of up-front preparation. If you're not ready to discuss the IEP program at the IEP eligibility meeting, ask for another meeting to give yourself time to prepare.

On the other hand, if you'd like to combine the meetings (assuming your child is found eligible), ask the school district to do so. Make your request well ahead of the scheduled eligibility meeting, so you and the school district will have enough time to prepare.

📄 A sample Request for Joint IEP Eligibility/ Program Meeting is below; a blank, tear-out copy is in Appendix 5.

F. If Your Child Is Not Found Eligible for Special Education

You may attend the IEP eligibility meeting, point out significant information that supports your child's eligibility, and argue your points in a manner worthy of Clarence Darrow, all to no avail. What then? You have two options.

1. Exercise Your Due Process Rights

As explained in Chapter 2, due process is your right to take any dispute you have with your child's district—whether a disagreement about an assessment, eligibility, or any part of the IEP—to a neutral third party to help you resolve your dispute. Due process is covered in Chapter 12.

2. Seek Eligibility Under Section 504 of the Rehabilitation Act

Section 504 of the federal Rehabilitation Act (29 U.S.C. § 794) is a disability rights law entirely separate from IDEA. It requires all agencies that receive federal financial assistance to provide "access" to individuals with disabilities. Historically, Section 504 has been used to require public agencies to install wheelchair accessible ramps, accessible restrooms, and other building features, and to provide interpreters at meetings. Section 504 also requires school districts to ensure that children with disabilities are provided access to educational programs and services through interpreters, note takers, readers, and the like.

Your child may be entitled to assistance under Section 504 even if he is not eligible under IDEA. The first step in the process is to refer your child for Section 504 services—this simply means asking the school to consider your child's eligibility under Section 504. Some school districts automatically consider children who are found ineligible under IDEA for Section 504 services; if yours does not, request—in writing—that it do so.

Once a child has been referred, the school will evaluate her eligibility. It will look at:

- whether the child has a physical or mental impairment
- whether the child's impairment substantially limits the child's "major life activities," including learning, and
- what types of accommodations the child needs in order to receive a free, appropriate public education.

If your child is found eligible for help under Section 504, the school must develop a written plan, describing the modifications, accommodations, and services your child will receive. Like an IEP, the Section 504 plan must be individually tailored to meet your child's needs. Many schools have developed a standard form for Section 504 plans; ask your school if it has one.

Because Section 504 tries to achieve the same result as IDEA—to give your child the help he needs to succeed in school—many of the tips and strategies described in this book will be useful to you as you develop a Section 504 plan for your child. The eligibility, procedural, and other requirements of Section 504 are different from IDEA's requirements, however. Because this book focuses on the IEP process, you'll need to get more information on Section 504 if you decide to proceed.

📖 For more information on Section 504, contact the U.S. Department of Education, Office of Civil Rights (contact information is in Appendix 2); your school district; your local community advisory committee; or one of the disability groups listed in Appendix 3. You can find a copy of the Section 504 regulations in Appendix 1.

Request for Joint IEP Eligibility/Program Meeting

Date: March 10, 20xx

To: Valerie Sheridan

McKinley Unified School District

1345 South Drive

Topeka, KS 00000

Re: Carl Ralston, 4th grade student at Eisenhower School

I believe there is sufficient information for us to discuss both my child's eligibility for special education and the specifics of my child's IEP at the same meeting. I would appreciate it if you would plan enough time to discuss both those important items at the April 14, 20xx IEP meeting. I would also like to see any and all reports and other written material that you will be introducing at the IEP meeting, at least two weeks before the meeting.

Thanks in advance for your help. I hope to hear from you soon.

Sincerely,

Albert Ralston

Albert Ralston

78 Elm Drive

Topeka, KS 00078

Phones: 555-1111 (home); 555-2222 (work)

8

Gathering Information and Evidence

Once your child is found eligible for special education, the IEP team must decide what types of instruction and assistance your child will receive. This is where the promise of special education is fulfilled or broken—the specifics of the IEP plan will spell out exactly what help you child will get to overcome her learning disability.

Your role in this process is vital—after all, no matter how kind and professional your child's teachers and school administrators may be, they are not going to understand your child as you do, nor will they likely have the time or energy to explore options as fully and passionately as you will. It is therefore vital that you do some legwork to find out what's available, decide what would be most effective for your child, and present your findings persuasively to the IEP team. This chapter will help you meet these challenges.

By now, you should have a copy of your child's school file (see Chapter 4) and the school district's assessment report (see Chapter 6). You should also have developed a rudimentary IEP blueprint for your child (see Chapter 5). In addition, you may have spoken to other parents, your child's teacher and classroom aide, your child's pediatrician, and others who have information about your child's learning disability and needs. In other words, you probably have a mountain of available information—and you may not know exactly how you can put it to use.

The key to a successful IEP meeting is developing and presenting information that supports your child's need for a particular program and class, services, and teaching methods. This chapter shows you how to:

- review your child's school file and the school district's assessment report (Section A)
- track your child's current progress in school (Section B)
- look into available special education programs, services, and methodologies—both within and outside of the school district—

that may be appropriate for your child (Sections C and D)

- figure out whether available programs and services fit your child's education needs and whether you need additional information to make your case (Section E), and
- make a list of other materials you might generate to support your position, such as an independent assessment, a statement from your child's teacher, or a statement from your child's pediatrician or other professional (Sections F and G).

Chapter 10 provides a system for organizing all of your materials—positive and negative—to best make your case at your child's IEP meeting.

A. Analyze the School District's Information

Your first step in preparing for the IEP program meeting is to figure out what position the school will probably take and whether you can use any of the school district's own documents and statements to show that your child needs a particular program. Start by reviewing all of the information you've received from the school district. As you look over your child's school file, assessment report, and other items, there are several issues to consider.

1. Read Between the Lines

Can you figure out what position the school district will take simply by reading your child's file and assessment report? For example, if the school district's materials say "Martha needs to be placed in a regular classroom with 1 hour a day of extra assistance to work on her reading" or "Henry needs speech therapy twice a week," you'll know exactly where the district stands.

Sometimes, you need to look for less direct statements, such as "Henry has difficulty understanding instructions given by the teacher" or "No matter how often I tell him about the homework, Henry does not follow through." Comments like these clue you in to how the district is thinking about your child. The statements in the example show that the district recognizes that your child is having trouble with basic learning processes, notably possible auditory processing or sequential thinking problems.

2. Where to Look For the School District's Position

You can find the school district's position in a variety of material. It is most likely to come up in an assessment report, but you may also come across the school district's position in a letter, teacher report, or memo, or another written item in your child's file. Your child's teacher, the school assessor, or another district employee may even have stated the school district's position in a conversation.

 If a school district employee says something to you that supports your position, be sure to send a confirming letter. (See Chapter 4.)

3. Sources of the School District's Information

It's important to figure out who is saying what in the school district's material. These speakers are the district's experts—and their opinions will greatly influence the IEP process. Specifically, you'll want to know each person's:

- name and position—for example, a teacher, teacher's aide, counselor, assessor, or learning disability or resource specialist
- training and expertise, and
- first-hand experience with your child.

Clearly, the most persuasive opinions come from those who know your child and have experience dealing with children who have learning disabilities. On the other hand, it may be easier to challenge the opinions of someone who hasn't taught or assessed your child, has very few years of experience, or has no special expertise in learning disabilities.

Make sure to figure out which school personnel (for example, a classroom teacher, school psychologist, reading specialist, or speech/language therapist) have the most experience and training in your child's particular type of learning disability.

4. Keeping Track of the School District's Statements

Once you've reviewed all of the information available from the school district, make a chart like the one below to highlight key elements of your child's program (see your blueprint), whether the school district agrees or disagrees with your position, and where in the school district's materials the issue is addressed. Note where the school district data support or oppose your position and where you have gaps that need to be filled—little or no information to show that a particular program or service is necessary for your child to receive an appropriate education. Finally, note the source of the information—was it in writing or did someone say it to you?

Key Elements for Child's Program

Child: R. Boston

Date: June 1, 20xx

Desired IEP Components	District Material	District Position
Placement in regular class	4-4-03 Assessment	Disagrees, p. 14
1:1 aide for regular class	4-4-03 Assessment	No position
	3-12-03 Bi-Weekly Teacher Report	Teacher agrees
LD Curricula	2-4-03 Teacher Report	Teacher responds to parents Qs about LD
LD Methodology	Assessment of Dr. Jones	No position yet
LD Strategies	Assessment of Dr. Jones	No position yet
Adaptive Physical Ed	5-2-03 Adaptive P.E. Assessment	Disagrees (but see comment on p. 5)

5. Changing a Report or Assessment

If there is something in your child's school file or the assessment report that is inaccurate or harmful to your child, find out whether the school district is willing to change the statement. Start with a phone call. For example:

> *"Hello Mr. Altman, I'm Von Williams's father. I read your assessment and I appreciate your help in evaluating Von's needs. I did want to ask you a question. You say on page 4 that Von does not need help with his reading comprehension. Did you review the report by Von's teacher, which states that he does need one-on-one reading help?"*

To make a formal request for a change, see Chapter 4B (changing something in a school file) and Chapter 6E (changing a draft assessment report).

B. Chart Your Child's Progress

As you prepare for an IEP program meeting, take some time to learn how your child is currently doing in school—in regular or special education. At the IEP meeting, you'll want to be able to describe exactly how your child is doing in the current program, what your child's strengths and weaknesses are, and what additional help your child needs. Pay special attention to those areas most likely affected by his learning disability (such as reading, spelling, language, or calculations).

Here are a few ways to get current information about your child:

- Ask the teacher(s), teacher's aide, and service provider for periodic reports focusing on key areas of need for your child—reading, behavior, language development, social interaction, spelling, physical mobility, and the like.

- Ask the teacher(s) for samples and reports of your child's work.
- Visit your child's class. (See Section C, below.)
- Set up periodic meetings with your child's teacher(s). If your child already has an IEP, ask the teacher whether the current IEP goals and objectives are being met.

Example:

One of your child's current IEP objectives is to read a three-paragraph story and demonstrate 80% comprehension by answering questions. First, ask the teacher whether your child can read a three-paragraph story. Then ask about your child's reading comprehension level. If it's not up to 80%, where is it: 60%? 40%? 20%?

To easily organize this material, you can create a chart for your child's teacher to update your child's progress regularly (once a month, for example) in key areas such as math, reading, behavior, and motor development, as well as emotional and psychological issues and self-help skills. Do remember that teachers have a remarkable amount of paperwork to complete—try to be sensitive to the teacher's time when you consider how often you want him to send you a written report. If the teacher can email reports to you, that might make the process easier.

A sample Progress Chart is below; a blank, tear-out copy is in Appendix 5. You can tailor this chart to your child's particular goals and objectives. This form will help you track your child's general progress, as well as whether your child is meeting the IEP goals and objectives. (See Chapter 9 for more details on developing goals and objectives.)

Progress Chart

Student: __Mary Hamilton__

Class: __Ms. Frank's 3rd Grade__

Date: __February 23, 20xx__

Key Goals and Objectives	Current Status	Comments
Math	Progressing appropriately? [X] yes　[ ] no	On schedule to complete goals and objectives.
Reading	Progressing appropriately? [X] yes　[ ] no	On schedule to complete goals and objectives. Needs to improve reading fluidity.
Writing	Progressing appropriately? [X] yes　[ ] no	On schedule to complete goals and objectives.
Spelling	Progressing appropriately? [ ] yes　[X] no	Reversals continue to be problem.
Social-Behavioral	Progressing appropriately? [ ] yes　[X] no	Still problems with focus; hard time not teasing others.
Language development	Progressing appropriately? [X] yes　[ ] no	On schedule, but some problems going from specific to general.
Motor development	Progressing appropriately? [ ] yes　[X] no	Small motor problems affecting handwriting.
Other	Progressing appropriately? [ ] yes　[X] no	When struggling with spelling and handwriting, seems to feel high level of stress.

C. Explore Available School Programs

To prepare for the IEP program meeting, you will want to gather information about your child's existing program and other programs that may be appropriate for your child. By finding out what's available, you'll have a better sense of what the best approach for your child might be.

Program possibilities include:

- placement in a regular classroom, perhaps with support services (such as a 1:1 aide, classroom accommodations such as seating in the front of the room, speech/language therapy, occupational therapy for small motor/handwriting difficulties)—ask about local options, including your child's neighborhood school

- placement in a program specifically designed for children with learning disabilities, difficulties with communication, or other disabling conditions—ask about special day classes at your neighborhood school, nearby schools, or other schools in the area, or

- placement in a specialized program, such as a private school or residential program—ask about the existence and location of any such programs (these more restrictive options won't be appropriate for many children with learning disabilities).

For students with learning disabilities, there may be some kind of "pull-out" program including a small group of students and one staff person with some expertise in learning disabilities. This person may be called a Resource Specialist (RSP), aide, or LD teacher. Many students with learning disabilities receive specific services—special help in or out of the regular classroom—but are not in a special classroom or separate program. As you read through this chapter, remember that your child's IEP program and services might include anything from a little extra help in a regular classroom to placement in a special school program.

When you gather information, explore every possible option—even those programs or services that don't seem to offer exactly what your child needs. Even if the program and services aren't right for your child, you'll have more information about what's out there. And you'll be able to respond effectively to any discussions about those programs and services at the IEP meeting. For example, if the school district recommends that your child use or attend one of these programs, you can respond, "With all due respect, I visited that classroom for children with learning disabilities and it is inappropriate for my child for the following reasons …."

1. Ask About Available Programs and Services

Contact your child's teacher, the school assessor, the district special education administrator, other parents, your PTA, and, local community advisory committee. Ask about programs and services for children with learning disabilities within your district.

Don't be surprised if the school administrator (or even the classroom teacher) is reluctant to tell you about programs. You may hear, for example, "It's way too early to be looking at programs for next year, Mr. and Mrs. Gough. We've just started this year." Or, "Let's wait until the IEP team meets and goals and objectives are drafted. Then we can talk about programs."

While school personnel may have reasons for making assertions like these, you have every right to find out about available program options. Emphasize that you are not looking to change programs or force an early IEP decision—you are merely trying to gather information. You might respond, "I appreciate what you are saying, Ms. Casey, but it will really be helpful to me and my child to get started as soon as possible, so we can plan ahead. I am not looking for a change in programs or for a commitment on your part. Is there some reason why I shouldn't be gathering information about programs in the district?"

2. Visit Programs

The best way to find out what a particular school or program has to offer is to spend some time there. However, while a school administrator may be willing to provide you with some information about existing programs, she may be reluctant for you to actually visit a program before the IEP meeting. Although the IEP team might not know which program will best meet your child's needs until after you have the IEP meeting, nothing in IDEA prevents you from visiting potential programs before the meeting, as long as your requests are reasonable.

"If the Law Doesn't Require It, We Don't Have to Do It"

Some school administrators will take the position that they don't have to do anything unless it is expressly required by IDEA. For example, because IDEA does not expressly state that a parent can visit programs at a specific time, some administrators will take the position that you have no legal right to visit before the IEP—and, therefore, that you can't do it. Technically, the administrator is correct that the IDEA doesn't require such visits, but that doesn't mean that the school can't allow you to visit. The fact that something is not required by law does not mean that it is not permitted.

It is reasonable and fair for you to visit available school programs. As a parent or guardian, a tax-paying citizen, and a member of the community in which your child's school district is located, you have the same right of access to school programs as anyone else (and your school's policy probably provides for this type of access). For the school district to deny a reasonable request is itself unreasonable, and you should approach the situation that way. Ultimately, the school will have to explain and justify its decision. And while there are certainly exceptions, most people want to be fair and reasonable. Your best strategy is to avoid getting tangled up in a debate about what "the law" requires or allows. Instead, simply approach the situation with the point of view that your request is reasonable and should be granted. This strategy usually works (and if it doesn't, the school district will end up looking bad for refusing your reasonable request).

If the administrator steadfastly refuses to let you visit programs, put your concerns in writing.

A sample Program Visitation Request letter is below; a blank, tear-out copy is in Appendix 5.

Program Visitation Request Letter

Date: April 6, 20xx

To: Mr. John White, Special Education Administrator

Carlson Unified School District

8709 Fourth Street

Helena, MT 00087

Re: Elizabeth Moore

I appreciate the concerns you have and realize that you can't know which programs are appropriate for my child until after the IEP meeting. Nonetheless, I think it would be very helpful for me to see existing programs so I can be a more effective member of the IEP team. I do not feel I can make an informed IEP decision without seeing, first-hand, all possible options. I want to assure you that I understand that by giving me the names of existing programs, you are not stating an opinion as to their appropriateness for my child.

I assure you that I will abide by all rules and regulations for parental visits. If those rules and regulations are in writing, please send me a copy.

Thanks in advance for your help. I hope to hear from you soon.

Sincerely,

Arnette Moore

Arnette Moore

87 Mission Road

Helena, MT 00087

Phones: 555-3334 (home); 555-4455 (work)

If the administrator still refuses your request, don't give up. Indicate that you understand her concerns but feel that you could not possibly make a decision about placement without some basic information about available programs. Make it clear that you are more than willing to visit programs again after the IEP meeting.

If you get nowhere, contact the administrator's superior. If that fails, contact your school board of education. If you don't make any progress, you can file a complaint with your state department of education or other appropriate educational agency, as discussed in Chapter 13. The complaint might not be processed until after the date set for the IEP meeting. If this happens, you'll have to decide whether to postpone the IEP meeting or ask (at the IEP meeting) to see the programs after the meeting. In that case, you may not be ready to sign the IEP at the meeting. (See Chapter 11E for more information on signing the IEP.)

a. When to Visit Programs

Ideally, you will want to visit programs in the fall of the school year. While it may seem logical to visit right before the IEP meeting, checking out possible program options earlier offers these advantages:

- The sooner you see a particular program, the sooner you'll have a sense of whether or not it is appropriate for your child.
- If you can't decide whether a program is a good fit for your child, there will be time for others, such as an independent assessor, to take a look and give you an opinion.
- You'll have time to visit a program more than once (and you should, if it's necessary).

b. Visitation Guidelines

The purpose of your visits is to gather information. As you plan your visits, keep these tips in mind:

- Ask to visit all program options.
- Follow the policies and rules established by the school district, school site administrator, and teacher.
- If an independent assessor or other professional will attend the IEP meeting, it is a good idea to have him visit with you. Be sure to inform the school district ahead of time.
- Do not ask for any personal information about the students, such as names of individual children. A teacher should not give you this information. You can (and should) talk with any parents you know who have children in the programs.
- Find out as many details as possible about each program or class. Include the same categories of information you use in your blueprint (see Chapter 5):
  - ▲ student description (number of students in the program; students' disabilities, age, cognitive range, and language range)
  - ▲ staff description (details on teachers and aides)
  - ▲ teacher-student instruction (teacher-to-class, small group, or individual instruction)

▲ curricula, methodology, and other teaching strategies used

▲ classroom environment (behavior problems, noise level, number of teachers and teacher aides, and how much time teacher aides spend in class)

▲ related services (how many children leave the class to go to another program and how often; how many children receive related services—such as help from a 1:1 aide—in the class), and

▲ any other comments you have on the program.

IDEA does not require the teacher to provide you with this information, so make sure to ask for it in a pleasant, matter-of-fact way. If the teacher balks, indicate that the information you seek is important and noncontroversial, and should be made available.

Write down your observations and the answers to your questions. You can write as you watch the class and talk to the teacher. If you "interview" the teacher with notebook in hand and pencil poised, however, the teacher may be intimidated. You might put the teacher at ease by saying something like, "I have a poor memory; do you mind if I take notes while we talk?" If not, try to take notes in an unobtrusive way or wait until you're outside and write down what you remember as soon as possible.

A sample Class Visitation Checklist is below; a blank, tear-out copy is in Appendix 5. Be sure to keep copies of this important form in your IEP binder.

D. Find Out About Related Services

Classroom programs are only one component of your child's IEP program. Related services, such as occupational, physical, or speech therapy, are also very important. (Related services are explained in Chapter 2.)

Gathering information about related services will be a little different from gathering information about programs. You'll still want to talk to your child's teacher, the school assessor, the district special education administrator, other parents, your PTA, and local parent groups for disabled children to find out about related services that will meet your child's needs. But the similarities end there.

Service providers, such as physical therapists or reading specialists, usually work one-on-one with individual children or in small groups. So visiting these specialists in action may not be possible. Instead, when you talk to people about the services available, ask about the background, training, and experience of the specialists. Candid conversations with other parents will probably be your most helpful source of information.

Keep detailed notes of your conversations and include them in your IEP binder.

E. Compare Your Blueprint With the Existing Program and Services

Once you have information about your school district's programs and services, compare what's available to what you believe your child needs. Obviously, if the school provides services you feel will meet your child's needs (as fleshed out in your blueprint), the IEP process should be relatively simple. On the other hand, if there is a gap between what your child needs and what is available, you will likely have to convince the IEP team that the school options are inappropriate.

You'll need to detail the shortcomings of the programs and services offered by the school district—the Classroom Visitation checklist will be of real help here. Be as specific as possible: Is the problem the frequency or location of a service, the pupil-teacher ratio, the qualifications of the teacher or service provider, the specific work to be done with a service provider, the class make-

Class Visitation Checklist

Date: _9/11/03_ _____ Time: _9:00-10:15_ _____ a.m./~~p.m.~~

School: _Jefferson School, Chicago_ _____

Class: _3rd Grade Special Day Class for Learning Disabled (Teacher: Sue Avery)_ ___

Student Description:

Total students: _17_ _____ Gender range: _12 boys; 5 girls_ _____

Age range: _7 - 10 (ten kids are nine or younger; seven ten-year-olds)_ ____

Cognitive range: _"Wide range; probably from pre-K through 5th grade skills," says S. Avery_

(teacher). _____

Language/communication range: _Two students with hearing impairment; two other students_

with delayed communication skills (1st grade level). _____

Disability range: _12 students have specific learning disability, three are borderline retarded,_

one has emotional disturbance, and one autistic-like behavior. _____

Behavioral range: _Five students acting out throughout class, four other students constantly_

demanding of teacher. Two students sent to principal because of behavior. Rest of class

generally cooperative, quiet. _____

Other observations: _Overall impression was of a class of children with varied needs and behavior,_

which made it difficult for the teacher to focus on any one group of children for very long. __

Staff Description:

Teachers: _Sue Avery has four years' experience working with learning disabled children. She_

was generally very patient with students (less so with the behaviorally troubled children), but

she seemed easily distracted. _____

Aides: _In class two hours per day; worked with all children, no one child more than few_

minutes. Seemed mostly to superficially check in with students, but not provide any sustained

1:1 help. Aide has no specific training working with learning disabled children. _____

Other observations: _Neither teacher nor aide seemed fully comfortable with curriculum,_

particularly given varied needs of students. Both were very nice to students. _____

Curricula/Classroom Strategies:

Curricula: "Using Mathematics," (Book 2) for math, teacher-developed materials for spelling, and "Project Explore" for science lessons.

Strategies: Teacher/aide when working 1:1 in reading divided words into simple sounds using much repetition; no overall strategy or specific curriculum designed for learning disabled children.

Classroom Environment:

Description: Classroom had tiled floor so sound echoed. Quite loud; no other apparent acoustical treatment to reduce noise; all added to a noisy room. Various work stations and cubicles set up so students can work 1:1 or by themselves. Somewhat effective, but noise was distracting to all students. Classroom situated near playground, so much visual stimulation outside classroom window and noise from outside.

Related Services:

At least four students received their related services in class, one had speech therapy, another had a special aide that worked with her in the corner.

Other Comments:

School site principal (Lee Parsons) is interested in special education, but has no training or expertise in the field. She did express reservations about excessive mainstreaming of children with disabilities into regular classrooms. Visited one mainstreamed class, teacher seemed interested, but expressed concern that the school had not provided any support or training for dealing with special education students in her regular class.

How This Program Relates to IEP Blueprint:

Program does not meet Tara's blueprint:
- Cognitive and behavioral range of students too wide
- Teacher unable to provide individual attention
- Aide not trained for working with L-D kids
- Question about curriculum

up, the teacher methodology, the curriculum, or other important features?

Make a comprehensive, side-by-side comparison of your blueprint and what you know about the school's options, and put the details on the bottom of the Class Visitation Checklist.

F. Generate Additional Supporting Information

Once you've reviewed your child's school file, developed your blueprint, reviewed the school assessment, evaluated your child's progress, and gathered information about program and service options, you may need further data to support your goals. This material will be invaluable in preparing for the IEP meeting.

1. Help From School Personnel

Contact any teachers, assessors, or service providers who you think are likely to support your position. You can do this by phone or in person. Explain the programs and services you want for your child (the items you included in your blueprint) and why you feel they are appropriate. Note any discrepancy between what you want and what you believe the school district has available. Ask for their ideas and opinions about what you plan to propose.

Ask if the teacher, assessor, or service provider would be willing to write a statement supporting what you want for your child or to state his position at the IEP meeting.

If you talk to someone who supports your point of view but doesn't want to put anything in writing, follow up the conversation with a confirming letter. (See Chapter 4.) For example, you might say, "Thank you for the chance to chat today. I appreciate your frankness and was glad to hear that you agree that Max needs an aide in order to function effectively in the regular class."

Be aware that a confirming letter can put the teacher in an awkward position. If the teacher says one thing to you (and you confirm it in a letter) and then says another thing at the IEP meeting, the letter may be important proof of what was originally said—but this may lead to some friction between you and the teacher. If the teacher will not speak frankly at the IEP meeting, however, the confirming letter will be valuable proof of what was said earlier—and might discourage the teacher from changing his tune.

No matter what, be sure to keep notes of who said what, including the date, time, and place of the conversation, in as much detail as possible. This is your record in case the school representative changes his mind later on.

2. Help From People Outside the School

Anyone who knows your child or has some expertise in special education or your child's disability may be of value. This includes your child's doctor, tutor, therapist, or other specialist.

Ask each person to write a letter to the IEP team stating:

- how she knows your child
- her specific expertise
- any specific comments on your child's condition as it relates to the educational experience, and
- her recommendation for your child in terms of program, services, or other IEP components.

Example:
"Teresa needs extensive help with small and large motor skills and should work with an occupational and physical therapist at least three times a week."

G. Independent Assessments

An independent assessment may be the best proof of what program and services your child needs. An independent assessment, like the school district's assessment, can be as comprehensive or as narrow as your child's needs dictate. In most cases, an independent assessment will use a variety of tests to evaluate your child's abilities and determine what teaching and program strategies would be most helpful.

An independent assessment will be useful—even if your child isn't eligible under IDEA—for figuring out your child's strengths, weaknesses, and educational needs. If your child is eligible under IDEA, it will help you prove that particular programs or services should be included in the IEP. If your child is not found eligible, it will help you develop a written Section 504 plan or come up with your own program to help your child. Section 504 is discussed in Chapter 7.

Under IDEA, you have an absolute right to have your child assessed independently. Moreover, your school district is required to provide you with information on where you can get an independent assessment. (34 C.F.R. § 300.502(a).)

Chapter 6 discusses assessments in general; Chapter 11 explains how to present an independent assessment at the IEP meeting.

While IDEA requires the school district to consider the results of the independent assessment in reaching any decision regarding your child's education, it does not require your school district to agree with the results. While an independent assessment may include persuasive information, your child's school district can reject the conclusions. You do have the right to go to due process (mediation session or hearing) to prove the district is wrong. (See Chapter 12.)

1. When to Use an Independent Assessment

You may want an independent assessment because you need more information about your child or, as we noted, because the school district's assessment does not support what you want. Before you hire an independent assessor, make sure you understand the district's position. If the district's position is clear—and you disagree with it—an outside assessment may very well be needed.

2. Finding Independent Assessors

Independent assessors generally work in private practice or are affiliated with hospitals, universities, or other large institutions. How do you find a qualified independent assessor? Here are a few tips:

- Ask parents of children with similar disabilities. Check with the PTA or your school district's advisory committee of parents with children in special education.
- Get recommendations from the school. A trusted teacher, aide, service provider, or other school employee may be able to give you the names of independent assessors.
- Talk to your child's pediatrician.
- Call a local hospital, particularly a university medical hospital. A department that employs experts in your child's disability may be able to do the assessment or refer you to an independent assessor.
- Call local private schools for disabled children; they often work with credible independent assessors.
- Check resources on learning disabilities, including local and regional support groups, Web links, and associations, for information on independent assessors who specialize in assessing children with learning disabilities. A good place to start is the

Learning Disabilities Association (LDA), an advocacy and educational group with national and state chapters. See Appendix 3 for information about LDA and other learning disability organizations.

How Not to Find an Independent Assessor

Assessors are often psychologists. If you look in the phone book, you will see a long list of psychologists. But choosing randomly from the phone book is a poor method for selecting a reputable and knowledgeable assessor—the only thing you really know about these people is that they could afford to pay for an ad in the yellow pages.

3. Selecting the Right Assessor

Speak to various independent assessors, and ask the following questions for each person:

- Does the assessor have significant expertise, training, and experience in dealing with learning disabilities?
- Is the assessor affiliated with a well-respected institution?
- Were you referred by someone who actually worked with the assessor?
- Do you trust the person (or institution) who recommended the assessor?
- Will the assessor give you references?
- Did the assessor's references like the results of the assessor's work and find the assessor easy to work with?
- Is the assessor impartial? (An assessor who has previously done work for—and been paid by—your child's school district may not be truly independent.)
- Which assessments and other tools does the assessor use for children with learning disabilities (see Chapter 6)?

- Can the assessor complete the assessment and written report well in advance of the IEP meeting?
- Will the assessor's report recommend specific programs and services that are appropriate for your child's learning disability?
- Can the assessor attend the IEP meeting, if necessary?
- Is the assessor familiar with testing, curricula, methodologies, and other strategies for kids with learning disabilities?
- What are the assessor's fees, and do they include a written report and attendance at the IEP meeting?

The answers to these questions, your own sense of the individual assessor, and recommendations from others are key factors in making your decision. It is also important that the independent assessor be able to clearly, professionally, and vigorously articulate her position.

4. Having the Independent Assessor on Your Side

The reason you are hiring an independent assessor is to support your goals for your child's education. Be very clear on your plans and perspectives.

Examples:

- Your child needs a multisensory approach to help him with his learning disability. Be sure the assessor's recommendations include 1) information showing that he needs that specific program, 2) specifically named multisensory programs, 3) a detailed explanation of the kind of multisensory work he needs (without referring to a named program), and 4) the time and teaching conditions needed for that program (for example, one hour a day, one-on-one with a teacher trained in a multisensory approach for your child's learning disability).

• You want your daughter placed in a private school for children with learning disabilities. Ideally, the assessor will write, "Jane requires placement in a program with no more than ten children on a small campus, a full-time aide, a teacher qualified to work with learning disabled children, and a class where there are no behavioral problems. The X School in Boston is the only program that can meet Jane's needs."

If the assessor can't or won't name a specific school or program, then make sure she will name the specific components of an appropriate program. Continuing Example 2 above, if the independent assessor won't say Jane needs to be placed in the X School, she should say that Jane needs a program that has the characteristics of the X School.

Of course, it's possible that the data will not support your goals. A good assessor will not write something he disagrees with or make a recommendation he does not believe in. A good assessor will tell you when the evidence—the testing data—does not support what you want. You want an assessor who will:

• show you a draft assessment report
• consider your concerns about the draft report
• make specific recommendations about your child's educational status and appropriate programs and related services to meet your child's needs, and
• provide a written rationale for these recommendations.

Independent Assessors and Learning Disabilities

As you undoubtedly know, learning disabilities can be complicated and difficult to pinpoint. If you anticipate a disagreement about placement or services with your school district, an expert in learning disabilities can be indispensable to you and your child. An independent assessor skilled in learning disability issues can not only make your case with careful and detailed analysis, but also give you a frank and objective sense of the real differences between the program the school offers and the one you want. A good assessor won't just help you win your case if you go to due process—he'll also let you know when the facts are not on your side and you might lose a due process claim. You may not always be happy with the assessor's conclusions, but it's better to know where you stand before you waste time and money fighting a losing battle with the school district.

5. How an Independent Assessment Proceeds

Most independent assessors will meet with you and review your child's school file, the school district's assessment, and other district material. The assessor will then explain what testing will be done, secure your approval, do the testing, and prepare a report. Depending on your child's characteristics and needs, the assessor may also want to observe her in class and visit some program options.

6. When to Submit the Independent Assessment

Just as you want to review the school district's assessments before the IEP meeting, the school district will likely want to see your independent assessment before the IEP meeting. Of course, the more time the school has to review the independent assessment, the more time the administration will have to find data to counter its conclusions. Does this mean you should delay giving the school district your assessment? While such a strategy has its attractions, the bottom line is that the school district is entitled to the same courtesy that you are.

Waiting to give the district a copy of your assessment could ultimately prove counterproductive. The district may distrust you and your assessment. The delay may be grounds for postponing the IEP meeting. And your relationship with the district may be affected. Because you will likely be working together for many years, you will want to maintain a positive relationship, if possible. If one party will be nasty, unfair, or untrustworthy, let it be someone other than you. While there is no hard-and-fast rule here, providing the independent assessment (and other key material) a week before the IEP meeting is usually appropriate.

7. Cost of an Independent Assessment

Independent assessments can be quite costly, anywhere from several hundred to several thousand dollars.

But you may not have to pay for the assessment. Under IDEA, you have the right to an independent educational evaluation of your child (by an assessor of your choosing) at public expense if you disagree with the school district's evaluation. The school district must pay for the independent assessment unless it goes to due process and convinces the hearing officer that the school district evaluation was appropriate. (34 C.F.R. § 300.502(b).)

School districts don't go to due process very often to argue about who should pay for an independent assessment, but that doesn't mean your school district won't. To win the due process hearing, the district has to show only that its own evaluation was appropriate, the appropriate tests were used, the assessor was properly trained and knowledgeable, and your child was evaluated in all areas of suspected disability. The district must either pay for the independent assessment or initiate due process "without unnecessary delay." (34 C.F.R. § 300.502(b)(2).)

The real problem for parents is how to get the district to pay for the assessment, particularly because IDEA does not require the district to pay in advance or to provide assurances that it will pay for the assessment. If you want the school district to foot the bill for the assessment, you will probably have to pay the assessor up front and seek reimbursement from the district (forcing it to either pay or go to due process).

Here are some ideas on how to get the school district to pay:

- Ask the assessor to bill the school district directly. Because the assessor wants to be paid, she may not be willing to do this. But there's no harm in asking.
- If the assessor won't bill the district, pay her bill and submit a copy to the district. Include a cover letter explaining that IDEA requires the district to pay for the independent assessment unless it pursues due process. Refer to the law—34 C.F.R. § 300.502.
- If the school district doesn't go to due process and still won't pay, file a complaint (as discussed in Chapter 13). ∎

9

Goals and Objectives

Goals and objectives are the nuts and bolts of your child's education: the academic, cognitive, linguistic, social, and vocational aims you have for your child (goals) and the specific things your child will need to accomplish (objectives) to reach those goals. Objectives might spell out the steps your child will have to take or the skills your child will need to master in order to achieve a particular goal—they describe what will take place in class each day. Objectives also give you a concrete way to measure your child's progress toward a goal. An IEP document usually includes many objectives for each broad goal.

Examples:

Goal. Tim will improve his reading comprehension.

Objective. Tim will read a four-paragraph story and demonstrate 75% comprehension using objective classroom tests.

Goal. Ellen will improve her peer relationships.

Objective. Ellen will initiate three positive peer interactions each day, per teacher observation.

Goal. Juan will master all third grade math skills.

Objective. Juan will identify sets of ones and tens with 90% accuracy, using appropriate textbook tests.

Goal. Jane will improve her writing skills.

Objective. Jane will write a three-sentence paragraph with subject and predicate sentences, per teacher evaluation.

Goal. Mark will improve short-term auditory memory.

Objective. Mark will be able to listen to a set of ten related items and list them with 75% accuracy.

Benchmarks Are Objectives

When IDEA was reauthorized in 1997, Congress added the term "benchmark" to the law—but only as a synonym for "objective." The two terms are used interchangeably. For example, IDEA requires the written IEP to include a "statement of measurable annual goals, including benchmarks **or** short-term objectives." (34 C.F.R. § 300.347(a)(2) and 20 U.S.C. § 1414(d)(1)(A)(ii).) Because the phrase "goals and objectives" has been used for such a long time, you're more likely to hear that phrase than "benchmarks."

IDEA requires an IEP program to include a statement of measurable annual goals, including benchmarks or short-term objectives, for two reasons (34 C.F.R. § 300.347(a)(2)):

- to ensure that the child is progressing in the general curriculum, and
- to meet the child's other educational needs resulting from his disability.

Goals and objectives are important because they are the guts of your child's daily program (and therefore central to the IEP document) *and* because your child's ability to meet her goals and objectives will largely determine whether your school district is providing your child an appropriate education.

What Goals and Objectives Are Not

- Goals and objectives are not used for students who are in regular education. They are written for special education students—even special education students who are mainstreamed into regular classes.
- Goals and objectives are not part of a contract between you and the school district—that is, the school is not legally liable if your child does not meet his goals and objectives. Goals and objectives are simply a way to measure your child's progress and to determine whether your child's program and services are working.
- Goals and objectives are not the totality of your child's instructional plan. They are important aims to be accomplished during the school year, but there will be other important components of your child's IEP—such as particular instruction techniques and methodologies, descriptions of the type of services and special help your child will receive, and information about your child's program.

A. Areas Covered by Goals and Objectives

IDEA does not dictate what areas goals and objectives must address. They can cover a wide variety of skills or topics (depending on your child's needs), including:

- academic skills, such as math computation, reading comprehension, spelling, and writing
- cognitive skills, such as abstract thinking and memory
- emotional and psychological issues, such as overcoming fears or improving self-esteem

- social-behavioral skills, such as relating to peers
- linguistic and communication skills, such as expressing oneself effectively
- self-help and independent living skills, such as using money, dressing, using transportation and, perhaps, for younger children, using the toilet
- physical and recreational skills, such as improving coordination and fine and large motor skills
- vocational skills, such as work skill development, and
- transition skills, such as exploring work or college options.

B. Developing Goals and Objectives

IDEA does not specify how to write goals and objectives, what subjects to cover, how many to include in the IEP, or how to implement or measure them. These details are up to the IEP team. This gives you the flexibility to develop goals and objectives that will be useful in conjunction with the programs and services you want for your child.

This section describes the typical elements of goals and objectives.

A sample Goals and Objectives form appears later in this chapter. You can also find examples of goals and objectives in the sample IEP in Appendix 4.

1. Child's Present Level of Performance

The IEP program should spell out your child's current level of skill in each goal-and-objective area. This "current level" can be described through assessment numbers or in more general terms. For example, for a reading comprehension goal and objective, a child's present level of performance may state, "Beth scored X on the Wood-cock-Johnson; her current reading comprehension is at the mid-fourth grade level. She enjoys reading, but requires help in maintaining focus." Or, "Matthew has completed his business math class." Make sure that the IEP addresses every area affected by your child's learning disability.

2. Who Implements Goals and Objectives

Normally, your child's classroom teacher is responsible for implementing your child's goals and objectives. Junior and senior high school students may have a different teacher for each subject area. If the teacher is working with other educational professionals, such as an aide, that person will be responsible as well. For example:

- A speech therapist may be responsible for a child's language goals and objectives.
- An occupational or physical therapist may oversee physical education or motor goals, such as handwriting improvement.
- A school counselor or therapist may cover emotional goals and objectives.
- A resource specialist or instructor in a special day class may be responsible for a child's goals and objectives that relate to a learning disability—for example, to work with the child on improving reading or handwriting. For a junior or senior high school student, the resource specialist may work on reading, math, spelling, or language skills and/or may work on specific class areas (for example, to assist a child who has short-term memory problems by developing strategies for remembering the scientific detail contained in the science class textbook).

3. Completion Dates for Goals and Objectives

Goals and objectives are normally written for a one-year period, but this is not set in stone. In fact, because objectives are supposed to be concrete, bite-sized, and manageable tasks, they may very well be completed in less than a year—and it may be a good idea to set a shorter timeframe in the written IEP.

Example:
Lily is in a special day class with no main-streaming in a regular classroom. Her IEP reading goal and objective has a completion time of one year. Lily's parents feel she could reach her reading goal and objective in a shorter time if she were in a regular classroom. If Lily's parents want her mainstreamed, it might help to set a shorter period for this goal in the IEP.

4. Measuring Goals and Objectives

IDEA requires a child's goals and objectives to be "measurable." There are a number of ways to measure goals and objectives, including objective testing, teacher or other staff observation, evaluating work samples, or any other method agreed to by the IEP team. Many IEP goals and objectives include a quantifiable accomplishment level, such as "Mia will read a four-paragraph story with 90% reading comprehension as measured by the Woodcock Reading Mastery Test" or "Bret will read the assigned novel in his English class and demonstrate comprehension of the novel's themes, describe the main characters, and explain what they represent."

IDEA does not require goals and objectives to be quantifiable—that is, capable of being measured in numbers. Of course, numbers can be of value, but not everything of value can be reduced to numbers. For example, how does one measure numerically whether goals and objectives were met in areas relating to emotions, psychology, self-help, or vocational skills?

Example:

Brian's IEP program states that he will improve his social skills. As goals and objectives, this is stated as follows:

Goal. Brian will improve his ability to interact appropriately with his peers.

Objective. Brian will improve his ability to read body and language cues from his peers and respond appropriately in 7 out of 10 situations as measured by teacher observation and with immediate feedback to Brian by the teacher.

5. Goals and Objectives and General Curriculum

IDEA states that a child's goals and objectives must allow the child to "be involved in and progress in the general curriculum"—the same curriculum offered to nondisabled children. The IEP team is free to determine how much involvement in the general curriculum is appropriate for a particular child. Indeed, there may be very important reasons why a child is not fully exposed to the general curriculum. Generally, however, Congress wants children with disabilities to have the opportunity to learn the same subjects and skills as all other children their age.

Don't Set Your Objectives Too Low

Be wary if an IEP team member from the school district suggests setting your child's objectives fairly low. The district may want to set low standards so your child can achieve them without too much help from the school. If the school wants to eliminate a particular support service (such as a one-on-one aide or reading specialist) or keep your child in a special day class rather than mainstreaming her in a regular class, it might propose objectives that your child can meet without this extra help.

C. When to Draft Goals and Objectives

While specific goals and objectives aren't discussed, approved, and included in the written IEP until the IEP meeting, it makes sense to draft them ahead of time.

In fact, it is not uncommon for school representatives to write goals and objectives in advance. Under IDEA, the school cannot simply present their goals and objectives at the IEP meeting, insist that you accept them, and refuse to discuss alternatives. That would violate a basic tenet of IDEA: that the IEP team makes all IEP decisions as a group, at the meeting. Still, you should anticipate that the school district might draft goals and objectives in advance. Prepare for the IEP meeting by asking the school district (in writing) for a copy of any predrafted goals and objectives at least two weeks in advance.

You should also draft goals and objectives before the IEP meeting. You do not have to give a copy to the school district before the IEP meeting unless it asks you to (which would be unlikely). However, even if you aren't asked for a copy, you can give your goals and objectives to the school district in advance. Some advocates argue that you shouldn't do this because it gives the district time to counter your goals and objectives. Others argue that if you present your goals and objectives for the first time at the IEP meeting, the school might need some extra time to review them—and might postpone the meeting.

In general, I think it's best to provide the school district information in advance, unless the element of surprise is necessary in your particular situation.

D. Writing Effective Goals and Objectives

Writing goals and objectives for the first time may seem as foreign to you as writing a medical prescription. But don't worry—it's not as tough as it might seem at first. Like much of the IEP process, writing effective goals and objectives requires gathering information, asking questions, and a little practice.

1. Get Your School's IEP Form

Every school district has its own form for the written IEP program. As mentioned earlier in this book, you should get a copy of your school's form and any guidelines or instructions that accompany it. As you begin to draft your child's goals and objectives, be sure to refer to the school's current IEP form for guidance.

2. Use Your Binder and Blueprint

Your dining room table or desk may be overrun with special education papers. If they are not already organized in a binder (as recommended in Chapter 4), take some time to gather them together. Make sure you have the following documents:

- your child's school file
- all assessment reports
- written reports from professionals, and
- your blueprint.

Start with your blueprint. While the blueprint won't show you how to write specific goals and objectives, it will help you think about what you want for your child. The goals and objectives you create will be the stepping stones your child uses to achieve these ultimate ends.

3. Talk to Professionals

Talk with your child's teacher(s), other support staff, your independent assessor, service providers, and others who know your child. They might be willing to suggest specific goals and objectives or at least to review yours. If a specific person will implement or be responsible for your child's goals, be sure to talk to that person.

If this is your child's first IEP, ask the professionals what areas your goals and objectives should cover and how to make them as specific as possible. Be sure to explore with them every area that you feel requires goals and objectives. Ask them about useful goals and objectives for children with learning disabilities. Most teachers and other educators who work with or assess children with learning disabilities will be able to provide you with goals and objectives that they have found helpful in addressing your child's areas of need.

If this is not your child's first IEP, ask the following questions.

- What previous goals and objectives should be retained?
- If previous goals and objectives are carried over, why were they not accomplished before? What can be done to better ensure completion this year? Using the Progress Chart in Chapter 8 will help you monitor goals and objectives throughout the year.
- What new goals and objectives should be developed?

By talking with your child's teacher and other staff members about goals and objectives, you may learn their opinions about your child's placement and services. You may also come to an informal agreement on goals and objectives before the IEP meeting, which is always preferable.

4. Talk to Other Parents

If you know other special education families, ask to see their IEPs, particularly if their child's needs are similar to your child's. Even if your child's needs are different, other parents may have valuable advice to offer about drafting goals and objectives that will pass muster with your school district. (Of course, a child who is in junior or senior high school may not want you talking to another parent about his problems.)

Also, check with the PTA, the school district's local advisory committee on special education, and local individuals or organizations that provide help to special education parents for written material on goals and objectives. Chapter 15 discusses parent organizations.

Finally, check Appendix 3 for support organizations and learning disability websites that can provide you with information and help.

5. List Your Goals and Objectives Areas

Your job is to develop general goals and specific objectives for each skill area that relates directly to your child's needs (eight such areas are listed in Section A, above). Be as precise as possible. For example, don't simply list "academic achievement" as a skill area—break it down into reading, writing, math, cognitive abilities, spelling, and so on. For junior and senior high school students, list specific academic areas such as biology, algebra, social studies, English, and computer skills. Under social and behavioral goals, you might include separate goals and objectives for peer relations and for self-control.

6. Connect Goals and Objectives to a Specific Program and Services

The best goals and objectives not only state your immediate expectations for your child's performance, but also provide support for the program and services you want for your child. You should draft them with this result in mind. Whether the school district is offering an appropriate program for your child will depend, in large part, on whether your child can meet her goals and objectives within that program. On the other hand, if your child can meet her goals and objectives without the program and services you want for her, you probably won't get the program and services. If the IEP team has created appropriate goals and objectives and your child is meeting them, that is strong evidence that the IEP is working and, therefore, that the district has met its legal requirements.

When referring to a specific program or service, be as precise as you can. If you can mention the name of a special school or the details of the service, so much the better. If you don't have the exact information, add something that will support your broad IEP program goals. Not all goals and objectives are written this way—schools often argue that the goals and objectives portion of the IEP is not the place to mention program or services. However, IDEA does not prevent such added language. You should include it in your draft goals and objectives and argue for it at the IEP meeting.

The key is to write the goals and objectives so that an objective reader will conclude that your child needs the particular program or service you want to meet the goals and objectives. Even if the school district doesn't include this language in the written IEP, you can use your draft as a reminder of what you want.

Write a variety of goals and objectives for each skill area, incorporating specific language and referring to the desired program and services. Then write a second set that describes what you want without referring to specific programs and services by name. For example, assume you want your child in a regular classroom with a one-to-one aide in order to improve her reading comprehension. The ideal goal would be "Mary, in Ms. Jones's regular third grade class at Spencer School, will improve her reading comprehension, using her full-time one-to-one aide." The alternative would be "With the assistance of her one-to-one aide and by modeling her regular peers, Mary will improve her reading comprehension." Or, "With the assistance of his 1:1 aide, Tim will demonstrate understanding of all basic concepts covered in his 10th grade social studies class, including sections on government and the U.S. Constitution." If the school district does not agree that Mary or Tim should be mainstreamed, suggest implicit, instead of explicit, language. For example, the phrases "modeling her regular peers" and "in his 10th grade social studies class" in the examples above suggest (without actually saying) that Mary and Tim will be in a regular classroom.

7. Sample Goals and Objectives for Children With Learning Disabilities

The goals and objectives developed for your child will be very specific to his needs, and will vary in complexity depending on his age and ability level.

Goals and objectives for children with learning disabilities can cover many areas. The most obvious are academic subjects, but goals and objectives may also cover social and behavior issues that relate to the learning disability or to underlying cognitive issues, such as memory and processing difficulties. Goals and objectives can also be tied to particular junior and senior high school classes. Some areas for goals and objectives for children with learning disabilities include:

- reading
- mathematics
- spelling
- language (reception and expression)
- writing
- speech production
- behavior and socialization
- visual, spatial, auditory, memory, or conceptual problems
- study skills
- fine and gross motor skills, and
- computer skills, including keyboarding

a. Reading

Goal: Steven will improve his phonemic awareness.

Objective: Steven will distinguish initial letter sounds, such as between cat, hat, and sat.

Goal: Margaret will increase her reading comprehension.

Objective: Margaret will read a five-paragraph story at grade level, then describe the main character and list at least five specific details from the story in sequential order.

Goal: Ted will increase his reading vocabulary.

Objective: Ted will recognize and define ten new vocabulary words each week.

Goal: Harry will increase his reading vocabulary.

Objective: Harry will recognize and define ten new vocabulary words each week as taken from the novel or other readings in his English class.

b. Mathematics

Goal: Carl will improve his ability to count.

Objective: Carl will be able to count by ones with 95% accuracy, count by fives with 70% accuracy, and count by tens with 50% accuracy.

Goal: Linda will improve her ability to use standard measurements.

Objective: Linda will measure by inches and feet, demonstrating 80% accuracy.

Goal: Mark will understand geometric concepts.

Objective: Mark will demonstrate understanding of the concepts of geometric shapes, area, and the difference between triangles, with 80% accuracy.

c. Spelling

Goal: Cindy will improve her spelling skills.

Objective: Cindy will spell correctly ten new spelling words per week as identified by her 2nd grade reader.

Goal: Cindy will improve her spelling skills.

Objective: Cindy will demonstrate 75% accuracy using a list of spelling words appropriately in a dictated sentence.

Goal: Cindy will improve her spelling skills.

Objective: Cindy will demonstrate 75% accuracy using a list of two-syllable words provided by her teacher.

d. Language

Goal: David will improve his language skills.

Objective: David will be given five nouns and five verbs and will demonstrate 75% accuracy in identifying which are nouns and which are verbs.

Goal: David will improve his language skills.

Objective: David will be given ten words and will demonstrate 75% accuracy generating short sentences with each of the 10 words.

Goal: Katie will improve her pragmatic language skills.

Objective: Katie will demonstrate 70% accuracy in using sentences to convey correct information about assigned reading topics in her English class.

e. Writing

Goal: Melannie will improve her writing.

Objective: Given a topic of interest, Melannie will describe, in writing, the main idea and 3 details that support her conclusion about the main idea.

Goal: Melannie will improve her writing.

Objective: Given a short work of fiction to read, Melannie will describe, in writing, the main character, providing both physical and personality traits.

Goal: Melannie will improve her writing.

Objective: Melannie will demonstrate, with 80% accuracy, the ability to print the letters b, d, l, m, n.

f. Speech

Goal: Sam will improve his speech.

Objective: Sam's speech therapist will read out loud ten words with a long "e" sound and Sam will repeat those words with 85% accuracy.

Goal: Sam will improve his speech.

Objective: Sam will demonstrate 80% accuracy in pronouncing the "th" sound.

Goal: Sam will improve his speech.

Objective: Sam will demonstrate 80% accuracy in pronouncing the "gh" sound.

Goal: David will improve his language skills.

Objective: David will be given ten words orally and will demonstrate 75% accuracy in repeating each word.

(Goals and objectives in the area of speech may often be the responsibility of a speech and language therapist, as well as the classroom teacher or aide/resource specialist.)

g. Behavior and Socialization

Goal: Carla will improve her relationships with peers and develop specific strategies for improving peer relationships.

Objective: After each negative encounter between Carla and a peer, Carla will articulate what happened and why, and discuss specific ways in which she and her peer might approach the same encounter in a more positive and constructive way.

Goal: Carla will improve her relationships with peers and develop specific strategies for improving peer relationships.

Objective: Carla will correctly recognize, two out of three times, body and other cues from her peers.

Goal: Carla will improve her relationships with peers and develop specific strategies for improving peer relationships.

Objective: Carla, with the assistance of her behavioral assistant, will recognize when she is becoming angry and will make use of the following strategies: ask to go to a "time out" area, take several deep breaths, or ask for help from an adult to discuss her anger before she acts.

h. Visual, Spatial, Auditory, Memory, and Conceptual Problems

Goal: Mark will improve his ability to maintain visual place.

Objective: With the use of visual aids (such as a pointer or bookmark), Mark will read two sentences without losing his place, with 90% accuracy.

Goal: Sheila will improve her awareness of her immediate environment.

Objective: Sheila will develop a simple map of her school, including her classroom, the main office, the gym, and outside areas, and will be able to show her classroom teacher or aide where the items on the map are and how to reach them.

Goal: Brad will improve his ability to input auditory information.

Objective: Brad will be provided a written description of classroom assignments and then, after the teacher describes that assignment orally, he will explain the assignment.

Goal: Nancy will improve her short-term memory.

Objective: Given a list of five words written on the board and then erased, Nancy will name all five words with 100% accuracy.

Goal: Ben will improve his understanding of visual concepts.

Objective: Ben will be provided three sets of similar objects (such as a pen and pencil) and describe their similarities and differences.

A sample Goals and Objectives Chart is below; Appendix 5 includes a blank, tear-out copy. This chart is intended to give you a feel for what goals and objectives look like—including sample entries for present performance level and measuring progress. For more goal and objective examples, see the sample IEP form in Appendix 4.

Goals and Objectives Chart

Skill Area	Annual Goal	Short-Term Objective (or Benchmark)	Present Performance Level	How Progress Measured	Date of Completion
Reading	Ted, in his sophomore English class, will improve reading comprehension.	Ted will demonstrate 90% comprehension of the assigned novel in his 10th grade English class.	Ted demonstrates 50% comprehension of the assigned novel.	Essays assigned for homework, tests, and teacher observation.	June 20xx
Math	Bob, in his mainstreamed class, will master fourth grade math skills.	Bob will subtract a one-digit number from a two-digit number with 90% accuracy.	Bob subtracts a one-digit number from a two-digit number with 25% accuracy.	Teacher material	June 20xx
Emotional and psychological	Leah, in a class of no more than 12 students in a small and protected educational environment, will reduce her outward anger.	Because Leah is adversely affected by acting out behavior of others, she will, in a quiet and safe school environment, develop a better self-awareness of her anger and reduce her angry out-bursts from five to two a day.	Leah averages five daily angry outbursts as observed.	Teacher and therapist observation and recording.	June 20xx

Skill Area	Annual Goal	Short-Term Objective (or Benchmark)	Present Performance Level	How Progress Measured	Date of Completion
Social-behavioral	Sara will improve her peer relationships.	With the support of her aide and in a class of no more than ten students, Sara will initiate three positive peer interactions per day.	Sara is unable to initiate positive peer interactions.	Teacher-aide observation and recording.	June 20xx
Linguistic and communication	Adam, in his tri-weekly, 45 minute, one-to-one speech therapy sessions, will improve articulation.	Adam will produce the s, sh, and c sounds.	Adam produces the s, sh, and c sounds irregularly.	Speech therapist observation and recording.	June 20xx
Self-help and independent living skills (transition services)	Nina will explore career options.	Nina will meet with the school guidance counselor each month, identify three fields of work that interest her, and arrange, with the counselor's help, to visit a workplace in each field by the end of the year.	Nina doesn't know what she wants to do when she graduates high school.	Parent and guidance counselor observation.	June 20xx

10

Preparing for the IEP Meeting

Now that you've gathered your evidence and figured out what kinds of help your child will need, it's time to prepare for the IEP meeting, where you and the school district will hammer out the details of your child's special education program. Preparing for this meeting will make you a better advocate for your child, allow you to influence the IEP meeting agenda effectively, and reduce your own anxieties. In short, preparation increases your chances of success.

If you are attending your first IEP meeting, be sure to read this entire chapter. If you've done IEPs before, you'll want to at least skim this chapter. You might find some new ideas that you can put to use.

While this chapter will help you prepare for the IEP meeting, everything that you've done to this point—gathering your child's school records, having your child assessed, drafting a blueprint, and so on—will be crucial to the success of the IEP meeting. If you've skipped any earlier chapters, you should go back and read them before reading this chapter.

A. Schedule the IEP Meeting

IDEA sets out rules about the IEP meeting (34 C.F.R. §§ 300.343, 300.349):

- It must be held at a time and location convenient for all parties, especially the parents. The school district cannot simply schedule a meeting on a morning when you must be at work or pick a time without your input.
- It must be held at least once a year.
- It must be long enough to cover all issues.

Do You Need an Interpreter?

The school district must take necessary steps to ensure that you understand the IEP proceedings, including hiring an interpreter if you are deaf or hard of hearing or if English is not your first language. Be sure to let the school district know in advance if you will need an interpreter at the IEP meeting. (34 C.F.R. § 300.345(a)(e).)

1. Date of the IEP Meeting

As discussed in Chapter 4, the best time for the IEP meeting is during the spring preceding the school year for which you are developing the IEP plan. Before you choose a date, you may have to make several calls to the district administrator and your attendees to make sure all key people can attend. Don't choose a date that won't give you enough preparation time—you'll want to give yourself at least a month to get ready for the meeting.

2. Length of the IEP Meeting

IDEA does not require the IEP meeting to last for a particular length of time. A few weeks before the meeting, you should ask the school administrator how much time has been set aside (two or three hours is common). If the administrator has allotted less time than you think is necessary, explain why you think a longer meeting is needed, particularly if it may eliminate the need for a second meeting. If the administrator insists that the time allotted is enough, put your concerns in writing and send a copy to the superintendent of schools. If you're really concerned, you can file a complaint (see Chapter 13), but there is no legal rule setting a minimum length for the IEP meeting.

Sample Letter Requesting More Time for IEP Meeting

Date: September 28, 20xx

To: Ms. Suzanne Warner
Director of Special Education
Monroe School District
892 South 4th Street
Salem, OR 97307

Re: Karen Jamison, student in 1st grade class
of Drew Bergman

You indicated that we had one hour for my daughter Karen's October 14 IEP meeting. As I mentioned on September 27, I believe the issues we have to discuss will require at least two hours. It would be a hardship on our family to attend two meetings.

I will be calling you within the next few days to discuss this. I appreciate your understanding in this matter.

Sincerely,

Denise Jamison

Denise Jamison
909 Hanson Street
Salem, OR 97307
Phones: 555-3090 (home); 555-5000 (work)

cc: School Superintendent Phyllis Bander

As discussed in Chapter 2, the initial IEP meeting must be held within 30 days after the school district determines your child is eligible for special education. (34 C.F.R. § 300.343(b)(2).) If this is your child's first IEP meeting and the administrator doesn't set aside enough time, you might have to schedule a second one. This means that the meeting might be more than 30 days after the eligibility determination and therefore in violation of IDEA. You should point this out to the school district when you lobby for a longer initial meeting.

B. The IEP Meeting Agenda

Knowing the IEP meeting agenda in advance will help you tremendously as you prepare for the meeting. Although IDEA does not require that the district provide you with an agenda, it does require that you be given the opportunity to participate in and understand the proceedings. (34 C.F.R. § 300.345(a)(e).) It would not be unreasonable, therefore, to ask that you be told what issues will be discussed.

Most IEP meetings cover the following issues:
- eligibilty, if it hasn't already been determined
- your child's current status—how he's doing, whether or not previous goals and objectives were fulfilled, and what the current assessments indicate
- specific goals and objectives
- specific support or related services, and
- specific program, including the type, make-up, and location of the class.

Ask the school district special education administrator for an agenda or a description of the specific issues that will be discussed at the meeting. After you receive it, check your blueprint to make sure that the issues you've pegged as important will be covered at the meeting. If a crucial item is not on the agenda, let the administrator know, preferably in writing.

C. Organize Your Materials

Having access to key material at your fingertips is vitally important in an IEP meeting. You don't want to be fumbling about, looking for that one report or quote that could really help. Following these steps will help you organize the mountain of material.

1. Review Your Blueprint and All Written Material

Your starting point in preparing for the IEP meeting is your blueprint. You should also gather all written material, such as assessments, previous IEPs, notes and reports from your child's teacher and other staff members, work samples, and letters to and from your child's school district. These should all be in your IEP binder, clearly labeled and organized for easy reference.

Review all of these documents. Plan to bring to the meeting everything that supports your child's blueprint. Also bring any materials that counter the negative points school district representatives are likely to raise.

2. Highlight Supportive Material

Go through your binder and highlight or underline every important positive or negative statement. You may want to tab certain key statements for easy reference. How do you know what statements to highlight? Focus on the following:

- Test results, staff observations, reports, and other information on your child's current educational status. Highlight descriptive statements, such as "Tom scored at the first grade level on the Brigance Test, Counting Subtest" or "Sheila has difficulty staying focused in class; any activity beyond three-five minutes can be quite taxing for her." Be sure to include all information relating to your child's specific learning problems.
- Recommendations about program placement, related services, goals and objectives, and methodology. Look for statements such as "Carla would benefit from 30 minutes of speech therapy a week" or "Jim needs to be in a small classroom in which there are minimal disturbances or acting out behavior." Make sure your material includes recommendations specific to your child's learning disability.

- The consequences of providing or not providing specific placements, services, methodology, and other program components —for example, "Teri has significant fears about large groups and open space; placing her in a larger class on a big campus will increase those fears and put her at risk for serious emotional difficulties."

As you go through all your IEP-related information, you probably will highlight a lot of what you read, making the task of organizing the material seem overwhelming. To make it manageable, use different colored highlighters or tabs to differentiate the important from the less important statements or items—such as yellow for very important, green for somewhat important, and blue for less important. You can also make second copies of all significant items and keep them as a separate section in your IEP binder.

3. Use an IEP Material Organizer Form

Once your material is highlighted, you should take the time to create an additional document that will help you organize and access important information. I call it, for want of a more creative term, an IEP Material Organizer form.

A sample IEP Material Organizer is below, and Appendix 5 includes a blank, tear-out copy. Use one page for each major issue (for example, programs, related services, and methodology).

An IEP Material Organizer divides your written information, notes, and reports into important topics (such as related services or methodologies) keyed to your blueprint. As you can see from the sample, the IEP Material Organizer form allows you to find specific information—such as an assessment report, pediatrician letter, or key statements made by a teacher or other potential witnesses—that support or dispute your blueprint items.

IEP Material Organizer Form

Use this form to track documents and persons that provide support for or opposition to your goals.

Issue: Related Service: 1:1 Aide

Document or Witness* Name(s):	Binder Location (if applicable)	Helps You	Hurts You	Key Supportive or Oppositional Information	Rebuttal Document or Witness Name(s) (If hurts) (If none, what will you say at meeting?)
Lee Portaro (District) 3/1/xx assessment	1C		✓	Recomm. #s 3, 6, 8, 10 (p. 8)	Brown Assessment
Suzanne Brown 2/4/xx Assessment (Independent)	1B	✓		Narrative (p. 3, ¶s 4, 5). Recomm. #s 1-7, p. 12	
Weekly Teacher Reports	1F	✓	✓	9/6/xx, 10/4/xx, 1/17/xx Support 10/14/xx, 11/5/xx, 2/2/xx Against	Portaro Report: No IEP Agreement on Aide
5/2/xx IEP	1A	✓	✓	Narrative (¶s 7, 8) Against Narrative (¶s 2, 5) Support	Portaro p. 3 (¶ 2)
Dr. Baker (Pediatrician) 1/22/xx letter	1G	✓		P. 2, Concerns for psychological impact if no aide	
Phil Anderson (tutor) 12/6/xx letter	1H	✓		Reports positive results with direct work, 1:1 work	
Karla Jones (District Psychologist)	1M		✓	Sees Steve once/month Reports no adverse psych. impact	Brown, p. 3, ¶s 6, 9
Student Work	1P	✓		Steve on 10/5 assignment writes "Don't understand, who cares."	

* A "witness" is someone (teacher, doctor, assessor, tutor, psychologist) who gives an oral or written opinion regarding your child's needs at the IEP meeting.

You can divide the IEP Material Organizer form into subtopics that track your child's specific needs and relate directly to your blueprint. For example, under "placement," you might have subtopics like class size, peer needs, type of class, and location of class. Under the related service of a one-to-one aide, you might add the length and number of sessions, the qualifications of the aide, and what the aide will do. Under a curricula/methodology issue such as a reading program, you might include the name of the reading program, when the reading work is done, at what pace, and how reading comprehension will be measured.

Feel free to use the IEP Material Organizer form to subdivide issues in a way that works for you.

4. Identify Negative Material and Prepare Rebuttals

Keeping in mind your blueprint and goals for your child, what materials hurt your position? Do test results, staff observations, or assessor recommendations state that your child doesn't need what you want for her—or needs something you don't want her to have? Do statements such as "Ben does not need any special education services now" or "Leo should be provided one hour of aide time a week" (when you believe he needs one hour per day) or "Nicole cannot function in a regular classroom at this time" (when you're in favor of mainstreaming) appear in the written materials?

Some negative material is less direct. For example, a test result may not reflect the difficulties your child is actually experiencing. If an assessment concludes that "Sandy is at age level for reading," you might face an uphill climb in convincing the school district she needs additional help. Or a teacher's observation may undermine a placement or service you want. For example, a teacher's statement that "Steven frequently acts out and disrupts classroom activities"

may make it very hard for you to have Steven mainstreamed.

Here are some ways to counter negative material:

- Look for anything that directly or indirectly contradicts a troublesome statement or report. For example, an aide's statement that "Steven's behavior is erratic, but with help he can control his behavior and focus effectively and quietly on his work" might help you convince the school that Steven can be mainstreamed.

- Look for professional opinions contrary to the school's position. Usually statements in an independent assessment can counter school data.

- Are the qualifications of the person who wrote the unfavorable statement appropriate? If a psychologist completed the school assessment, find out if she has expertise in your child's learning disability and the specific subjects of her negative comments.

- Is the negative statement crystal clear? For example, what exactly does the following observation mean: "While Jane does not need a small class, there is some indication that she has a difficult time in a large school environment"? The reference to a large school environment may indirectly support a small class placement.

- Is the unfavorable statement supported by data, testing results, or anecdotal information? If not, be prepared to point that out. For example, if a teacher says that "Mark seems to understand basic math concepts," but Mark's independent assessment and your experience helping him with homework demonstrate that he can't perform simple multiplication and division, you should challenge the teacher's conclusion.

Use the IEP Material Organizer form to identify negative statements and rebuttal information. As a general rule, you shouldn't bring up negative statements unless the school district raises them first.

5. Provide Documents Before the IEP Meeting

In preparation for the IEP meeting, have everything in your binder marked, tabbed, highlighted, and referenced in your IEP Material Organizer. Also, make copies of material you want to show to school district representatives at the IEP meeting. This includes anything that supports your blueprint or rebuts negative information. The material can be in any form—a letter, report, independent assessment, teacher's report, work sample, or anything else. You may want to make a copy for each person who will attend the meeting.

Provide the school district with a copy of all material you've generated, such as an independent assessment. Give these to the district a week before the meeting. This way, school representatives can't argue that they need more time to review your material and, therefore, must postpone the meeting.

D. Draft Your Child's IEP Program

IDEA requires you and the school district to develop the IEP program as a joint endeavor. This does not mean, however, that you cannot—or should not—draft key portions of what you want to see in the IEP program beforehand. Drafting some language ahead of time can help you organize your arguments and recognize any potential roadblocks to getting what you want for your child.

The major portions of the IEP program are:
- goals and objectives
- specific programs and placement
- related services, and
- other items, including curricula, methodology, and a description of the placement.

Can Your School District Write the IEP Before the Meeting?

All IEP team members, including you, must have a full opportunity to discuss all aspects of your child's IEP. This means that the district cannot just present you with a completed IEP at the start of the IEP meeting and tell you to take it or leave it. Like you, however, the district can prepare draft statements ahead of time. School district representatives will probably have discussed the IEP agenda and their thoughts on your child's needs before the meeting as well—and they have every right to do so.

Writing out your IEP program will not only help you learn your material, but it will also force you to think again about how to make your case for the key issues. When you prepare your draft, you can either fill out a blank school district IEP form—you should get a copy early in the process—or you can simply write out your statements so you're ready to discuss them at the IEP meeting. As the IEP team proceeds, bring up the specific components you want in the IEP program.

You can use your blueprint and IEP Material Organizer form to help you draft an IEP and be an active participant at the IEP meeting. Chapter 11 explains how to use the IEP form and blueprint to put together the final IEP document—including how to get as much of your blueprint as possible included in the IEP.

1. Goals and Objectives

Goals and objectives refer both to the broad goals for your child—usually involving reading, math and language skills, social development, behavior issues, and other cognitive areas of need—and to the specific tasks your child will have to complete in order to reach those goals. Chapter 9 covers goals and objectives in detail.

2. Specific Programs and Placement

Program and placement refer to the exact school, class, and classroom characteristics (number and type of students, teacher qualifications, and so on) you want for your child.

Examples:

- Placement in the special day class for learning disabled students at Hawthorne School.
- Placement in a special day class for learning disabled children, no more than 12 students, students with no disruptive behaviors, and a teacher qualified to work with learning disabled students; SDC at Laurel or Martin Schools would be appropriate.
- Placement in Tina's home school, the regular third grade class.

3. Related Services

Related services are developmental, corrective, and other supportive services (such as transportation, one-on-one help from an aide, or special teaching strategies geared to children with learning disabilities) that your child needs to benefit from special education or to be placed in a regular class.

Examples:

- Jason needs three speech/language therapy sessions per week, each session for 30 minutes, one-on-one with a qualified speech therapist.
- Maria needs a full-time one-on-one aide in order to be mainstreamed in a regular fifth grade class, the aide to be qualified to assist Maria specifically in the areas of reading comprehension, spelling, fifth grade math, and developing positive peer relationships.

4. Other Components

Other components of the IEP program include:

- curricula, including how your child will be involved and progress in the general curriculum found in the regular classroom, and whether specific related services or special education are needed to assure your child's involvement and progress in the general curriculum
- teacher methodology and strategies (this is particularly important for children with learning disabilities—and you should be as specific as possible; see Chapters 3 and 5 for more information)
- transition plans, including vocational needs, and
- extracurricular activities such as after-school clubs, lunchtime activities, and sports activities.

 Chapter 2 provides details on each of these components of the IEP.

Child Profile

School district representatives might balk if you present them with a fully drafted IEP program or a blueprint. Instead, you might prepare a statement for the IEP meeting that incorporates important information without necessarily triggering school district opposition. Instead of emphasizing goals, objectives, placement, and services, emphasize your child and her needs.

Example:

Sally has a learning disability that creates problems with auditory memory, spelling, and reading comprehension. She has some emotional difficulties because of her learning disability, which appear in the forms of anxiety, fear of other children, and concern with safety. She has run off campus on a few occasions. When placed in a large classroom, her fears can be increased.

Sally needs a program in which the environment is not overly active, with no children who have behavioral problems. She should not be on a large campus, which might overwhelm her. She needs to be in a classroom of no more than 15 children. She benefits from the Slingerland method and requires instruction in simple, small steps. She needs one-on-one help with reading for at least two hours a day, and does best when this help is provided in continuous segments that are at least 30 minutes long.

This child profile combines parts of the blueprint with a description of your child and her needs. It is not unlike a school district's assessment, which normally includes a narrative section describing your child. Although you will want to draft the child profile for the meeting, do not give it to the school district in advance. Focus on:

- describing your child (quiet, kind, determined, afraid)
- explaining your child's areas of need, including academic, social, and environmental, and
- weaving in references to specific service and placement needs.

This profile provides another way to incorporate important information about your child into the IEP, which will help you argue for your blueprint goals.

E. Establish Who Will Attend the IEP Meeting

Under IDEA, any person with knowledge or expertise about your child may attend the IEP meeting. This includes the following people (34 C.F.R. § 300.344):

- you
- your child, if appropriate (see Section 2, below)
- a representative of the school district who is qualified to provide or supervise your child's special education and is knowledgeable about the general curriculum
- your child's special education teacher
- your child's regular classroom teacher(s), if your child is or may be in a regular class
- a person who can interpret the assessments and their impact on instructional strategies
- at your discretion or the discretion of the school district, other people who have knowledge or expertise regarding your child or her needs, and
- if your child is 14 or older, someone who knows about transitional services.

Representatives From Non-Educational Public Agencies

Sometimes, representatives from public agencies (other than the school district) may attend an IEP meeting. This generally happens if responsibility for certain IEP services is entrusted to an agency other than the school district. In California, for example, the county mental health department is responsible for providing mental health services, and a representative from that agency will often be present at IEP meetings. In Vermont, a representative of an agency other than the school district will attend to discuss transition services. And if your child has been involved with the juvenile authorities, a probation officer may attend, depending on the laws in your state.

Prior to the IEP meeting, talk with any of these additional folks and find out why they are attending the meeting, what they will do there (such as report on your child), and what position (if any) they plan to take on your child's needs.

1. Representing the School District

Finding out who will attend the IEP meeting on behalf of the school district will help you know what to expect. The school district should give you a written list of attendees, but if you are not told at least two weeks before the meeting, write the district and ask for the following information for each person who will attend:

- name
- reasons for attending
- qualifications and specific title, and
- whether or not he or she knows your child and, if so, in what capacity.

Prepare a list of all participants, including the positions they are likely to take on your child's special education needs.

A sample IEP Meeting Participants form is shown below; you can find a blank, tear-out copy in Appendix 5.

a. Your Child's Teacher(s)

If your child is in a regular class, his current teacher must attend the IEP meeting. (34 C.F.R. § 300.344(a)(2)(3).) Your child's teacher has the most information about your child's education—and the most experience with your child. The teacher may write reports about your child's progress, help write goals and objectives, be responsible for seeing that these goals are met, and make recommendations for the next school year.

The teacher can be your best ally or your worst enemy in the IEP process. Either way, the teacher is often the most convincing team member. The teacher's opinion may carry the most weight and influence how far your school district will pursue a dispute. If the teacher supports your position, you have a better chance of success. If the teacher does not, the school district may feel that it would win any due process dispute and, therefore, may decide to stand its ground at the IEP meeting.

Making sure the teacher understands your concerns and is prepared to speak frankly about them is crucial, but not always easy to achieve. Teachers work for their school districts; at times, a teacher's professional opinion may conflict with what an administrator believes to be right or feasible given budgetary or other constraints. A teacher who speaks frankly regardless of what a school administrator thinks is invaluable. It is therefore vital that you keep in contact with the teacher, ask his opinion, and indicate your specific concerns. Be specific, respectful, and always conscious of the teacher's time.

IEP Meeting Participants

Name	Position/Employer	Purpose for Attending	Point of View
Fred Brown	Third grade teacher, Kentington School District	Gene's teacher	Supports Gene's placement in regular class; does not think Gene needs aide
Diana Hunt	Psychologist, Kentington School District	Did assessment	Recommends placement in special day class
Violet King	Psychologist, Independent assessor	Did independent assessment	Supports regular class and aide
Jane Gough	Speech therapist, Kentington School District	Representative of school district	Agrees with need for speech therapy, but not on amount
Phil Chase	Administrator, Kentington School District	Representative of school district	No stated position

b. School Administrator

In most cases, someone representing the school district will attend the IEP meeting. This may be the district special education coordinator, student services director, county or regional office of education administrator, or school principal. There are all kinds of administrators, just like there are all kinds of parents. The administrator may be a kind, cooperative advocate for your child—or may be a burned-out, unpleasant bureaucrat.

You will be working with the administrator a good deal and will want to know where he stands on your child's IEP. Your inclination might be to ask the administrator before the meeting what position he will take on key issues for your child. Is it a good idea to do so? Many a wise administrator will let you know when he agrees with you, but will not let you know in advance if he disagrees. That doesn't mean you can't ask, but it does mean you should consider the pros and cons of asking the administrator's position prior to the IEP meeting.

Pros

- You will find out if the administrator agrees with you.
- If you get an honest answer, you'll know what the administrator thinks and how determined he is that the IEP plan reflect his position.
- If you disagree with the answer, you may convince him to change his mind, or you will have a better idea how to prepare for the IEP meeting.
- You may learn about options you like.

Cons

- The administrator will learn your plans and be able to counter them if he disagrees.
- You may put the administrator on guard, making it difficult for you to communicate with staff, visit programs, and the like.

If you decide to ask and the administrator says he opposes your goals for your child, consider the following:

- If the administrator says that he will not support you on a particular item, he may have violated IDEA by making a decision before the IEP meeting. This may be the basis of a formal complaint against the school district. (see Chapter 13.) This doesn't mean that you should "trap" the administrator into making a decision outside of the IEP meeting. But if he does, be aware of your rights.
- If the administrator has not made a decision, you may want to share the materials you have that support your position. You might give the administrator some ideas that will allow the district to agree with you. On the other hand, you may help the administrator prepare to rebut you at the IEP meeting. You'll have to judge the odds of making the administrator into an ally rather than a well-prepared adversary.

c. School Psychologist and Other Specialists

Depending on your child's condition and needs, other professionals may be involved in the IEP meeting, such as a school psychologist, speech/language therapist, occupational therapist, physical therapist, adaptive physical education specialist, or resource specialist. Most likely there will be someone from the district who has some knowledge about learning disabilities, including assessments, programs, and services. Like your child's teacher, these specialists may be great allies or formidable foes.

As with the teacher or administrator, speak with the specialists ahead of time to find out their positions on key issues.

d. Limits on School Representatives

Are there limits to who can attend the meeting? Federal policy states that a school may not invite

Sample IEP Meeting Attendance Objection Letter

Date: May 15, 20xx

To: Dr. Sean Gough
Hamilton School District
1456 Howard Avenue
Little Rock, AR 72212

From: Eva Crane
88 2nd Street
Little Rock, AR 72212

Re: Amy Crane, student in third grade class of Carol Smith

I understand that Joan Green, the district's psychologist, will be at Amy's IEP meeting. Ms. Green knows nothing about Amy and appears to have no knowledge that might be of use to the IEP team. I am formally requesting that Ms. Green not attend, unless there is some clear reason that makes her attendance appropriate and necessary for the development of Amy's IEP plan. As you know, IEP meetings can be particularly difficult for parents. We are already anxious about ours and would prefer that you not take action that will heighten our stress level.

If you insist on Ms. Green attending without a good reason, then we will file a complaint with the state and federal departments of education.

I will call you in a few days t o find out your decision on this issue. Thank you for considering my request.

Sincerely,

Eva Crane
Eva Crane
88 2nd Street
Little Rock, AR 72212

so many people as to make the IEP intimidating. State laws and policies, too, may also speak to the issue; California, for example, requires that the IEP meeting be "nonadversarial." A meeting full of district employees may violate these rules.

The 1999 IDEA regulations require individuals who attend the IEP meeting at the invitation of the parent or the school district to have knowledge or special expertise regarding the child. (34 C.F.R. § 300.344(a)(6).) If it seems inappropriate for a particular person to attend based on this standard, notify the school in writing (even if you initially call) of your concern. State why the person is not qualified to attend, why her attendance is not necessary or helpful, or why her presence may make the meeting intimidating. If the school insists that the person attend, see Chapter 13 on filing a complaint. And at the IEP meeting, state for the record, without being personal, that you feel so-and-so should not be there. When it's time to sign the IEP plan, reiterate your objection.

A sample letter objecting to a particular person's attendance at the IEP meeting is shown above; you can find a blank, tear-out copy in Appendix 5.

One Teacher Too Many

I once represented a child at an IEP meeting where there were a dozen school representatives, including several administrators, the school nurse, and the "teacher of the day." I asked the "teacher of the day" if he knew my client, Laura. The answer was no—he had neither met her nor knew anything about her. I asked him why he was there. Without hesitation he said he was there to "represent the teachers of the area." His involvement—or the presence of anybody else who doesn't have knowledge of your child or the relevant educational issues—would be contrary to federal policy and the purpose of the IEP meeting.

2. Representing the Parents

While some of the people representing the school district may support your goals for your child, you may want some or all of the following people to attend the IEP meeting on your behalf:

- your spouse or partner
- your child
- others who know your child, such as a relative or close family friend
- independent assessors or other professionals who have worked with your child, and
- an attorney.

Contact these people well in advance to let them know the date, time, location, and likely duration of the meeting. Make sure they understand the key topics that will arise during the IEP meeting and the issues and solutions they are there to discuss. Let them know the positions of the various school representatives on the key issues. Show them copies of materials that both support and are contrary to your goals.

Remind your attendees that the IEP meeting is informal and that points of view should be stated in a positive but firm way. Disagreements can be spirited, but should remain professional and respectful.

Some of the people you ask to attend—such as an independent assessor, a pediatrician, or a lawyer—might charge you a fee. Find out the cost ahead of time. If you can't afford to have the person stay for the entire meeting, let the school administrator know in advance that you will have someone attending who needs to make a statement and leave. Before the meeting, ask the administrator to set aside a specific time for that person to speak.

Some people you want to attend might not be able to, or you might not be able to afford to pay them to attend. In either situation, ask the person to prepare a written statement for you to read at the meeting. Some people's testimony may actually be better in writing rather than it would be live—for example, someone who is timid or reluctant to strongly state a position in person might come across better in writing.

Chapter 8 discusses items to include in a written statement from your child's doctor or other people from outside the school.

a. Parents

While work schedules or living arrangements may make attending the IEP meeting difficult, it is generally best if both parents attend, even if you are divorced or separated. If you have differences of opinion, resolve them before the IEP meeting. If you argue with each other during the IEP meeting, you will most likely damage your credibility and chances of success.

I strongly recommend that you attend all IEP meetings. By allowing the IEP to proceed without you, you are giving up your right to be involved–and increasing the chance that an IEP will be developed that doesn't meet your child's unique needs. If one of you cannot attend, be sure to prepare a strong and emotional statement for the other to read.

Can an IEP Meeting Be Held Without You?

Your school district has a duty to ensure that you are present at the IEP meeting. It can hold an IEP meeting without your involvement only in unusual situations, and only after following very specific procedures, including:

- notifying you early enough of the meeting to ensure you have the opportunity to attend
- scheduling the meeting at a mutually convenient time and place, and
- finding ways of including you—such as individual or conference telephone calls—if you cannot attend.

The district can proceed without you only if it can prove that it took specific steps to convince you to attend, by keeping records of its attempts to arrange a mutually agreeable time and place by phone, correspondence, and even visits to the parent's home or workplace. (20 U.S.C. § 1414(d); 34 C.F.R. § 300.345.)

Sample Statement to IEP Team

To: Marilyn Haversham's IEP Team

From: Claudine Haversham (Marilyn's mom)

Date: March 1, 20xx

I cannot attend the March 15 IEP meeting, but I wanted you to know that I am very concerned that Marilyn might be removed from her regular program. She is such a happy child now that she is mainstreamed. As her mother, I see the joy in her eyes when she gets up in the morning to get ready for school. A placement in a more restrictive environment would be devastating to my daughter. I must be frank and tell you that we will vigorously oppose any efforts to remove Marilyn from her current program.

I greatly appreciate your sensitivity to Marilyn's needs and your past assistance in making her educational experience a positive one.

Sincerely,

Claudine Haversham

Claudine Haversham

b. Your Child

IDEA says that the student shall attend the IEP meeting if it is appropriate or if the IEP team is considering transition services for a child. (34 C.F.R. §§ 300.344(a)(7).)

When is it considered appropriate for a child to attend? If your child can speak about his hopes and needs, he may be a compelling self-advocate. But be careful—if he's unpredictable or unsure of the importance of the meeting, you may not want to risk him giving a "wrong" answer. For example, you want your child to remain in his mainstreamed program. A school district representative says, "Tell me Tommy, do you want to stay in your class?" You're not going to be happy if Tommy responds, "Nope."

If your child does attend, have him focus on his feelings and hopes. For example, "Carl, the school assessor says you had a hard time in Ms. Shaver's class, particularly with other students. Why do you think that was so?" Be sure you know what his answer will be.

c. Relatives, Friends, and Child Care Workers

It is important to limit the number of people who attend the IEP meetings—the more people in attendance, the longer the meeting will drag on. Therefore, you'd ordinarily not bring a relative, friend, or child care worker to the meeting. But if someone can present a view of your child that wouldn't otherwise be presented, you might want him or her to come. For example, if your child's regular babysitter can describe how your otherwise shy and reserved child talks nonstop about how she loves being in a regular class, it may be powerful testimony.

Generally, a sibling or peer of your child, particularly a young one, should not attend unless she is the only person who can speak to an issue or has a really powerful presence. Preparing young attendees will be very important, with focus on the sibling or peer's "feelings" about your child, rather than more formal information.

Bring Someone to Take Notes

Ask a friend or relative to attend the IEP meeting and take notes for you—paying careful attention to who says what regarding important items. Having a note taker can be invaluable, particularly if you anticipate a controversial meeting. See Section F, below, for information on taping the meeting.

d. Independent Assessors and Other Professionals

Because the conclusions reached by any independent assessor who tested your child will probably be instrumental in helping you secure the right services and placement, it is crucial that the assessor attend the IEP meeting. The assessor must be able to clearly articulate her professional opinion on the key blueprint items, as well as her opinion on all assessment data. She must also be prepared to rebut contradictory information presented by the school district.

Other professionals, such as a pediatrician, private tutor, therapist, or psychological counselor, can be important witnesses on your behalf if they know your child and can speak to your child's learning disability and any other key issues affecting the IEP plan. Prepare these individuals as you would prepare an independent assessor.

You may also have worked with a specialist, an educational consultant, or another professional to address your child's learning disabilities. This person may make the strongest case for including components specific to your child's learning disabilities in the IEP and should certainly attend the IEP meeting.

e. An Attorney

If you hire or consult an attorney during the IEP process, that person can attend the IEP meeting. You can also hire a lawyer just for the IEP meeting. (See Chapter 14 for information on working with lawyers.) As a general rule, you might want an attorney at the IEP meeting if your relationship with the school district has deteriorated and you anticipate a complicated and difficult IEP meeting.

If you bring an attorney to the IEP meeting, school representatives are more likely to be on guard and less likely to speak frankly. On the other hand, if the school administrators haven't been cooperative and you feel the plan that will emerge from the IEP meeting will be harmful to your child, bringing an attorney shows that you mean business. You're much better off not using an attorney—it does change the entire experience—but if you must, then find one who is reasonable and cooperative.

If you plan to have an attorney at the IEP meeting, you should notify the school district reasonably in advance. Except in unusual situations, you will be responsible for paying your attorney with little chance of reimbursement. (See Chapter 14 for information about attorney fees and reimbursement.)

F. Final Preparation Concerns

As you finish your IEP preparation, consider these additional recommendations.

1. Taping the IEP Meeting

You (and the school district) have the right to tape record the meeting. While a tape recording may be the best proof of what was said, it may have an inhibiting effect. People don't always want to make a particular statement if it is going "on record." In addition, tape recordings are not always of great quality; participants are not always audible, and it can be hard to discern what was said and who said it.

If you decide to tape record, bring a good quality recorder. Bring extra tapes and batteries in case an outlet is not accessible. The school district can tape record even if you object—just as you can tape over the objections of school representatives. If the school district tapes the meeting, you are entitled to a copy of the tape, and it will become part of your child's file—just as the district can ask for a copy of your tape.

You should notify the district in advance that you want to tape record the meeting.

School Resistance to Tape Recording

The U.S. Department of Education, Office of Special Education Programs has issued several statements reinforcing the right of parents to tape record IEP meetings. If, once you get to the meeting, the special education administrator says you cannot tape record, state that the district's refusal to allow you to tape is against the law and that you will file a complaint. If tape recording is crucial, your only choice may be to postpone the meeting until this issue is resolved. See Chapter 13 for advice on filing a complaint.

---

2. Reducing Your Anxiety

Since it is a given that you will be nervous at the meeting, don't worry about being anxious. But do give some thought to what you might do before the IEP meeting to relax: taking a walk or jogging, soaking in the bathtub, going out for breakfast, or any other activity that helps you settle your nerves. If you need to get a babysitter or take time off from work, set it up well in advance, so you're not scrambling the day before the meeting.

By preparing—knowing your material, completing your IEP blueprint, drafting your IEP plan, and talking to your IEP participants ahead of time—you will do much to reduce your anxiety.

IEP Preparation List

Things to do before the IEP meeting:
- Find out the date, time, and location.
- Get a copy of the school's agenda.
- Make your own agenda.
- Prepare your IEP Material Organizer.
- Draft IEP plan.
- Find out who is attending on behalf of school district.
- Invite and prepare your own IEP participants.
- Give the school a copy of the following:
  ▲ independent assessments
  ▲ documents such as reports and work samples
  ▲ names and titles of people attending IEP, and
  ▲ notice of intent to tape record IEP meeting (if applicable).
- Create meeting reminder list of items you want to be sure to remember:
  ▲ "Make sure we read statements of Dr. Wilson and Rona (babysitter), who can't attend."
  ▲ "Make sure Dr. Ramirez covers Lydia's physical therapy needs."
  ▲ "Remember we don't have to sign all of the IEP—we can object."

11

The IEP Meeting

Your IEP meeting is soon. You'll enter the room, sit down, put your binder on the table, take a deep breath, and do just fine. You'll do fine because being nervous is natural, the school administrator probably feels the same way, and, most important, you are prepared for this meeting. You've developed your child's blueprint and drafted an ideal IEP, supported by various documents. You're familiar with the school's IEP form, policies, programs, and services. You know who will attend the meeting and where each person stands on key issues. You have people with you who are ready to help you make your case. Even if you don't have every one of these items nailed down, you'll do your best. And if you can't reach an agreement on some or all of the IEP, you'll know your options.

Chapter 10 provides valuable advice on preparing for the IEP meeting. Chapter 7 gives you tips on preparing for and attending an IEP eligibility meeting.

A. Getting Started

IEP meetings can take a lot of time. Therefore, it's very important that you be prompt. In fact, you'll want to be at least ten to 15 minutes early so you can get the lay of the land, see the meeting room, and perhaps say a few words to the teacher or school administrator. More important, being early will give you the chance to talk to your participants and make sure everyone is clear about their roles at the meeting.

1. What to Bring

Bring your IEP binder and the written material you've gathered, including assessments, letters, reports, and your IEP Material Organizer form. Make sure you have extra copies of key documents, such as an independent assessment.

2. Get the Note Taker Organized

As recommended in Chapter 10, it's a good idea to bring someone to take notes, particularly if you anticipate a controversial meeting. Make sure you provide your note taker with paper and pens (unless he's using a laptop computer). Remind your note taker to get the details on important items, particularly those that relate to your blueprint— what was said and who said it are especially important. These notes, particularly on items that you and the school district dispute, will be extremely important should you end up filing for due process (see Chapter 12) or making a formal complaint (see Chapter 13). If you do not have a note taker, make sure you give yourself time to jot down important statements—don't hesitate to ask participants to slow down or repeat what they said, or to ask for a pause so you can complete your note taking.

3. Set Up the Tape Recorder

If you're planning to tape record the meeting, set up the equipment and make sure that it's working. Also, make sure you have extra tape and batteries, just in case.

Chapter 10 explains how to notify the school district in advance of your intent to tape record the IEP meeting and how to deal with any dispute that arises about taping the meeting.

4. How the Meeting Will Begin

The IEP meeting is typically led by the school administrator responsible for special education programs, although it may be led by the school site principal, the school district assessor, or even, on some occasions, a teacher.

Most IEP meetings begin with the introduction of all participants. School representatives will probably explain their roles at the meeting. You should do the same with your participants. If, for example, a friend will take notes or an outside assessor will explain her report, make that clear.

After introductions, the administrator will probably explain the agenda, how the meeting will run, and how decisions will be made. If the agenda is different from what you anticipated or omits issues you want to cover, bring up your concerns at the beginning of the meeting. You have the right to raise any issue you want at the IEP meeting. Also, if the agenda appears too long for the allotted time, explain that you don't think there will be enough time to cover everything and ask that certain items be discussed first. If your request is denied, do your best to keep the meeting moving forward.

Hitting the Wall

You may not be able to convince the school district that your position is correct. Unfortunately, there are times when no matter what you say or how persuasive you are, the other side won't budge. Many parents fear that if they are not able to come up with some remarkable statement that will cause the administrator to change her mind, there will be some dire consequence. But this is rarely the case, so just make your point and then add your concern about the unresolved matter to the addendum. (See Section F.)

While most IEP meetings follow a certain pattern, (discussed in Section D, below), don't be surprised if yours seems to have a life of its own, going in directions you did not anticipate. Just make sure your key issues are covered before the meeting ends.

IEP Meeting Dos and Don'ts

Is there etiquette to the IEP meeting? There should be. As in any potentially difficult encounter, try to proceed in a positive way.

Dos
- Do respect other opinions.
- Do try to include all IEP team members in the process.
- Do ask questions in a fair and direct way.
- Do state your position firmly, but fairly.
- Do explore ways of reaching consensus.

Don'ts
- Don't interrupt.
- Don't accuse.
- Don't make personal attacks.
- Don't raise your voice (too high).
- Don't question another's motives.

You might begin by saying that you appreciate everyone's attendance, the time and energy they're spending on your child, and their professional dedication. Emphasize that you are determined to discuss all issues in a fair and thorough way, and that you are looking forward to a challenging but ultimately positive meeting in which everyone's point of view is respected.

B. Simple Rules for a Successful IEP Meeting

Several simple rules can help you get the most out of the IEP meeting.

1. Know Your Rights

IDEA was created for your child. As you undoubtedly know by now, it gives your child the right to:
- a free appropriate public education (FAPE) in the
- least restrictive environment (LRE), based on an

• individualized education program (IEP).

Parents are co-equal decisionmakers—their opinions are just as important as everyone else at the IEP meeting.

Chapter 2 explains your child's legal rights under IDEA. Appendix 1 includes the relevant statutes and regulations.

2. Don't Be Intimidated

You have special knowledge of your child's needs. School personnel are not the only experts. In fact, if you have documents to support each item you want in the IEP plan, you may be better prepared than the school district.

At the same time, don't automatically assume that teachers or other school officials are wrong. There are many dedicated teachers and school administrators who want to provide the best education for your child, have expertise in educating children with disabilities, and have been through this process numerous times before. This doesn't mean you won't encounter opposing opinions or perhaps even run up against someone who is just plain nasty or incorrect. But as a general rule, most of the folks in special education are there because they care for your child and want to do the best they can for her.

How to Deal With Intimidating or Nasty Comments

For many parents, dealing with teachers and school administrators in an IEP meeting can be intimidating. You don't want to (but may) hear:
- *I'm sorry, Mr. Walker, but you're wrong.*
- *I'm sorry, Ms. Richards, the law doesn't say that.*
- *Your assessment report is incorrect.*
- *Our policy precludes that.*
- *Maybe they do that in another school district, but we don't.*
- *I will not agree to that!*
- *That's enough on that subject!*
- *That's not the way it works.*

In most cases, you can ignore these kinds of comments or make a simple response. (Section B5, below, discusses how to challenge blanket assertions.) Try to determine whether the comment is anything more than just an impolite or negative remark. If it is unimportant, say your piece and move on.

"I don't appreciate your tone of voice, Ms. Hanson. I have treated you with respect and expect the same from you. Even if we disagree, we can do it in a civil way. More important, your statement is not correct (or reasonable or productive or conducive to a positive IEP meeting)."

If the comment seems important, you may need to be more assertive.

"Ms. Hanson, I resent your comment and believe you are undermining this IEP meeting. Please understand, I will do what is necessary to ensure my child receives the program she needs and bring your behavior to the attention of the appropriate individuals."

If you don't feel calm and your voice is shaky, that's okay, too. Just don't yell or get overly aggressive. If necessary, you may want to raise the possibility of filing a formal complaint regarding something that seems illegal—for example, if the district won't allow you to discuss your independent assessment. (Chapter 13 covers complaints.) But don't make a threat without first thinking it through. Do you really have grounds to file a formal complaint? Is there any validity to the school representative's comment? Know the difference between an opposing point of view or even a bad style and a patently intimidating statement or action. Is it worth alienating the school district and changing the atmosphere of the IEP meeting? In most cases, you can make your point without threatening to file a formal complaint.

3. Focus on Your Child's Needs—Not Cost or Administrative Constraints

IDEA recognizes that each child's needs are unique and, therefore, that each individual program will be different. If you can show that your child needs a specific service, such as a one-on-one assistance from an aide or two hours of occupational therapy each week, then the law requires it.

If the school district does not have the staff to provide the related service your child needs, such as a speech therapist, then the school should pay for a private therapist.

A child's needs—not cost—should influence all IEP decisions. For example, the school administrator cannot refuse to discuss or provide a service or placement because it "costs too much." Given recent budgetary problems and state deficits, you may hear this comment more frequently. Reduced funding does put school districts in a tough fiscal bind, but neither you nor your child is responsible for that. IDEA still requires a "free" and "appropriate" education for your child.

An administrator may try to get the point across indirectly, by saying something like "If we provide that service for your child, another child will not get services she needs." Don't argue the issue; simply respond with something like this:

> *Mr. Keystone, I do understand and feel the same frustration you do with existing fiscal problems, but it is wrong for you to make my child responsible for your budgetary difficulties. I won't be put in the position of making a choice between my child's needs and the needs of other children. The law is clear that we should be discussing an appropriate education for my child, not the cost.*

If you can't reach agreement, and the school district representative continues to admit that there is an administrative or budget problem, be sure you (or your note taker) has written this down in case you end up in due process.

This is not to say that cost is never a legitimate issue. Let's say you want your child in Program X and the school offers to put your child in Program Y, which is less costly for the district. You're unable to reach an agreement and decide to resolve the matter through due process. If the district can prove Program Y is appropriate for your child, it will likely prevail at the due process hearing. You won't win a fight for the ideal program when an appropriate one is available.

 Don't describe the program you want as the "best" or "optimum" or "maximum." The school district might use these types of statements as evidence that you want more than the "appropriate" education to which your child is entitled under IDEA. If you feel that a program or service offered by the school isn't right, characterize it as "inappropriate"—this will signal that you don't think the school district is meeting its legal obligations. And always remember to characterize your desired program as appropriate.

4. Know When to Fight and When to Give In

Understanding the IEP process and having a clear, step-by-step strategy does not guarantee that every issue will be resolved as you want. It is important to realize when you don't have a case. You may be fully prepared, do a superb job in the IEP meeting, and still not have enough evidence to support your position. Knowing the strength of your case will help you figure out when to fight and when to concede.

Fight for the crucial issues and be more flexible on others. For instance, goals and objectives and test protocol may be important, but, ultimately, the related services, placement, and methodology are what matter in your child's education. Spending an hour fighting over the wording of one goal or objective is probably a waste of time; spending half of the meeting on a major issue like placement is probably worth it.

5. Ask Questions

You should always feel comfortable asking questions—and there will undoubtedly be times during the IEP meeting when you need more information or clarification. There are several very good reasons to ask questions: to obtain basic information, to persuade someone of your position, or to question a blanket assertion.

a. Obtain Basic Information

During the IEP meeting, many technical terms will be used. If you don't understand something, ask what it means. It's better to ask—even for the tenth time—than to proceed without understanding.

Most important, find out what these terms mean for your child. Knowing that your child scores at the 42 percentile on the Wechsler is useless unless it tells you something about your child's abilities and opportunities to improve.

b. Persuade

Asking questions can be an effective way to persuade someone that your position is right and his should be changed. State your questions positively, such as "Do you [IEP team members] agree with the recommendations on page eight of Dr. Calderon's report?" or "Ms. Porter, do you agree that Amy should be placed in a regular eighth grade class with a one-to-one aide?"

You may need to establish agreement on preliminary matters before asking these kinds of big questions.

Example:

You want a particular IEP member to agree with you on placement. You realize that you must first establish agreement on the assessment supporting that placement. You first ask, "You read Dr. Harper's report. She states that Carolyn needs, and I am quoting, 'a quiet environment in which there are no behavioral problems or acting out by other students.' Do you agree with Dr. Harper?" The IEP member agrees and you follow up by asking, "Given Dr. Harper's report and our desire that Carolyn be placed in the special day class at the Manning School, do you agree with that placement?"

Someone may chafe at being asked such a pointed question and may feel like they are being cross-examined. One good way to respond would be to say, "I certainly don't mean to cross-examine you and appreciate you reminding me of that. Please understand that I am not a lawyer but a parent. What is important to Carolyn is not the nature of the question but the answer. I will certainly try not to be too formal; would you like me to try to put it another way?"

c. Challenge Blanket Assertions

Nothing is more frustrating for a parent than hearing lines like these:

- *"Unfortunately, we are not allowed to discuss that issue."*
- *"We don't provide that service."*
- *"That's not our policy."*
- *"Sorry, but you can't do that."*
- *"That's not the law."*

If an assertion seems illegal or illogical, ask what it's based on. If the administrator says something vague like "It's our policy," "It's the law," "It's our best judgment" or "It's the way things are," keep asking why. Request a copy of the law or policy.

If possible, refer to your documentation. For example, the district administrator says that, as a general rule, the district doesn't provide more than two hours of a related service per week. An assessment states that your child needs three hours. Point that out and ask how the district's rule complies with IDEA, which requires that the specifics of a service be determined by the IEP team.

The administrator may say something like "Mrs. Wasserman, that is just the way it is and I won't respond any further to that question." You'll want to follow up with something like "I'm sorry you won't answer my question; it is a fair and important question and I plan to ask your superintendent or the school board to answer it." If the issue is crucial to your child's education, you may want to file a complaint as discussed in Chapter 13.

Or the school district may not agree with you on an important IEP component. For example, you feel there is clear support for a specific placement, but the administrator disagrees. Ask her to tell you why and to provide you a detailed explanation supported by appropriate materials.

Note any unresolved matter on your addendum. (See Section F, below.)

6. Pay Attention to What's Written on the IEP Form

Make sure you know what statements are entered onto the IEP document and voice any objections immediately—whether it's about a particular goal or objective or a general statement made on the narrative page of the IEP form. (Section D, below, covers the narrative page.)

7. Keep Your Eye on the Clock

Whether the school has allotted two hours or five hours for the IEP meeting, keep track of time. If you are 45 minutes into a 90-minute meeting and the IEP team is still talking in generalities, you should say, "We need to move on to a specific discussion of Cora's goals and objectives, placement, and related services."

A good school administrator will keep the meeting on schedule. If she's not doing so, take the lead. Be ready to suggest moving on to the next topic when the discussion on a particular issue has gone on long enough.

8. Don't Limit Your Options to All or Nothing

At some point during the IEP meeting, you may realize that you will not reach agreement on all issues. For example, you feel your child needs at least two sessions with a reading specialist each week, one hour per session. The district offers one hour-long session. You've done your best to persuade them, to no avail. What do you do?

The school district cannot present you with a "take-or-leave-it" position—for example, "We've offered help from a reading specialist once a week. You want it twice a week. You can either agree with us and sign the IEP or disagree and go to a hearing." Furthermore, the school district cannot insist that you give up your right to due process—for instance, "We've offered help from a reading specialist once a week and that's all we'll offer. We'd advise you to sign the IEP form and not make waves."

Your best bet is to make sure the IEP document specifically states that you agree that a specific service is needed—or that a particular placement is appropriate—and that your child will receive at least what the school district has offered. Then make sure your opinions are reflected on the parent addendum page.

There are no magic phrases you need to use, no legal language required by IDEA. State that you are accepting the district's "offer" but then indicate exactly why the offer falls short and what you believe would be appropriate for your child. For example, your district offers your child one hour a week of 1:1 assistance in her 11th grade social studies class so she can meet her reading and language goals and objectives. You feel she needs two hours a week. You should state clearly on the IEP (probably on the addendum page) that "Nicole needs two hours a week of 1:1 assistance in her 11th grade social studies class. We have accepted the district's offer of one hour per week, but we do *not* agree that she only needs one hour per week. We reserve the right to go to due process and seek an additional hour of assistance per week."

9. Don't Be Rushed Into Making a Decision

If you're on the fence about a particular issue, don't be rushed into making a decision. Ask for a break and go outside for a few minutes to think about what the school has offered. If you are concerned that pausing on some issues may mean delay on others, ask for a day or two to make up your mind on a particular issue so that the IEP team can proceed with other items. This may require a second IEP meeting, unless you eventually agree with the rest of the IEP team on the issue. If an item is that important, however, then a second meeting is worth the time. Sometimes, it's easier to figure out what to do once you have gone home and had a chance to think things over.

C. Become Familiar With Your School's IEP Form

As we've already suggested, you should get a copy of your school district's IEP form before the IEP meeting. While forms vary, they will almost always have sections on the following:
- present levels of educational performance
- goals and objectives (and evaluation procedures)
- related services
- placement/program
- effective dates of the IEP

- summer school or an extended school year, and
- a narrative page or pages for recording various important statements (such as comments on assessments) or keeping a running account of the meeting discussion. (This important part of the IEP is described in Section D, below.)

In addition, IEP forms typically include the following types of information:
- identifying information, such as your child's name, gender, date of birth, grade and school district, and parents' names and addresses
- the type of IEP (eligibility or annual review) and date of IEP meeting
- your child's eligibility status and disability category
- the amount of time your child will spend in a regular or mainstreamed program, if applicable
- your child's English proficiency, and
- signatures of IEP team members and parents.

The IEP team may include other important information in the IEP, such as a specific curriculum or teaching methodology, a specific classroom setting, peer needs, or a child profile.

 You can find a sample completed IEP form in Appendix 4.

The IEP Form and Your IEP Blueprint

The IEP form itself and your blueprint (your list of desired program components) will have a similar structure, but won't be identical.

Most of your blueprint items, such as related services and placement, have a corresponding section in the IEP. In some cases, however, you may find that the IEP form does not have space for all the details you included on your blueprint. For example, the IEP form will allow you to specify the kind of program or placement—such as a regular class or special day class—but might not provide space for the details of the placement—such as peer numbers and make-up, classroom environment, and school environment. Other blueprint items, such as methodology and curricula, may not have a corresponding section on the IEP form. And the school administrator may not be familiar with a blueprint like yours.

As you prepare for the IEP meeting, keep in mind that while the IEP form may not reference all of your blueprint items, IDEA allows the IEP team to discuss and agree on any element it feels is necessary for your child. These types of details can go on the IEP narrative page (see Section D, below) or, if the school disagrees, a parent addendum page (see Section F, below).

D. Writing the IEP Plan

Usually, someone from the school district will write the IEP plan as the meeting progresses, by checking off boxes on the form, filling in specific sections, and completing a narrative or descriptive page.

You should frequently ask to see what has been written, to make sure it accurately reflects what was discussed or agreed upon. You may want to check every 30 minutes or so, with a simple "Excuse me, but can we break for just a few minutes? I want to see what the IEP looks like so far." If 30-minute breaks seem forced, ask to review the form each time you complete a section. Pay special attention to the narrative page—this will be more subjective than other parts of the IEP.

Your goal is to create an IEP—including the narrative page, goals and objectives, placement, and related services—that reflects your point of view.

1. Child's Current Educational Status

If your child is presently enrolled in school, the IEP team will review your child's current educational statue and IEP goals and objectives, program, and related services. Your child's current status may be reflected in testing data, grades, and teacher reports or observations. If this is an eligibility IEP meeting, the team will review assessment data; it will do the same every three years when your child is reassessed. Discussion of your child's current status may be broad or specific. It may occur at the beginning of the IEP meeting or as you review specific items, such as goals and objectives, for the upcoming year.

What goes onto the IEP about your child's current situation is very important. For example, if you are concerned about the current program, you won't want the IEP narrative page to state that "Sam's placement has been highly successful this past year." If such a statement is made and entered onto the IEP document—perhaps on the narrative page—be sure to object, with something like "I'm sorry, but I don't think that statement is accurate, and here's why." Perhaps the ensuing discussion will result in a change of this statement. If not, say, "I certainly cannot agree with it. It should not be on the IEP as our consensus." If the district insists, then you will have another item for your addendum. (See Section F, below.)

2. Assessments

A school district representative (most likely the assessor) will either read or summarize the school district's assessment. If the assessor starts reading the report, ask her to synthesize the salient points rather than spend precious time reading the assessment verbatim—especially if you have already seen a copy of the assessment.

This may be a good time to use your IEP Material Organizer (see Chapter 10) to point to other documents—such as previous IEP plans, an independent assessment, other reports, teacher notes, and the like—to support or contradict the school assessment.

If you haven't already introduced the independent assessment, you will do so once the district has finished presenting its assessment. You or your assessor should provide a synopsis of the report, focusing on:

- the assessor's credentials
- the reason for the assessment
- the tests used
- the key conclusions regarding the testing, and
- the specific recommendations.

Be sure to highlight the test results and recommendations not covered in the school assessment. This is also the time to introduce any other supporting material, including letters, work samples, and other professional opinions.

Most IEP forms refer to the assessments on the narrative page. The IEP plan might specify the sections, results, and/or statements in the assessments on which you all agree. Even if there is only one statement in the assessment you all agree on, make sure it gets into the IEP document if it is essential to your child's needs. If the person drafting the IEP plan includes something from an assessment with which you disagree, make sure your objections are noted.

Sometimes, the assessments are attached to the IEP document. This can work in your favor if you agree with the assessment. Attaching the assessment suggests that its findings and recommendations have been incorporated into the IEP.

If an assessment is not attached or there is some disagreement over the accuracy or usefulness of the assessment, the narrative page should specify what parts of the assessments are included or excluded.

Examples:

- The IEP team agrees with Sections 1, 2, 4, 6, and 8 of the school assessment and Sections 3, 5, 9, 10, and 12 of the independent assessment and incorporates them into the IEP.
- The IEP team disagrees with the rest of both assessments and does not incorporate them into the IEP.

You can use the parent addendum page to state the reasons for your disagreement. (See Section F, below.)

3. Goals and Objectives

If this is not your child's first IEP, the IEP team will next review the previous year's goals and objectives. This discussion is likely to lead to one of four different outcomes:

- You and the school district agree that the goals and objectives were met.
- You and the school district agree that certain goals and objectives were met, but others were not. You may also agree that an objective was met, but not the larger goal. For example, if John met the objective of successfully adding two-digit numbers 75% of the time, it does not necessarily mean that John achieved the larger goal of doing third grade math or that John understood the process.
- You and the school district agree that the goals and objectives were not met.
- You and the school district disagree on whether the goals and objectives were met.

Although you won't be working on placement and services during this part of the meeting, keep in mind that your child's success or failure in meeting the goals and objectives will likely affect whether the placement and services are changed. For example, if your child met the goals and objectives, perhaps it means her placement is correct and should continue. Or maybe it means she is ready to be mainstreamed. If she didn't meet the goals and objectives, she may need a smaller class. Or maybe the placement is fine, but she needs more tutoring (a related service).

Once you finish reviewing the previous goals and objectives—or if this is your child's first time in special education—it's time to write goals and objectives for the coming year. Chapter 9 explains how to draft goals and objectives—and recommends that you do so in advance. It's possible that school representatives have also prepared some ahead of time.

Remember, your goal is for the IEP team to agree on goals and objectives that support the placement and related services you want for your child.

What if you disagree with each other's goals and objectives? Try these tips:

- Do your best to convince school members of the IEP team that your goals and objectives are consistent with the recommendations made by others, such as the assessor, the classroom teacher, or your child's aide.
- Ask school members what they specifically disagree with in your goals and objectives.
- If you can't agree on all goals and objectives, try to reach consensus on some—half a loaf is better than no loaf at all.
- If attempts to compromise fail, suggest dropping all predrafted goals and objectives and coming up with something new.

If you and the school representatives disagree about past or future goals and objectives, be sure the IEP document clearly states that. At the very least, record your concerns on your parent addendum. (See Section F, below.)

The Pros and Cons of Quantifying Educational Progress

Goals and objectives frequently refer to numbers to determine whether your child (and the school district) has succeeded—for example, your child might have a goal that says "Mary will spell three-syllable words with 85% accuracy." These numbers are important indicators of your child's educational health. On the other hand, not all educational goals are measurable. Of course, once you set a numeric goal, your child should strive for it—and you and the school district should fully support that effort—but failing to hit that mark is not necessarily a sign that your child isn't learning. None of us learn in a straight line; progress often takes those classic two steps forward, one step back. And Mary should not feel she has failed because she spelled those three-syllable words with 78% accuracy.

4. Transition Services

If your child is 14 or older, the IEP team must discuss transition services regarding her course of study, including advanced courses and vocational classes. The IEP team should consider strategies to assist your child in assessing, securing information about, and taking steps to participate in vocational, employment, independent living, and post-high school educational plans. Your child can investigate transition services in a variety of ways, including looking at potential jobs, learning how to function in the community, accessing other agencies that will provide support for adults with disabilities, and researching college opportunities.

5. Related Services

Your discussions regarding related services (and placement, covered in the next section) are likely to generate the most debate. You and the school district may have very different notions of the type and amount of related services that are appropriate for your child. Your child cannot be denied related services because of the school's monetary or administrative constraints. However, the school district may try to argue that your child needs fewer services, or less expensive services, in an effort to stay within its budget.

Under IDEA, related services are the developmental, corrective, and other supportive services, including transportation, that a disabled child needs to benefit from special education. They also include the services your child needs to be educated in a regular classroom. Children wtih learning disabilities use a wide variety of relating services, including 1:1 classroom assistance (for reading, spelling, or math), language and speech therapy and service, occupational and physical therapy (for fine and gross motor skills), and psychological counseling. Remember, the burden is on the school district to demonstrate that your child cannot achieve satisfactorily in a regular classroom even with the use of some related services. (See Chapter 2A.)

Independent assessors and others who support your position should be prepared to state their opinions in detail—for example, "Given Hank's difficulty in language and reading, he needs to work one-to-one with an aide trained in a multisensory approach, for 30 minutes, three times per week." If someone is not there to make this statement, be prepared to point to written materials that show your child's need for the particular related service.

The related services section of the IEP document requires more detail than any other. It's not enough to say "Hank will be assisted in a multisensory approach"; the IEP team should specify how often (three sessions per week), how long (30-minute sessions), the ratio of pupils to related service provider (one-to-one), and the qualifications of the aide (trained in a multisensory approach to developing language and reading skills).

The more vague the description, the more flexibility the school district has to give your child something less than (or different from) what he needs. Assistance from a one-to-one aide two to three times a week is very different from assistance three times per week. Try to avoid terminology such as "or," "about," "to be determined," or "as needed." When in doubt, be specific; it's that simple.

Other Agencies May Be Responsible for Providing Some Related Services

In some states, certain related services, such as mental health services or occupational or physical therapy, may be the responsibility of a public agency other than the school district. Still, these services should be discussed at the IEP meeting, and the school district is responsible for making sure representatives of those other agencies attend the meeting. These other agencies have the same responsibilities as the school district—and therefore the same role to play at the meeting—regarding the services they must provide.

6. Placement or Program

Placement or program refers both to the kind of class (such as a regular class, special day class, or residential placement) and to the specific location of the program (such as a regular fifth grade class at Abraham Lincoln School). Placement or program, sometimes referred to on the IEP form as the instructional setting, is central to a successful IEP and an effective educational experience.

Placement or program is most often some kind of public program, but IDEA requires placement in a private school if there is no appropriate public option. Placement or program is generally the last item discussed at the IEP meeting.

As explained in Chapter 2, IDEA requires that your child be educated in the "least restrictive environment." This means that to the maximum extent appropriate, children with disabilities are to be educated with children who are nondisabled. Special classes, separate schooling, or other placements that remove children with disabilities from a regular class are appropriate only if the nature or severity of the disability is such that education in a regular class would not be satisfactory, even with the use of supplementary aids and services.

There is no absolute rule that your child must be mainstreamed. For many students with learning disabilities, however, a mainstreamed program will be the least restrictive environment—and the school district has a substantial burden to prove that a different placement would be appropriate.

If you don't want your child mainstreamed, point out that although the law favors regular classroom placement, individual need determines whether a particular placement is appropriate for a particular child. Courts have clearly stated that there is no prohibition to placing a child in a non-regular class—in fact, if a child needs such a placement, it is by definition the least restrictive environment. (See *Geis v. Board of Education*, 774 F.2d 575 (3d Cir. 1985) and *Stockton by Stockton v. Barbour County Bd. of Educ.*, 25 IDELR 1076 (4th Cir. 1997)—for more on court cases and legal research, see Chapter 14.)

If you want your child mainstreamed, you should emphasize your child's basic right to the least restrictive environment. You should also emphasize your child's right to be as close to home as possible, and to be educated in the school the child would attend if not disabled. (34 C.F.R. § 300.550-552.) Ultimately, the burden is on the school district to prove that your child should be removed from a regular classroom.

School representatives may be prepared to discuss a specific program in a named school. Or, they may propose a kind of class, such as a special day class, but want to leave the specific location up to the school administration. If this happens, object. The IEP team should decide both the kind of class (such as a special day class for language-delayed children) and the specific location (such as a regular class at King School).

More likely, you and the school administrator will know before the meeting where each of you stands on placement. Still, an open-minded IEP team should fully discuss your child's placement needs. The school administrator will probably state that the IEP team has reviewed your child's record, agreed on goals and objectives, resolved related services, and decided that a particular placement is called for—such as, "We recommend placement in the special day class at John School."

If you disagree with the administrator's conclusion, state your preference and refer to supportive materials—particularly items that are very persuasive about placement. Then ask (or have your independent assessor ask) pointed questions, such as:

Ms. Parton, you said Betsy should be placed at Johnson School in the special day class. We believe Betsy should be placed in the regular class at Thompson School with a one-to-one aide. The assessment by Dr. Jones recommends that placement specifically, and Betsy's current teacher agrees. Can you explain why you disagree?

If the school administrator is not persuaded or does not adequately answer your question, be direct and frank:

With all due respect, I think your answer is vague and does not address the specifics in Dr. Jones's report and your own teacher's comment about Betsy's readiness for a regular classroom. I feel very strongly about this, and we will go to due process on the issue of placement if we have to. I also think that with the documentation and the law on mainstreaming, we will be successful in due process. I really feel like going in that direction is a bad use of school resources and will only make the ultimate move that much more expensive for you. I just don't understand—given the evidence—why you want to put me and my wife, your district personnel, and, most important, our child through that.

7. Narrative Page

The narrative page is the place to record information that can't be included by way of a checkbox or is too long for the space provided on the IEP form. The narrative page can include information on any topic, whether covered by the IEP document or not. Here some examples of narrative page statements.

Examples:

- The IEP team agrees that the school district and outside assessments are complete and appropriate and are incorporated into the IEP.
- The IEP team incorporates the child profile provided by Steven's parents into the IEP.
- The IEP team agrees that Melissa needs a school environment in which there are no behavioral problems.
- The IEP team agrees that Henry is beginning to show signs of emotional distress; the classroom teacher will report on a weekly basis to the family about any signs of such distress. The district psychologist will observe Henry in class. The IEP team agrees to meet in three months to review this matter and to discuss the possible need for more formal assessment or the need for additional related services.
- The IEP team agrees with the recommendations made by Dr. Jones on page 4 of her report.
- Ms. Brown [Steve's teacher] is concerned about Steve's lack of focus.

- The IEP team agrees with recommendations 1, 2, 5, 7, and 9 made by Dr. Jones on page 4 of her report.
- Carolyn's parents expressed concern about class size.

Sometimes, the person recording the IEP document may write something that the parents and school personnel disagree about. Make sure the narrative is changed to reflect your disagreement or to indicate that the statement reflects only the point of view of the school personnel. Basically, you don't want the narrative to imply agreement when there is none.

Check the narrative page throughout the meeting to see what has been written. If something is included that you disagree with or something important was left out, raise the issue: "We all agreed that William had a successful year at Kennedy High School and that his mainstreaming helped his sense of self. That sentiment should be included in the narrative page—it is a vitally important bit of information about William."

Include a Child Profile in the IEP Plan

In Chapter 10, we suggested that you create a child profile to give school officials a perspective on your child beyond numbers and test results. The school administrator may question whether law or policy allows a child profile to be included in the IEP document. Since IDEA does not prohibit it, nothing prevents the IEP team from discussing and including a child profile.

Emphasize that your statement about your child will help the school staff implement the goals and objectives, and for that reason it should be included in the IEP document. If the school administrator disagrees, ask specifically what is objectionable. Try to convince the team of the importance of the profile. If the administrator continues to refuse, use the parent addendum to include it.

8. How Decisions Are Made at the IEP Meeting

How does the IEP team make an actual decision on IEP components? Do you vote? IDEA establishes no set method for reaching agreement, so it's really up to the IEP team. The school administrator may not even raise the question of how agreement is reached.

You can request voting, but in most IEP meetings, the team tries to reach consensus through discussion. Asking members to vote may be self-defeating—there are usually more folks on the school district's side of the table than on yours. No matter how decisions are reached, you are an equal partner in the process. If you don't agree on an item, there is no consensus and, therefore, the team has not reached a decision on that topic.

E. Sign the IEP Document

At the end of the IEP meeting, the school administrator will ask you to sign the IEP document. School officials will be signing the form as well. You don't have to sign the IEP document on the spot. You may want to take it home and return it in 24 hours. This will give you time to decide whether you agree or disagree with each aspect of the plan. It will also give you time to record your concerns coherently on a parent addendum (discussed in Section F, below).

Of course, if you have reached complete agreement with the school representatives on all issues and don't need time to mull anything over, go ahead and sign. Read the document carefully, however, to make sure the statements and information accurately reflect the IEP team's intentions. Also, make sure that the team covered everything on your agenda and resolved all important issues.

If you do take the IEP document home, be sure that other participants have already signed off on each item to which they agreed.

Every IEP form has a signature page with a variety of checkboxes, including:

- a box to indicate you attended
- a box to indicate that you were provided your legal rights
- a box to indicate your approval of the IEP document, and
- a box to indicate your disapproval.

There may also be boxes to show partial approval and indicate that you do or do not plan to initiate due process.

Make sure to check the right boxes. If you partially agree, check the partial agreement box—but carefully and clearly write next to it: "Approval in part only; see parent addendum." (Section F discusses the parent addendum.)

You must state your position clearly on the IEP. There are no legally required phrases to use—plain and direct English will do fine.

1. Full Agreement

Congratulations! Check the correct box and sign the form.

2. Nearly Full Agreement

It's possible that the IEP team will agree on all important items concerning related services, methodology, and program or placement, but disagree on some secondary issues, such as goals and objectives or statements in an assessment. In this situation, you have two choices:

- You can check the box to indicate your approval and sign your name. This might make sense if the issues on which you disagree are minor and you want to foster a good relationship with the school district.
- You can check the box to indicate partial approval, list the items you dispute (on the signature page if there's room or on the parent addendum), and sign your name.

Sample

Date: April 24, 20xx

Signature: *Lucinda Crenshaw*

I agree with all of the IEP except for:

- items 3, 4, and 6 on the district's assessment
- goals and objectives numbers 2 and 5.

You Don't Have to Accept "All or Nothing"

Remember that the school district cannot present you with an "all or nothing" choice. For example: "We're offering two sessions of occupational therapy. If you don't agree to the two sessions, there will be no occupational therapy for your child." You can agree to the two sessions without giving up your right to seek more. See Sections B and F.

3. Partial Agreement

In this situation, you agree on some, but not all, of the big issues (related services, methodology, and program or placement). You should check the box to indicate partial approval, state that your disagreements are on the parent addendum, spell out your disagreements on the parent addendum, spell out your disagreements on the parent addendum, and sign your name.

Sample

Date: April 24, 20xx

Signature: *Lucinda Crenshaw*

I agree with all of the IEP except for those items listed on the parent addendum page, designated as "Attachment A" and attached to the IEP.

4. Nearly Total Disagreement

In this case, you don't agree on any of the major items concerning related services, curricula-methodology, and program or placement, but do agree on certain goals and objectives, parts of the assessment, and minor items. Again, you can check the box to indicate partial approval, state that your disagreements are on the parent addendum, spell out your disagreements on the parent addendum (see Section F, below), and sign your name.

5. Total Disagreement

In some instances, there is total disagreement. If so, sign your name after checking both the box acknowledging that you attended the meeting and the disapproval box. You could also refer to the parent addendum page.

At this stage, your options are informal negotiations, mediation, or a fair hearing.

See Chapter 12 for information on due process, including your child's status when there is no IEP agreement.

F. Parent Addendum Page

When you disagree with any aspect of the IEP deliberations, including specific items such as related services, a statement on the narrative page, a portion of the school's assessment report, or even the administrator's refusal to discuss an item you raised, make sure to state your position clearly. You or your note taker should keep a list of every issue you dispute on a separate piece of paper.

A parent addendum page is an attachment to the IEP where you can record these disagreements and give your point of view. There is no IDEA requirement for an addendum page, although your district's IEP form may have one. The addendum page need not be a formal document—a blank piece of paper will do.

You will most likely complete the addendum page at or near the end of the meeting. The content of the addendum page is vastly more important than its format. Your statement should:

- relate specifically to issues concerning your child's education and the IEP meeting; don't use the addendum to state general complaints
- be in plain English, and
- state specifically your point of view on all key items of dispute.

As shown in Section E, above, you should indicate on the signature page that you disagree with part of the IEP document and refer to the attached addendum page for the detail of the disagreement.

Date: _____

Parent Signature**: _____

** See Addendum page (designated as "A") for a statement regarding what we are agreeing to and not agreeing to. My signature above is to be read only in conjunction with the statement on "A."

If your school's IEP form includes an addendum page, use it; otherwise, mark "Attachment A" at the top of a blank piece of paper and write something like the following.

Sample Heading for Addendum Page

> Parent Addendum Page of Carol and Steven Stack
> IEP for Beatrice Stack
> March 12, 20xx

You have an absolute right to state your position, but if, for some reason, the school district does not allow you to attach an addendum, indicate on the signature page that you do not agree with everything in the IEP document, and that you want to attach an addendum but the school administration will not let you. Mail your addendum to the school—certified mail if you can (keep copies)—with a cover letter stating that you asked to include this at the IEP meeting, were denied by the administrator, and are now sending it to to be attached to the IEP. Then, file a complaint. (See Chapter 13.)

Example Addendum Statements:

- The district does not agree with the recommendations of Dr. Jones's independent assessment, but has refused to state why. We believe that her assessment is valid and should be fully incorporated into the IEP as representing useful and valid information about Tonya.

- We do not agree with recommendations 3, 6, 9, and 14 of Dr. Lee's assessment of January 21, 20xx. We do agree with the rest of her report.

- The IEP team agrees with sections 3, 7, 8, and 9 of the school's report and all of Dr. Friedman's assessment, but the school will not put this agreement into the IEP. We believe those agreed-to sections should be incorporated into the IEP.

- Dr. Pentan of the school district stated that we have no right to include a child profile in the IEP. IDEA does not say that and if the IEP team agrees, the profile can be part of the IEP. We believe the profile provides valid and important information regarding Fernando.

- While the teacher reported that Stanley increased his reading comprehension (this relates to goal #4 on page 2), we have observed at home, over a long period of time, that his reading comprehension seems substantially below the test results.

- We don't agree that Sandy's goals and objectives were met because the evaluation of the goals and objectives was inaccurate.

- The district offered multisensory work one time a week, 20 minutes per ses-

sion. Moira needs three sessions per week, each session to be 40 minutes long, conducted one-to-one with an aide trained in one of the multisensory approaches. This is supported by the May 2, 20xx report of Dr. Shawn Waters. We accept the one session and give permission for that to begin, but this acceptance is not to be construed as agreement about the amount of the related services, only agreement as to the need.

- The IEP agrees that Nick be placed in the regular fifth grade class at Kennedy School. We agree with placement in the regular fifth grade class at Kennedy School, but we believe Nick needs an aide to meet his needs and allow him to achieve satisfactorily in that regular class.

- We believe that the regular ninth grade class program at Roosevelt School is the only appropriate placement for Tony. We believe placement in the special day class at Roosevelt as offered by the school district is inappropriate. We agree to placement in the regular classroom at Roosevelt for three periods a day, although such agreement is not to be construed as agreement on partial mainstreaming. We will proceed to due process on the issue of full-time mainstreaming in the regular ninth grade class at Roosevelt.

■

12

Resolving IEP Disputes Through Due Process

The purpose of this book is to help you successfully develop an IEP plan for your child, and thereby make this chapter irrelevant. But the nature of the IEP process is such that disagreements do arise, and some cannot be resolved informally.

Under IDEA, you have the right to resolve these disputes with your school district through "due process." (20 U.S.C. § 1415; 34 C.F.R. §§ 300.500-517.) There are two ways to resolve disputes through due process: mediation and/or a hearing.

In mediation, you and representatives of the school district meet with a neutral third party, who tries to help you reach a compromise. The mediator has no authority to impose a decision on you—her job is to help you and the school district come up with a mutually agreeable resolution to your dispute.

If you cannot reach an agreement in mediation or you'd prefer to skip mediation altogether, you can request a due process hearing—often referred to as a "fair hearing"—where you and school district personnel present written evidence and have witnesses testify about the disputed issues before a neutral third party, called a hearing officer. Much like a judge, the hearing officer considers the evidence, makes a decision, and issues a binding order within 45 days after you formally requested due process. (34 C.F.R. § 300.511.) If you or school district representatives disagree with the decision, you can appeal to a state or federal court.

Due process is available to resolve factual disputes—that is, when you and your child's school district cannot agree on eligibility or some part of the IEP plan. If the school district has violated a legal rule— for example failing to hold an IEP meeting, do an assessment, meet a time limit, or provide an agreed-to part of the IEP—you must file a complaint rather than use due process. (Complaints are covered in Chapter 13.)

There are many types of due process disputes that might arise for children with learning disabili-

ties. Some of the more common areas of conflict are:

- whether the assessments used to test for a learning disability are appropriate and/or accurate
- eligibility: whether the child qualifies as a child with a specific learning disability
- placement: the district may want to place the child in a special day class or nonregular placement, while the family believes the child's learning disability needs can be meet in a regular classroom with support
- methodology: the parent wants a specific methodology (such as a multisensory approach) and the district disagrees
- related services: the parent wants 1:1 help or other support services (language/speech therapy, occupational therapy for handwriting problems, and so on) and the district disagrees about the need for services or the amount of services to be provided.

Don't Delay Filing for Due Process

If you wait too long to file for due process, you may lose your right to do so. IDEA does not establish a time limit for filing for due process, submitting a complaint, or appealing a due process decision to a court. The general rule for IDEA due process is that the state "statutes of limitations" applies. Statutes of limitations set time limits for filing a lawsuit or initiating a similar action (like a due process). Depending on the state and the kind of case, the time limit may be anywhere from a few months to several years after the disputed event took place. If you fail to bring your legal action within your state's time limit, you will likely be barred from taking any legal action at all.

To avoid losing your right to file for due process, it is therefore very important that you check with your state department of education or a local lawyer regarding your state's statute of limitations—and be sure to file for due process well within that timeline.

A. Before Due Process: Informal Negotiations

Before invoking due process, you may want to try to resolve your dispute through informal discussions or negotiations with the school. While resolving some problems might require formal action, many of these issues can be settled informally.

In addition, some disputes may not even qualify for due process because they do not involve factual disputes. (See Section B, below.) For example, you and the school principal may disagree about when you can visit the classroom or why the assessor had to reschedule your child's testing. Because you can't take these disputes to due process, you'll have to hash them out informally or not at all.

Alternatives to Informal Negotiations and Formal Due Process

Informal discussions with the school district and formal due process aren't the only ways to resolve disputes. Other methods, such as building parent coalitions and becoming involved in the local political process, can also be effective. These options are discussed in Chapter 15.

In addition, IDEA provides that a state or local school district can establish "alternative dispute resolution" (ADR) procedures for parents who choose not to use due process. In ADR, you meet with a neutral third party who is under contract with a parent training center, community parent resource center, or appropriate alternative dispute resolution entity. (20 U.S.C. § 1415(e)(2)(B).) The purpose of the meeting is for you to explore alternative ways to resolve your dispute and for the third party to explain the benefits of mediation. This ADR meeting is intended to be nonadversarial, while mediation is the first step in formal due process. Be aware, however, that using ADR may delay resolution of the dispute—so if you need immediate action or the time limit for pursuing due process is coming up, you might want to skip this step.

If you're interested in ADR, call your school district or state department of education (see Appendix 2) to find out if ADR is available.

1. Pros and Cons of Informal Negotiation

Informal negotiation (including ADR) is useful for several reasons. It if works well, it may save you stress, time, and money. It will also help you maintain a more positive relationship with the school district, and will keep problems from escalating. Finally, informal negotiation is easier to pursue than due process.

Even if you eventually pursue your due process rights, it might be a good idea to start with informal negotiation. This will show that you are reasonable and fair-minded, and don't immediately look to an adversarial method of settlement. Informal negotiations will also help you understand the school district's position, which will be valuable if you end up in mediation or at a fair hearing.

In limited situations, however, it might make sense to go immediately to due process. For example, skip the informal negotiations if:

- You need an immediate resolution of an issue that affects your child's well-being, safety, or health. For example, if you think your child needed psychological counseling for depression but the district disagrees, you may not have time for informal meetings.

- The school administrator is so unpleasant or inflexible that you just don't want to deal with her. For example, you want your 10th grader in a regular academic high school setting, but the administrator is pushing for a special class comprised only of children with learning disabilities and has said she won't budge under any circumstances.

- The IEP meeting made it clear that it would be a waste of time to try to resolve things informally. For example, you want three hours a week of speech therapy for your child, the district's assessment recommends 1 hour, the administrator has said that it will not go beyond the assessor's recommendation, and you know other parents who have faced similar situations without success.

- You're facing a time limit. For example, your child is already many weeks behind in reading and each day she goes without a reading specialist will set her back even farther. Informal negotiation will almost always eat up some time—and may not be successful. By trying to handle the dispute informally, you will likely use up weeks or even months before the more formal due process steps begin—weeks and months

when your child will not have that daily help she needs.

- You want to push the school district towards a settlement. For example, they have hinted that they are considering giving your child three hours a week of 1:1 aide time for her reading problems, but have not taken any concrete steps to set it up. Even if you try to resolve things informally, you might want to file for due process to motivate the school district to settle informally. Remember, however, that pursuing due process, with its time limits and requirements, will also put pressure on you.

2. Basics of Informal Negotiation

To begin informal negotiations, call or write your child's teacher, school principal, or special education administrator and ask for a meeting to discuss your concerns. You can raise the issues in your phone conversation or letter, but ideally you'll want an appointment to discuss the problem face to face.

Before the meeting, prepare a clear written description of the problem and a recommended solution. Also, find out if any school personnel support you. If so, ask them to attend the meeting or ask for permission to present their opinions at the meeting.

During the meeting, emphasize problem solving, not winning. Try to structure the negotiation as a mutual attempt to solve a problem. Avoid personal attacks on school personnel. Respect the school's point of view even if you disagree. Acknowledge the school representatives' concerns. Even if you strongly disagree, you don't lose anything by saying, "I understand your concerns, but I think we can address those by doing ...."

Be respectful, but firm—for example, you can say, "It is clear we disagreed at the IEP meeting. I am open to trying to solve this informally, but I will not hesitate to pursue my due process rights if we cannot." When you enter the meeting, you should know what you are willing to compromise and what is not negotiable. If you know your bottom line, you'll have an easier time presenting your point of view and evaluating what the school district has to say.

Good Books on Negotiation

Getting to Yes: Negotiating Agreement Without Giving In, by Roger Fisher and William Ury (Penguin Books). This classic book offers a strategy for coming to mutually acceptable agreements in all kinds of situations.

Getting Past No: Negotiating Your Way From Confrontation to Cooperation, by William Ury (Bantam Books). This sequel to *Getting to Yes* suggests techniques for negotiating with difficult people.

---

3. After Meeting Informally

If you do not resolve your dispute informally, send a letter briefly stating the problem, the solution you think makes sense, and what you are considering next, such as contacting an attorney, pursuing mediation or a fair hearing, or filing a complaint with your school board or the state department of education.

If you resolve your problem informally, it is very important to follow up the meeting with a confirming letter.

A sample letter confirming the results of an informal negotiation is shown below; a blank, tear-out copy of this form is in Appendix 5.

If the meeting does not resolve the problem to your satisfaction, then you may proceed to due process (either mediation or a fair hearing) or file a complaint.

Use the Law to Make Your Case

As you try to persuade your school district—in writing or in person—that you are correct, cite the legal authority for your position, if possible. Referring to a section in IDEA or even a court decision may help convince the school district that you're in the right. See Chapter 14 for tips on legal research.

B. Typical Due Process Disputes

Remember, due process (mediation or fair hearing) is used to resolve only factual disputes, not disagreements over what the law requires or allows. Here are some common IEP factual disputes:

- eligibility for special education
- results of an assessment
- goals and objectives
- specific placement or program
- related services
- proposed changes to your child's current IEP program, and
- suspension or expulsion of your child.

Certain kinds of disputes are simply not appropriate for due process because 1) they are generally not covered by IDEA and 2) if you pursue due process, you will almost always lose. These disputes include:

- requesting a specific teacher or service provider by name for your child
- hiring or firing school staff
- assigning a different school administrator to your case, or
- requesting that a specific person represent the school district in the IEP process.

These concerns may be addressed through non-IDEA activities, such as parent organizing (see Chapter 15) or informal negotiations with the school.

Sample Letter Confirming Informal Negotiation

Date: June 1, 20xx

To: Michael Chan, Principal
       Truman High School
       803 Dogwood Drive
       Patterson, NJ 07506

Re: Tasha Kincaid, Sophomore

I appreciated the chance to meet on May 28 and discuss Tasha's placement. I also appreciated your point of view and the manner in which we solved the problem. I want to confirm our agreement that Tasha will be placed in the regular academic track at Truman High School with 1 hour per day of resource specialist help in math, English, and Social Studies for the upcoming school year. [If you have already requested due process, add: Once you have confirmed this in writing to me, I will formally withdraw my due process request.]

I greatly appreciate the manner in which you helped solve this problem. Please tell all of Tasha's teachers that I would be delighted to meet with them before school starts to discuss effective ways to work with Tasha.

Thank you.

Sincerely,

André Kincaid

André Kincaid
4500 Fair Street
Patterson, NJ 07506
555-3889 (home); 555-2330 (work)

C. When to Pursue Due Process

As noted, due process can be hard; it takes time, energy, and sometimes money, and it can be quite stressful. When you consider whether to go forward, you should be careful and objective. Consider these five factors:

- **The precise nature of the problem**. You will have to pinpoint exactly what your disagreement is about—and make sure it is a factual dispute. For example, if you feel your child's education is generally not working (and you have not yet gone to an IEP meeting), or you object to the attitude of the school administrator, your concern is not yet ready for due process. If, however, your child has fallen behind in her regular class and you want her placed in a special class but the IEP team did not agree, you have a problem that qualifies for due process resolution.

Don't File for Due Process Until After the IEP Meeting

Many parents make the mistake of requesting a fair hearing before the issue is considered at an IEP meeting. Unless there are very unusual circumstances—for example, a threat to your child's health or well-being—you must go to an IEP meeting and reach an impasse there before you can request due process.

- **The importance of the issue to your child**. Placement or related service disputes are often central to your child's educational well-being. On the other hand, disputes over goals and objectives or assessment conclusions may not be significant enough to merit due process, because they do not directly impact your child's placement and related services.

- **The strength of your case**. Can you win? Is the district's position unreasonable, when you step back and consider the arguments from every angle? What evidence do you have to support your position? What evidence undercuts it? What are the qualifications of the people making supportive or contrary statements? Remember that the district is required to provide your child with an appropriate education, not the best possible one. After the IEP meeting, review and update your IEP Material Organizer form (discussed in Chapter 10) to evaluate the evidence for and against you. If you want other opinions on the strength of your case, consider these sources:

  s Nonschool employees, your independent assessor, an outside tutor, or an attorney. Describe the disputed issue, your evidence, and the evidence against you, and ask if they think you have a good chance of winning.

  s Other parents, particularly those who have been through due process with your school district. How does the school district react? Is the school likely to take a hard line position or might it offer a compromise after you show you are determined to go forward?

  s Local parent and disability organizations. (Chapter 15 discusses how to find and work with a parents' group.) If you need help finding a local group, start by contacting a national organization (see the list in Appendix 3).

- **The bottom line concerns for the school district**. For any disputed issue, the school district will have some bottom line concerns—notably, the cost and administrative difficulty of providing what you want. For example, the school administrator may be willing to compromise on a dispute between two public school program options, rather than pay for costly private school placement. The school's bottom line may affect your bottom line—and how far you'll go to get it.

- **The cost of going forward**. Due process witnesses (including independent assessors) and attorneys will charge for their time. You can be reimbursed for those costs, but only if you win at the hearing. (See Chapter 14 for information on using an attorney and attorney's fees.) It is therefore crucial that you objectively weigh the cost of the hearing in light of your chance of winning.

D. Your Child's Status During Due Process

During due process, your child is entitled to remain in her current placement until you reach an agreement with the school, settle the matter through mediation, receive a fair hearing decision rendered that neither you nor the school district appeals or get a final court decision. This is called the "stay put" provision. (34 C.F.R. § 300.514; 20 U.S.C. § 1415(j).) "Stay put" can be a complicated legal right. If you are concerned about whether your child is allowed to stay put in a particular situation, see an attorney or contact a nonprofit disability rights organization right away.

Example:
Your child is in a regular sixth grade class with a one-to-one aide, two hours a day. At the IEP meeting, the school district offers a special day class, not a regular class, for seventh grade. You want your child to continue in a regular class. You are unable to reach an agreement at the IEP meeting. You initiate due process, during which time your child is entitled to remain in a regular classroom with the aide until the matter is resolved.

Exceptions to the Stay Put Rule

IDEA entitles your child to remain in her current placement pending due process unless your child carries a weapon to school or a school function, or knowingly possesses, uses, sells, or solicits illegal drugs while at school or a school function. In these situations, the school district can change your child's placement to an appropriate interim alternative educational setting for up to 45 days, or suspend your child for up to ten school days. (20 U.S.C. § 1415 (k); 340 C.F.R. § 300.520.) See Chapter 2A for more information on discipline for students in special education.

E. Using a Lawyer During Due Process

Using an attorney in due process certainly escalates the adversarial nature of the dispute, but by the time you've reached due process that is probably not your primary concern. Using an attorney may also speed things along and increase your chances of success.

In mediation, an attorney will present your case and counter the school district's arguments. In a fair hearing, an attorney should prepare witnesses, submit exhibits, make the opening statement, and direct the proceeding. An attorney can also play a less active role, such as giving advice and helping you organize your case material, without attending the proceeding. Once you hire an attorney, she will contact the district to let them know that she is involved in the case.

Not surprisingly, legal costs can be considerable. To prepare for and attend a one-day mediation session, legal fees will likely range from $500 to $1,000—sometimes less, sometimes more. The cost for a two- to three-day fair hearing may range from $1,500 to $7,500 or more. It is not unusual for an attorney to spend ten to 25 hours preparing for a three-day hearing. If you use an attorney for advice only—for example, to help organize your case—your legal costs will be lower.

 See Chapter 14 for a thorough discussion of attorneys and legal fees.

Check Out Free or Low-Cost Legal Services

The school district must provide you with a list of free or low-cost legal services available in your area. See Chapter 14 for advice on finding and working with an attorney.

1. Attorney Fees in Mediation

During mediation, you should ask the school district, as part of your proposed settlement, to pay your attorney fees. Your legal fees are one of many bargaining chips you can use to negotiate a settlement in mediation. However, the school district doesn't have to pay your fees, just as it doesn't have to agree to any particular settlement terms. Because mediation (and any settlement you reach as a result of it) is voluntary, the school district may or may not agree to pay attorney fees. Remember, a mediation is usually a settlement in which neither party gets everything it wants; attorney's fees may be one of those things you are willing to forgo in order to get something more important.

The school district's decision will depend largely on how strong your case is and how motivated the school district is to settle. The school district may try to avoid having to reimburse you by agreeing to provide the education you want, if you agree to drop your demand for attorney's fees. You will need to assess the strength of your case to decide whether you are willing to forgo your legal fees. If your case is very strong, the school district may decide that they are better off paying your

attorney's fees now rather than later, when they will be much higher. Your attorney can advise you of the pros and cons in this situation.

Courts have ruled that attorney's fees in mediation can be awarded to parents. See, for example, *Jose Louis R. v. Joliet Township H.S. Dist. 204*, 35 IDELR 151.

2. Attorney Fees in Fair Hearing

If your case goes to fair hearing and you win, you will be entitled to reimbursement of your attorney's fees. If you lose the hearing, you're responsible for your own attorney's fees, but you will not have to pay the school district's attorney's fees. This is often referred to as the "prevailing party" rule. If you win, or "prevail," you will be reimbursed for your attorney's fees.

If you win on some issues but not on others, you will be reimbursed for the time your lawyer spent on the winning issues (but not for time spent on the losing issues).

3. Other Legal Advocates

There are many nonattorney advocates who are quite skilled in due process. Their fees are usually lower than a lawyer's fees, but you are not entitled to reimbursement of an advocate's fees if you prevail in a fair hearing.

Special education attorneys, nonprofit law centers, and disability and parent support groups may know the names of special education advocates in your area.

F. How to Request Due Process

You must formally request due process in order for a mediation or fair hearing to be scheduled. The agency responsible for due process varies from state to state, but it is usually the state department of education. Your school district must provide you with the name, address, and phone number of the appropriate state agency. Call the agency and ask how to initiate due process. Usually, you will have to either complete a form provided by the agency or send a letter providing the following information:

- your name and address
- your child's name and grade
- the name of your child's school and the address of the school district
- a description of the disputed issues
- your desired resolution—what you want for your child's education, as well as reimbursement for your due process costs, such as attorney's fees, witness fees, and independent assessment costs, and
- whether you want to mediate or to go directly to a fair hearing.

(This information is required under IDEA (34 C.F.R. § 300.507(c)(2)).) Keep a copy of your completed form or letter for your records.

A sample letter requesting due process is shown below; a blank, tear-out copy is in Appendix 5. Your school district is required to have a model due process request letter for you to use. (34 C.F.R. § 300.507(c)(3).)

G. Prepare for Due Process

While a mediation session and a fair hearing are different, preparing for the former will help as you get ready for the latter. The preparation you did for the IEP meeting will also be of enormous help as you go through due process. The recommendations in this section apply to both mediation and the due process hearing.

1. Organize Your Evidence

First, pull out your child's file and the reports, assessments, and other documents in your IEP binder (Chapter 4), your blueprint (Chapter 5), and your IEP Material Organizer form (Chapter 10).

Make a list of the disputed issues. Using a blank IEP Material Organizer form, write next to each disputed issue the witnesses, documents, or facts that support your point of view—and those that oppose it. You should make a separate list of all of your potential witnesses and think about who the district's witnesses will be.

Now find every piece of evidence you have that supports your position. Review your binder, original Material Organizer forms, and notes from the IEP meeting. Focus not only on reports and assessments, but also on comments made at the meeting. Gather all your supportive evidence together or tab it in your binder and highlight key statements. Make photocopies of all written materials that support your point of view to have available during the mediation or hearing.

Now work on the school district's case—that is, figure out what evidence contradicts your point of view. Think about any evidence you can use (including comments made during the IEP meeting) to rebut the district's likely arguments.

2. Make a List of Expenses

Once you've gathered evidence, make a list of expenses you've incurred throughout the IEP process, such as the costs of:

- independent assessments
- tutors
- lost wages for attending IEPs
- private school or private related service costs
- personal transportation costs, such as those incurred driving your child to a private school
- attorney's fees
- costs for other professionals (such as a private speech therapist or counselor), and
- photocopying.

Note the date a payment was made or cost incurred, name of the payee, and purpose of the expense. Attach all receipts.

Sample Letter Requesting Due Process

Date: March 1, 20xx

To: Phillip Jones
       Due Process Unit
       Wisconsin Department of Education
       8987 Franklin Avenue
       La Crosse, WI 54601

Re: Steven Howard

Our son, Steven Howard, is a fourth grader at Clinton School in La Crosse. His school district is the Central La Crosse Elementary School District, 562 5th Avenue, La Crosse, Wisconsin.

We are formally requesting due process, beginning with mediation. We believe that Steven requires a full-time, on-on-one aide in order to be fully mainstreamed in next year's regular fifth grade class at Clinton School. The school district has refused to provide that aide.

We believe an appropriate solution would include, but should not be limited to, the following:

- A qualified full-time academic aide, to work one-on-one with Steven in the regular fifth grade class at Clinton School for the coming school year.

- Reimbursement for all attorney's fees, witnesses, independent assessments, and other costs accrued for the February 14, 20xx IEP meeting and subsequent due process.

We understand IDEA (34 C.F.R. § 300.511) requires that a fair hearing decision be rendered within 45 days after you receive this request. We would appreciate it if you would contact us at once to schedule the mediation.

Sincerely,

William Howard   *Kate Howard*

William and Kate Howard
1983 Smiley Lane
La Crosse, WI 54601
555-5569 (home); 555-2000 (work)

There are no IDEA rules on how you must prepare or present these expenses. At mediation or the fair hearing, you will want to request payment of the expenses; if the district agrees to pay some or all of them, or if the hearing officer rules in your favor, the receipts will be your proof that you really spent this money.

3. Prepare an Opening Statement

At the beginning of a mediation session or fair hearing, you will need to make an opening statement explaining why you're there and what you want. Some people are comfortable making notes and then talking extemporaneously; others write out a complete statement and read it. Do what's easiest for you. Whatever method you choose, your opening statement should cover these topics:

Your child. Briefly describe your child, including her age, current educational program, general areas of educational concern, and disabling conditions. Give a short explanation of your child's educational history.

The dispute. Briefly describe the specific items in dispute—for example, the amount of a related service or the placement.

What you want and why. Summarize what your child needs—for example, speech therapy three times a week, in a one-to-one setting with a therapist qualified to work with students with language delays; placement in the Smith School; or the use of the Lindamood-Bell program or the Orton-Gillingham method.

Your evidence. You'll want to end with a strong statement briefly summarizing evidence you have for your position. In some mediations, however, you may decide not to reveal all of your evidence right away. You will have to judge the best approach, based on the situation, the personalities involved, and even your intuition. See Section H, below, for more on how much to reveal in mediation.

H. Mediation Specifics

Mediation is the first official step in due process. It is less confrontational than a fair hearing, and is intended to help you and the school district explore ways to compromise and settle your dispute. The IDEA requires all states to offer you mediation. (20 U.S.C. § 1415(e); 34 C.F.R. § 300.506.)

The mediator is a neutral third party, usually hired by the state department of education, who is knowledgeable about IDEA and special education matters. The mediator has no authority to force a settlement on you. If you reach settlement, however, your agreement will be put into writing and will be made binding on you and the district—you both must abide by and follow the settlement.

While mediation is fairly similar from one place to another, the way the sessions proceed will vary depending on the style of the mediator and rules established by your state.

 Contact your state department of education to find out the details of your state's laws on mediation. See Appendix 2.

Mediation must be made available to you at no cost. Mediation is completely voluntary—if you don't want to mediate, you don't have to. If you prefer, you can go straight to a fair hearing and skip mediation altogether.

If mediation is not successful, any settlement offers and other comments made during the mediation cannot be used as evidence at the fair hearing or any subsequent legal proceedings. This rule allows you to discuss matters frankly, without fear that your statements will later be used against you. (34 C.F.R. § 300.506(b)(6).)

1. Pros and Cons of Mediation

You may be asking yourself why you would try mediation, particularly because it ends in a compromise rather than a clear victory for one side or the other. There are some compelling reasons to go to mediation:

- **Know thine enemy.** Mediation gives you a chance to better understand the school district's arguments. Of course, the school district gets the same opportunity to hear about your case, but sharing information in this way may bring you closer to a solution.

- **The school district may be motivated to compromise.** Mediation takes the school district one step closer to a fair hearing and the possibility of a ruling against the school, with all of the costs that entails (including possible attorney's fees). The school administrator may be far more flexible in mediation than she was at the IEP meeting, feeling that a compromise now is better than an expensive loss later. Remember, the school will have to pay your legal fees if you win at the hearing (you will not have to pay their fees if you lose).

- **Mediation is constructive.** Mediation requires the parties to work out their disagreements and increases the chances you can retain a positive relationship with your school district. You also keep control over the outcome—you must agree to any solution proposed in mediation. When you go to fair hearing, the decision-making power is out of your hands.

- **Mediation is cheap.** As a general rule, you will have few or even no costs at mediation. In contrast, fair hearings can be expensive, particularly if you use an attorney.

- **Mediation can provide a reality check.** Even if you don't settle the case, mediation gives you a chance to have a neutral party assess your case and point out its strengths and weaknesses.

- **You get two bites of the apple**. By going to mediation, you give yourself two chances at success. If the mediation is unsuccessful, you can move on to a fair hearing.

But there are also downsides to mediation, including:

- **Half a loaf can be disappointing**. Ideally, you can settle in mediation and get everything your child needs. In reality, however, mediation usually involves compromise, meaning you will probably settle for less than what you would have gotten if you won at fair hearing.

- **Mediation may delay resolution of your dispute.** IDEA's requirement that a fair hearing decision be issued within 45 days after you request due process applies whether you go through mediation or go straight to fair hearing. In reality, however, extensions of that 45-day rule can be granted if you spend significant time in mediation. If you have a real time problem—for example, your child must be placed in a specific program by a certain date or he will suffer dire consequences—you may not want to go to mediation. If you decide to mediate, be sure to oppose any requests to extend the 45-day time limit.

- **You do things twice.** If you go to mediation and then a fair hearing, you will have been involved in two procedures, doubling the time, inconvenience, stress, and possible costs.

The bottom line about mediation. Although there are some downsides to mediation, they are almost always outweighed by its benefits. Unless there's some compelling reason to go straight to a hearing—like a serious time crunch or a truly uncompromising opponent—you should give mediation a try. The vast majority of cases I've been involved in are resolved at mediation (or before).

Reality Check: What to Expect From Due Process

Parents often expect to get everything their child needs if they go forward with informal negotiations, mediation, a fair hearing, or even litigation. After all, if you want certain IEP components and you have evidence and arguments to back up your claims, you can look forward to total victory, right? Well, not necessarily. Even if you have a strong case, you may not get everything that you want. What is fair or right and what will actually happen are usually very different things.

This is especially important to remember when you consider a settlement offer from your school district (whether through informal negotiations or through mediation). You may be thinking, "I know I'm right and I know a hearing officer or judge will agree, so I'm going to go for the full loaf and reject the school district's offer of 80%." But you have to weigh the school district's offer against the chances of winning at a fair hearing—and, if you win, whether you'll get more than the school district offered. You also have to weigh the financial, emotional, and educational cost of going forward rather than getting things resolved now.

2. Mediators

The mediator's job is to help you and the school district reach a settlement. The mediator will not decide who is right and who is wrong.

A good mediator will:

- put you and school representatives at ease
- try to establish an atmosphere in which compromise is possible
- be objective
- give you and the school district a frank assessment of the strengths and weaknesses of your positions, and

- go beyond your stated positions to explore possible settlements that may not be initially apparent.

Some mediators play a more limited role—they simply present everyone's positions and hope that the weight of the evidence and formality of the process will lead to a settlement.

3. Who, Where, and When of Mediation

Mediation sessions must be held at a time and place convenient for you. They are often held at the school district's main office, but they can be held elsewhere. Some people are concerned that having the mediation at a school office gives the district an advantage, but I have found it usually does not matter.

The length of the mediation can vary, but sessions generally take many hours and often a full day. The mediation sessions almost always take more time than you would think.

Most school districts send the special education administrator and perhaps another person who has direct knowledge of your child to the mediation. While you can bring outside assessors, aides, tutors, and any other individuals you want (including a lawyer), you will generally want to save them for the fair hearing.

Bringing in experts might make mediation more expensive and difficult to schedule. Whether you should include (or exclude) experts will depend on:

- how forceful the experts can be
- whether there is any chance to change the district's mind, and
- the risks of revealing some of your evidence prior to the fair hearing.

If you expect to go to a fair hearing and don't want to put all your cards on the table at mediation, don't bring the experts. On the other hand, if you want to settle quickly and your experts can aid in that process, bring them along.

4. The Mediation Session Itself

You, the mediator, and the school representatives will gather in a conference or meeting room. After brief introductions, the mediator will explain how the mediation process works, stressing that mediation is a voluntary attempt to resolve your disagreement.

a. Your Opening Statement

You begin by briefly explaining your side of the dispute. (Section G, above, shows how to prepare an opening statement.) Do not hesitate to express your feelings. Your child has important needs and his well-being is at stake. Express how worried you are. Explain why you feel the school district has not effectively served your child or has failed to provide an appropriate education. It's important to show the mediator how imperative the matter is to you and your child. This does not mean tirades or irrational, off-the-wall, unfocused monologues. Give your opinion, but don't question the honesty, professionalism, or decency of the school personnel. Don't berate anyone.

Your opening statement should not go on and on or discuss every possible problem. It should be clear and succinct and run from five to 20 minutes.

If the school has committed any legal violations, you can raise these in your opening statement. While legal violations are subject to the complaint procedure (see Chapter 13), evidence of a legal violation may be a powerful addition to your case, showing the school district's disregard or lack of understanding of the law, and possibly the district's lack of reliability. Nothing in IDEA prevents you from raising legal issues in the mediation. While the mediator cannot look to remedy legal violations, the mediator can say to district personnel, "You are in trouble because you clearly violated the law; you might want to think about settling this case now."

How Much Evidence Do You Reveal in Mediation?

Section G, above, suggests that you describe your evidence as a part of your opening statement. But you may not want to reveal all of your supporting evidence at mediation. By telling all, you may help the school prepare for the fair hearing. On the other hand, if your evidence is very strong, revealing it may lead to a settlement in your favor. If you're not sure what to do, ask the mediator's opinion in your private meeting. If the mediator feels that the school realizes its case is weak or for some other reason is close to settling, then it may be wise to lay all your cards on the table. On the other hand, if the mediator feels the school is rigid and unlikely to settle, then it may be better not to reveal all of your evidence.

No matter what, you'll want to provide at least a synopsis of your evidence, noting where a professional (teacher, related service provider, administrator, doctor, outside assessor, or private tutor) has made a clear statement about the disputed issue. Also note the credentials of the person, particularly if he is well known and loaded with degrees and experience. Stress all documents or statements by school district representatives that support your position.

b. School District's Opening Statement

After you make your opening statement, the school district's representative usually presents the district's point of view, perhaps responding to what you have said. Don't interrupt or respond, even though the school's version of the dispute may be very different from yours. Take notes of the main points.

Sometimes the district will choose not to make an opening statement—in that case, you'll move right on to private sessions with the mediator.

After the school representative finishes, the mediator may invite you to add anything you forgot or to respond to the school's statement. If you respond, make it brief and to the point, focusing on why you disagree with the school's position.

c. Private Sessions With the Mediator

After you and the school representative make your opening statements, the mediator will meet privately with you, then with the school representatives, then back with you, then back with the school representatives, continuing back and forth as necessary. When you meet privately with the mediator, speak frankly. The mediator cannot disclose anything you say to the school representatives, unless you give the mediator permission. Be sure of this by clearly telling the mediator what you want conveyed to the school district and what you want kept between you and the mediator.

In your first meeting, the mediator may want to clarify issues and begin exploring whether you're willing to compromise. As the mediator shuttles back and forth, specific evidence related to each disputed issue may come up. For example, you and the school district may have very different views on the validity of the district's assessment versus your independent assessment. You can tell the mediator something like "Please convey to Mr. Roberts that my assessor is a recognized expert and is clear in her recommendations; the district's expert has limited knowledge of my child's learning disability."

After a few of these private sessions, the mediator should be able to tell you how far the school will go to settle the dispute. At this point, you will have to think about your bottom line. Think about what is essential, what you can give up, how strong your case is, and how hard a line the school is taking. Make use of the mediator by asking direct questions, such as:

- What do you think the school will do on the placement issue?

- Do they understand that Dr. Parnell said Victor needs placement in the private school?
- What is their bottom line?
- Do you think we have a case if we go to a fair hearing?
- I want to push for everything; given the district's last offer, how do you think they'll react to a take-it-or-leave-it last offer?

The strength of the evidence and the work of the mediator will convince the district to settle (or not). If the district has moved somewhat from the position it held at the IEP meeting, but some issues remain unresolved, you'll have to decide what to do. You'll have to weigh the importance of the outstanding issues, your willingness to go to a fair hearing, and the likelihood of ultimate victory.

Bargaining in Mediation

Bargaining is part of mediation. When presenting what you want, make your list as strong and inclusive as possible. Put in everything you could possibly want, including your expenses and even minor items. But know your priorities—including what you can live without and can therefore use as bargaining chips.

Example:

You feel your child should be in a private school, which costs $15,000 per year. You also want the school district to pay for your private assessment, which was $1,000. You also have some reimbursement costs, including a tutor, totaling several hundred dollars. Your case is strong enough to go after all of these items. But to settle the case, the district wants you to forgo the assessment and other costs. Is it worth giving up $1,000 in costs for the $15,000? It depends on the strength of your evidence. No matter how strong your case is, there is always a risk that the hearing could go against you.

d. Wrapping Up the Mediation Session

After various private meetings with the mediator, there will be four possible outcomes:

- full settlement of all issues: for example, the school district agrees to provide three hours a week of speech/language therapy so your child can strengthen his expressive and receptive language skills
- partial settlement: you agree on some issues and disagree on others—for example, the district agrees to mainstream your 11th grader for three hours a week for aide help in English and social studies, but will not reimburse you for your independent assessment, which cost $2,500.
- no settlement, but you agree to try again with the mediator at a later date: for example, you want large-print materials for your child, but the district needs to check the process for securing them or you decide to let the matter sit for a week and reconvene to see if one or both parties have moved from their original position, or
- no settlement and no further mediation sessions scheduled: for example, if you want a private school and the district disagrees, the issue will have to go to a hearing officer.

A mediation settlement can contain anything you and the school district agree to—including that the school district will provide all or part of what you want for your child and pay your attorney's fees.

Whatever the outcome, you will all return to the meeting room and the mediator will fill out a mediation form. The mediator will write down what the parties agreed to (if anything), what issues are unresolved (if any), and what the next steps will be if full agreement was not reached.

If you don't reach a settlement on all or some issues, you have three options:

- go to a fair hearing
- drop the matter—this may make sense if only minor issues remain unresolved, or

- go directly to court—this highly unusual approach requires you to prove that the problem is so serious you can't spend time at a fair hearing and need a judge to look at the matter immediately; you will need a lawyer's help (see Chapter 14).

Once you and the school district sign the mediation form, both of you are bound by whatever agreement you reached.

I. Fair Hearing

A fair hearing is like a court trial, although it won't be held in a courtroom. You and the school district submit evidence in the form of written documents and sworn testimony from witnesses. A neutral third party (called a hearing officer) reviews the evidence and decides who is right and who is wrong. That decision is binding on you and the district. The hearing officer has the authority to act independently of you and the school district—in essence, as a judge. The hearing officer cannot be an employee of the school district or the state educational agency if either agency is involved in the education of your child. (34 C.F.R. § 300.508.)

Although IDEA establishes specific rules for fair hearings (34 C.F.R. §§ 300.507-511), states can vary some of the procedural details. For example, Ohio provides that attorneys will act as hearing officers; other states specify qualifications rather than requiring that officers be members of particular professions. In most states, the department of education provides a list of hearing officers or contracts with a qualified agency to do so. For instance, in California, the state department of education has contracted with a law school, which in turn hires the hearing officers.

 Contact your state department of education to find out the details of your state's laws on fair hearings. See Appendix 2.

Settling Your Case Once the Fair Hearing Begins

Fair hearings are expensive, difficult, and risky for both parties. Recognizing this, some hearing officers will start the hearing by suggesting that you try one more time to settle the case. If both sides are interested, you might even meet, with or without the hearing officer, to try to work out the details. There are no rules to these discussions—it is a lot like mediation in that neither side has to agree to anything. If you do reach a compromise, the hearing officer will write up a formal agreement for you and the school district to sign.

A fair hearing is used to resolve factual disputes between you and your child's school district, normally disagreements about placement, a related service, curricula, or methodology. Section B, above, lists typical IEP due process disputes.

Often, a factual dispute includes a legal dispute. For example, say you want your child in a private school and the school district offers a special day class in the public school. The factual dispute is over which placement is appropriate for your child. The legal issue is whether IDEA allows a private school placement when supported by the facts (it does).

Or perhaps the school district wants to place your child in a special school 15 miles from your home; you want your child placed in a regular class at the local school. Again, the factual dispute involves finding the appropriate placement. The legal issue is IDEA's requirement that your child be placed in the least restrictive environment and as close to home as possible.

At this point, you may be thinking, "I thought legal problems were only subject to the complaint process." Here's how it works: In a fair hearing, there may be legal issues that are pertinent to the factual analysis and outcome. In a complaint, you are only claiming that the school district broke the law—there is no factual dispute regarding an IEP issue.

In some cases, you may simultaneously file a complaint and pursue due process. These situations are discussed at the end of Chapter 13.

A witness may testify about a legal issue, or you or the school district may raise a legal issue in your opening statements. In most cases, however, legal issues are addressed in a post-hearing brief. (See Section 6, below.) Discussing legal issues at the hearing or in a brief may seem quite daunting. If you anticipate major legal disputes, see Chapter 14 on lawyers and legal research, or contact an attorney for help on this part of the process.

Fear of Fair Hearings

It's natural to be afraid of a fair hearing—after all, it's like a trial and can be difficult and complicated. But many parents conduct fair hearings. So how do you get through one with your nerves intact? Here are a few tips:

- Be organized.
- Take some time to think through the issues and your evidence.
- Know that everybody else is nervous, too.

Never doubt that you can do it. Lots of parents have had these same fears—and done just fine in the hearing. In preparing for the IEP meeting (and perhaps mediation), you already did a good deal of the hard work.

---

1. Your Fair Hearing Rights and Responsibilities

IDEA sets out several rights and responsibilities you *and* the school district have during the fair hearing process. (20 U.S.C. § 1415(h)(i); 34 C.F.R. §§ 508-511.) These include:

- You have the right to be advised and accompanied by an attorney or another person with special knowledge or training.
- At least five days before the hearing, you and the school district must provide each other with a list of your witnesses and copies of all written evidence—exhibits—you will submit at the hearing, including any assessments. The hearing officer can refuse to hear the testimony of anyone not on the witness list or to consider any document not exchanged before the hearing.
- Before the hearing, you can subpoena witnesses to ensure that they will attend. (Most state educational agencies have subpoena forms.)
- Before the hearing, you have the right to declare the fair hearing closed or open to the public, including the press. In most cases, I'd opt for a closed hearing—there's little to be gained from an open hearing, and it may greatly increase your level of stress.
- After the hearing, you are entitled to a verbatim record of the hearing (in either written or electronic format). The hearing officer will tape the proceedings and the agency responsible for due process will give you a transcript of that tape.
- After the hearing, you're entitled to a written decision, including findings of fact, within 45 days of when you first requested due process.
- You have the right to appeal a fair hearing decision to a state or federal court.

Check your state laws and regulations for any different or additional rules or requirements. For example, California requires each party to a fair hearing to submit a statement of issues and their proposed resolutions at least 10 days before the hearing. (California Education Code § 56505(e)(6).)

2. Pros and Cons of a Fair Hearing

There are several good reasons to request a fair hearing:

- If you win, your child will receive the education he needs.
- If you win, it's unlikely you will have to fight the battle again.
- If you win, your attorney's fees and other costs will be reimbursed for every issue you prevail on.
- Whether or not you win, you buy time. If your child is currently in a placement you want to maintain, your child is entitled to remain there until the issue is finally resolved —either through the fair hearing decision or a final court decision, if you appeal. (Section D, above, discusses this "stay put" provision.)

Of course, there are also some disadvantages to a fair hearing:

- Fair hearings are difficult, time-consuming, emotionally draining, and contentious.
- You might lose.
- Your relationship with your school district will likely be strained and formal. Future IEPs may be hard. If you lose, the school district may feel invincible.
- If you lose, you won't be entitled to reimbursement for your costs and attorney's fees (although you won't have to pay the school district's attorney's fees).

3. Who, What, and Where of Fair Hearings

A fair hearing must be held at a time and place that are convenient for you. Normally, fair hearings are held at the school district office and last anywhere from one to several days.

Once you request a fair hearing, you will be sent a notice of the date and location of the hearing, as well as the name of the hearing officer. You will also be given the name, address, and phone number of the school district representative. You have to send your exhibits and witness lists to this representative as well as the hearing officer.

4. Preparing for a Fair Hearing

If you go to mediation first, much of your preparation will be done by the time you go to fair hearing. But you still have some very important and time-consuming work to do. Give yourself several weeks to prepare, more if you skip mediation and go straight to fair hearing.

a. Know Your Case

Review your child's file (Chapter 4), your binder (Chapter 4), and your IEP blueprint (Chapter 5). Be clear on the disputed issues: what you want, what the school district is offering, and how you disagree.

b. Determine Your Strategy

At the hearing, you must clearly state your position on each disputed issue and offer evidence to support it. (In your request for due process, you listed the issues. See Section F, above.) You will present your evidence in the form of witnesses and documents.

You should have a clear strategy that connects your evidence to the disputed issues. For example, you want your child to have a one-to-one aide, two hours each day, to work on reading comprehension and language acquisition. How can you convince the hearing officer to give you what you want? Hopefully, you have specific evidence about your child's needs, written reports as exhibits, and/or testimony from your witnesses. But there may be other important, if indirect, evidence as well. For example, the school district may not have assessed your child in a timely manner or may have failed to test in certain areas.

Or the district may not have up-to-date assessment material to prove an alternative to the aide would be sufficient. Or the district may have cut off the discussion of your proposal in the IEP meeting. None of this evidence proves or disproves that your child needs a 1:1 aide, but it does show that the district did not allow the IEP process to proceed appropriately—and, therefore, adds weight to your argument that the district is wrong.

> Example:
> You want your child mainstreamed with a one-to-one aide, but your school district offers a special class. At the hearing, you will have to show that:
> - The school district failed to offer mainstreaming placement.
> - An aide will help your child function in the mainstream classroom.
> - Your child will do well socially because her friends are in the class.
> - A special class will be detrimental to your child because it will not address your child's unique needs—and is contrary to IDEA's least restrictive environment requirement.

c. Prepare Exhibits of Written Material

Any written document that contains evidence supporting your position or provides information that the hearing officer will need to make a decision can be used as an exhibit. But be choosy—you don't necessarily want to turn over your entire IEP binder. The issues in dispute will guide you. Review all of your documents, looking for everything that supports your position, such as an assessment or teacher's report. Note the specific page number and paragraph in each document where the supportive statement is made. You have probably done much of this work with the Material Organizer form you developed for the IEP meeting.

⚠️ **Do not submit material that damages your case or reveals private information you don't want known.** The school district may submit evidence that harms your case or point out the gaps in your evidence; obviously, you should not. Remember that the school district and hearing officer will get to examine whatever you submit as evidence—if it contains personal or confidential information you don't want to reveal, you should try to find a different way to make your point or submit only portions of the document.

Example of exhibits typically presented at fair hearings include:

- IEP documents
- assessments and evaluations
- letters or reports from your child's teacher or physician
- articles about your child's disability, appropriate teaching methods, or any other issues in your case
- witnesses résumés and articles they've written that relate to the issues in dispute, and
- your child's classroom work.

If in doubt, include the item. You never know when you might want to refer to something during the hearing. If you don't include the item when you prepare your exhibit exchange (at least five days before the hearing), you will probably be barred from using it at the hearing.

Arrange your exhibits in an order that makes sense to you, such as the order in which you plan to introduce them or alphabetical order. Place them in a folder or binder with tabs and a table of contents. Be sure to put page numbers on each individual exhibit, too, so you can easily find specific statements.

You'll refer to these exhibits in your own testimony and when you question witnesses. At this stage, it is unlikely that you will have to develop new evidence. But if you do not yet have support for a disputed item, you may need new material—for example, a supportive letter or even an independent evaluation.

d. Choose and Prepare Witnesses

Witnesses are crucial to the outcome of a fair hearing. Choose and prepare your witnesses with care.

i. Choosing Witnesses

Double check your list of *all* potential witnesses, those who support you and those who might testify for the school district (including participants at the IEP meeting). Try to anticipate what each witness can testify about. One witness may be able to testify about several issues, while others may focus on only one disputed matter. In choosing your witnesses, look for the following:

- The strength of the witness's testimony.
- The witness's experience, training, education, and direct knowledge of your child.
- The witness's willingness to testify under oath. You must make sure a person is willing to testify at the hearing before you put her on your witness list. A witness's favorable or supportive report won't help if she equivocates in her testimony at the hearing. In that case, submit the person's written material and have other witnesses refer to that report.

Sometimes, an important witness refuses to testify voluntarily at the hearing. For example, your child's former tutor—who could testify in detail about your child's reading problems—may now work for the school district and be reluctant to support you in a due process fight over eligibility. In these cases, you may need to subpoena a reluctant witness to testify at the hearing. A subpoena is an order that requires the witness to appear. You can get subpoena forms from your state department of education.

ii. Preparing Witness Questions

Write out a list of questions for each witness. Here is a general outline (of course, the specific questions you ask each witness will depend on what he knows about your child):

- Ask the witness to identify herself—for example, "Please state your name, occupation, and place of employment."
- Ask about the witness's experience, education, training, and specific expertise in the area of dispute—you can refer the witness to his résumé or written articles that you included in your exhibits. In a fair hearing for a child with learning disabilities, the witness might be an expert in reading, language, or strategies used to address learning disabilities. It is important to establish your witness's credentials so that his testimony will carry a lot of weight with the hearing officer.
- Establish the witness's knowledge of your child—for example:
  - s *"Have you met my son, Philip Jones?"*
  - s *"Please tell us when, for how long, and for what purpose."*
  - s *"Did you also observe him in school?"*
  - s *"Please tell us when that was and for how long."*
- Ask questions to elicit your witness's opinion about the issues in dispute, for example:
  - s *"You stated that you tested Philip. What tests did you administer?"*
  - s *"What were the results?"*
  - s *"What do those results mean?"*
  - s *"What conclusions did you draw regarding Philip's reading difficulties?"*
  - s *"How severe are his difficulties?"*

- s *"In your professional opinion, what is the appropriate way to help Philip improve his reading?"*
- s *"Do you have any specific recommendations regarding Philip's reading needs?"*
- s *"What is your professional opinion regarding Philip's prognosis as a successful reader if he is not provided the help you recommend?"*

Keys to preparing your witnesses. As a general rule, witnesses must be able to clearly state what your child needs and why, the benefits to your child if those needs are met, and the detriment to your child if they are not.

iii. Preparing Your Witnesses

Before the hearing, meet with your witnesses and go over your questions. Their answers may lead to new questions you'll want to ask, trigger a new strategy or approach, and help you and your witnesses prepare for the hearing. Explain that after you're done asking questions, the school district representative will cross-examine the witness by asking additional questions.

Some witnesses, particularly any school employees who agree to testify for your child, may be unwilling to meet during school hours. You may have to arrange to meet them at their home. Others may not want to meet at all. What should you do about witnesses who can help your case but won't talk to you ahead of time? If you can't discuss the case before the hearing, you won't know exactly how the witness will testify, which can be risky. One strategy is to leave the person off your witness list, then hope that the district calls her so you can cross-examine her. Of course, if the witness is the only person who can testify about a certain element of your case, then you'll probably need to take a chance and use the witness, even though you didn't talk to her before the hearing.

Another strategy is to include the person on your witness list but don't ask him to testify during your presentation. Then you can either cross-examine him (if he is called as a witness by the school) or use him as a "rebuttal witness"—a witness you call after the school district presents its evidence, to counter the testimony of the district's witnesses.

Just before the hearing date, get back in touch with your witnesses to tell them:

- the date, time, and location of the hearing
- what time you need them to arrive to be ready to testify—be sure to let them know that they might not be called on time if an earlier witness takes longer than expected or the hearing officer breaks early, and
- how long you expect their testimony to take.

iv. Preparing Yourself as a Witness

You will most likely be a witness at the hearing. You have valuable information about your child, her history, her previous programs, her needs, your worries, your frustrations, and what teachers have said to you about your child.

Your testimony must cover those matters about which you have first-hand knowledge, although you can also testify about issues others will cover in their testimony. For example, you can testify about the assessment done on your child and what the assessor told you, even though the assessor is in a better position to give detailed testimony about this issue.

You can present your testimony in one of two ways: You can respond to questions (just like you will be asking questions of your witnesses) asked by your spouse, a relative, or a close friend, or you can make a statement covering all issues of importance. You can either read your statement or give it from notes. After you're done answering questions or making your statement, the school district representative will cross-examine you.

Your testimony should be clear, specific, and objective. Break down your points into the following areas, using your mediation statement (if you made one) as a starting point:

- a general description of your child, including his age, strengths, and weaknesses (your child profile, discussed in Chapter 10, can help here)
- your child's disability and the effect of that disability—for example, your child has a learning disability, and, as a result, he has difficulty with simple computations, reading comprehension, and visual memory
- any secondary difficulties due to the disability —such as emotional problems
- your child's educational history—that is, the classes he's been in, including his current program
- the particular issues in dispute and your desired resolution (remember, you child is entitled to an "appropriate"—not an ideal—education; your testimony should explain why the program, related services, and other items you want for your child are appropriate)
- your observations at class visits, meetings with teachers and other professionals, and the IEP meeting (for example, "On February 12, 20xx, I visited the second grade class at Tower School and I observed ....")
- statements others have made to you that support your point of view, including your reaction to those statements—for instance, "On November 3, 20xx, Mr. Mastin of the school district told me there was no room for my child in the second grade class at Tower School; I confirmed this conversation in a letter which is my Exhibit F. Mr. Mastin did not respond to my letter."
- your child's specific educational needs and the consequences if those needs are not met—for example, "Given the assessment by Dr. Pollack, I believe a placement in a program other than the second grade class at Tower School will have serious emotional and cognitive consequences for my child."

e. Prepare Questions for School Witnesses

Preparing questions for school witnesses is more difficult than preparing for your own witnesses because you don't know exactly what they'll say. Still, you can probably guess what many witnesses will say, because you heard their opinions at the IEP meeting.

Start by reviewing your files, the transcript or your notes of the IEP meeting, and the school district's exhibits (you'll get them five days before the hearing). Then make a list of questions to strengthen your case or at least undermine what the school district's witnesses might say.

Example:

Your child's teacher said something very important to you when you visited your child's class. You sent a letter confirming what was said ("Thanks for talking to me today. I was glad to hear that you agreed Jake should remain in a regular class with the help of an aide."). The teacher never objected to your confirming letter, but you now believe she will say the opposite at the hearing. Be ready to point out the discrepancy—for instance, "Ms. Jenkins, you testified this morning that you feel Jake should be placed in a special education class. Do you recall when we met on October 15 and you told me that Jake was doing well in the regular class but needed an aide to keep up? You don't recall that meeting? Please look at Exhibit B, my November 1 letter to you."

Rules of Evidence

You may have heard of something called the "rules of evidence." These formal rules, which are very specific and sometimes quite arcane, are used in courts to guide judges in deciding what evidence can be included and what must be excluded. These rules don't have to be followed at fair hearings, but the hearing officer can use them as appropriate.

For example, some rules relate to hearsay evidence—information that a witness did not hear or receive directly. "I saw Jack hit Frank" is not hearsay; "Jack told me that Frank hit Bill" is hearsay evidence and can be excluded at a fair hearing.

Don't worry too much about formal rules of evidence. If the other side "objects" to a question you ask because it violates a rule of evidence, ask the hearing officer to explain the rule and then rephrase your question or move on.

f. Exchange Witness Lists and Evidence

Remember, you must submit a list of your witnesses and copies of written exhibits at least five days before the hearing begins. (34 C.F.R. §§ 300.509 (a)(3), (b)(1).) Once you have your exhibits (organized in binders) and your list of witnesses, make two copies. Keep the originals for yourself, send one copy to the fair hearing officer, and send the other copy to the school district representative. To make sure you have proof that they received the items at least five days before the hearing, send them certified mail, return receipt requested.

5. The Fair Hearing Itself

The fair hearing normally proceeds as follows:

1. The hearing officer opens the hearing and explains the process, including the order in

which the hearing will proceed. The hearing officer will usually identify and confirm the written testimony or exhibits you and the school district submitted. Finally, the officer will set up the tape recorder and make sure the parties are ready.

2. The parties introduce themselves.

3. The hearing officer turns on the tape recorder and the formal hearing begins.

4. You make your opening statement.

5. The school district makes its opening statement.

6. You question (direct examine) your witnesses.

7. The school representative questions (cross-examines) your witnesses.

8. You ask more questions of your witnesses (redirect) if you want, the school representative cross-examines again (called recross), and so on.

9. The school district calls its witnesses with the same pattern of direct examination, cross-examination, redirect, and recross.

10. You call back any witnesses after the school finishes, if you want. These are called rebuttal witnesses and are used to clarify or contradict testimony raised by the other side. The school district has the same right.

11. You give a closing statement, if you want.

12. The school district gives a closing statement, if it wants.

13. You and the school district agree to submit written briefs discussing the facts presented at the hearing and any applicable law. (See Section 6, below.)

14. The hearing officer issues a decision within 45 days after you requested due process.

Keeping Track During the Fair Hearing

You want to have an ongoing record of the testimony during the hearing because you may need to refer back to previous testimony. For example, say the district calls a witness who testifies for 45 minutes on various issues. When you cross-examine this witness, you want to refer back to a specific statement he made that contradicted other testimony or ask him to clarify something in his testimony. You need to be able to refer to earlier statements.

Taking notes is the logical way to keep track; however, it can be difficult to get everything down while you're also conducting the hearing. The better plan is to let someone else take notes for you, recording statements of each witness, while you also take notes on key statements. (You can do this on paper or a laptop computer.) If you had a note taker at the IEP meeting, consider using the same person, who is probably very familiar with the issues by nows. You can tape the hearing, but you won't have time to review taped testimony while the hearing is going on. Also, it is more difficult to try to find an exact statement on a tape than to simply refer to written notes. If you don't have a note taker, be sure to keep notes as the other side questions witnesses. Highlight key statements.

How do you use the notes? During your cross-examination you'd say something like "Mr. Adams, you testified, let me see [look at your notes], that and I quote, 'I don't think James needs an aide in class.' Is that correct?" If he agrees, then point out evidence that contradicts him, such as "In her testimony yesterday, Dr. Markham stated that you told her on April 29, 20xx that James needed an aide."

a. Make an Opening Statement

You can use the opening statement you prepared for mediation as a starting point, but you will need to change it somewhat for a fair hearing. At mediation, you can say anything; your aim is to reach a compromise. At a fair hearing, however, your aim is to prove your case. Your opening statement, therefore, should emphasize what you want for your child and how that is supported by evidence. This doesn't mean you shouldn't include items for which your evidence is weak, but it does mean that you should carefully think about what you're requesting—and how likely you are to get it. The hearing officer will consider not only your evidence, but your credibility. If you ask for something unsupported by any evidence, your credibility may be affected.

Be sure to include these details in your opening statement:

- basic facts about your child, including her age, disability, and current educational program
- a clear statement of your child's needs and the dispute that brought you to the hearing, and
- a brief statement that what you want is supported by evidence, such as "Cheryl needs a full-time aide, as we will clearly show with evidence, including the testimony of several different professionals and exhibits B, D, and M."

Opening statements can be any length, but five to 15 minutes is typical. If you can, don't read a verbatim statement—instead, use notes to guide you in making your points. If you're very nervous, however, it's okay to read the statement. It is important to express your feelings and bring the human element into the hearing. Be careful not to go off on an unfocused monologue or use your statement to launch a personal attack on school district representatives, but don't hesitate to make a strong, clear statement of what your child needs.

b. Questioning Your Witnesses

After opening statements, your witnesses will testify. Think carefully about the order in which you want to present their testimony. You are telling a story, and you need to present the details of the story in an order that will make sense to someone who has little or no prior knowledge of the situation. It's often best to begin with someone (possibly you) who can give general background information about your child. Next, you might want a witness who can present the assessment data, such as your independent assessor.

After that, you want to go to the core of the dispute and make your case. For example, say you and the school district disagree on placement and a related service. During the past year, your child was in a regular class, with no assistance. You want your child to stay in that class with an aide; the school district has offered placement in a special day class. Your first witness can give the details of the regular class. The second can talk about why your child needs that class. The third can describe the services offered by the aide. The fourth can explain why your child needs that aide.

Of course, you may have to modify the presentation and go out of order if a witness is available only on a certain day or at a certain time. Or, you may choose a different order to maximize impact. In some instances, the witness who will give the most dramatic and effective testimony should go last, so the hearing officer is left with that impression. Or that person might go first, to set a tone for the rest of the hearing. Only you can decide which strategy will be most effective in your situation.

c. Questioning Reluctant Witnesses

Question reluctant witnesses with care. First, ask the hearing officer to note that the witness is not cooperative. To ensure the person's attendance at the hearing, you should have issued a subpoena.

At the hearing, ask something like "Mr. Jones are you testifying voluntarily?" The response will be something like "No. As you know I was subpoenaed by you."

Another possibility is to begin your questioning with a statement such as "This witness, Mr. Hobson, the fourth grade teacher, would not talk to me prior to the hearing. I am calling him as a hostile witness."

d. How to Use Your Exhibits

Have your exhibits available so you can use them when you question witnesses. For example, "Tell me, Dr. Whitland, you said Monroe does not need psychotherapy. Would you please look at Exhibit B, page 4? You reported last year that Monroe had severe emotional difficulties that were interfering with his education. Aren't severe emotional difficulties usually addressed in some kind of psychological therapy?"

e. Closing Statements

After all the evidence has been presented and all witnesses have testified, the hearing officer will likely ask if you want to make closing arguments or submit a written brief.

A closing statement, like the opening statement, is a powerful and precise summary of your arguments, but now you can refer to useful testimony from the hearing itself as proof of what you want. For example, you might say, "Every witness we called agreed that Michele needs four sessions each week with a reading specialist; not one of the school district's witnesses contradicted that. This is fully consistent with Dr. Hanover's written report, Exhibit L." Your closing statement might also note that the recommended education is consistent with IDEA, and point out what would happen to your child if the hearing officer rules against you.

Further Suggestions on Questioning Witnesses

No matter how much you prepare, you won't be able to anticipate exactly how the questioning will go. Be ready to depart from your planned questions. For example, a witness might answer in a way slightly different from what you expected, requiring you to ask follow-up questions. Or the witness may say the opposite of what you expect.

Here are some tips on dealing with surprises when questioning witnesses:

- Ask for a brief break if you need to gather yourself or consider new questions.
- Keep track of your questions. If you veer off on a line of questioning you had not planned, mark where you are on your list of questions so you can come back to it later.
- Be very, very careful about asking a question unless you know how the witness will answer, particularly of a school witness.
- Don't overwhelm the hearing officer with a ton of facts. Parents tend to try to get everything into the record at the hearing. Know the difference between important facts and minutiae.
- Know when to stop. Stop asking questions when something powerful has been stated. Further questioning will only dilute the impact.
- Don't badger a witness. Ask questions in a firm way and repeat them if necessary. But don't become hostile, belligerent, or belittling.
- Don't play lawyer. You'll do fine with your own style and language.

---

6. Post-Hearing Briefs

If you agree to submit briefs, the parties, with the help of the hearing officer, will set a short timeframe (usually no more than one week) to submit the briefs. The purposes of the briefs are to highlight the evidence that supports your case and bring any supportive law and legal cases to the attention of the hearing officer.

To develop your brief, first review your notes, your memory, and the evidence. The written brief should point out the evidence that supports your case and the evidence that contradicts the school district's point of view. If there are legal issues, you should review IDEA and any court cases that support your analysis of the law. (See Chapter 14 for advice on legal research.) You may also want to contact a lawyer or support organization for help.

J. Fair Hearing Decision and Appeals

After the hearing, you're entitled to a written decision, including findings of fact, within 45 days after you first requested due process.

Both you and the school district have the right to appeal the hearing decision, theoretically all the way to the U.S. Supreme Court. (34 C.F.R. § 300.512.) While the purpose of this book is to help you get through the IEP process without an attorney, you should seriously consider getting some legal advice if you're contemplating an appeal. If you lost, several factors will help you decide whether or not to appeal:

- **Strength of your case.** You should already have considered this as part of your decision to pursue due process. For an appeal,

you must look at your situation with a more critical eye. Many reviewing courts will defer to the administrative decision and won't want to rehear the evidence anew. Even if your court takes a fresh look at the evidence, remember that a neutral third party has already ruled against you, which suggests some problems with your case.

- **Costs of an appeal.** There are various costs in appealing a fair hearing decision to court, including filing fees, fees for serving papers on the school district, witness fees, and other trial costs (such as copying exhibits). And there's one more cost: potential attorney's fees. While nonattorneys can represent themselves in court, I strongly recommend that you hire an attorney. At the very least, have an attorney who specializes in IDEA review your case and advise you of your chances on appeal.

- **Time.** State laws vary as to when you must file your appeal (depending on their statute of limitations). Once your case is filed, court workloads may affect how soon your appeal is heard in court. Anticipate a lengthy process, taking many months at least. Remember, too, that as long as the case is active, your child must stay where she is. Thus, if you lost at hearing—for example, the district offered a new placement and the hearing officer agreed—appealing that decision will allow your child to remain in her previous placement. Deciding to go to court, however, is a very serious step. You shouldn't decide to take it solely because you want your child to stay put, particularly if your case is not strong. ■

13

Filing a Complaint

As discussed in Chapter 12, factual disputes with the school district are usually resolved through informal negotiation and due process. But what if the school district has violated a legal requirement under IDEA? For legal disputes like this, IDEA provides a complaint process. (34 C.F.R. §§ 300.660-662; see Appendix 1.)

Avoid Factual Disputes With a Carefully Written IEP

Sometimes it's hard to tell whether you're dealing with a factual dispute (and therefore something that is subject to due process) or a legal violation that must be resolved by filing a complaint. For example, let's say your child needs a multisensory approach to his learning disability needs. The IEP might refer to a specific multisensory approach, such as Slingerland. In this case, if the district does not provide Slingerland, then it has violated the IEP. On the other hand, if the IEP does not specifically require Slingerland, then the dispute may be over what the IEP requires. For example, say the IEP says only that your child will have a multisensory approach or (even more vaguely) that the teacher will try to approach Mary's problems by helping her visual, auditory, and kinesthetic abilities. If the district does not use Slingerland, it has not violated IDEA; because the IEP did not specifically require Slingerland, this is a factual dispute (subject to due process).

To avoid factual disputes over what the IEP requires, make sure that your child's IEP is clear and precise. Generally, an IEP that both parties have agreed to and signed is legally binding. If the school district doesn't provide what the IEP requires, your remedy will probably be to file a complaint charging a legal violation, rather than initiating due process.

A. When to File a Complaint

IDEA statutes and regulations set out the school district's legal obligations. Excerpts of key sections of IDEA are contained in Appendix 1. Here are some common school district actions (or inactions) that are legal violations of IDEA:

- failure to provide a child's records
- failure to do assessments
- failure to meet assessment and IEP timelines
- failure to hold an IEP meeting
- failure to allow a parent to effectively represent her child in the IEP meeting—for example, by limiting who can attend or by intimidating the parent
- failure to follow certain procedures before suspending or expelling a special education student (see Chapter 2A)
- failure to discuss all elements in an IEP meeting—including goals and objectives, placement, related services, and transition plans
- failure to implement an agreed-to IEP—for example, if your child's IEP calls for three sessions of speech/language therapy and the school district provides only one session, and
- failure to give notice before changing, or refusing to change, a child's IEP. Your district cannot change your child's IEP without giving you notice of that change and holding an IEP meeting, nor can it refuse you the right to have an IEP meeting if you want a change.

Collective Complaints: There's Strength in Numbers

If your school district is violating the law in a way that affects a group of children, consider filing a complaint together. A complaint filed by more than one family can be that much more effective. Your state department of education has a legal duty under IDEA to monitor all school districts to make sure they are following the law—and to take any necessary steps to force a recalcitrant district to shape up. States are usually more sensitive to what may be a pattern of IDEA violations. If you are able to show that many children are being hurt by the district's failure to follow the law, your state department of education may be quicker to step in and take action. And it's much less costly for a group of parents to hire one attorney to draft and submit a complaint than for each family to hire its own lawyer. See Chapter 15 for a more detailed discussion about the value of parent groups.

B. Where to File a Complaint

Section A, above, lists common violations of IDEA, but it is not an exhaustive list. If you believe your school district has violated IDEA or any state special education law, contact your state department of education (or a locally designated agency) or the U.S. Department of Education, Office for Civil Rights (OCR). Contact information for both is in Appendix 2.

You can file a complaint with either the state or federal education agency. Both handle violations of IDEA, state law, or Section 504 of the Rehabilitation Act of 1973.

 See Chapter 7 for a brief description of Section 504, which prohibits schools from denying access to children with disabilities.

State departments of education primarily focus on IDEA violations, but will also look into complaints regarding Section 504. In contrast, the federal OCR is primarily concerned with Section 504 or discrimination violations, but will also investigate IDEA complaints.

Before deciding where to file a complaint, contact your state department of education and the regional office of the OCR and ask the following questions:

- What kinds of complaints do they investigate?
- What is the deadline for filing a complaint? Section 504 complaints must be filed within 180 days of the last alleged act of discrimination against your child. IDEA complaints must be filed within the time established in your state statute of limitations (discussed in Chapter 12).
- How do they handle complaints? In some states, an IDEA or Section 504 complaint is initially investigated by the school district. If you have a choice, opt for an investigator (one who is not associated with your school district) or the state department of education rather than the local school district—you're likely to find greater neutrality the further you move away from the "offending" entity.
- What are their timelines for investigating complaints?
- What remedies are available if the district is found in violation of the law? For example, are you entitled to reimbursement for attorney's fees or the cost of related services?

Notifying the U.S. Department of Education

In addition to filing a complaint, you can notify the U.S. Department of Education, Office of Special Education and Rehabilitation Services, Office of Special Education Programs (OSEP). OSEP won't investigate the problem or issue a decision, but it has overall responsibility for monitoring how states implement IDEA and might consider your comments when conducting its annual review of the programs in your state. You can find contact information in Appendix 2.

C. What to Include in a Complaint

Your state department of education may have a complaint form for you to use. OCR has one, but you aren't required to use it. Whether you use a form or simply write a letter, include the following information:

- Your name and address (a telephone number where you may be reached during business hours is helpful, but not required).
- Your child's name and school district.
- As precise a description as possible of the violation, including the date, time, and location. If you cite more than one violation or you have very broad concerns, be as detailed as possible, describing each violation separately.
- The applicable section of IDEA or any state law, if you know it. Key sections of IDEA are cited throughout this book, and Appendix 1 includes excerpts of IDEA and its regulations. Contact your state department of education (Appendix 2) for state special education laws and regulations.
- The remedy you want, including reimbursement for costs incurred due to the district's violations.

A sample complaint letter is shown below.

Sample Complaint Letter

February 5, 20xx

John Harrington, Director
Compliance Unit
Special Education Division
Department of Education
721 Capitol Mall
Sacramento, CA 95814

Dear Mr. Harrington:

I am formally requesting that you investigate legal violations by the Valley Unified School District, 458 4th Street, Visalia, California. I am making this request pursuant to 34 C.F.R. § 300.660.

The facts in this matter are as follows:

I requested an IEP meeting on October 14, 20xx, just after my child was determined eligible for special education. The school district did not contact us to schedule an IEP meeting until February 2, 20xx, at which time I was told that the meeting would be March 5, 20xx. This violates 34 C.F.R. § 300.343, which provides that an IEP will be held within 30 days of a determination that a child needs special education and related services. I request that an IEP meeting be held within 15 days of the conclusion of your investigation. I also request reimbursement for the cost we incurred to hire a private physical therapist because of the school district's failure to address my child's needs.

Please contact me to confirm receipt of this request, set up times for me to meet with your investigator, and establish timelines for completing the investigation.

Sincerely,

Becky Masteron

Becky Masteron
6004 Green Street
Visalia, CA 95800

Hiring a Lawyer to File a Complaint

Nothing in IDEA prevents you from hiring an attorney to file and pursue a complaint on behalf of your child. If the issues are particularly complex, it might be a good idea to bring in a lawyer. Keep in mind, however, that you are less likely to be reimbursed for your legal fees in the complaint process. While there is always a chance that the school district will pay your attorney fees (particularly if you have a strong case), most families have to pay their own fees if they use an attorney to bring a complaint. If your state department of education investigates your complaint and finds in your favor, nothing in IDEA prevents the department from requiring the school district to pay your legal fees as part of the resolution. Be aware, however that departments are not used to addressing this issue—they may not even know that they can award legal fees.

D. What Happens When You File a Complaint

After you file your complaint, the investigating agency will most likely meet with you to discuss the case, review evidence and records, meet with the school district, and then issue a decision. IDEA requires that the state issue a decision within 60 days after the complaint is filed. If the district is found to have violated IDEA, the agency will make recommendations that the school district must follow to comply with the law. The decision can be appealed to the U.S. Secretary of Education (contact information in Appendix 2).

Due Process and Complaints

You can simultaneously go through due process and file a complaint alleging a legal violation. If the district is found to have violated the law, you would certainly want the fair hearing officer to know. Indeed, if timing permits, you may want to file your complaint first so you can submit the decision as an exhibit at the due process hearing.

14

Lawyers and Legal Research

Lawyers can play an important role in the special education process. While the purpose of this book is to guide you through the IEP process without an attorney, there may be times when you will might need to hire or at least consult a lawyer.

This chapter covers:

- how a lawyer can help with the IEP and other IDEA processes
- whether you need a lawyer
- finding an effective attorney
- how lawyers are paid
- resolving problems with your lawyer, and
- doing your own legal research.

A. How a Lawyer Can Help

Generally speaking, an attorney can help you in one of two ways: A lawyer can provide advice and assistance as needed throughout the IEP process while you do most of the work, or a lawyer can be directly involved as your formal representative.

Here are some of the specific tasks a lawyer can help you with:

- securing your child's school files
- requesting an assessment or an IEP meeting
- helping you find specialists and programs for children with learning disabilities
- preparing for the IEP eligibility meeting
- preparing for the IEP program meeting—including drafting goals and objectives, your child's profile, and program and service descriptions as they relate to her learning disability; reviewing supportive evidence and materials; suggesting who should attend and what material will be most effective; and providing pointers that will help you present your ideas persuasively
- attending an IEP meeting (remember to notify your school district before the meeting if your lawyer will attend)
- reviewing assessments and IEP forms before you sign them
- researching a specific legal issue that applies to your situation
- helping you informally resolve a dispute with the school district
- assessing the strength of your case, if you're considering filing a complaint or pursuing due process
- preparing for and attending mediation and the due process hearing
- writing a post-hearing brief
- preparing a complaint for you to file with the appropriate educational agency, and
- representing you in court.

You may choose to have a lawyer do everything from beginning to end in the IEP process or only handle certain tasks. For example, you might want to attend the IEP meeting yourself but have an attorney review the IEP document before you sign it.

B. Do You Need an Attorney?

Because lawyers can be expensive—and because hiring a lawyer definitely makes the IEP process more adversarial—you'll want to think carefully before bringing in an attorney. Here are some factors to consider:

- **Complexity of the case.** The more complex your case is, the more likely it is that you could benefit from some legal advice. If your dispute involves complicated placement and service issues, for example, it might make sense to bring in a lawyer. Fighting about the difference between two and three hours a week of occupational therapy is pretty straightforward; a dispute over whether your child's learning disabilities require a private school may justify the use of an attorney.
- **Strength of your case.** If you really don't know whether you have a good case against the school district, consider schedul-

ing a consultation with a recommended attorney. (See Section C.) A good attorney should tell you how strong he thinks the case is and, therefore, whether your situation justifies hiring him.

- **Your time and energy.** If you work full-time, are a single parent, or have a difficult schedule, you may want someone else to take charge. On the other hand, if you have the time and energy to represent yourself and your child, hiring an attorney may not be necessary.

- **Your budget.** Attorneys aren't cheap. Can you afford the help? Even though you might be entitled to reimbursement for your legal costs, you must assume your legal costs may not be recouped (See Section D, below.)

- **Your self-confidence.** The purpose of this book is not only to help you advocate for your child, but also to give you the confidence to be an effective advocate. Still, you may prefer to hire a lawyer rather than waging the battle on your own.

- **Who represents the school district.** If the school district is using an attorney, you may want the same protection and leverage.

- **Your relationship with the district.** Hiring a lawyer may change your relationship with the school district. When you involve attorneys, the atmosphere becomes more formal and potentially combative. School personnel will likely be more guarded and may view you as the troublemaker or squeaky wheel. Of course, if you are at the point where you may need an attorney, your relationship with the school district has probably already changed. Ultimately, your child's welfare is more important than maintaining a cordial relationship with the school district. And, as attorneys have become more common participants in IEPs and due process, most school districts have become quite used to us, if not fully happy to see us.

Should Your Lawyer Be an Expert in Learning Disabilities?

If you find a qualified special education attorney who has handled many cases for kids with learning disabilities and has a solid working knowledge of learning disabilities, you've found the best of two worlds. Most special education attorneys will likely have had cases involving learning disabilities. If you find a special education attorney who is not that conversant with learning disability issues, but you really feel she is the right lawyer for your case, ask her how she will develop the learning disability arguments in the case. Remember, your lawyer doesn't have to be an expert in learning disabilities, but should have enough working knowledge to be able to understand the issues, prepare witnesses, and make the necessary factual and legal arguments required in the hearing.

If you are unable to find a special education attorney—which is more likely if you live in a less populated area—your counsel is not likely to know much about learning disabilities. You and others who know your child's needs will have to bring your attorney up to speed. Ultimately, you and your experts will make or break your child's case in mediation or a hearing, not your lawyer. However, your lawyer will need to understand enough about your child's learning disability to know what questions to ask and what answers to seek.

C. Finding an Attorney

Special education attorneys are not as numerous as personal injury or business lawyers. It is also unlikely that attorneys working in more standard areas of law—such as wills and estates, criminal law, family matters, or corporation law—will know anything about special education law.

You may be tempted to hire the attorney who did your will, your sister-in-law who just graduated from law school, or the attorney whose ad in the phone book promises the lowest rates. But special education law is highly specialized. Hiring an attorney who does not know the law or have experience in special education will significantly increase your chance of failure and can ultimately cost you more rather than less. When you pay an attorney, you are paying for all the time she spends on your case, including the time she spends doing research. You don't want to pay an attorney for on-the-job training, nor do you want to hire an attorney who won't be able to master the subject matter and legal issues quickly enough to serve you and your child well.

1. Compile a List of Potential Attorneys

To find the "right" lawyer, you'll need to compile a list of potential candidates. Here's how:

- Ask other parents in the school district.
- Ask your pediatrician or other health care professionals.
- If you are working with or know learning disability specialists, ask them.
- Ask school district personnel—the district is required to maintain a list of special education attorneys and other advocacy resources for parents.
- Contact your state special education advisory commission. IDEA requires each state to have a special education commission, comprised of educators and parents, which advises the state about special education. The commissioners should have numerous special education contacts.
- Contact your state department of education and ask for referrals. (See Appendix 2.)
- Contact a nearby Parent Training and Information Center (PTI). (See Appendix 3.)
- Contact a local disability rights advocacy organization. (See Appendix 3.)

- Contact a low-cost or free legal clinic, such as legal aid—while most offices focus on common civil issues (such as domestic disputes or evictions), some offices do special education work for low-income people.
- Use your personal network—friends, colleagues, neighbors, or coworkers who know special education lawyers or who know lawyers who can recommend good special education lawyers.

Nonprofit Legal Clinics

There are nonprofit organizations that provide legal assistance in special education, disability rights, or what is generally called "public interest law." Your school district should have a list of disability-specific or special education nonprofit legal clinics in your area. Also see the organizations listed in Appendix 3.

There are advantages and disadvantages to using a nonprofit legal clinic rather than a private attorney. Advantages to using a nonprofit include:

- The attorneys probably have worked in special education and handled many cases.
- Nonprofits often do not charge for their services or have significantly reduced rates.
- Nonprofits, particularly disability-focused offices, have special knowledge and often a strong passion about the issues.

But there are disadvantages to using a nonprofit:

- Demand is often greater than supply; you may have to wait some time for an appointment, even to have someone assess your case.
- Nonprofit organizations often have limited resources—some focus on either precedent-setting cases (unusual disputes) or cases that will have an impact on a large number of children—and may not handle individual cases.

How Not to Find a Special Education Lawyer

There are several bad ways to find a special education lawyer. Avoid these traps for the unwary:

- **Heavily advertised legal clinics.** While they may offer low flat rates for routine services such as drafting a will, most make their money on personal injury cases. We are not aware of any such clinics offering special education help.
- **Referral panels set up by local bar associations.** Bar association panels do only minimal (if any) screening before qualifying lawyers as experts in certain areas. While you might get a good referral from these panels, it is highly unlikely there will even be a special education attorney listed.
- **Private referral services.** When it comes to services that advertise on TV and billboards, forget it. It is highly unlikely they offer any special education help. Even if they say they do, we would still avoid this route.

2. Call the Attorneys on Your List

Once you have a list of recommended attorneys, either you can narrow it down to one or two individuals who were enthusiastically recommended or you can make initial contact with everyone on your list.

Try to have a brief phone conversation or ask for a short meeting. Some attorneys will briefly chat with you over the phone to determine the nature of your case and whether or not you need an attorney. Other attorneys may have you speak with an assistant, complete a form describing your case, or make an appointment to come in and talk about the case. Some attorneys will not talk to you without at least a minor retainer or fee; others will not charge for the first discussion. Before making an appointment, find out the following information:

- the attorney's fee
- how the attorney will review the case and decide whether or not you should proceed
- how much the initial review costs, and
- whether you can talk briefly to decide if it's worth sending in a retainer. (If your case is complicated, this might not be an option—you can't expect an attorney to listen to an hour-long explanation of your child's situation during an initial screening call.)

3. Meet With the Best Candidates

Make an appointment with those candidates who seem like the best prospects. Naturally, if there is a fee for the initial intake, you may only want to see a few attorneys. Be sure to ask the attorney what records she needs to evaluate your case.

When you meet with an attorney, you should ask about your specific case, of course. You should also ask about the attorney's:

- years of experience
- specific experience with special education and learning disabilities
- experience with your particular legal issue (such as a due process hearing)
- knowledge of special education law and the IEP process
- experience with your school district
- general style—is the attorney confrontational or cooperative (for example, does he like mediation or think it's a waste of time?)
- references (you may ask for references when you first call), and
- fees.

Does the attorney clearly answer your questions about fees, experience, and your specific legal issues? Does the attorney objectively assess your chances in due process? If the lawyer makes you uncomfortable, think carefully about whether his expertise and success rate is worth putting up with a difficult style.

Will the attorney provide the type of help you want? Is the attorney willing to advise you now, but hold off on full participation unless and until you need it? If the attorney wants to take over the case but you only want a consultant, you have the wrong attorney.

Will the attorney be accessible? This is important: The most common complaint about lawyers is that they don't return phone calls, respond to faxes or email, or make themselves available when a client calls. Discuss the attorney's response time. While no attorney should be expected to respond instantly, you shouldn't have to wait more than a day or two, except in rare circumstances.

Client's Responsibility in Working With an Attorney

Your attorney should be responsive and courteous, and keep you informed. But the client-attorney relationship is a two-way street. Keep the following in mind:

- Vague questions are likely to receive vague responses; be clear and specific when you discuss matters or ask questions.
- No matter how good an attorney is, the quality of the case—that is, the strength of the evidence—is the key to success. Your attorney cannot transform a bad case into a good one.
- You have responsibility for controlling your legal bill. Be especially aware of time. If you talk to your lawyer for 30 minutes, you will normally be billed for 30 minutes, even if you feel you were "just chatting." Remember that legal time seems to add up in a parallel universe—one where minutes turn into hours in the blink of an eye.
- You cannot call up an attorney, chat for five minutes, and have your problem resolved. I frequently receive phone calls that go something like this:

  "Hello. I have a question about special education. Do you know special education law?"

  "Yes."

"My daughter has an IEP on Thursday. She is learning disabled and I want her placed in a private school. The school district has offered a special day class. What do you recommend?"

Any attorney who tries to answer that question without knowing all of the facts is doing a disservice to himself and the caller. And the caller is being remarkably unfair. I will try to answer simple questions over the phone from first-time callers—such as, "Can you tell me if a school has to do an assessment of a child before the child enters special education?"—but most questions are more complicated than that. It is unfair to assume that an attorney can either provide a simple answer to a complex question or provide free advice.

One final suggestion from an attorney: Courtesy and respect for the attorney's time go a long way. It can be very off-putting to get a call from someone who presumes that I am prepared to provide free advice. On the other hand, when strangers call and say something like "Can I take 2 minutes of your time," or "Do you have a moment? I'd be happy to pay for a brief call," I will do my best to try to answer the caller's questions, without any thought about my fee.

4. Ask for a Case Evaluation

A good attorney will evaluate the evidence before giving you any advice. After reviewing your case materials, a good special education attorney should be able to:

- tell you the strength of your case
- explain the process
- evaluate your documents and potential witnesses

- tell you if additional supportive material is needed
- estimate the cost of hiring an attorney for due process or beyond
- estimate how long your case may take
- provide insights into school district personnel, particularly if the attorney has worked with the district before, and
- provide a cost-benefit analysis of hiring the attorney to represent you versus using the attorney as an advisor only.

5. A Word on an Attorney's Style

Some attorneys are pleasant, patient, and good listeners. Others are unpleasant, impatient, and bad listeners. Although you may want the former, you may get the latter. Whatever the style of your attorney, make it clear that you know the attorney is busy, but you expect him to treat you courteously, explain matters, keep you fully posted about what is happening, and include you as an active partner in the process. An effective professional relationship must be based on mutual respect.

Furthermore, the attorney should contact you regarding any decision to be made, whether scheduling a meeting, deciding on tactics, reviewing a key issue, or considering a possible resolution of the dispute.

If at any time you don't understand what your attorney has said, requested, or planned, ask for clarification. If the answer isn't clear, ask again. Although you hired the attorney because of his professional expertise and knowledge—and therefore have relinquished a certain amount of control—it does not mean you should be kept in the dark.

D. How Attorneys Are Paid

How you pay your lawyer depends on the type of legal services you need and the amount of legal work involved. Once you choose a lawyer, ask for a written agreement explaining how fees and costs will be billed and paid. In some states, a written agreement is required by law; even if it isn't, you should always ask for one. A good attorney will provide you with a written contract (whether you ask or not). Be sure to tell the lawyer how much you are able (and willing) to spend—if you and the lawyer agree on a cap or limit on legal fees, that should also go into your fee agreement.

As your case progresses, you'll want to make sure you receive a bill or statement at least once a month. If your lawyer will be delegating some of the work to a less experienced associate, paralegal, or secretary, the delegated work should be billed at a lower hourly rate. Make sure this is stated in your written fee agreement.

1. Lawyers' Billing Methods

Lawyers charge for their services in three different ways.

Hourly rate. Most special education attorneys charge by the hour. In most parts of the U.S., you can secure competent representation for $100-$250 an hour. Many clients prefer an hourly rate to a flat fee (discussed next) because you pay only for the actual time the lawyer spends on your case. Comparison shopping among lawyers can help you avoid overpaying, but only if you compare lawyers with similar expertise. A highly experienced special education attorney (who has a higher hourly rate) may be cheaper in the long run than a general practitioner (at a lower rate). The special education attorney won't have to research routine questions and usually can evaluate your case quickly.

SO MUCH FOR THE SMALL TALK! HOW MUCH DO YOU CHARGE?

Legal Time

How much time your attorney will spend on your case depends on the nature of your dispute. Here are some general guidelines for the amount of time it might take a good lawyer to do some common legal tasks in the IEP process:

- initial review of your records and interview with you .... 2-3 hours
- helping you with the IEP process— developing a blueprint; contacting assessors and school personnel; drafting goals and objectives .... 2-5 hours
- attending the IEP meeting .... 2-4 hours (per meeting)
- preparing for and attending mediation session .... 3-8 hours
- preparing for and attending fair hearing .... 10-35 hours

Flat rate. A flat rate is a single fee that will cover all the work the lawyer has agreed to do—for example, prepare for and attend the IEP meeting or prepare for and conduct the fair hearing. You are obligated to pay the flat fee no matter how many hours the lawyer spends on your case, assuming the lawyer does the work. A flat fee can be quite economical if the fee is reasonable and you anticipate a lot of work. On the other hand, if the case is resolved early in the process, you may end up paying much more than you would have paid in hourly fees. Most special education attorneys charge by the hour and may be unwilling to work on a flat fee.

Contingency fee. Contingency fee arrangements are rarely used in special education cases. A contingency fee is a percentage of whatever money the party wins; if you don't win anything, the attorney gets nothing. Because almost all successful special education cases will require the school district to provide a program or service rather than pay an award of money, don't expect a special education attorney to work on a contingency.

Legal Costs

In addition to the fees they charge for their time, lawyers bill for a variety of expenses they incur. These costs, which can add up quickly, may include charges for:

- photocopies
- faxes
- postage
- overnight mail
- messenger services
- expert witness fees
- court filing fees
- long distance phone calls
- process servers
- work by investigators
- work by legal assistants or paralegals
- deposition transcripts
- online legal research, and
- travel.

Some lawyers absorb the cost of photocopies, faxes, online legal research, and local phone calls as normal office overhead, but that's not always the case. When working out the fee arrangement, ask for a list of costs you'll be expected to pay. If the lawyer seems intent on nickel-and-diming you or hitting you with a $5 per page fax charge, you should talk to him. While this may not reflect the attorney's skills or ability to win a case, it does raise some red flags about how he does business.

2. Reimbursement for Legal Fees and Costs

If you hire an attorney and pay for his services, *and* you prevail in due process (at a mediation or fair hearing), you are entitled to be reimbursed by the school district for your attorney's fees and other due process costs. (20 U.S.C. § 1415(i)(3); 34 C.F.R. § 300.513.)

But your right to reimbursement can be limited. First, you are not entitled to reimbursement for the fees you paid an attorney to attend the IEP meeting, unless the meeting was required as part of due process. This might happen if the fair hearing officer orders a second IEP meeting to discuss matters that were improperly omitted from the first meeting.

Second, you are not entitled to reimbursement if the school district makes a settlement offer ten days before the due process hearing, you reject the offer, *and* the hearing officer finds that what you actually won in due process is no better than the school district's settlement offer. If the hearing officer finds that you were substantially justified in rejecting the settlement offer, however, you are entitled to full reimbusement. What constitutes "substantially justified" is not defined in IDEA.

Third, the hearing officer can reduce the amount of attorney's fees to which you are entitled if the officer finds that any of the following are true:

- You unreasonably protracted or extended the final resolution of the controversy.
- The attorney's fees unreasonably exceed hourly rates charged by other attorneys in the community for similar services.
- The time and services provided by the attorney were excessive.
- The attorney failed to provide certain information required by law. (34 C.F.R. § 300.513 (c)(4).)

You should carefully discuss these reimbursement issues with your attorney before you evaluate any settlement offers or decide whether to request a fair hearing.

3. Reducing Legal Fees

There are several ways to control legal fees.

Be organized. Especially when you are paying by the hour, it's important to gather important documents, write a short chronology of events, and concisely explain the problem to your lawyer. Keep a copy of everything you give to the lawyer.

Be prepared before you meet your lawyer. Whenever possible, put your questions in writing and mail, fax, or deliver them to your lawyer before all meetings or phone conversations. Early preparation also helps focus the meeting so there is less chance of digressing (at your expense) into unrelated topics.

Carefully review lawyer bills. Like everyone else, lawyers make mistakes. For example, .1 of an hour (six minutes) may be transposed into a 1. (one hour) when the data is entered into the billing system. That's $200 instead of $20 if your lawyer charges $200 per hour. Don't hesitate to question your bill. You have the right to a clear explanation of costs.

Ask your lawyer what work you can do. There are some things you can do to save time. For example, you could go through the school's record and highlight key statements. Or you could talk with important witnesses to find out their attitudes about key issues in the case. Some attorneys may be comfortable with you doing substantial work, others won't. Be sure to discuss this ahead of time.

Listen to your lawyer. Certainly, lawyers deserve some of the criticism that comes their way; there's a reason why lawyers are the subject of a separate book of New Yorker jokes. But large legal bills are sometimes the result of clients losing track of time and/or ignoring advice. I have had clients to whom I have carefully, clearly, and repeatedly explained why I thought pursuing a particular argument was a waste of time or had little chance of success, yet the client persisted in pressing forward, despite my advice. When the argument ultimately failed, all that was left was a legal bill. As a client, you should not be afraid to question your attorney's recommendation. But part of what you're paying for is reasonable and objective advice—and when she says not to waste time on an issue, you should probably listen.

E. Resolving Problems With a Lawyer

If you see a problem brewing with your lawyer, don't just sit back and fume. Call or write your lawyer. Whatever it is that rankles—a high bill, a missed deadline, or a strategic move you don't understand—have an honest discussion about your feelings. Be prepared to state your concerns and listen objectively to your lawyer's side of the misunderstanding.

If you can't frankly discuss these matters with your lawyer or you are unsatisfied with the outcome of any discussion, it's time to consider finding another attorney. If you don't, you may waste money on unnecessary legal fees and risk having matters turn out badly.

If you decide to change lawyers, be sure to end the first professional relationship before you hire a new attorney. If you don't, you could find yourself being billed by two lawyers at the same time. Also, be sure all important legal documents are returned to you. Tell your new lawyer what your old one has done to date and pass on the file.

Here are some tips on resolving specific problems:

- If you have a dispute over fees, the local bar association may be able to mediate it for you.
- If a lawyer has violated legal ethics—for example, had a conflict of interest, over-billed you, or didn't represent you professionally—the state agency that licenses lawyers may discipline the lawyer.
- Where a major mistake has been made—for example, a lawyer missed the fair hearing deadline for submitting the witness list and exhibits—you might even consider suing for malpractice. Lawyers carry malpractice insurance.

Remember, while there will be times when you question your attorney's tactics, you have hired someone because of his expertise and experience. Before confronting the attorney, ask yourself whether the attorney misfired or you are overreacting.

Your Rights as a Client

As a client, you have the right to expect the following:

- courteous treatment by your lawyer and staff members
- an itemized statement of services rendered and a full explanation, in advance, of billing practices
- charges for agreed-upon fees and nothing more
- prompt responses to phone calls and letters
- confidential legal conferences, free from unwarranted interruptions
- up-to-date information on the status of your case
- diligent and competent legal representation, and
- clear answers to all questions.

A final word on attorneys: We live in a time when public attitudes about attorneys are negative, to some degree rightfully so. There are, however, many conscientious attorneys, particularly in special education. A high percentage of the special education attorneys I've run across in my 25 years of practice have been compassionate, able, and decent professionals.

F. Doing Your Own Legal Research

Using this book is a good way to educate yourself about the laws that affect your rights as a parent of a special education child. Chapter 2 has already provided you with much of the key legal language of IDEA. Because the laws and court decisions of 50 states are involved, however, no one book can give you all the information you might need.

There's a lot you can do on your own, once you understand a few basics about law libraries, statute books, court opinions, and the general reference books that lawyers use to learn about issues. Some basic legal research skills can help you determine how strong your case is and the best and most effective way to go forward. Whether the issue is private school placement, the type or amount of a related service, an assessment question, or an eligibility issue, IDEA and judicial decisions can help you judge the strength of your case.

Using the Library

Look for a law library that's open to the public—there may be one in your main county courthouse or at your state capitol. Law librarians, who increasingly have experience working with nonlawyers, can help you find the appropriate resources. Publicly funded law schools generally permit the public to use their libraries, and some private law schools grant access to the public, sometimes for a modest fee.

If you can't find an accessible law library, don't overlook the public library. Many large public libraries have sizable legal reference collections, including state and federal statutes. Also, if you work with a lawyer, ask about using the research materials at your lawyer's office.

Examples:

- You want your child in a private school that has an identical program to the one available in your school district. Legal research should lead you to the conclusion that your position isn't a winning one. The law is clear: There is no right to a private school in this situation.
- Your child needs a multisensory approach to address his learning disability. You do some research and find that IDEA does not require the IEP team to include a teaching methodology, but you also find cases stating that, if the evidence supports the need, the hearing officer can rule in your favor.
- Your child is going into the 10th grade and continues to have significant difficulties with handwriting and using the computer keyboard. He also has had some behavioral problems and was suspended in the 9th grade. The district wants to place him in a special class for learning disabled students at a small alternative high school. You visit a law library and discover that in the case of *Board of Education v. Holland*, 4 F.3d 1398 (9th Circuit, 1994), the court established rules for determining whether a child is entitled to be mainstreamed, including:
  - ▲ the academic and nonacademic benefits to the child
  - ▲ the effect of the placement on the teacher and other students, and
  - ▲ the cost of the aids and services needed to mainstream.

The materials you can research include:

- IDEA statutes and regulations (excerpts are in Appendix 1)
- state statutes
- court cases interpreting IDEA and other relevant statutes
- explanatory documents, such as the U.S. Department of Education policy guidelines and correspondence—these documents do not have the authority of a statute or court case, but they reflect the Department's analysis of the law.
- fair hearing decisions (available through your state department of education and the *Individuals with Disabilities Education Law Reporter*, discussed below)—although these are binding only on the parties to that specific hearing, they may be of value to you in showing how hearing officers make decisions in your state, and
- law review and other articles about IDEA and special education issues.

1. Individuals With Disabilities Education Act (IDEA): Where to Find It

Like all federal laws, IDEA is found in a multivolume series of books called the United States Code (U.S.C.), which is available in most libraries or online. The U.S.C. consists of separate numbered titles, each covering a specific subject matter. IDEA is found in Title 20, beginning with Section 1400. Appendix 1 includes a copy of key sections of the IDEA statute and regulations.

You can find annotated versions of the U.S.C., which include not only the text of the IDEA, but also summaries of cases that interpret IDEA and a reference to where each case can be found. Annotated codes also list articles that discuss IDEA. Annotated codes have comprehensive indexes by topic and are kept up to date with paperback supplements (called pocket parts) found inside the back cover of each volume or in a separate

paperback volume. Supplements include changes to IDEA and recent cases.

Your school district is required to provide you with copies of federal law—that is, the statutes and regulations of IDEA. Your school district, however, is not required to inform you of any legal decisions on IDEA. One source of up-to-date information, including policy guidelines on the IDEA, is the U.S. Department of Education. (See Appendix 2.) But that's not the only source.

Special newsletters provide extensive detail about most fields of law. Special education has one such publication called the *Individuals with Disabilities Education Law Reporter* (IDELR). It is published by LRP Publications (contact information is in Appendix 3). IDELR issues a bimonthly highlights newsletter, along with the written decisions of IDEA court rulings, fair hearing decisions, Department of Education policy statements, and other information. IDELR has a subject index, making it easy to locate the specific cases you want to review. At a current cost of $890 per year, IDELR is aimed at special education lawyers and school districts.

Some law libraries subscribe to IDELR—call the nearest law libraries and ask. Some school districts also subscribe. If this fails, contact a local nonprofit special education or disability organization in your area and ask if they receive IDELR.

2. State Statutes

As noted in Chapter 2, each state has passed a law that parallels or even exceed the rights under IDEA. You should take a look at your state's special education laws, which are available in many public libraries and all law libraries.

Most states also make their statutes available online. (See Section G, below.) In some states, statutes are organized by subject matter, with each title, chapter, or code covering a particular legal area—for example, the vehicle code or the corporations code. Most states have some kind of education code. In some states, statutes are simply numbered sequentially without regard to subject matter, which means that you'll have to use the index to find what you need. State codes are like the federal U.S.C., with annotated volumes, indexes, and pocket parts.

Some states have their own regulations implementing special education laws; check with your state department of education for information about these regulations.

Appendix 2 includes addresses, phone numbers, and websites of state departments of education.

3. Court Decisions

When Congress passes a law, it cannot address every possible situation or clarify what each section of the law means. It is the job of a court—federal or state—to interpret the applicable laws and apply them to particular facts. The court will often explain, clarify, and even expand or limit what actually appears in a statute. These court decisions are often referred to as "case law."

Court decisions are published in state or federal reporters. Each decision has a name and a citation, indicating the volume, name, and page of the reporter in which it appears the court that issued the decision, and the year of the decision. With the citation, you can locate the printed decision.

Example:

The first special education case to reach the U.S. Supreme Court was *Rowley v. Board of Education*. It concerned a deaf child who needed a sign language interpreter in her regular classroom. The U.S. Supreme Court said she didn't need one, because she was passing from grade to grade (even though not having an interpreter caused her to miss 40% of classroom communication).

The case was first decided by a federal trial court: the case citation is 483 F. Supp.

536 (S.D.N.Y. 1980). This means that the case can be found in volume 483 of a reporter called the Federal Supplement, starting at page 536. The court that issued the decision was the federal court for the Southern District of New York. The case was decided in 1980.

That decision was appealed, and the case citation of the appeal is 623 F.2d 945 (2d Cir. 1980). This means that the decision of the appellate court can be found in volume 623 of the Federal Report (2d Series), starting at page 945. The court that ruled on the appeal was the Second Circuit Court of Appeals. The appeal was decided in 1980.

The citation for the U.S. Supreme Court decision is 102 S.Ct 3034 (1982). The decision can be found in volume 102 of the Supreme Court Reports, starting at page 3034. The court decided the case in 1982.

Although IDEA gives you or the school district the option of appealing a due process decision to a state court, most cases involving a federal law such as IDEA are decided by the federal courts. Each state has a unique case reporting system, but decisions are usually found in regional reporters. For example, in the case of *State of Connecticut v. Bruno*, 673 A.2d 1117 (Conn. 1996), the decision was published in volume 673 of the regional law reporter called the Atlantic Second Series and begins on page 1117. The case comes from the state of Connecticut (not surprising given the name of the case) and was decided in 1996.

4. Finding Cases About Learning Disabilities

Every decision a court issues is specific to the facts of that case. Even though a case addresses the same underlying legal concepts as yours, it might be very different, factually, from your child's situation. When you come across a case involving a learning disabled student, remember that the facts of the case will dictate the extent to which it applies to your child and your claims.

You'll find learning disability cases that interpret every aspect of IDEA, including assessment, educational methodology, eligibility, placement, services, suspension, and expulsion. Because the facts of each case are different and because IDEA requires an appropriate education for each individual child, you will not find any court saying that a particular kind of methodology or placement is always required for students with learning disabilities. Instead, the court will be deciding whether IDEA procedures and rules were followed in the context of a particular factual situation and for one particular child.

On rare occasions, a court will make a very broad and important decision. For example, in a famous case in 1986, a federal court ruled that IQ tests were not valid for determining whether African-American students have learning disabilities. (*Larry P. v. Riles*, 793 F2d 969 (9th Cir. 1984).) It is very unusual, however, for a court to make this kind of blanket ruling.

If you use IDELR, you can find cases on learning disabilities in the *Topical Index/Current Decisions*. Each Topical Index/Current Decision book will cover those cases reprinted in particular IDELR volumes; as of the writing of this chapter, IDELR is up to Volume 38. Most of the Indexes cover two to three volumes. The topics are arranged alphabetically. You can find learning disability cases under the heading "Specific Learning Disability," which in turn is divided up into subcategories such as Educational Methodologies, Eligibility Criteria, Identification and Evaluation, Placement, and so on. Cases are listed under each of the subcategories.

IDELR reprints not only court case decisions but also decisions made by fair hearing officers (usually referred to as SEA or state educational agency decisions) and the Office of Civil Rights (which investigates § 504 complaints). IDELR also includes IDEA policy analysis by the U.S. Department of Education, Office of Special Education Programs (OSEP). Court decisions will have the

most potential impact, but the SEA, OCR, and OSEP decisions and policy determinations, particularly the OSEP letters, can be of real value to you and your child. The OSEP letters on policy indicate how the department interprets IDEA. Because court cases, SEA decisions, and even OCR complaints are so fact-specific, their application to your child's case may be limited. The OSEP letters have a broader application because they deal not so much with particular facts, but with policy and the meaning of IDEA.

 Further Reading on Legal Research. *Legal Research: How to Find & Understand the Law*, by Stephen Elias and Susan Levinkind (Nolo), gives easy-to-use, step-by-step instructions on how to find legal information.

When you research cases, make sure the case you find has not been overturned or replaced by a more recent court decision. You can check this through a set of books known as Shepard's. A friendly law librarian might have the time and patience to guide you through this process—if not, Nolo's *Legal Research* book has an easy-to-follow explanation of how to use the Shepard's system to expand and update your research.

When you find a court decision, there will be a short synopsis of the decision at the beginning. This synopsis not only will help you determine whether the case is relevant to your situation, but also will tell you what the court decided. After the case synopsis there will be a list of numbered items, each item followed by a short summary. The numbers (1, 2, 3, and so on) refer to the location in the written decision where that legal issue is discussed.

Keep in mind that your situation may or may not relate exactly to a particular court decision. It will depend on how similar the facts are and whether your situation and the legal decision involve the same sections of IDEA. The more alike the facts and pertinent parts of IDEA, the more you can use the decision to your advantage. But the existence of a case that supports your position does not mean that the school district has to apply or even abide by that decision. It is certainly a very persuasive precedent, but it is just an example of how one court has ruled in a similar situation.

If the decision was reached by the U.S. Supreme Court, the federal court of appeals covering your state, your federal district court, or your state supreme court, the case represents the law in your area. Decisions in other federal circuits can be useful as long as there is not a different legal standard in your circuit.

If you find a case that is similar to yours and the decision is a good one, think about discussing the case in a letter to your school district, explaining why you believe you will prevail in due process.

⚠ **Do legal research with care.** Analyzing case law and the meaning and reach of legal statutes can be complicated. Make sure you know what you're talking about before you cite the law. While you can learn a good deal, becoming expert at legal research requires care, time, and training. Proceed carefully and use what you learn with real caution.

Letter Encouraging School Board Settlement

Date: April 20, 20xx

To: Howard Yankolon, Superintendent
     Eugene School District
     15578 South Main Street
     Eugene, OR 00000

Re: Clara Centler, student in Westside School, 5th grade

I appreciated your efforts at the April 14, 20xx IEP meeting; as you know, we are in disagreement about Clara's need for a one-to-one aide so she can be mainstreamed.

I have requested a fair hearing. I have also done some research on this matter and determined that the facts and the law in the U.S. Supreme Court's decision in *Board of Education v. Holland* are almost identical to our dispute. I strongly believe that with the Supreme Court's direction in that case, it would be a real waste of time and district money to go to due process.

I am therefore requesting that you consider this and meet with me to discuss a possible settlement of our differences.

Sincerely,

Stuart Centler

Stuart Centler
78 Pine Avenue
Eugene, OR 00000
Phones: 555-5543 (home); 555-0933 (work)

G. Online Legal Research

Every day, a growing number of basic legal resources are available online through the Internet. There are a number of different ways to use the Internet to search for material, but by far the most important and common tool for doing research on the Internet is the World Wide Web. The Web provides links among documents and makes it easy to jump from one resource to another. Each resource is organized graphically like a book, allowing you to skip from topic to topic.

In addition, a wide variety of secondary sources intended for both lawyers and the general public have been posted on the Internet by law schools and firms. If you are on the Web, for example, a good way to find these sources is to visit any of the following websites, each of which provides links to legal information by specific subject.

- www.nolo.com. Nolo's Internet site contains helpful articles, information about new legislation, and a legal reseach center you can use to find state and federal statutes.
- www.law.cornell.edu. This site is maintained by Cornell Law School. You can find the text of the U.S. Code, federal court decisions, and some state court decisions. You can also search for material by topic.

- www.law.indiana.edu/v-lib. This site is maintained by Indiana University's School of Law at Bloomington. You can search by organization, including the U.S. government, state governments, and law journals, or by topic.
- www.access.gpo.gov/nara/cfr/. This site provides the entire Federal Code of Regulations.
- www.statelocalgov.net/index.cfm. This comprehensive site provides links to state and local government websites. Look here to find a link to your state's department of education, your county government's site, and perhaps even a website for your city or town.

In addition, Appendix 3 includes a section entitled "Legal Resources for Parents of a Special Education Child." These resources include websites that offer a wealth of legal and practical material on special education. ■

15

Parent Organizations

The first word in IDEA is "Individuals." Special education law, philosophy, and approach are based on the individual child, which makes it somewhat difficult to approach special education from a collective or group perspective. Each IEP is different, which is why this book has focused on strategies and procedures for parents who are acting alone.

There are, however, situations in which a group of parents working together can have a tremendous impact on a school district and the programs available for children with learning disabilities. Because the "specific learning disability" category under IDEA is the largest, you are going to find some parents in your school district whose children have learning disabilities. When a group of parents approaches a school to recommend changes, the school is more likely to take notice. A parent group can also serve as an invaluable resource for information and support as you navigate the special education process.

A. Join a Parent Organization

There are many ways to find an existing parent group. You can start by getting in touch with the local PTA. In addition, most school districts have a parent advisory committee (sometimes referred to as CACs or Community Advisory Committees) specifically formed for special education matters. If you haven't already done so, contact your school district to find out about that committee. Usually, these committees are composed of special education professionals and other parents. If you can't find information on a local group, try the state level. Appendix 3 contains a state-by-state list of Parent Training and Information Centers (PTIs). PTIs are parent-to-parent organizations that can provide advice, training, and even advocacy help.

Because a majority of children in special education have learning disabilities, you may be able to find a local parents' group that deals only with learning disability issues. You should also take a look at Appendix 3 for a list of national organizations serving children with learning disabilities. You can contact them to determine if there are any local, regional, or state affiliates.

A parent organization can help you in several ways:

- There is strength in numbers. School districts often pay more attention to two parents than one, four parents than two, ten parents than five.
- A parent group can provide you with all kinds of important information about the school administrator, staff, existing classes, the local IEP process, and outside support professionals, such as independent assessors, private service providers, private schools, and attorneys.
- A parent group can offer you plenty of information and resources for you, can suggest successful educational strategies and methodologies geared for your child, and may even have sophisticated knowledge about IDEA and its legal mandates.
- A parent group can provide the emotional support and advice you will need as you wind your way through the special education process.

⚠️ **Community advisory committees may include school district representatives.** School personnel regularly attend meetings of these committees, so parents may find it difficult to speak frankly. This is not to say you shouldn't trust or include school personnel, but you should recognize that there may be times when the presence of school personnel inhibit honest discussion of certain issues. If this is the only organization in your area, consider forming an independent parent organization.

B. Form a Parent Organization

If your community doesn't have a parent organization, the existing group is too tied to or influenced by the school district, or the existing group doesn't meet your needs, you can organize a new group. How do you begin?

First, consider how wide or narrow you want your focus to be. If you want to form a specialized group that deals only with learning disabilities, you may have to sacrifice size for specificity. If you open your group up to parents whose children have any type of disability, you'll have a larger group, with more general goals. The strength that comes from a large group can often offset the challenges that come with a diversity of concerns. But even if you can only put together a small group, you should find it helpful. You don't need a lot of people. Three or four parents can be quite effective.

Sometimes a few simple phone calls will lead to very useful recommendations. Here's how to get started and prepare for your first meeting:

- Invite all possible parents who fit within your chosen scope.
- Ask them for agenda ideas, focusing on common issues and concerns.
- Ask them for the names of other parents to invite.
- Ask your child's teacher or pediatrician for names of other parents to invite.
- Ask the PTA and your school district to announce the meeting or to include information on it in any mailings.
- Place an announcement in your local newspaper.
- Contact local disability organizations. They may be able to connect you with other parent support groups in your state. They may also be able to advise you if you encounter problems. (Appendix 3 lists learning disability organizations.)

Your Child's Privacy

Before you get involved in a parents' group, you should consider your older child's feelings about privacy. We all know that the teenage years are a time of significant emotional and physical growth, when your child will have to face important social and identity issues. Will your active involvement in a parent group compromise her sense of independence? Should you talk to her before proceeding to be sure that her sense of privacy and self-confidence won't be compromised? Does she want you to take such a high profile stance and is she comfortable with you using her name as you become involved in school organizing? There are of course no hard and fast answers—you'll have to talk to your child to figure out how to proceed.

At your first meeting, you can decide how formal you want to be and what issues you want to focus on. If you take the formal route, you'll need to select a name, elect officers, decide whether to charge dues (and, if so, how much), collect those dues, and establish regular meetings.

No matter how formal or informal you are, you will need to spend some time discussing your purpose and what you hope to accomplish. Do you simply want to establish better ties with the school administration? Do you want to address specific concerns, such as the quality of a particular class, intimidation by school personnel during the IEP process, or certain procedures that you find unfair? Once you decide which issues you want to tackle, you can figure out how to formally contact the district and raise your concerns.

At later meetings, consider inviting guests, such as representatives of the school district or a local special education attorney. The attorney will probably charge for his time. Your dues or an additional contribution from each family can cover the cost. Also, consider developing a newsletter (online is easiest) to stay in touch and share ideas with other parents in your area.

Ultimately, a successful group will develop important contacts with the district, represent a collective "strength" that can affect district decision-making, and provide a way to express specific concerns directly and powerfully.

Get Involved With the School District

Whether you work alone or with a group, there are many ways to improve your child's educational program through direct involvement with the school district. Volunteer at school or in the administrative office, run for school board, or assist in school fundraisers. Generally, this kind of activity gets you involved, opens doors, and allows you to meet the people in charge. This often can foster a good relationship with school personnel, making it easier for you to pick up the phone and call about—and resolve—a problem.

The same advice goes for your parent group. You should meet with the district on a somewhat regular basis, to find out how you can help the school. Build a relationship between your group and the school. Ultimately, you and the school district really do have the same goal (if unfortunately not the necessary budget or time): to help your child grow into an effective, productive, and happy adult.

Appendix 1

Special Education Law and Regulations

Individuals With Disabilities Education Act (Key Sections)

Sec. 1401. Definitions

Except as otherwise provided, as used in this chapter:

(1) Assistive technology device. The term "assistive technology device" means any item, piece of equipment, or product system, whether acquired commercially off the shelf, modified, or customized, that is used to increase, maintain, or improve functional capabilities of a child with a disability.

(2) Assistive technology service. The term "assistive technology service" means any service that directly assists a child with a disability in the selection, acquisition, or use of an assistive technology device. Such term includes:

(A) the evaluation of the needs of such child, including a functional evaluation of the child in the child's customary environment;

(B) purchasing, leasing, or otherwise providing for the acquisition of assistive technology devices by such child;

(C) selecting, designing, fitting, customizing, adapting, applying, maintaining, repairing, or replacing of assistive technology devices;

(D) coordinating and using other therapies, interventions, or services with assistive technology devices, such as those associated with existing education and rehabilitation plans and programs;

(E) training or technical assistance for such child, or, where appropriate, the family of such child; and

(F) training or technical assistance for professionals (including individuals providing education and rehabilitation services), employers, or other individuals who provide services to, employ, or are otherwise substantially involved in the major life functions of such child.

(3) Child with a disability

(A) *In general.* The term "child with a disability" means a child:

(i) with mental retardation, hearing impairments (including deafness), speech or language impairments, visual impairments (including blindness), serious emotional disturbance (hereinafter referred to as "emotional disturbance"), orthopedic impairments, autism, traumatic brain injury, other health impairments, or specific learning disabilities; and

(ii) who, by reason thereof, needs special education and related services.

(B) *Child aged 3 through 9.* The term "child with a disability" for a child aged 3 through 9 may, at the discretion of the State and the local educational agency, include a child:

(i) experiencing developmental delays, as defined by the State and as measured by appropriate diagnostic instruments and procedures, in one or more of the following areas: physical development, cognitive development, communication development, social or emotional development, or adaptive development; and

(ii) who, by reason thereof, needs special education and related services.

(4) Educational service agency. The term "educational service agency":

(A) means a regional public multiservice agency:

(i) authorized by State law to develop, manage, and provide services or programs to local educational agencies; and

(ii) recognized as an administrative agency for purposes of the provision of special education and related services provided within public elementary and secondary schools of the State; and

(B) includes any other public institution or agency having administrative control and direction over a public elementary or secondary school.

(5) Elementary school. The term "elementary school" means a nonprofit institutional day or residential school that provides elementary education, as determined under State law.

(6) Equipment. The term "equipment" includes:

(A) machinery, utilities, and built-in equipment and any necessary enclosures or structures to house such machinery, utilities, or equipment; and

(B) all other items necessary for the functioning of a particular facility as a facility for the provision of educational services, including items such as instructional equipment and necessary furniture; printed, published, and audio-visual instructional materials; telecommunications, sensory, and other technological aids and devices; and books, periodicals, documents, and other related materials.

(7) Excess costs. The term "excess costs" means those costs that are in excess of the average annual per-student expenditure in a local educational agency during the preceding school year for an elementary or secondary school student, as may be appropriate, and which shall be computed after deducting:

(A) amounts received:

(i) under subchapter II of this chapter;

(ii) under part A of title I of the Elementary and Secondary Education Act of 1965 (20 U.S.C. 6311 et seq.); or

(iii) under part A of title VII of that Act (20 U.S.C. 7401 et seq.); and

(B) any State or local funds expended for programs that would qualify for assistance under any of those parts.

(8) Free appropriate public education. The term "free appropriate public education" means special education and related services that:

(A) have been provided at public expense, under public supervision and direction, and without charge;

(B) meet the standards of the State educational agency;

(C) include an appropriate preschool, elementary, or secondary school education in the State involved; and

(D) are provided in conformity with the individualized education program required under section 1414(d) of this title.

(9) Indian. The term "Indian" means an individual who is a member of an Indian tribe.

(10) Indian tribe. The term "Indian tribe" means any Federal or State Indian tribe, band, rancheria, pueblo, colony, or community, including any Alaska Native village or regional village corporation (as defined in or established under the Alaska Native Claims Settlement Act (43 U.S.C. 1601 et seq.)).

(11) Individualized education program. The term "individualized education program" or "IEP" means a written statement for each child with a disability that is developed, reviewed, and revised in accordance with section 1414(d) of this title.

(12) Individualized family service plan. The term "individualized family service plan" has the meaning given such term in section 1436 of this title.

(13) Infant or toddler with a disability. The term "infant or toddler with a disability" has the meaning given such term in section 1432 of this title.

(14) Institution of higher education. The term "institution of higher education":

(A) has the meaning given that term in section 1141(a) of this title; and

(B) also includes any community college receiving funding from the Secretary of the Interior under the Tribally Controlled Community College Assistance Act of 1978 (25 U.S.C. 1801 et seq.).

(15) Local educational agency

(A) The term "local educational agency" means a public board of education or other public authority legally constituted within a State for either administrative control or direction of, or to perform a service function for, public elementary or secondary schools in a city, county, township, school district, or other political subdivision of a State, or for such combination of school districts or counties as are recognized in a State as an administrative agency for its public elementary or secondary schools.

(B) The term includes:

(i) an educational service agency, as defined in paragraph (4); and

(ii) any other public institution or agency having administrative control and direction of a public elementary or secondary school.

(C) The term includes an elementary or secondary school funded by the Bureau of Indian Affairs, but only to the extent that such inclusion makes the school eligible for programs for which specific eligibility is not provided to the school in another provision of law and the school does not have a student population that is smaller than the student population of the local educational agency receiving assistance under this chapter with the smallest student population, except that the school shall not be subject to the jurisdiction of any State educational agency other than the Bureau of Indian Affairs.

(16) Native language. The term "native language", when used with reference to an individual of limited English proficiency, means the language normally used by the individual, or in the case of a child, the language normally used by the parents of the child.

(17) Nonprofit. The term "nonprofit", as applied to a school, agency, organization, or institution, means a school, agency, organization, or institution owned and operated by one or more nonprofit corporations or associations no part of the net earnings of which inures, or may lawfully inure, to the benefit of any private shareholder or individual.

(18) Outlying area. The term "outlying area" means the United States Virgin Islands, Guam, American Samoa, and the Commonwealth of the Northern Mariana Islands.

(19) Parent. The term "parent":

(A) includes a legal guardian; and

(B) except as used in sections 1415(b)(2) and 1439(a)(5) of this title, includes an individual assigned under either of those sections to be a surrogate parent.

(20) Parent organization. The term "parent organization" has the meaning given that term in section 1482(g) of this title.

(21) Parent training and information center. The term "parent training and information center" means a center assisted under section 1482 or 1483 of this title.

(22) Related services. The term "related services" means transportation, and such developmental, corrective, and other supportive services (including speech-language pathology and audiology services, psychological services, physical and occupational therapy, recreation, including therapeutic recreation, social work services, counseling services, including rehabilitation counseling, orientation and mobility services, and medical services, except that such medical services shall be for diagnostic and evaluation purposes only) as may be required to assist a child with a disability to benefit from special education, and includes the early identification and assessment of disabling conditions in children.

(23) Secondary school. The term "secondary school" means a nonprofit institutional day or residential school that provides secondary education, as determined under State law, except that it does not include any education beyond grade 12.

(24) Secretary. The term "Secretary" means the Secretary of Education.

(25) Special education. The term "special education" means specially designed instruction, at no cost to parents, to meet the unique needs of a child with a disability, including:

(A) instruction conducted in the classroom, in the home, in hospitals and institutions, and in other settings; and

(B) instruction in physical education.

(26) Specific learning disability

(A) *In general.* The term "specific learning disability" means a disorder in one or more of the basic psychological processes involved in understanding or in using language, spoken or written, which disorder may manifest itself in imperfect ability to listen, think, speak, read, write, spell, or do mathematical calculations.

(B) *Disorders included.* Such term includes such conditions as perceptual disabilities, brain injury, minimal brain dysfunction, dyslexia, and developmental aphasia.

(C) *Disorders not included.* Such term does not include a learning problem that is primarily the result of visual, hearing, or motor disabilities, of mental retardation, of emotional disturbance, or of environmental, cultural, or economic disadvantage.

(27) State. The term "State" means each of the 50 States, the District of Columbia, the Commonwealth of Puerto Rico, and each of the outlying areas.

(28) State educational agency. The term "State educational agency" means the State board of education or other agency or officer primarily responsible for the State supervision of public elementary and secondary schools, or, if there is no such officer or agency, an officer or agency designated by the Governor or by State law.

(29) Supplementary aids and services. The term "supplementary aids and services" means aids, services, and other supports that are provided in regular education classes or other education-related settings to enable children with disabilities to be educated with nondisabled children to the maximum extent appropriate in accordance with section 1412(a)(5) of this title.

(30) Transition services. The term "transition services" means a coordinated set of activities for a student with a disability that:

(A) is designed within an outcome-oriented process, which promotes movement from school to post-school activities, including post-secondary education, vocational training, integrated employment (including supported employment), continuing and adult education, adult services, independent living, or community participation;

(B) is based upon the individual student's needs, taking into account the student's preferences and interests; and includes instruction, related services, community experiences, the development of employment and other post-school adult living objectives, and, when appropriate, acquisition of daily living skills and functional vocational evaluation.

Sec. 1412. State eligibility

(a) In general. A State is eligible for assistance under this subchapter for a fiscal year if the State demonstrates to the satisfaction of the Secretary that the State has in effect policies and procedures to ensure that it meets each of the following conditions:

(1) *Free appropriate public education*

(A) *In general.* A free appropriate public education is available to all children with disabilities residing in the State between the ages of 3 and 21, inclusive, including children with disabilities who have been suspended or expelled from school.

(B) *Limitation.* The obligation to make a free appropriate public education available to all children with disabilities does not apply with respect to children:

(i) aged 3 through 5 and 18 through 21 in a State to the extent that its application to those children would be inconsistent with State law or practice, or the order of any court, respecting the provision of public education to children in those age ranges; and

(ii) aged 18 through 21 to the extent that State law does not require that special education and related services under this subchapter be provided to children with disabilities who, in the educational placement prior to their incarceration in an adult correctional facility:

(I) were not actually identified as being a child with a disability under section 1401(3) of this title; or

(II) did not have an individualized education program under this subchapter.

(2) *Full educational opportunity goal.* The State has established a goal of providing full educational opportunity to all children with disabilities and a detailed timetable for accomplishing that goal.

(3) *Child find*

(A) I*n general.* All children with disabilities residing in the State, including children with disabilities attending private schools, regardless of the severity of their disabilities, and who are in need of special education and related services, are identified, located, and evaluated and a practical method is developed and implemented to determine which children with disabilities are currently receiving needed special education and related services.

(B) *Construction.* Nothing in this chapter requires that children be classified by their disability so long as each child who has a disability listed in section 1401 of this title and who, by reason of that disability, needs special education and related services is regarded as a child with a disability under this subchapter.

(4) *Individualized education program.* An individualized education program, or an individualized family service plan that meets the requirements of section 1436(d) of this title, is developed, reviewed, and revised for each child with a disability in accordance with section 1414(d) of this title.

(5) *Least restrictive environment*

(A) *In general.* To the maximum extent appropriate, children with disabilities, including children in public or private institutions or other care facilities, are educated with children who are not disabled, and special classes, separate schooling, or other removal of children with disabilities from the regular educational environment occurs only when the nature or severity of the disability of a child is such that education in regular classes with the use of supplementary aids and services cannot be achieved satisfactorily.

(B) *Additional requirement*

(i) In general. If the State uses a funding mechanism by which the State distributes State funds on the basis of the type of setting in which a child is served, the funding mechanism does not result in placements that violate the requirements of subparagraph (A).

(ii) Assurance. If the State does not have policies and procedures to ensure compliance with clause (i), the State shall provide the Secretary an assurance that it will revise the funding mechanism as soon as feasible to ensure that such mechanism does not result in such placements.

(6) *Procedural safeguards*

(A) *In general.* Children with disabilities and their parents are afforded the procedural safeguards required by section 1415 of this title.

(B) *Additional procedural safeguards.* Procedures to ensure that testing and evaluation materials and procedures utilized for the purposes of evaluation and placement of children with disabilities will be selected and administered so as not to be racially or culturally discriminatory. Such materials or procedures shall be provided and administered in the child's native language or mode of communication, unless it clearly is not feasible to do so, and no single procedure shall be the sole criterion for determining an appropriate educational program for a child.

(7) *Evaluation.* Children with disabilities are evaluated in accordance with subsections (a) through (c) of section 1414 of this title.

(8) *Confidentiality.* Agencies in the State comply with section 1417(c) of this title (relating to the confidentiality of records and information).

(9) *Transition from subchapter III to preschool programs.* Children participating in early-intervention programs assisted under subchapter III of this chapter, and who will participate in preschool programs assisted under this subchapter, experience a smooth and effective transition to those preschool programs in a manner consistent with section 1437(a)(8) of this title. By the third birthday of such a child, an individualized education program or, if consistent with sections 1414(d)(2)(B) and 1436(d) of this title, an individualized family service plan, has been developed and is being implemented for the child. The local educational agency will participate in transition planning conferences arranged by the designated lead agency under section 1437(a)(8) of this title.

(10) *Children in private schools*

(A) Children enrolled in private schools by their parents

(i) In general. To the extent consistent with the number and location of children with disabilities in the State who are enrolled by their parents in private elementary and secondary schools, provision is made for the participation of those children in the program assisted or carried out under this subchapter by providing for such children special education and related services in accordance with the following requirements, unless the Secretary has arranged for services to those children under subsection (f) of this section:

(I) Amounts expended for the provision of those services by a local educational agency shall be equal to a proportionate amount of Federal funds made available under this subchapter.

(II) Such services may be provided to children with disabilities on the premises of private, including parochial, schools, to the extent consistent with law.

(ii) Child-find requirement. The requirements of paragraph (3) of this subsection (relating to child find) shall apply with respect to children with disabilities in the State who are enrolled in private, including parochial, elementary and secondary schools.

(B) Children placed in, or referred to, private schools by public agencies

(i) *In general.* Children with disabilities in private schools and facilities are provided special education and related services, in accordance with an individualized education program, at no cost to their parents, if such children are placed in, or referred to, such schools or facilities by the State or appropriate local educational agency as the means of carrying out the requirements of this subchapter or any other applicable law requiring the provision of special education and related services to all children with disabilities within such State.

(ii) *Standards.* In all cases described in clause (i), the State educational agency shall determine whether such schools and facilities meet standards that apply to State and local educational agencies and that children so served have all the rights they would have if served by such agencies.

(C) Payment for education of children enrolled in private schools without consent of or referral by the public agency

(i) *In general.* Subject to subparagraph (A), this subchapter does not require a local educational agency to pay for the cost of education, including special education and related services, of a child with a disability at a private school or facility if that agency made a free appropriate public education available to the child and the parents elected to place the child in such private school or facility.

(ii) Reimbursement for private school placement. If the parents of a child with a disability, who previously received special education and related services under the authority of a public agency, enroll the child in a private elementary or secondary school without the consent of or referral by the public agency, a court or a hearing officer may require the agency to reimburse the parents for the cost of that enrollment if the court or hearing officer finds that the agency had not made a free appropriate public education available to the child in a timely manner prior to that enrollment.

(iii) Limitation on reimbursement. The cost of reimbursement described in clause (ii) may be reduced or denied:

(I) if:

(aa) at the most recent IEP meeting that the parents attended prior to removal of the child from the public school, the parents did not inform the IEP Team that they were rejecting the placement proposed by the public agency to provide a free appropriate public education to their child, including stating their concerns and their intent to enroll their child in a private school at public expense; or

(bb) 10 business days (including any holidays that occur on a business day) prior to the removal of the child from the public school, the parents did not give written notice to the public agency of the information described in division (aa);

(II) if, prior to the parents' removal of the child from the public school, the public agency informed the parents, through the notice requirements described in section 1415(b)(7) of this title, of its intent to evaluate the child (including a statement of the purpose of the evaluation that was appropriate and reasonable), but the parents did not make the child available for such evaluation; or

(III) upon a judicial finding of unreasonableness with respect to actions taken by the parents.

(iv) *Exception.* Notwithstanding the notice requirement in clause (iii)(I), the cost of reimbursement may not be reduced or denied for failure to provide such notice if:

(I) the parent is illiterate and cannot write in English;

(II) compliance with clause (iii)(I) would likely result in physical or serious emotional harm to the child;

(III) the school prevented the parent from providing such notice; or

(IV) the parents had not received notice, pursuant to section 1415 of this title, of the notice requirement in clause (iii)(I).

(11) *State educational agency responsible for general supervision*

(A) *In general.* The State educational agency is responsible for ensuring that:

(i) the requirements of this subchapter are met; and

(ii) all educational programs for children with disabilities in the State, including all such programs administered by any other State or local agency:

(I) are under the general supervision of individuals in the State who are responsible for educational programs for children with disabilities; and

(II) meet the educational standards of the State educational agency.

(B) Limitation Subparagraph (A) shall not limit the responsibility of agencies in the State other than the State educational agency to provide, or pay for some or all of the costs of, a free appropriate public education for any child with a disability in the State.

(C) *Exception.* Notwithstanding subparagraphs (A) and (B), the Governor (or another individual pursuant to State law), consistent with State law, may assign to any public agency in the State the responsibility of ensuring that the requirements of this subchapter are met with respect to children with disabilities who are convicted as adults under State law and incarcerated in adult prisons.

(12) *Obligations related to and methods of ensuring services*

(A) *Establishing responsibility for services.* The Chief Executive Officer or designee of the officer shall ensure that an inter-agency agreement or other mechanism for interagency coordination is in effect between each public agency described in subparagraph (B) and the State educational agency, in order to ensure that all services described in subparagraph (B)(i) that are needed to ensure a free appropriate public education are provided, including the provision of such services during the pendency of any dispute under clause (iii). Such agreement or mechanism shall include the following:

(i) Agency financial responsibility. An identification of, or a method for defining, the financial responsibility of each agency for providing services described in subparagraph (B)(i) to ensure a free appropriate public education to children with disabilities, provided that the financial responsibility of each public agency described in subparagraph (B), including the State Medicaid agency and other public insurers of children with disabilities, shall precede the financial responsibility of the local educational agency (or the State agency responsible for developing the child's IEP).

(ii) Conditions and terms of reimbursement. The conditions, terms, and procedures under which a local educational agency shall be reimbursed by other agencies.

(iii) Interagency disputes. Procedures for resolving inter-agency disputes (including procedures under which local educational agencies may initiate proceedings) under the agreement or other mechanism to secure reimbursement from other agencies or otherwise implement the provisions of the agreement or mechanism.

(iv) Coordination of services procedures. Policies and procedures for agencies to determine and identify the interagency coordination responsibilities of each agency to promote the coordination and timely and appropriate delivery of services described in subparagraph (B)(i).

(B) *Obligation of public agency*

(i) *In general.* If any public agency other than an educational agency is otherwise obligated under Federal or State law, or assigned responsibility under State policy or pursuant to subparagraph (A), to provide or pay for any services that are also considered special education or related services (such as, but not limited to, services described in sections 1401(1) relating to assistive technology devices, 1401(2) relating to assistive technology services, 1401(22) relating to related services, 1401(29) relating to supplementary aids and services, and 1401(30) of this title relating to transition services) that are necessary for ensuring a free appropriate public education to children with disabilities within the State, such public agency shall fulfill that obligation or responsibility, either directly or through contract or other arrangement.

(ii) Reimbursement for services by public agency. If a public agency other than an educational agency fails to provide or pay for the special education and related services described in clause (i), the local educational agency (or State agency responsible for developing the child's IEP) shall provide or pay for such services to the child. Such local educational agency or State agency may then claim reimbursement for the services from the public agency that failed to provide or pay for such services and such public agency shall reimburse the local educational agency or State agency pursuant to the terms of the interagency agreement or other mechanism described in subparagraph (A)(i) according to the procedures established in such agreement pursuant to subparagraph (A)(ii).

(C) *Special rule.* The requirements of subparagraph (A) may be met through:

(i) state statute or regulation;

(ii) signed agreements between respective agency officials that clearly identify the responsibilities of each agency relating to the provision of services; or

(iii) other appropriate written methods as determined by the Chief Executive Officer of the State or designee of the officer.

(13) *Procedural requirements relating to local educational agency eligibility.* The State educational agency will not make a final determination that a local educational agency is not eligible for assistance under this subchapter without first affording that agency reasonable notice and an opportunity for a hearing.

(14) *Comprehensive system of personnel development.* The State has in effect, consistent with the purposes of this chapter and with section 1435(a)(8) of this title, a comprehensive system of personnel development that is designed to ensure an adequate supply of qualified special education, regular education, and related services personnel that meets the requirements for a State improvement plan relating to personnel development in subsections (b)(2)(B) and (c)(3)(D) of section 1453 of this title.

(15) *Personnel standards*

(A) *In general.* The State educational agency has established and maintains standards to ensure that personnel necessary to carry out this subchapter are appropriately and adequately prepared and trained.

(B) *Standards described.* Such standards shall:

(i) be consistent with any State-approved or State-recognized certification, licensing, registration, or other comparable requirements that apply to the professional discipline in which those personnel are providing special education or related services;

(ii) to the extent the standards described in subparagraph (A) are not based on the highest requirements in the State applicable to a specific profession or discipline, the State is taking steps to require retraining or hiring of personnel that meet appropriate professional requirements in the State; and

(iii) allow paraprofessionals and assistants who are appropriately trained and supervised, in accordance with State law, regulations, or written policy, in meeting the requirements of this subchapter to be used to assist in the provision of special education and related services to children with disabilities under this subchapter.

(C) *Policy*. In implementing this paragraph, a State may adopt a policy that includes a requirement that local educational agencies in the State make an ongoing good-faith effort to recruit and hire appropriately and adequately trained personnel to provide special education and related services to children with disabilities, including, in a geographic area of the State where there is a shortage of such personnel, the most qualified individuals available who are making satisfactory progress toward completing applicable course work necessary to meet the standards described in subparagraph (B)(i), consistent with State law, and the steps described in subparagraph (B)(ii) within three years.

(16) *Performance goals and indicators*. The State:

(A) has established goals for the performance of children with disabilities in the State that:

(i) will promote the purposes of this chapter, as stated in section 1400(d) of this title; and

(ii) are consistent, to the maximum extent appropriate, with other goals and standards for children established by the State;

(B) has established performance indicators the State will use to assess progress toward achieving those goals that, at a minimum, address the performance of children with disabilities on assessments, drop-out rates, and graduation rates;

(C) will, every two years, report to the Secretary and the public on the progress of the State, and of children with disabilities in the State, toward meeting the goals established under subparagraph (A); and

(D) based on its assessment of that progress, will revise its State improvement plan under part A of subchapter IV of this chapter as may be needed to improve its performance, if the State receives assistance under that part.

(17) *Participation in assessments*

(A) *In general*. Children with disabilities are included in general State and district-wide assessment programs, with appropriate accommodations, where necessary. As appropriate, the State or local educational agency:

(i) develops guidelines for the participation of children with disabilities in alternate assessments for those children who cannot participate in State and district-wide assessment programs; and

(ii) develops and, beginning not later than July 1, 2000, conducts those alternate assessments.

(B) *Reports*. The State educational agency makes available to the public, and reports to the public with the same frequency and in the same detail as it reports on the assessment of nondisabled children, the following:

(i) The number of children with disabilities participating in regular assessments.

(ii) The number of those children participating in alternate assessments.

(iii)

(I) The performance of those children on regular assessments (beginning not later than July 1, 1998) and on alternate assessments (not later than July 1, 2000), if doing so would be statistically sound and would not result in the disclosure of performance results identifiable to individual children.

(II) Data relating to the performance of children described under subclause (I) shall be disaggregated:

(aa) for assessments conducted after July 1, 1998; and

(bb) for assessments conducted before July 1, 1998, if the State is required to disaggregate such data prior to July 1, 1998.

(18) *Supplementation of State, local, and other Federal funds*

(A) *Expenditures*. Funds paid to a State under this subchapter will be expended in accordance with all the provisions of this subchapter.

(B) *Prohibition against commingling*. Funds paid to a State under this subchapter will not be commingled with State funds.

(C) *Prohibition against supplantation and conditions for waiver by Secretary*. Except as provided in section 1413 of this title, funds paid to a State under this subchapter will be used to supplement the level of Federal, State, and local funds (including funds that are not under the direct control of State or local educational agencies) expended for special education and related services provided to children with disabilities under this subchapter and in no case to supplant such Federal, State, and local funds, except that, where the State provides clear and convincing evidence that all children with disabilities have available to them a free appropriate public education, the Secretary may waive, in whole or in part, the requirements of this subparagraph if the Secretary concurs with the evidence provided by the State.

(19) *Maintenance of State financial support*

(A) *In general*. The State does not reduce the amount of State financial support for special education and related services for children with disabilities, or otherwise made available because of the excess costs of educating those children, below the amount of that support for the preceding fiscal year.

(B) *Reduction of funds for failure to maintain support*. The Secretary shall reduce the allocation of funds under section 1411 of this title for any fiscal year following the fiscal year in which the State fails to comply with the requirement of subparagraph (A) by the same amount by which the State fails to meet the requirement.

(C) *Waivers for exceptional or uncontrollable circumstances*. The Secretary may waive the requirement of subparagraph (A) for a State, for one fiscal year at a time, if the Secretary determines that:

(i) granting a waiver would be equitable due to exceptional or uncontrollable circumstances such as a natural disaster or a precipitous and unforeseen decline in the financial resources of the State; or

(ii) the State meets the standard in paragraph (18)(C) of this section for a waiver of the requirement to supplement, and not to supplant, funds received under this subchapter.

(D) *Subsequent years.* If, for any year, a State fails to meet the requirement of subparagraph (A), including any year for which the State is granted a waiver under subparagraph (C), the financial support required of the State in future years under subparagraph (A) shall be the amount that would have been required in the absence of that failure and not the reduced level of the State's support.

(E) *Regulations*

(i) The Secretary shall, by regulation, establish procedures (including objective criteria and consideration of the results of compliance reviews of the State conducted by the Secretary) for determining whether to grant a waiver under subparagraph (C)(ii).

(ii) The Secretary shall publish proposed regulations under clause (i) not later than 6 months after June 4, 1997, and shall issue final regulations under clause (i) not later than 1 year after June 4, 1997.

(20) *Public participation.* Prior to the adoption of any policies and procedures needed to comply with this section (including any amendments to such policies and procedures), the State ensures that there are public hearings, adequate notice of the hearings, and an opportunity for comment available to the general public, including individuals with disabilities and parents of children with disabilities.

(21) *State advisory panel*

(A) *In general.* The State has established and maintains an advisory panel for the purpose of providing policy guidance with respect to special education and related services for children with disabilities in the State.

(B) *Membership.* Such advisory panel shall consist of members appointed by the Governor, or any other official authorized under State law to make such appointments, that is representative of the State population and that is composed of individuals involved in, or concerned with, the education of children with disabilities, including:

(i) parents of children with disabilities;

(ii) individuals with disabilities;

(iii) teachers;

(iv) representatives of institutions of higher education that prepare special education and related services personnel;

(v) State and local education officials;

(vi) administrators of programs for children with disabilities;

(vii) representatives of other State agencies involved in the financing or delivery of related services to children with disabilities;

(viii) representatives of private schools and public charter schools;

(ix) at least one representative of a vocational, community, or business organization concerned with the provision of transition services to children with disabilities; and

(x) representatives from the State juvenile and adult corrections agencies.

(C) *Special rule.* A majority of the members of the panel shall be individuals with disabilities or parents of children with disabilities.

(D) *Duties.* The advisory panel shall:

(i) advise the State educational agency of unmet needs within the State in the education of children with disabilities;

(ii) comment publicly on any rules or regulations proposed by the State regarding the education of children with disabilities;

(iii) advise the State educational agency in developing evaluations and reporting on data to the Secretary under section 1418 of this title;

(iv) advise the State educational agency in developing corrective action plans to address findings identified in Federal monitoring reports under this subchapter; and

(v) advise the State educational agency in developing and implementing policies relating to the coordination of services for children with disabilities.

(22) *Suspension and expulsion rates*

(A) *In general.* The State educational agency examines data to determine if significant discrepancies are occurring in the rate of long-term suspensions and expulsions of children with disabilities:

(i) among local educational agencies in the State; or

(ii) compared to such rates for nondisabled children within such agencies.

(B) *Review and revision of policies.* If such discrepancies are occurring, the State educational agency reviews and, if appropriate, revises (or requires the affected State or local educational agency to revise) its policies, procedures, and practices relating to the development and implementation of IEPs, the use of behavioral interventions, and procedural safeguards, to ensure that such policies, procedures, and practices comply with this chapter.

(b) State educational agency as provider of free appropriate public education or direct services. If the State educational agency provides free appropriate public education to children with disabilities, or provides direct services to such children, such agency:

(1) shall comply with any additional requirements of section 1413(a) of this title, as if such agency were a local educational agency; and

(2) may use amounts that are otherwise available to such agency under this subchapter to serve those children without regard to section 1413(a)(2)(A)(i) of this title (relating to excess costs).

(c) Exception for prior State plans

(1) *In general.* If a State has on file with the Secretary policies and procedures that demonstrate that such State meets any requirement of subsection (a) of this section, including any policies and procedures filed under this subchapter as in effect before the effective date of the Individuals with Disabilities Education Act Amendments of 1997, the Secretary shall consider such State to have met such requirement for purposes of receiving a grant under this subchapter.

(2) *Modifications made by State.* Subject to paragraph (3), an application submitted by a State in accordance with this section shall remain in effect until the State submits to the Secretary such modifications as the State deems necessary. This section shall apply to a modification to an application to

the same extent and in the same manner as this section applies to the original plan.

(3) *Modifications required by Secretary.* If, after the effective date of the Individuals with Disabilities Education Act Amendments of 1997, the provisions of this chapter are amended (or the regulations developed to carry out this chapter are amended), or there is a new interpretation of this chapter by a Federal court or a State's highest court, or there is an official finding of noncompliance with Federal law or regulations, the Secretary may require a State to modify its application only to the extent necessary to ensure the State's compliance with this subchapter.

(d) Approval by Secretary

(1) *In general.* If the Secretary determines that a State is eligible to receive a grant under this subchapter, the Secretary shall notify the State of that determination.

(2) *Notice and hearing.* The Secretary shall not make a final determination that a State is not eligible to receive a grant under this subchapter until after providing the State:

(A) with reasonable notice; and

(B) with an opportunity for a hearing.

(e) Assistance under other Federal programs. Nothing in this chapter permits a State to reduce medical and other assistance available, or to alter eligibility, under titles V and XIX of the Social Security Act (42 U.S.C. 701 et seq., 1396 et seq.) with respect to the provision of a free appropriate public education for children with disabilities in the State.

(f) By-pass for children in private schools

(1) *In general.* If, on December 2, 1983, a State educational agency is prohibited by law from providing for the participation in special programs of children with disabilities enrolled in private elementary and secondary schools as required by subsection (a)(10)(A) of this section, the Secretary shall, notwithstanding such provision of law, arrange for the provision of services to such children through arrangements which shall be subject to the requirements of such subsection.

(2) *Payments*

(A) *Determination of amounts.* If the Secretary arranges for services pursuant to this subsection, the Secretary, after consultation with the appropriate public and private school officials, shall pay to the provider of such services for a fiscal year an amount per child that does not exceed the amount determined by dividing:

(i) the total amount received by the State under this subchapter for such fiscal year; by

(ii) the number of children with disabilities served in the prior year, as reported to the Secretary by the State under section 1418 of this title.

(B) Withholding of certain amounts. Pending final resolution of any investigation or complaint that could result in a determination under this subsection, the Secretary may withhold from the allocation of the affected State educational agency the amount the Secretary estimates would be necessary to pay the cost of services described in subparagraph (A).

(C) *Period of payments.* The period under which payments are made under subparagraph (A) shall continue until the Secretary determines that there will no longer be any failure or inability on the part of the State educational agency to meet the requirements of subsection (a)(10)(A) of this section.

(3) *Notice and hearing*

(A) *In general.* The Secretary shall not take any final action under this subsection until the State educational agency affected by such action has had an opportunity, for at least 45 days after receiving written notice thereof, to submit written objections and to appear before the Secretary or the Secretary's designee to show cause why such action should not be taken.

(B) *Review of action.* If a State educational agency is dissatisfied with the Secretary's final action after a proceeding under subparagraph (A), such agency may, not later than 60 days after notice of such action, file with the United States court of appeals for the circuit in which such State is located a petition for review of that action. A copy of the petition shall be forthwith transmitted by the clerk of the court to the Secretary. The Secretary thereupon shall file in the court the record of the proceedings on which the Secretary based the Secretary's action, as provided in section 2112 of title 28.

(C) *Review of findings of fact.* The findings of fact by the Secretary, if supported by substantial evidence, shall be conclusive, but the court, for good cause shown, may remand the case to the Secretary to take further evidence, and the Secretary may thereupon make new or modified findings of fact and may modify the Secretary's previous action, and shall file in the court the record of the further proceedings. Such new or modified findings of fact shall likewise be conclusive if supported by substantial evidence.

(D) *Jurisdiction of court of appeals; review by United States Supreme Court.* Upon the filing of a petition under subparagraph (B), the United States court of appeals shall have jurisdiction to affirm the action of the Secretary or to set it aside, in whole or in part. The judgment of the court shall be subject to review by the Supreme Court of the United States upon certiorari or certification as provided in section 1254 of title 28.

Sec. 1414. Evaluations, eligibility determinations, individualized education programs, and educational placements

(a) Evaluations and reevaluations

(1) *Initial evaluations*

(A) *In general.* A State educational agency, other State agency, or local educational agency shall conduct a full and individual initial evaluation, in accordance with this paragraph and subsection (b) of this section, before the initial provision of special education and related services to a child with a disability under this subchapter.

(B) *Procedures.* Such initial evaluation shall consist of procedures:

(i) to determine whether a child is a child with a disability (as defined in section 1401(3) of this title); and

(ii) to determine the educational needs of such child.

(C) *Parental consent*

(i) *In general.* The agency proposing to conduct an initial evaluation to determine if the child qualifies as a child with a disability as defined in section 1401(3)(A) or 1401(3)(B) of this title shall obtain an informed consent from the parent of such child before the evaluation is conducted. Parental consent for evaluation shall not be construed as consent for placement for receipt of special education and related services.

(ii) *Refusal.* If the parents of such child refuse consent for the evaluation, the agency may continue to pursue an evaluation by utilizing the mediation and due process procedures under section 1415 of this title, except to the extent inconsistent with State law relating to parental consent.

(2) *Reevaluations.* A local educational agency shall ensure that a reevaluation of each child with a disability is conducted:

(A) if conditions warrant a reevaluation or if the child's parent or teacher requests a reevaluation, but at least once every 3 years; and

(B) in accordance with subsections (b) and (c) of this section.

(b) Evaluation procedures

(1) *Notice.* The local educational agency shall provide notice to the parents of a child with a disability, in accordance with subsections (b)(3), (b)(4), and (c) of section 1415 of this title, that describes any evaluation procedures such agency proposes to conduct.

(2) *Conduct of evaluation.* In conducting the evaluation, the local educational agency shall:

(A) use a variety of assessment tools and strategies to gather relevant functional and developmental information, including information provided by the parent, that may assist in determining whether the child is a child with a disability and the content of the child's individualized education program, including information related to enabling the child to be involved in and progress in the general curriculum or, for preschool children, to participate in appropriate activities;

(B) not use any single procedure as the sole criterion for determining whether a child is a child with a disability or determining an appropriate educational program for the child; and

(C) use technically sound instruments that may assess the relative contribution of cognitive and behavioral factors, in addition to physical or developmental factors.

(3) *Additional requirements.* Each local educational agency shall ensure that:

(A) tests and other evaluation materials used to assess a child under this section:

(i) are selected and administered so as not to be discriminatory on a racial or cultural basis; and

(ii) are provided and administered in the child's native language or other mode of communication, unless it is clearly not feasible to do so; and

(B) any standardized tests that are given to the child:

(i) have been validated for the specific purpose for which they are used;

(ii) are administered by trained and knowledgeable personnel; and

(iii) are administered in accordance with any instructions provided by the producer of such tests;

(C) the child is assessed in all areas of suspected disability; and

(D) assessment tools and strategies that provide relevant information that directly assists persons in determining the educational needs of the child are provided.

(4) *Determination of eligibility.* Upon completion of administration of tests and other evaluation materials:

(A) the determination of whether the child is a child with a disability as defined in section 1401(3) of this title shall be made by a team of qualified professionals and the parent of the child in accordance with paragraph (5); and

(B) a copy of the evaluation report and the documentation of determination of eligibility will be given to the parent.

(5) *Special rule for eligibility determination.* In making a determination of eligibility under paragraph (4)(A), a child shall not be determined to be a child with a disability if the determinant factor for such determination is lack of instruction in reading or math or limited English proficiency.

(c) Additional requirements for evaluation and reevaluations

(1) *Review of existing evaluation data.* As part of an initial evaluation (if appropriate) and as part of any reevaluation under this section, the IEP Team described in subsection (d)(1)(B) of this section and other qualified professionals, as appropriate, shall:

(A) review existing evaluation data on the child, including evaluations and information provided by the parents of the child, current classroom-based assessments and observations, and teacher and related services providers observation; and

(B) on the basis of that review, and input from the child's parents, identify what additional data, if any, are needed to determine:

(i) whether the child has a particular category of disability, as described in section 1401 (3) of this title, or, in case of a reevaluation of a child, whether the child continues to have such a disability;

(ii) the present levels of performance and educational needs of the child;

(iii) whether the child needs special education and related services, or in the case of a reevaluation of a child, whether the child continues to need special education and related services; and

(iv) whether any additions or modifications to the special education and related services are needed to enable the child to meet the measurable annual goals set out in the individualized education program of the child and to participate, as appropriate, in the general curriculum.

(2) *Source of data.* The local educational agency shall administer such tests and other evaluation materials as may be needed to produce the data identified by the IEP Team under paragraph (1)(B).

(3) *Parental consent.* Each local educational agency shall obtain informed parental consent, in accordance with subsection (a)(1)(C) of this section, prior to conducting any reevaluation of a child with a disability, except that such informed parent consent need not be obtained if the local educational agency can demonstrate that it had taken reasonable measures to obtain such consent and the child's parent has failed to respond.

(4) *Requirements if additional data are not needed.* If the IEP Team and other qualified professionals, as appropriate, determine that no additional data are needed to determine whether the child continues to be a child with a disability, the local educational agency:

(A) shall notify the child's parents of:

(i) that determination and the reasons for it; and

(ii) the right of such parents to request an assessment to determine whether the child continues to be a child with a disability; and

(B) shall not be required to conduct such an assessment unless requested to by the child's parents.

(5) *Evaluations before change in eligibility.* A local educational agency shall evaluate a child with a disability in accordance with this section before determining that the child is no longer a child with a disability.

(d) Individualized education programs.

(1) *Definitions*

As used in this chapter:

(A) *Individualized education program.* The term "individualized education program" or "IEP" means a written statement for each child with a disability that is developed, reviewed, and revised in accordance with this section and that includes:

(i) a statement of the child's present levels of educational performance, including:

(I) how the child's disability affects the child's involvement and progress in the general curriculum; or

(II) for preschool children, as appropriate, how the disability affects the child's participation in appropriate activities;

(ii) a statement of measurable annual goals, including benchmarks or short-term objectives, related to:

(I) meeting the child's needs that result from the child's disability to enable the child to be involved in and progress in the general curriculum; and

(II) meeting each of the child's other educational needs that result from the child's disability;

(iii) a statement of the special education and related services and supplementary aids and services to be provided to the child, or on behalf of the child, and a statement of the program modifications or supports for school personnel that will be provided for the child:

(I) to advance appropriately toward attaining the annual goals;

(II) to be involved and progress in the general curriculum in accordance with clause (i) and to participate in extracurricular and other nonacademic activities; and

(III) to be educated and participate with other children with disabilities and nondisabled children in the activities described in this paragraph;

(iv) an explanation of the extent, if any, to which the child will not participate with nondisabled children in the regular class and in the activities described in clause (iii);

(v)

(I) a statement of any individual modifications in the administration of State or districtwide assessments of student achievement that are needed in order for the child to participate in such assessment; and

(II) if the IEP Team determines that the child will not participate in a particular State or districtwide assessment of student achievement (or part of such an assessment), a statement of:

(aa) why that assessment is not appropriate for the child; and

(bb) how the child will be assessed;

(vi) the projected date for the beginning of the services and modifications described in clause (iii), and the anticipated frequency, location, and duration of those services and modifications;

(vii) a statement of:

(I) beginning at age 14, and updated annually, a statement of the transition service needs of the child under the applicable components of the child's IEP that focuses on the child's courses of study (such as participation in advanced-placement courses or a vocational education program);

(II) beginning at age 16 (or younger, if determined appropriate by the IEP Team), a statement of needed transition services for the child, including, when appropriate, a statement of the interagency responsibilities or any needed linkages; and

(III) beginning at least one year before the child reaches the age of majority under State law, a statement that the child has been informed of his or her rights under this chapter, if any, that will transfer to the child on reaching the age of majority under section 1415(m) of this title; and

(viii) a statement of:

(I) how the child's progress toward the annual goals described in clause (ii) will be measured; and

(II) how the child's parents will be regularly informed (by such means as periodic report cards), at least as often as parents are informed of their nondisabled children's progress, of:

(aa) their child's progress toward the annual goals described in clause (ii); and

(bb) the extent to which that progress is sufficient to enable the child to achieve the goals by the end of the year.

(B) *Individualized education program team.* The term "individualized education program team" or "IEP Team" means a group of individuals composed of:

(i) the parents of a child with a disability;

(ii) at least one regular education teacher of such child (if the child is, or may be, participating in the regular education environment);

(iii) at least one special education teacher, or where appropriate, at least one special education provider of such child;

(iv) a representative of the local educational agency who:

(I) is qualified to provide, or supervise the provision of, specially designed instruction to meet the unique needs of children with disabilities;

(II) is knowledgeable about the general curriculum; and

(III) is knowledgeable about the availability of resources of the local educational agency;

(v) an individual who can interpret the instructional implications of evaluation results, who may be a member of the team described in clauses (ii) through (vi);

(vi) at the discretion of the parent or the agency, other individuals who have knowledge or special expertise regarding the child, including related services personnel as appropriate; and

(vii) whenever appropriate, the child with a disability.

(2) *Requirement that program be in effect*

(A) *In general.* At the beginning of each school year, each local educational agency, State educational agency, or other State agency, as the case may be, shall have in effect, for each child with a disability in its jurisdiction, an individualized education program, as defined in paragraph (1)(A).

(B) *Program for child aged 3 through 5.* In the case of a child with a disability aged 3 through 5 (or, at the discretion of the State educational agency, a 2-year-old child with a disability who will turn age 3 during the school year), an individualized family service plan that contains the material described in section 1436 of this title, and that is developed in accordance with this section, may serve as the IEP of the child if using that plan as the IEP is:

(i) consistent with State policy; and

(ii) agreed to by the agency and the child's parents.

(3) *Development of IEP*

(A) *In general.* In developing each child's IEP, the IEP Team, subject to subparagraph (C), shall consider:

(i) the strengths of the child and the concerns of the parents for enhancing the education of their child; and

(ii) the results of the initial evaluation or most recent evaluation of the child.

(B) *Consideration of special factors.* The IEP Team shall:

(i) in the case of a child whose behavior impedes his or her learning or that of others, consider, when appropriate, strategies, including positive behavioral interventions, strategies, and supports to address that behavior;

(ii) in the case of a child with limited English proficiency, consider the language needs of the child as such needs relate to the child's IEP;

(iii) in the case of a child who is blind or visually impaired, provide for instruction in Braille and the use of Braille unless the IEP Team determines, after an evaluation of the child's reading and writing skills, needs, and appropriate reading and writing media (including an evaluation of the child's future needs for instruction in Braille or the use of Braille), that instruction in Braille or the use of Braille is not appropriate for the child;

(iv) consider the communication needs of the child, and in the case of a child who is deaf or hard of hearing, consider the child's language and communication needs, opportunities for direct communications with peers and professional personnel in the child's language and communication mode, academic level, and full range of needs, including opportunities for direct instruction in the child's language and communication mode; and

(v) consider whether the child requires assistive technology devices and services.

(C) *Requirement with respect to regular education teacher.* The regular education teacher of the child, as a member of the IEP Team, shall, to the extent appropriate, participate in the development of the IEP of the child, including the determination of appropriate positive behavioral interventions and strategies and the determination of supplementary aids and services, program modifications, and support for school personnel consistent with paragraph (1)(A)(iii).

(4) *Review and revision of IEP*

(A) *In general.* The local educational agency shall ensure that, subject to subparagraph (B), the IEP Team:

(i) reviews the child's IEP periodically, but not less than annually to determine whether the annual goals for the child are being achieved; and

(ii) revises the IEP as appropriate to address:

(I) any lack of expected progress toward the annual goals and in the general curriculum, where appropriate;

(II) the results of any reevaluation conducted under this section;

(III) information about the child provided to, or by, the parents, as described in subsection (c)(1)(B) of this section;

(IV) the child's anticipated needs; or

(V) other matters.

(B) *Requirement with respect to regular education teacher.* The regular education teacher of the child, as a member of the IEP Team, shall, to the extent appropriate, participate in the review and revision of the IEP of the child.

(5) *Failure to meet transition objectives.* If a participating agency, other than the local educational agency, fails to provide the transition services described in the IEP in accordance with paragraph (1)(A)(vii), the local educational agency shall reconvene the IEP Team to identify alternative strategies to meet the transition objectives for the child set out in that program.

(6) *Children with disabilities in adult prisons*

(A) *In general.* The following requirements do not apply to children with disabilities who are convicted as adults under State law and incarcerated in adult prisons:

(i) The requirements contained in section 1412(a)(17) of this title and paragraph (1)(A)(v) of this subsection (relating to participation of children with disabilities in general assessments).

(ii) The requirements of subclauses (I) and (II) of paragraph (1)(A)(vii) of this subsection (relating to transition planning and transition services), do not apply with respect to such children whose eligibility under this subchapter will end, because of their age, before they will be released from prison.

(B) *Additional requirement.* If a child with a disability is convicted as an adult under State law and incarcerated in an adult prison, the child's IEP Team may modify the child's IEP or placement notwithstanding the requirements of section 1412 (a)(5)(A) of this title and subsection (d)(1)(A) of this section if the State has demonstrated a bona fide security or compelling penological interest that cannot otherwise be accommodated.

(e) Construction. Team to include information under one component of a child's IEP that is already contained under another component of such IEP.

(f) Educational placements. Each local educational agency or State educational agency shall ensure that the parents of each child with a disability are members of any group that makes decisions on the educational placement of their child.

Sec. 1415. Procedural safeguards

(a) Establishment of procedures. Any State educational agency, State agency, or local educational agency that receives assistance under this subchapter shall establish and maintain procedures in accordance with this section to ensure that children with disabilities and their parents are guaranteed procedural safeguards with respect to the provision of free appropriate public education by such agencies.

(b) Types of procedures. The procedures required by this section shall include:

(1) an opportunity for the parents of a child with a disability to examine all records relating to such child and to participate in meetings with respect to the identification, evaluation, and educational placement of the child, and the provision of a free appropriate public education to such child, and to obtain an independent educational evaluation of the child;

(2) procedures to protect the rights of the child whenever the parents of the child are not known, the agency cannot, after reasonable efforts, locate the parents, or the child is a ward of the State, including the assignment of an individual (who shall not be an employee of the State educational agency, the local educational agency, or any other agency that is involved in the education or care of the child) to act as a surrogate for the parents;

(3) written prior notice to the parents of the child whenever such agency:

(A) proposes to initiate or change; or

(B) refuses to initiate or change; the identification, evaluation, or educational placement of the child, in accordance with subsection (c) of this section, or the provision of a free appropriate public education to the child;

(4) procedures designed to ensure that the notice required by paragraph (3) is in the native language of the parents, unless it clearly is not feasible to do so;

(5) an opportunity for mediation in accordance with subsection (e) of this section;

(6) an opportunity to present complaints with respect to any matter relating to the identification, evaluation, or educational placement of the child, or the provision of a free appropriate public education to such child;

(7) procedures that require the parent of a child with a disability, or the attorney representing the child, to provide notice (which shall remain confidential):

(A) to the State educational agency or local educational agency, as the case may be, in the complaint filed under paragraph (6); and

(B) that shall include:

(i) the name of the child, the address of the residence of the child, and the name of the school the child is attending;

(ii) a description of the nature of the problem of the child relating to such proposed initiation or change, including facts relating to such problem; and

(iii) a proposed resolution of the problem to the extent known and available to the parents at the time; and

(8) procedures that require the State educational agency to develop a model form to assist parents in filing a complaint in accordance with paragraph (7).

(c) Content of prior written notice. The notice required by subsection (b)(3) of this section shall include:

(1) a description of the action proposed or refused by the agency;

(2) an explanation of why the agency proposes or refuses to take the action;

(3) a description of any other options that the agency considered and the reasons why those options were rejected;

(4) a description of each evaluation procedure, test, record, or report the agency used as a basis for the proposed or refused action;

(5) a description of any other factors that are relevant to the agency's proposal or refusal;

(6) a statement that the parents of a child with a disability have protection under the procedural safeguards of this subchapter and, if this notice is not an initial referral for evaluation, the means by which a copy of a description of the procedural safeguards can be obtained; and

(7) sources for parents to contact to obtain assistance in understanding the provisions of this subchapter.

(d) Procedural safeguards notice

(1) *In general.* A copy of the procedural safeguards available to the parents of a child with a disability shall be given to the parents, at a minimum:

(A) upon initial referral for evaluation;

(B) upon each notification of an individualized education program meeting and upon reevaluation of the child; and

(C) upon registration of a complaint under subsection (b)(6) of this section.

(2) *Contents.* The procedural safeguards notice shall include a full explanation of the procedural safeguards, written in the native language of the parents, unless it clearly is not feasible to do so, and written in an easily understandable manner, available under this section and under regulations promulgated by the Secretary relating to:

(A) independent educational evaluation;

(B) prior written notice;

(C) parental consent;

(D) access to educational records;

(E) opportunity to present complaints;

(F) the child's placement during pendency of due process proceedings;

(G) procedures for students who are subject to placement in an interim alternative educational setting;

(H) requirements for unilateral placement by parents of children in private schools at public expense;

(I) mediation;

(J) due process hearings, including requirements for disclosure of evaluation results and recommendations;

(K) State-level appeals (if applicable in that State);

(L) civil actions; and

(M) attorneys' fees.

(e) Mediation

(1) *In general.* Any State educational agency or local educational agency that receives assistance under this subchapter shall ensure that procedures are established and implemented to allow parties to disputes involving any matter described in subsection (b)(6) of this section to resolve such disputes through a mediation process which, at a minimum, shall be available whenever a hearing is requested under subsection (f) or (k) of this section.

(2) *Requirements.* Such procedures shall meet the following requirements:

(A) The procedures shall ensure that the mediation process:

(i) is voluntary on the part of the parties;

(ii) is not used to deny or delay a parent's right to a due process hearing under subsection (f) of this section, or to deny any other rights afforded under this subchapter; and

(iii) is conducted by a qualified and impartial mediator who is trained in effective mediation techniques.

(B) A local educational agency or a State agency may establish procedures to require parents who choose not to use the mediation process to meet, at a time and location convenient to the parents, with a disinterested party who is under contract with:

(i) a parent training and information center or community parent resource center in the State established under section 1482 or 1483 of this title; or

(ii) an appropriate alternative dispute resolution entity; to encourage the use, and explain the benefits, of the mediation process to the parents.

(C) The State shall maintain a list of individuals who are qualified mediators and knowledgeable in laws and regulations relating to the provision of special education and related services.

(D) The State shall bear the cost of the mediation process, including the costs of meetings described in subparagraph (B).

(E) Each session in the mediation process shall be scheduled in a timely manner and shall be held in a location that is convenient to the parties to the dispute.

(F) An agreement reached by the parties to the dispute in the mediation process shall be set forth in a written mediation agreement.

(G) Discussions that occur during the mediation process shall be confidential and may not be used as evidence in any subsequent due process hearings or civil proceedings and the parties to the mediation process may be required to sign a confidentiality pledge prior to the commencement of such process.

(f) Impartial due process hearing

(1) *In general.* Whenever a complaint has been received under subsection (b)(6) or (k) of this section, the parents involved in such complaint shall have an opportunity for an impartial due process hearing, which shall be conducted by the State educational agency or by the local educational agency, as determined by State law or by the State educational agency.

(2) *Disclosure of evaluations and recommendations*

(A) *In general.* At least 5 business days prior to a hearing conducted pursuant to paragraph (1), each party shall disclose to all other parties all evaluations completed by that date and recommendations based on the offering party's evaluations that the party intends to use at the hearing.

(B) *Failure to disclose.* A hearing officer may bar any party that fails to comply with subparagraph (A) from introducing the relevant evaluation or recommendation at the hearing without the consent of the other party.

(3) *Limitation on conduct of hearing.* A hearing conducted pursuant to paragraph (1) may not be conducted by an employee of the State educational agency or the local educational agency involved in the education or care of the child.

(g) Appeal. If the hearing required by subsection (f) of this section is conducted by a local educational agency, any party aggrieved by the findings and decision rendered in such a hearing may appeal such findings and decision to the State educational agency. Such agency shall conduct an impartial review of such decision. The officer conducting such review shall make an independent decision upon completion of such review.

(h) Safeguards. Any party to a hearing conducted pursuant to subsection (f) or (k) of this section, or an appeal conducted pursuant to subsection (g) of this section, shall be accorded:

(1) the right to be accompanied and advised by counsel and by individuals with special knowledge or training with respect to the problems of children with disabilities;

(2) the right to present evidence and confront, cross-examine, and compel the attendance of witnesses;

(3) the right to a written, or, at the option of the parents, electronic verbatim record of such hearing; and

(4) the right to written, or, at the option of the parents, electronic findings of fact and decisions (which findings and decisions shall be made available to the public consistent with the requirements of section 1417(c) of this title (relating to the confidentiality of data, information, and records) and shall also be transmitted to the advisory panel established pursuant to section 141 (a)(21) of this title).

(i) Administrative procedures

(1) *In general*

(A) *Decision made in hearing.* A decision made in a hearing conducted pursuant to subsection (f) or (k) of this section shall be final, except that any party involved in such hearing may appeal such decision under the provisions of subsection (g) of this section and paragraph (2) of this subsection.

(B) *Decision made at appeal.* A decision made under subsection (g) of this section shall be final, except that any party may bring an action under paragraph (2) of this subsection.

(2) *Right to bring civil action*

(A) *In general.* Any party aggrieved by the findings and decision made under subsection (f) or (k) of this section who does not have the right to an appeal under subsection (g) of this section, and any party aggrieved by the findings and decision under this subsection, shall have the right to bring a civil action with respect to the complaint presented pursuant to this section, which action may be brought in any State court of competent jurisdiction or in a district court of the United States without regard to the amount in controversy.

(B) *Additional requirements.* In any action brought under this paragraph, the court:

(i) shall receive the records of the administrative proceedings;

(ii) shall hear additional evidence at the request of a party; and

(iii) basing its decision on the preponderance of the evidence, shall grant such relief as the court determines is appropriate.

(3) *Jurisdiction of district courts; attorneys' fees*

(A) *In general.* The district courts of the United States shall have jurisdiction of actions brought under this section without regard to the amount in controversy.

(B) *Award of attorneys' fees.* In any action or proceeding brought under this section, the court, in its discretion, may award reasonable attorneys' fees as part of the costs to the parents of a child with a disability who is the prevailing party.

(C) *Determination of amount of attorneys' fees.* Fees awarded under this paragraph shall be based on rates prevailing in the community in which the action or proceeding arose for the kind and quality of services furnished. No bonus or multiplier may be used in calculating the fees awarded under this subsection.

(D) *Prohibition of attorneys' fees and related costs for certain services*

(i) Attorneys' fees may not be awarded and related costs may not be reimbursed in any action or proceeding under this section for services performed subsequent to the time of a written offer of settlement to a parent if:

(I) the offer is made within the time prescribed by Rule 68 of the Federal Rules of Civil Procedure or, in the case of an administrative proceeding, at any time more than 10 days before the proceeding begins;

(II) the offer is not accepted within 10 days; and

(III) the court or administrative hearing officer finds that the relief finally obtained by the parents is not more favorable to the parents than the offer of settlement.

(ii) Attorneys' fees may not be awarded relating to any meeting of the IEP Team unless such meeting is convened as a result of an administrative proceeding or judicial action, or, at the discretion of the State, for a mediation described in subsection (e) of this section that is conducted prior to the filing of a complaint under subsection (b)(6) or (k) of this section.

(E) *Exception to prohibition on attorneys' fees and related costs.* Notwithstanding subparagraph (D), an award of attorneys' fees and related costs may be made to a parent who is the prevailing party and who was substantially justified in rejecting the settlement offer.

(F) *Reduction in amount of attorneys' fees.* Except as provided in subparagraph (G), whenever the court finds that:

(i) the parent, during the course of the action or proceeding, unreasonably protracted the final resolution of the controversy;

(ii) the amount of the attorneys' fees otherwise authorized to be awarded unreasonably exceeds the hourly rate prevailing in the community for similar services by attorneys of reasonably comparable skill, reputation, and experience;

(iii) the time spent and legal services furnished were excessive considering the nature of the action or proceeding; or

(iv) the attorney representing the parent did not provide to the school district the appropriate information in the due process complaint in accordance with subsection (b)(7) of this section; the court shall reduce, accordingly, the amount of the attorneys' fees awarded under this section.

(G) *Exception to reduction in amount of attorneys' fees.* The provisions of subparagraph (F) shall not apply in any action or proceeding if the court finds that the State or local educational agency unreasonably protracted the final resolution of the action or proceeding or there was a violation of this section.

(j) Maintenance of current educational placement. Except as provided in subsection (k)(7) of this section, during the pendency of any proceedings conducted pursuant to this section, unless the State or local educational agency and the parents otherwise agree, the child shall remain in the then-current educational placement of such child, or, if applying for initial admission to a public school, shall, with the consent of the parents, be placed in the public school program until all such proceedings have been completed.

(k) Placement in alternative educational setting

(1) *Authority of school personnel*

(A) School personnel under this section may order a change in the placement of a child with a disability:

(i) to an appropriate interim alternative educational setting, another setting, or suspension, for not more than 10 school days (to the extent such alternatives would be applied to children without disabilities); and

(ii) to an appropriate interim alternative educational setting for the same amount of time that a child without a disability would be subject to discipline, but for not more than 45 days if:

(I) the child carries a weapon to school or to a school function under the jurisdiction of a State or a local educational agency; or

(II) the child knowingly possesses or uses illegal drugs or sells or solicits the sale of a controlled substance while at school or a school function under the jurisdiction of a State or local educational agency.

(B) Either before or not later than 10 days after taking a disciplinary action described in subparagraph (A):

(i) if the local educational agency did not conduct a functional behavioral assessment and implement a behavioral intervention plan for such child before the behavior that resulted in the suspension described in subparagraph (A), the agency shall convene an IEP meeting to develop an assessment plan to address that behavior; or

(ii) if the child already has a behavioral intervention plan, the IEP Team shall review the plan and modify it, as necessary, to address the behavior.

(2) *Authority of hearing officer.* A hearing officer under this section may order a change in the placement of a child with a disability to an appropriate interim alternative educational setting for not more than 45 days if the hearing officer:

(A) determines that the public agency has demonstrated by substantial evidence that maintaining the current placement of such child is substantially likely to result in injury to the child or to others;

(B) considers the appropriateness of the child's current placement;

(C) considers whether the public agency has made reasonable efforts to minimize the risk of harm in the child's current placement, including the use of supplementary aids and services; and

(D) determines that the interim alternative educational setting meets the requirements of paragraph (3)(B).

(3) *Determination of setting*

(A) *In general.* The alternative educational setting described in paragraph (1)(A)(ii) shall be determined by the IEP Team.

(B) *Additional requirements.* Any interim alternative educational setting in which a child is placed under paragraph (1) or (2) shall:

(i) be selected so as to enable the child to continue to participate in the general curriculum, although in another setting, and to continue to receive those services and modifications, including those described in the child's current IEP, that will enable the child to meet the goals set out in that IEP; and

(ii) include services and modifications designed to address the behavior described in paragraph (1) or paragraph (2) so that it does not recur.

(4) *Manifestation determination review*

(A) *In general.* If a disciplinary action is contemplated as described in paragraph (1) or paragraph (2) for a behavior of a child with a disability described in either of those paragraphs, or if a disciplinary action involving a change of placement for more than 10 days is contemplated for a child with a disability who has engaged in other behavior that violated any rule or code of conduct of the local educational agency that applies to all children:

(i) not later than the date on which the decision to take that action is made, the parents shall be notified of that decision and of all procedural safeguards accorded under this section; and

(ii) immediately, if possible, but in no case later than 10 school days after the date on which the decision to take that action is made, a review shall be conducted of the relationship between the child's disability and the behavior subject to the disciplinary action.

(B) *Individuals to carry out review.* A review described in subparagraph (A) shall be conducted by the IEP Team and other qualified personnel.

(C) *Conduct of review.* In carrying out a review described in subparagraph (A), the IEP Team may determine that the behavior of the child was not a manifestation of such child's disability only if the IEP Team:

(i) first considers, in terms of the behavior subject to disciplinary action, all relevant information, including:

(I) evaluation and diagnostic results, including such results or other relevant information supplied by the parents of the child;

(II) observations of the child; and

(III) the child's IEP and placement; and

(ii) then determines that:

(I) in relationship to the behavior subject to disciplinary action, the child's IEP and placement were appropriate and the special education services, supplementary aids and services, and behavior intervention strategies were provided consistent with the child's IEP and placement;

(II) the child's disability did not impair the ability of the child to understand the impact and consequences of the behavior subject to disciplinary action; and

(III) the child's disability did not impair the ability of the child to control the behavior subject to disciplinary action.

(5) *Determination that behavior was not manifestation of disability*

(A) *In general.* If the result of the review described in paragraph (4) is a determination, consistent with paragraph (4)(C), that the behavior of the child with a disability was not a manifestation of the child's disability, the relevant disciplinary procedures applicable to children without disabilities may be applied to the child in the same manner in which they would be applied to children without disabilities, except as provided in section 1412(a)(1) of this title.

(B) *Additional requirement.* If the public agency initiates disciplinary procedures applicable to all children, the agency shall ensure that the special education and disciplinary records of the child with a disability are transmitted for consideration by the person or persons making the final determination regarding the disciplinary action.

(6) *Parent appeal*

(A) *In general*

(i) If the child's parent disagrees with a determination that the child's behavior was not a manifestation of the child's disability or with any decision regarding placement, the parent may request a hearing.

(ii) The State or local educational agency shall arrange for an expedited hearing in any case described in this subsection when requested by a parent.

(B) *Review of decision*

(i) In reviewing a decision with respect to the manifestation determination, the hearing officer shall determine whether the public agency has demonstrated that the child's behavior was not a manifestation of such child's disability consistent with the requirements of paragraph (4)(C).

(ii) In reviewing a decision under paragraph (1)(A)(ii) to place the child in an interim alternative educational setting, the hearing officer shall apply the standards set out in paragraph (2).

(7) *Placement during appeals*

(A) *In general.* When a parent requests a hearing regarding a disciplinary action described in paragraph (1)(A)(ii) or paragraph (2) to challenge the interim alternative educational setting or the manifestation determination, the child shall remain in the interim alternative educational setting pending the decision of the hearing officer or until the expiration of the time period provided for in paragraph (1)(A)(ii) or paragraph (2), whichever occurs first, unless the parent and the State or local educational agency agree otherwise.

(B) *Current placement.* If a child is placed in an interim alternative educational setting pursuant to paragraph (1)(A)(ii) or paragraph (2) and school personnel propose to change the child's placement after expiration of the interim alternative placement, during the pendency of any proceeding to challenge the proposed change in placement, the child shall remain in the current placement (the child's placement prior to the interim alternative educational setting), except as provided in subparagraph (C).

(C) *Expedited hearing*

(i) If school personnel maintain that it is dangerous for the child to be in the current placement (placement prior to removal to the interim alternative education setting) during the pendency of the due process proceedings, the local educational agency may request an expedited hearing.

(ii) In determining whether the child may be placed in the alternative educational setting or in another appropriate placement ordered by the hearing officer, the hearing officer shall apply the standards set out in paragraph (2).

(8) *Protections for children not yet eligible for special education and related services*

(A) *In general.* A child who has not been determined to be eligible for special education and related services under this subchapter and who has engaged in behavior that violated any rule or code of conduct of the local educational agency, including any behavior described in paragraph (1), may assert any of the protections provided for in this subchapter if the local educational agency had knowledge (as determined in accordance with this paragraph) that the child was a child with a disability before the behavior that precipitated the disciplinary action occurred.

(B) *Basis of knowledge.* A local educational agency shall be deemed to have knowledge that a child is a child with a disability if:

(i) the parent of the child has expressed concern in writing (unless the parent is illiterate or has a disability that prevents compliance with the requirements contained in this clause) to personnel of the appropriate educational agency that the child is in need of special education and related services;

(ii) the behavior or performance of the child demonstrates the need for such services;

(iii) the parent of the child has requested an evaluation of the child pursuant to section 1414 of this title; or

(iv) the teacher of the child, or other personnel of the local educational agency, has expressed concern about the behavior or performance of the child to the director of special education of such agency or to other personnel of the agency.

(C) *Conditions that apply if no basis of knowledge*

(i) In general. If a local educational agency does not have knowledge that a child is a child with a disability (in accordance with subparagraph (B)) prior to taking disciplinary measures against the child, the child may be subjected to the same disciplinary measures as measures applied to children without disabilities who engaged in comparable behaviors consistent with clause (ii).

(ii) Limitations. If a request is made for an evaluation of a child during the time period in which the child is subjected to disciplinary measures under paragraph (1) or (2), the evaluation shall be conducted in an expedited manner. If the child is determined to be a child with a disability, taking into consideration information from the evaluation conducted by the agency and information provided by the parents, the agency shall provide special education and related services in accordance with the provisions of this subchapter, except that, pending the results of the evaluation, the child shall remain in the educational placement determined by school authorities.

(9) *Referral to and action by law enforcement and judicial authorities*

(A) Nothing in this subchapter shall be construed to prohibit an agency from reporting a crime committed by a child with a disability to appropriate authorities or to prevent State law enforcement and judicial authorities from exercising their responsibilities with regard to the application of Federal and State law to crimes committed by a child with a disability.

(B) An agency reporting a crime committed by a child with a disability shall ensure that copies of the special education and disciplinary records of the child are transmitted for consideration by the appropriate authorities to whom it reports the crime.

(10) *Definitions.* For purposes of this subsection, the following definitions apply:

(A) *Controlled substance.* The term "controlled substance" means a drug or other substance identified under schedules I, II, III, IV, or V in section 20 (c) of the Controlled Substances Act (21 U.S.C. 81 (c)).

(B) *Illegal drug.* The term "illegal drug":

(i) means a controlled substance; but

(ii) does not include such a substance that is legally possessed or used under the supervision of a licensed health-care professional or that is legally possessed or used under any other authority under that Act (21 U.S.C. 801 et seq.) or under any other provision of Federal law.

(C) *Substantial evidence.* The term "substantial evidence" means beyond a preponderance of the evidence.

(D) *Weapon.* The term "weapon" has the meaning given the term "dangerous weapon" under paragraph (2) of the first subsection (g) of section 930 of title 18.

(l) Rule of construction. Nothing in this chapter shall be construed to restrict or limit the rights, procedures, and remedies available under the Constitution, the Americans with Disabilities Act of 1990 (42 U.S.C. 12101 et seq.), title V of the Rehabilitation Act of 1973 (29 U.S.C. 790 et seq.), or other Federal laws protecting the rights of children with disabilities, except that before the filing of a civil action under such laws seeking relief that is also available under this subchapter, the procedures under subsections (f) and (g) of this section shall be exhausted to the same extent as would be required had the action been brought under this subchapter.

(m) Transfer of parental rights at age of majority

(1) *In general.* A State that receives amounts from a grant under this subchapter may provide that, when a child with a disability reaches the age of majority under State law (except for a child with a disability who has been determined to be incompetent under State law):

(A) the public agency shall provide any notice required by this section to both the individual and the parents;

(B) all other rights accorded to parents under this subchapter transfer to the child;

(C) the agency shall notify the individual and the parents of the transfer of rights; and

(D) all rights accorded to parents under this subchapter transfer to children who are incarcerated in an adult or juvenile Federal, State, or local correctional institution.

(2) *Special rule.* If, under State law, a child with a disability who has reached the age of majority under State law, who has not been determined to be incompetent, but who is determined not to have the ability to provide informed consent with respect to the educational program of the child, the State shall establish procedures for appointing the parent of the child, or if the parent is not available, another appropriate individual, to represent the educational interests of the child throughout the period of eligibility of the child under this subchapter.

IDEA Regulations (Key Sections)

Assistance to States for the Education of Children With Disabilities

34 C.F.R. Part 300

Assistance to States for the Education of Children With Disabilities

Subpart A: General Purposes, Applicability, and Regulations That Apply to This Program

Sec. 300.1. Purposes.

The purposes of this part are—

(a) To ensure that all children with disabilities have available to them a free appropriate public education that emphasizes special education and related services designed to meet their unique needs and prepare them for employment and independent living;

(b) To ensure that the rights of children with disabilities and their parents are protected;

(c) To assist States, localities, educational service agencies, and Federal agencies to provide for the education of all children with disabilities; and

(d) To assess and ensure the effectiveness of efforts to educate children with disabilities.

(Authority: 20 U.S.C. 1400 note)

Sec. 300.2 Applicability of this part to State, local, and private agencies.

(a) States. This part applies to each State that receives payments under Part B of the Act.

(b) Public agencies within the State. The provisions of this part—

(1) Apply to all political subdivisions of the State that are involved in the education of children with disabilities, including—

(i) The State educational agency (SEA);

(ii) Local educational agencies (LEAs), educational service agencies (ESAs), and public charter schools that are not otherwise included as LEAs or ESAs and are not a school of an LEA or ESA;

(iii) Other State agencies and schools (such as Departments of Mental Health and Welfare and State schools for children with deafness or children with blindness); and

(iv) State and local juvenile and adult correctional facilities; and

(2) Are binding on each public agency in the State that provides special education and related services to children with disabilities, regardless of whether that agency is receiving funds under Part B.

(c) Private schools and facilities. Each public agency in the State is responsible for ensuring that the rights and protections under Part B of the Act are given to children with disabilities—

(1) Referred to or placed in private schools and facilities by that public agency; or

(2) Placed in private schools by their parents under the provisions of Sec. 300.403(c).

(Authority: 20 U.S.C. 1412)

Sec. 300.3. Regulations that apply.

The following regulations apply to this program:

(a) 34 CFR part 76 (State-Administered Programs) except for Secs. 76.125-76.137 and 76.650-76.662.

(b) 34 CFR part 77 (Definitions).

(c) 34 CFR part 79 (Intergovernmental Review of Department of Education Programs and Activities).

(d) 34 CFR part 80 (Uniform Administrative Requirements for Grants and Cooperative Agreements to State and Local Governments).

(e) 34 CFR part 81 (General Education Provisions Act—Enforcement).

(f) 34 CFR part 82 (New Restrictions on Lobbying).

(g) 34 CFR part 85 (Government-wide Debarment and Suspension (Nonprocurement) and Government-wide Requirements for Drug-Free Workplace (Grants)).

(h) The regulations in this part—34 CFR part 300 (Assistance for Education of Children with Disabilities).

(Authority: 20 U.S.C. 1221e-3(a)(1))

Sec. 300.5. Assistive technology device.

As used in this part, Assistive technology device means any item, piece of equipment, or product system, whether acquired commercially off the shelf, modified, or customized, that is used to increase, maintain, or improve the functional capabilities of a child with a disability.

(Authority: 20 U.S.C. 1401(1))

Sec. 300.6. Assistive technology service.

As used in this part, Assistive technology service means any service that directly assists a child with a disability in the selection, acquisition, or use of an assistive technology device.

The term includes—

(a) The evaluation of the needs of a child with a disability, including a functional evaluation of the child in the child's customary environment;

(b) Purchasing, leasing, or otherwise providing for the acquisition of assistive technology devices by children with disabilities;

(c) Selecting, designing, fitting, customizing, adapting, applying, maintaining, repairing, or replacing assistive technology devices;

(d) Coordinating and using other therapies, interventions, or services with assistive technology devices, such as those associated with existing education and rehabilitation plans and programs;

(e) Training or technical assistance for a child with a disability or, if appropriate, that child's family; and

(f) Training or technical assistance for professionals (including individuals providing education or rehabilitation services), employers, or other individuals who provide services to, employ, or are otherwise substantially involved in the major life functions of that child.

(Authority: 20 U.S.C. 1401(2))

Sec. 300.7. Child with a disability.

(a) General. (1) As used in this part, the term child with a disability means a child evaluated in accordance with Secs. 300.530-300.536 as having mental retardation, a hearing impairment including deafness, a speech or language impairment, a visual impairment including blindness, serious emotional disturbance (hereafter referred to as emotional disturbance), an orthopedic impairment, autism, traumatic brain injury, an other health impairment, a specific learning disability, deaf-blindness, or multiple disabilities, and who, by reason thereof, needs special education and related services.

(2)(i) Subject to paragraph (a)(2)(ii) of this section, if it is determined, through an appropriate evaluation under Secs. 300.530-300.536, that a child has one of the disabilities identified in paragraph (a)(1) of this section, but only needs a related service and not special education, the child is not a child with a disability under this part.

(ii) If, consistent with Sec. 300.26(a)(2), the related service required by the child is considered special education rather than a related service under State standards, the child would be determined to be a child with a disability under paragraph (a)(1) of this section.

(b) Children aged 3 through 9 experiencing developmental delays. The term child with a disability for children aged 3 through 9 may, at the discretion of the State and LEA and in accordance with Sec. 300.313, include a child—

(1) Who is experiencing developmental delays, as defined by the State and as measured by appropriate diagnostic instruments and procedures, in one or more of the following areas: physical development, cognitive development, communication development, social or emotional development, or adaptive development; and

(2) Who, by reason thereof, needs special education and related services.

(c) Definitions of disability terms. The terms used in this definition are defined as follows:

(1)(i) Autism means a developmental disability significantly affecting verbal and nonverbal communication and social interaction, generally evident before age 3, that adversely affects a child's educational performance. Other characteristics often associated with autism are engagement in repetitive activities and stereotyped movements, resistance to environmental change or change in daily routines, and unusual responses to sensory experiences. The term does not apply if a child's educational performance is adversely affected primarily because the child has an emotional disturbance, as defined in paragraph (b)(4) of this section.

(ii) A child who manifests the characteristics of "autism" after age 3 could be diagnosed as having "autism" if the criteria in paragraph (c)(1)(i) of this section are satisfied.

(2) Deaf-blindness means concomitant hearing and visual impairments, the combination of which causes such severe communication and other developmental and educational needs that they cannot be accommodated in special education programs solely for children with deafness or children with blindness.

(3) Deafness means a hearing impairment that is so severe that the child is impaired in processing linguistic information through hearing, with or without amplification, that adversely affects a child's educational performance.

(4) Emotional disturbance is defined as follows:

(i) The term means a condition exhibiting one or more of the following characteristics over a long period of time and to a marked degree that adversely affects a child's educational performance:

(A) An inability to learn that cannot be explained by intellectual, sensory, or health factors.

(B) An inability to build or maintain satisfactory interpersonal relationships with peers and teachers.

(C) Inappropriate types of behavior or feelings under normal circumstances.

(D) A general pervasive mood of unhappiness or depression.

(E) A tendency to develop physical symptoms or fears associated with personal or school problems.

(ii) The term includes schizophrenia. The term does not apply to children who are socially maladjusted, unless it is determined that they have an emotional disturbance.

(5) Hearing impairment means an impairment in hearing, whether permanent or fluctuating, that adversely affects a child's educational performance but that is not included under the definition of deafness in this section.

(6) Mental retardation means significantly subaverage general intellectual functioning, existing concurrently with deficits in adaptive behavior and manifested during the developmental period, that adversely affects a child's educational performance.

(7) Multiple disabilities means concomitant impairments (such as mental retardation-blindness, mental retardation-orthopedic impairment, etc.), the combination of which causes such severe educational needs that they cannot be accommodated in special education programs solely for one of the impairments. The term does not include deaf-blindness.

(8) Orthopedic impairment means a severe orthopedic impairment that adversely affects a child's educational performance. The term includes impairments caused by congenital anomaly (e.g., clubfoot, absence of some member, etc.), impairments caused by disease (e.g., poliomyelitis, bone tuberculosis, etc.), and impairments from other causes (e.g., cerebral palsy, amputations, and fractures or burns that cause contractures).

(9) Other health impairment means having limited strength, vitality or alertness, including a heightened alertness to environmental stimuli, that results in limited alertness with respect to the educational environment, that—

(i) Is due to chronic or acute health problems such as asthma, attention deficit disorder or attention deficit hyperactivity disorder, diabetes, epilepsy, a heart condition, hemophilia, lead poisoning, leukemia, nephritis, rheumatic fever, and sickle cell anemia; and

(ii) Adversely affects a child's educational performance.

(10) Specific learning disability is defined as follows:

(i) General. The term means a disorder in one or more of the basic psychological processes involved in understanding or in using language, spoken or written, that may manifest itself in an imperfect ability to listen, think, speak, read, write, spell, or to do mathematical calculations, including conditions such as perceptual disabilities, brain injury, minimal brain dysfunction, dyslexia, and developmental aphasia.

(ii) Disorders not included. The term does not include learning problems that are primarily the result of visual, hearing, or motor disabilities, of mental retardation, of emotional disturbance, or of environmental, cultural, or economic disadvantage.

(11) Speech or language impairment means a communication disorder, such as stuttering, impaired articulation, a language impairment, or a voice impairment, that adversely affects a child's educational performance.

(12) Traumatic brain injury means an acquired injury to the brain caused by an external physical force, resulting in total or partial functional disability or psychosocial impairment, or both, that adversely affects a child's educational performance. The term applies to open or closed head injuries resulting in impairments in one or more areas, such as cognition; language; memory; attention; reasoning; abstract thinking; judgment; problem-solving; sensory, perceptual, and motor abilities; psychosocial behavior; physical functions; information processing; and speech. The term does not apply to brain injuries that are congenital or degenerative, or to brain injuries induced by birth trauma.

(13) Visual impairment including blindness means an impairment in vision that, even with correction, adversely affects a child's educational performance. The term includes both partial sight and blindness.

(Authority: 20 U.S.C. 1401(3)(A) and (B); 1401(26))

Sec. 300.9. Day; business day; school day.

As used in this part, the term—

(a) Day means calendar day unless otherwise indicated as business day or school day;

(b) Business day means Monday through Friday, except for Federal and State holidays (unless holidays are specifically included in the designation of business day, as in Sec. 300.403(d)(1)(ii)); and

(c)(1) School day means any day, including a partial day, that children are in attendance at school for instructional purposes.

(2) The term school day has the same meaning for all children in school, including children with and without disabilities.

(Authority: 20 U.S.C. 1221e-3)

Sec. 300.10. Educational service agency.

As used in this part, the term educational service agency—

(a) Means a regional public multiservice agency—

(1) Authorized by State law to develop, manage, and provide services or programs to LEAs; and

(2) Recognized as an administrative agency for purposes of the provision of special education and related services provided within public elementary and secondary schools of the State;

(b) Includes any other public institution or agency having administrative control and direction over a public elementary or secondary school; and

(c) Includes entities that meet the definition of intermediate educational unit in section 602(23) of IDEA as in effect prior to June 4, 1997.

(Authority: 20 U.S.C. 1401(4))

Sec. 300.11. Equipment.

As used in this part, the term equipment means—

(a) Machinery, utilities, and built-in equipment and any necessary enclosures or structures to house the machinery, utilities, or equipment; and

(b) All other items necessary for the functioning of a particular facility as a facility for the provision of educational services, including items such as instructional equipment and necessary furniture; printed, published and audio-visual instructional materials; telecommunications, sensory, and other technological aids and devices; and books, periodicals, documents, and other related materials.

(Authority: 20 U.S.C. 1401(6))

Sec. 300.13. Free appropriate public education.

As used in this part, the term free appropriate public education or FAPE means special education and related services that—

(a) Are provided at public expense, under public supervision and direction, and without charge;

(b) Meet the standards of the SEA, including the requirements of this part;

(c) Include preschool, elementary school, or secondary school education in the State; and

(d) Are provided in conformity with an individualized education program (IEP) that meets the requirements of Secs. 300.340-300.350.

(Authority: 20 U.S.C. 1401(8))

Sec. 300.18. Local educational agency.

(a) As used in this part, the term local educational agency means a public board of education or other public authority legally constituted within a State for either administrative control or direction of, or to perform a service function for, public elementary or secondary schools in a city, county, township, school district, or other political subdivision of a State, or for a combination of school districts or

counties as are recognized in a State as an administrative agency for its public elementary or secondary schools.

(b) The term includes—

(1) An educational service agency, as defined in Sec. 300.10;

(2) Any other public institution or agency having administrative control and direction of a public elementary or secondary school, including a public charter school that is established as an LEA under State law; and

(3) An elementary or secondary school funded by the Bureau of Indian Affairs, and not subject to the jurisdiction of

any SEA other than the Bureau of Indian Affairs, but only to the extent that the inclusion makes the school eligible for programs for which specific eligibility is not provided to the school in another provision of law and the school does not have a student population that is smaller than the student population of the LEA receiving assistance under this Act with the smallest student population.

(Authority: 20 U.S.C. 1401(15))

Sec. 300.19. Native language.

(a) As used in this part, the term native language, if used with reference to an individual of limited English proficiency, means the following:

(1) The language normally used by that individual, or, in the case of a child, the language normally used by the parents of the child, except as provided in paragraph (a)(2) of this section.

(2) In all direct contact with a child (including evaluation of the child), the language normally used by the child in the home or learning environment.

(b) For an individual with deafness or blindness, or for an individual with no written language, the mode of communication is that normally used by the individual (such as sign language, braille, or oral communication).

(Authority: 20 U.S.C. 1401(16))

Sec. 300.20. Parent.

(a) General. As used in this part, the term parent means—

(1) A natural or adoptive parent of a child;

(2) A guardian but not the State if the child is a ward of the State;

(3) A person acting in the place of a parent (such as a grandparent or stepparent with whom the child lives, or a person who is legally responsible for the child's welfare); or

(4) A surrogate parent who has been appointed in accordance with Sec. 300.515.

(b) Foster parent. Unless State law prohibits a foster parent from acting as a parent, a State may allow a foster parent to act as a parent under Part B of the Act if—

(1) The natural parents' authority to make educational decisions on the child's behalf has been extinguished under State law; and

(2) The foster parent—

(i) Has an ongoing, long-term parental relationship with the child;

(ii) Is willing to make the educational decisions required of parents under the Act; and

(iii) Has no interest that would conflict with the interests of the child.

(Authority: 20 U.S.C. 1401(19))

Sec. 300.24. Related services.

(a) General. As used in this part, the term related services means transportation and such developmental, corrective, and other supportive services as are required to assist a child with a disability to benefit from special education, and includes speech-language pathology and audiology services, psycho-

logical services, physical and occupational therapy, recreation, including therapeutic recreation, early identification and assessment of disabilities in children, counseling services, including rehabilitation counseling, orientation and mobility services, and medical services for diagnostic or evaluation purposes. The term also includes school health services, social work services in schools, and parent counseling and training.

(b) Individual terms defined. The terms used in this definition are defined as follows:

(1) Audiology includes—

(i) Identification of children with hearing loss;

(ii) Determination of the range, nature, and degree of hearing loss, including referral for medical or other professional attention for the habilitation of hearing;

(iii) Provision of habilitative activities, such as language habilitation, auditory training, speech reading (lip-reading), hearing evaluation, and speech conservation;

(iv) Creation and administration of programs for prevention of hearing loss;

(v) Counseling and guidance of children, parents, and teachers regarding hearing loss; and

(vi) Determination of children's needs for group and individual amplification, selecting and fitting an appropriate aid, and evaluating the effectiveness of amplification.

(2) Counseling services means services provided by qualified social workers, psychologists, guidance counselors, or other qualified personnel.

(3) Early identification and assessment of disabilities in children means the implementation of a formal plan for identifying a disability as early as possible in a child's life.

(4) Medical services means services provided by a licensed physician to determine a child's medically related disability that results in the child's need for special education and related services.

(5) Occupational therapy—

(i) Means services provided by a qualified occupational therapist; and

(ii) Includes—

(A) Improving, developing or restoring functions impaired or lost through illness, injury, or deprivation;

(B) Improving ability to perform tasks for independent functioning if functions are impaired or lost; and

(C) Preventing, through early intervention, initial or further impairment or loss of function.

(6) Orientation and mobility services—

(i) Means services provided to blind or visually impaired students by qualified personnel to enable those students to attain systematic orientation to and safe movement within their environments in school, home, and community; and

(ii) Includes teaching students the following, as appropriate:

(A) Spatial and environmental concepts and use of information received by the senses (such as sound, temperature and vibrations) to establish, maintain, or regain orientation and line of travel (e.g., using sound at a traffic light to cross the street);

(B) To use the long cane to supplement visual travel skills or as a tool for safely negotiating the environment for students with no available travel vision;

(C) To understand and use remaining vision and distance low vision aids; and

(D) Other concepts, techniques, and tools.

(7) Parent counseling and training means—

(i) Assisting parents in understanding the special needs of their child;

(ii) Providing parents with information about child development; and

(iii) Helping parents to acquire the necessary skills that will allow them to support the implementation of their child's IEP or IFSP.

(8) Physical therapy means services provided by a qualified physical therapist.

(9) Psychological services includes—

(i) Administering psychological and educational tests, and other assessment procedures;

(ii) Interpreting assessment results;

(iii) Obtaining, integrating, and interpreting information about child behavior and conditions relating to learning;

(iv) Consulting with other staff members in planning school programs to meet the special needs of children as indicated by psychological tests, interviews, and behavioral evaluations;

(v) Planning and managing a program of psychological services, including psychological counseling for children and parents; and

(vi) Assisting in developing positive behavioral intervention strategies.

(10) Recreation includes—

(i) Assessment of leisure function;

(ii) Therapeutic recreation services;

(iii) Recreation programs in schools and community agencies; and

(iv) Leisure education.

(11) Rehabilitation counseling services means services provided by qualified personnel in individual or group sessions that focus specifically on career development, employment preparation, achieving independence, and integration in the workplace and community of a student with a disability. The term also includes vocational rehabilitation services provided to a student with disabilities by vocational rehabilitation programs funded under the Rehabilitation Act of 1973, as amended.

(12) School health services means services provided by a qualified school nurse or other qualified person.

(13) Social work services in schools includes—

(i) Preparing a social or developmental history on a child with a disability;

(ii) Group and individual counseling with the child and family;

(iii) Working in partnership with parents and others on those problems in a child's living situation (home, school, and community) that affect the child's adjustment in school;

(iv) Mobilizing school and community resources to enable the child to learn as effectively as possible in his or her educational program; and

(v) Assisting in developing positive behavioral intervention strategies.

(14) Speech-language pathology services includes—

(i) Identification of children with speech or language impairments;

(ii) Diagnosis and appraisal of specific speech or language impairments;

(iii) Referral for medical or other professional attention necessary for the habilitation of speech or language impairments;

(iv) Provision of speech and language services for the habilitation or prevention of communicative impairments; and

(v) Counseling and guidance of parents, children, and teachers regarding speech and language impairments.

(15) Transportation includes—

(i) Travel to and from school and between schools;

(ii) Travel in and around school buildings; and

(iii) Specialized equipment (such as special or adapted buses, lifts, and ramps), if required to provide special transportation for a child with a disability.

(Authority: 20 U.S.C. 1401(22))

Sec. 300.26. Special education.

(a) General. (1) As used in this part, the term special education means specially designed instruction, at no cost to the parents, to meet the unique needs of a child with a disability, including—

(i) Instruction conducted in the classroom, in the home, in hospitals and institutions, and in other settings; and

(ii) Instruction in physical education.

(2) The term includes each of the following, if it meets the requirements of paragraph (a)(1) of this section:

(i) Speech-language pathology services, or any other related service, if the service is considered special education rather than a related service under State standards;

(ii) Travel training; and

(iii) Vocational education.

(b) Individual terms defined. The terms in this definition are defined as follows:

(1) At no cost means that all specially-designed instruction is provided without charge, but does not preclude incidental fees that are normally charged to nondisabled students or their parents as a part of the regular education program.

(2) Physical education—

(i) Means the development of—

(A) Physical and motor fitness;

(B) Fundamental motor skills and patterns; and

(C) Skills in aquatics, dance, and individual and group games and sports (including intramural and lifetime sports); and

(ii) Includes special physical education, adapted physical education, movement education, and motor development.

(3) Specially-designed instruction means adapting, as appropriate to the needs of an eligible child under this part, the content, methodology, or delivery of instruction—

(i) To address the unique needs of the child that result from the child's disability; and

(ii) To ensure access of the child to the general curriculum, so that he or she can meet the educational standards within the jurisdiction of the public agency that apply to all children.

(4) Travel training means providing instruction, as appropriate, to children with significant cognitive disabilities, and any other children with disabilities who require this instruction, to enable them to—

(i) Develop an awareness of the environment in which they live; and

(ii) Learn the skills necessary to move effectively and safely from place to place within that environment (e.g., in school, in the home, at work, and in the community).

(5) Vocational education means organized educational programs that are directly related to the preparation of individuals for paid or unpaid employment, or for additional preparation for a career requiring other than a baccalaureate or advanced degree.

(Authority: 20 U.S.C. 1401(25))

Sec. 300.28. Supplementary aids and services.

As used in this part, the term supplementary aids and services means, aids, services, and other supports that are provided in regular education classes or other education-related settings to enable children with disabilities to be educated with nondisabled children to the maximum extent appropriate in accordance with Secs. 300.550-300.556.

(Authority: 20 U.S.C. 1401(29))

Sec. 300.29. Transition services.

(a) As used in this part, transition services means a coordinated set of activities for a student with a disability that—

(1) Is designed within an outcome-oriented process, that promotes movement from school to post-school activities, including postsecondary education, vocational training, integrated employment (including supported employment), continuing and adult education, adult services, independent living, or community participation;

(2) Is based on the individual student's needs, taking into account the student's preferences and interests; and

(3) Includes—

(i) Instruction;

(ii) Related services;

(iii) Community experiences;

(iv) The development of employment and other post-school adult living objectives; and

(v) If appropriate, acquisition of daily living skills and functional vocational evaluation.

(b) Transition services for students with disabilities may be special education, if provided as specially designed instruction, or related services, if required to assist a student with a disability to benefit from special education.

(Authority: 20 U.S.C. 1401(30))

Subpart B: State and Local Eligibility

Sec. 300.125. Child find.

(a) General requirement. (1) The State must have in effect policies and procedures to ensure that—

(i) All children with disabilities residing in the State, including children with disabilities attending private schools, regardless of the severity of their disability, and who are in need of special education and related services, are identified, located, and evaluated; and

(ii) A practical method is developed and implemented to determine which children are currently receiving needed special education and related services.

(2) The requirements of paragraph (a)(1) of this section apply to—

(i) Highly mobile children with disabilities (such as migrant and homeless children); and

(ii) Children who are suspected of being a child with a disability under Sec. 300.7 and in need of special education, even though they are advancing from grade to grade.

(b) Documents relating to child find. The State must have on file with the Secretary the policies and procedures described in paragraph (a) of this section, including—

(1) The name of the State agency (if other than the SEA) responsible for coordinating the planning and implementation of the policies and procedures under paragraph (a) of this section;

(2) The name of each agency that participates in the planning and implementation of the child find activities and a description of the nature and extent of its participation;

(3) A description of how the policies and procedures under paragraph (a) of this section will be monitored to ensure that the SEA obtains—

(i) The number of children with disabilities within each disability category that have been identified, located, and evaluated; and

(ii) Information adequate to evaluate the effectiveness of those policies and procedures; and

(4) A description of the method the State uses to determine which children are currently receiving special education and related services.

(c) Child find for children from birth through age 2 when the SEA and lead agency for the Part C program are different. (1) In States where the SEA and the State's lead agency for the Part C program are different and the Part C lead agency will be participating in the child find activities described in paragraph (a) of this section, a description of the nature and extent of the Part C lead agency's participation must be included under paragraph (b)(2) of this section.

(2) With the SEA's agreement, the Part C lead agency's participation may include the actual implementation of child find activities for infants and toddlers with disabilities.

(3) The use of an interagency agreement or other mechanism for providing for the Part C lead agency's participation does not alter or diminish the responsibility of the SEA to ensure compliance with the requirements of this section.

(d) Construction. Nothing in the Act requires that children be classified by their disability so long as each child who has a disability listed in Sec. 300.7 and who, by reason of that disability, needs special education and related services is regarded as a child with a disability under Part B of the Act.

(e) Confidentiality of child find data. The collection and use of data to meet the requirements of this section are subject to the confidentiality requirements of Secs. 300.560-300.577.

(Authority: 20 U.S.C. 1412 (a)(3)(A) and (B))

Sec. 300.136. Personnel standards.

(a) Definitions. As used in this part—

(1) Appropriate professional requirements in the State means entry level requirements that—

(i) Are based on the highest requirements in the State applicable to the profession or discipline in which a person is providing special education or related services; and

(ii) Establish suitable qualifications for personnel providing special education and related services under Part B of the Act to children with disabilities who are served by State, local, and private agencies (see Sec. 300.2);

(2) Highest requirements in the State applicable to a specific profession or discipline means the highest entry-level academic degree needed for any State-approved or -recognized certification, licensing, registration, or other comparable requirements that apply to that profession or discipline;

(3) Profession or discipline means a specific occupational category that—

(i) Provides special education and related services to children with disabilities under Part B of the Act;

(ii) Has been established or designated by the State;

(iii) Has a required scope of responsibility and degree of supervision; and

(iv) Is not limited to traditional occupational categories; and

(4) State-approved or -recognized certification, licensing, registration, or other comparable requirements means the requirements that a State legislature either has enacted or has authorized a State agency to promulgate through rules to establish the entry-level standards for employment in a specific profession or discipline in that State.

(b) Policies and procedures. (1)(i) The State must have on file with the Secretary policies and procedures relating to the establishment and maintenance of standards to ensure that personnel necessary to carry out the purposes of this part are appropriately and adequately prepared and trained.

(ii) The policies and procedures required in paragraph (b)(1)(i) of this section must provide for the establishment and maintenance of standards that are consistent with any State-approved or -recognized certification, licensing, registration, or other comparable requirements that apply to the profession or discipline in which a person is providing special education or related services.

(2) Each State may—

(i) Determine the specific occupational categories required to provide special education and related services within the State; and

(ii) Revise or expand those categories as needed.

(3) Nothing in this part requires a State to establish a specified training standard (e.g., a masters degree) for personnel who provide special education and related services under Part B of the Act.

(4) A State with only one entry-level academic degree for employment of personnel in a specific profession or discipline may modify that standard as necessary to ensure the provision of FAPE to all children with disabilities in the State without violating the requirements of this section.

(c) Steps for retraining or hiring personnel. To the extent that a State's standards for a profession or discipline, including standards for temporary or emergency certification, are not based on the highest requirements in the State applicable to a specific profession or discipline, the State must provide the steps the State is taking and the procedures for notifying public agencies and personnel of those steps and the timelines it has established for the retraining or hiring of personnel to meet appropriate professional requirements in the State.

(d) Status of personnel standards in the State. (1) In meeting the requirements in paragraphs (b) and (c) of this section, a determination must be made about the status of personnel standards in the State. That determination must be based on current information that accurately describes, for each profession or discipline in which personnel are providing special education or related services, whether the applicable standards are consistent with the highest requirements in the State for that profession or discipline.

(2) The information required in paragraph (d)(1) of this section must be on file in the SEA and available to the public.

(e) Applicability of State statutes and agency rules. In identifying the highest requirements in the State for purposes of this section, the requirements of all State statutes and the rules of all State agencies applicable to serving children with disabilities must be considered.

(f) Use of paraprofessionals and assistants. A State may allow paraprofessionals and assistants who are appropriately trained and supervised, in accordance with State law, regulations, or written policy, in meeting the requirements of this part to be used to assist in the provision of special education and related services to children with disabilities under Part B of the Act.

(g) Policy to address shortage of personnel.

(1) In implementing this section, a State may adopt a policy that includes a requirement that LEAs in the State make an ongoing good faith effort to recruit and hire appropriately and adequately trained personnel to provide special education and related services to children with disabilities, including, in a geographic area of the State where there is a shortage of personnel that meet these qualifications, the most qualified individuals available who are making satisfactory progress toward completing applicable course work necessary to meet the standards described in paragraph (b)(2) of this section, consistent with State law and the steps described in paragraph (c) of this section, within three years.

(2) If a State has reached its established date under paragraph (c) of this section, the State may still exercise the option

under paragraph (g)(1) of this section for training or hiring all personnel in a specific profession or discipline to meet appropriate professional requirements in the State.

(3)(i) Each State must have a mechanism for serving children with disabilities if instructional needs exceed available personnel who meet appropriate professional requirements in the State for a specific profession or discipline.

(ii) A State that continues to experience shortages of qualified personnel must address those shortages in its comprehensive system of personnel development under Sec. 300.135.

(Authority: 20 U.S.C. 1412(a)(15))

Sec. 300.245. School-based improvement plan.

(a) General. Each LEA may, in accordance with paragraph (b) of this section, use funds made available under Part B of the Act to permit a public school within the jurisdiction of the LEA to design, implement, and evaluate a school-based improvement plan that—

(1) Is consistent with the purposes described in section 651(b) of the Act; and

(2) Is designed to improve educational and transitional results for all children with disabilities and, as appropriate, for other children consistent with Sec. 300.235(a) and (b) in that public school.

(b) Authority. (1) General. An SEA may grant authority to an LEA to permit a public school described in Sec. 300.245 (through a school-based standing panel established under Sec. 300.247(b)) to design, implement, and evaluate a school-based improvement plan described in Sec. 300.245 for a period not to exceed 3 years.

(2) Responsibility of LEA. If an SEA grants the authority described in paragraph (b)(1) of this section, an LEA that is granted this authority must have the sole responsibility of oversight of all activities relating to the design, implementation, and evaluation of any school-based improvement plan that a public school is permitted to design under this section.

(Authority: 20 U.S.C. 1413(g)(1) and (g)(2)).

Sec. 300.246. Plan requirements.

A school-based improvement plan described in Sec. 300.245 must—

(a) Be designed to be consistent with the purposes described in section 651(b) of the Act and to improve educational and transitional results for all children with disabilities and, as appropriate, for other children consistent with Sec. 300.235(a) and (b), who attend the school for which the plan is designed and implemented;

(b) Be designed, evaluated, and, as appropriate, implemented by a school-based standing panel established in accordance with Sec. 300.247(b);

(c) Include goals and measurable indicators to assess the progress of the public school in meeting these goals; and

(d) Ensure that all children with disabilities receive the services described in their IEPs.

(Authority: 20 U.S.C. 1413(g)(3))

Sec. 300.247. Responsibilities of the LEA.

An LEA that is granted authority under Sec. 300.245(b) to permit a public school to design, implement, and evaluate a school-based improvement plan shall—

(a) Select each school under the jurisdiction of the agency that is eligible to design, implement, and evaluate the plan;

(b) Require each school selected under paragraph (a) of this section, in accordance with criteria established by the LEA under paragraph (c) of this section, to establish a school-based standing panel to carry out the duties described in Sec. 300.246(b);

(c) Establish—

(1) Criteria that must be used by the LEA in the selection of an eligible school under paragraph (a) of this section;

(2) Criteria that must be used by a public school selected under paragraph (a) of this section in the establishment of a school-based standing panel to carry out the duties described in Sec. 300.246(b) and that ensure that the membership of the panel reflects the diversity of the community in which the public school is located and includes, at a minimum—

(i) Parents of children with disabilities who attend a public school, including parents of children with disabilities from unserved and underserved populations, as appropriate;

(ii) Special education and general education teachers of public schools;

(iii) Special education and general education administrators, or the designee of those administrators, of those public schools; and

(iv) Related services providers who are responsible for providing services to the children with disabilities who attend those public schools; and

(3) Criteria that must be used by the LEA with respect to the distribution of funds under Part B of the Act to carry out this section;

(d) Disseminate the criteria established under paragraph (c) of this section to local school district personnel and local parent organizations within the jurisdiction of the LEA;

(e) Require a public school that desires to design, implement, and evaluate a school-based improvement plan to submit an application at the time, in the manner and accompanied by the information, that the LEA shall reasonably require; and

(f) Establish procedures for approval by the LEA of a school-based improvement plan designed under Part B of the Act.

(Authority:1413(g)(4))

Sec. 300.280. Public hearings before adopting State policies and procedures.

Prior to its adoption of State policies and procedures related to this part, the SEA shall—

(a) Make the policies and procedures available to the general public;

(b) Hold public hearings; and

(c) Provide an opportunity for comment by the general public on the policies and procedures.

(Authority: 20 U.S.C. 1412(a)(20))

Subpart C: Services

Sec. 300.300. Provision of FAPE.

(a) General. (1) Subject to paragraphs (b) and (c) of this section and Sec. 300.311, each State receiving assistance under this part shall ensure that FAPE is available to all children with disabilities, aged 3 through 21, residing in the State, including children with disabilities who have been suspended or expelled from school.

(2) As a part of its obligation under paragraph (a)(1) of this section, each State must ensure that the requirements of Sec. 300.125 (to identify, locate, and evaluate all children with disabilities) are implemented by public agencies throughout the State.

(3)(i) The services provided to the child under this part address all of the child's identified special education and related services needs described in paragraph (a) of this section.

(ii) The services and placement needed by each child with a disability to receive FAPE must be based on the child's unique needs and not on the child's disability.

(b) Exception for age ranges 3-5 and 18-21. This paragraph provides the rules for applying the requirements in paragraph (a) of this section to children with disabilities aged 3, 4, 5, 18, 19, 20, and 21 within the State:

(1) If State law or a court order requires the State to provide education for children with disabilities in any disability category in any of these age groups, the State must make FAPE available to all children with disabilities of the same age who have that disability.

(2) If a public agency provides education to nondisabled children in any of these age groups, it must make FAPE available to at least a proportionate number of children with disabilities of the same age.

(3) If a public agency provides education to 50 percent or more of its children with disabilities in any disability category in any of these age groups, it must make FAPE available to all its children with disabilities of the same age who have that disability. This provision does not apply to children aged 3 through 5 for any fiscal year for which the State receives a grant under section 619(a)(1) of the Act.

(4) If a public agency provides education to a child with a disability in any of these age groups, it must make FAPE available to that child and provide that child and his or her parents all of the rights under Part B of the Act and this part.

(5) A State is not required to make FAPE available to a child with a disability in one of these age groups if—

(i) State law expressly prohibits, or does not authorize, the expenditure of public funds to provide education to nondisabled children in that age group; or

(ii) The requirement is inconsistent with a court order that governs the provision of free public education to children with disabilities in that State.

(c) Children aged 3 through 21 on Indian reservations. With the exception of children identified in Sec. 300.715(b) and (c), the SEA shall ensure that all of the requirements of Part B of the Act are implemented for all children with disabilities aged 3 through 21 on reservations.

(Authority: 20 U.S.C. 1412(a)(1), 1411(i)(1)(C), S. Rep. No. 94—168, p. 19 (1975))

Sec. 300.302. Residential placement.

If placement in a public or private residential program is necessary to provide special education and related services to a child with a disability, the program, including non-medical care and room and board, must be at no cost to the parents of the child.

(Authority: 20 U.S.C. 1412(a)(1), 1412(a)(10)(B))

Sec. 300.303. Proper functioning of hearing aids.

Each public agency shall ensure that the hearing aids worn in school by children with hearing impairments, including deafness, are functioning properly.

(Authority: 20 U.S.C. 1412(a)(1))

Sec. 300.304. Full educational opportunity goal.

Each SEA shall ensure that each public agency establishes and implements a goal of providing full educational opportunity to all children with disabilities in the area served by the public agency.

(Authority: 20 U.S.C. 1412(a)(2)

Sec. 300.305. Program options.

Each public agency shall take steps to ensure that its children with disabilities have available to them the variety of educational programs and services available to nondisabled children in the area served by the agency, including art, music, industrial arts, consumer and homemaking education, and vocational education.

(Authority: 20 U.S.C. 1412(a)(2), 1413(a)(1))

Sec. 300.306. Nonacademic services.

(a) Each public agency shall take steps to provide nonacademic and extracurricular services and activities in the manner necessary to afford children with disabilities an equal opportunity for participation in those services and activities.

(b) Nonacademic and extracurricular services and activities may include counseling services, athletics, transportation, health services, recreational activities, special interest groups or clubs sponsored by the public agency, referrals to agencies that provide assistance to individuals with disabilities, and employment of students, including both employment by the public agency and assistance in making outside employment available.

(Authority: 20 U.S.C. 1412(a)(1))

Sec. 300.307. Physical education.

(a) General. Physical education services, specially designed if necessary, must be made available to every child with a disability receiving FAPE.

(b) Regular physical education. Each child with a disability must be afforded the opportunity to participate in the regular physical education program available to nondisabled children unless—

(1) The child is enrolled full time in a separate facility; or

(2) The child needs specially designed physical education, as prescribed in the child's IEP.

(c) Special physical education. If specially designed physical education is prescribed in a child's IEP, the public agency responsible for the education of that child shall provide the services directly or make arrangements for those services to be provided through other public or private programs.

(d) Education in separate facilities. The public agency responsible for the education of a child with a disability who is enrolled in a separate facility shall ensure that the child receives appropriate physical education services in compliance with paragraphs (a) and (c) of this section.

(Authority: 20 U.S.C. 1412(a)(25), 1412(a)(5)(A))

Sec. 300.308. Assistive technology.

(a) Each public agency shall ensure that assistive technology devices or assistive technology services, or both, as those terms are defined in Secs. 300.5-300.6, are made available to a child with a disability if required as a part of the child's—

(1) Special education under Sec. 300.26;

(2) Related services under Sec. 300.24; or

(3) Supplementary aids and services under Secs. 300.28 and 300.550(b)(2).

(b) On a case-by-case basis, the use of school-purchased assistive technology devices in a child's home or in other settings is required if the child's IEP team determines that the child needs access to those devices in order to receive FAPE.

(Authority: 20 U.S.C. 1412(a)(12)(B)(i))

Sec. 300.309. Extended school year services.

(a) General. (1) Each public agency shall ensure that extended school year services are available as necessary to provide FAPE, consistent with paragraph (a)(2) of this section.

(2) Extended school year services must be provided only if a child's IEP team determines, on an individual basis, in accordance with Secs. 300.340-300.350, that the services are necessary for the provision of FAPE to the child.

(3) In implementing the requirements of this section, a public agency may not—

(i) Limit extended school year services to particular categories of disability; or

(ii) Unilaterally limit the type, amount, or duration of those services.

(b) Definition. As used in this section, the term extended school year services means special education and related services that—

(1) Are provided to a child with a disability—

(i) Beyond the normal school year of the public agency;

(ii) In accordance with the child's IEP; and

(iii) At no cost to the parents of the child; and

(2) Meet the standards of the SEA.

(Authority: 20 U.S.C. 1412(a)(1))

Sec. 300.311 FAPE requirements for students with disabilities in adult prisons.

(a) Exception to FAPE for certain students. Except as provided in Sec. 300.122(a)(2)(ii), the obligation to make FAPE available to all children with disabilities does not apply with respect to students aged 18 through 21 to the extent that State law does not require that special education and related services under Part B of the Act be provided to students with disabilities who, in the last educational placement prior to their incarceration in an adult correctional facility—

(1) Were not actually identified as being a child with a disability under Sec. 300.7; and

(2) Did not have an IEP under Part B of the Act.

(b) Requirements that do not apply. The following requirements do not apply to students with disabilities who are convicted as adults under State law and incarcerated in adult prisons:

(1) The requirements contained in Sec. 300.138 and Sec. 300.347(a)(5)(i) (relating to participation of children with disabilities in general assessments).

(2) The requirements in Sec. 300.347(b) (relating to transition planning and transition services), with respect to the students whose eligibility under Part B of the Act will end, because of their age, before they will be eligible to be released from prison based on consideration of their sentence and eligibility for early release.

(c) Modifications of IEP or placement.

(1) Subject to paragraph (c)(2) of this section, the IEP team of a student with a disability, who is convicted as an adult under State law and incarcerated in an adult prison, may modify the student's IEP or placement if the State has demonstrated a bona fide security or compelling penological interest that cannot otherwise be accommodated.

(2) The requirements of Secs. 300.340(a) and 300.347(a) relating to IEPs, and 300.550(b) relating to LRE, do not apply with respect to the modifications described in paragraph (c)(1) of this section.

(Authority: 20 U.S.C. 1412(a)(1), 1414(d)(6))

Sec. 300.312 Children with disabilities in public charter schools.

(a) Children with disabilities who attend public charter schools and their parents retain all rights under this part.

(b) If the public charter school is an LEA, consistent with Sec. 300.17, that receives funding under Secs. 300.711-300.714, that charter school is responsible for ensuring that the requirements of this part are met, unless State law assigns that responsibility to some other entity.

(c) If the public charter school is a school of an LEA that receives funding under Secs. 300.711-300.714 and includes other public schools—

(1) The LEA is responsible for ensuring that the requirements of this part are met, unless State law assigns that responsibility to some other entity; and

(2) The LEA must meet the requirements of Sec. 300.241.

(d)(1) If the public charter school is not an LEA receiving funding under Secs. 300.711-300.714, or a school that is part of an LEA receiving funding under Secs. 300.711-300.714, the SEA is responsible for ensuring that the requirements of this part are met.

(2) Paragraph (d)(1) of this section does not preclude a State from assigning initial responsibility for ensuring the requirements of this part are met to another entity; however, the SEA must maintain the ultimate responsibility for ensuring compliance with this part, consistent with Sec. 300.600.

(Authority: 20 U.S.C. 1413(a)(5))

Sec. 300.313 Children experiencing developmental delays.

(a) Use of term developmental delay.

(1) A State that adopts the term developmental delay under Sec. 300.7(b) determines whether it applies to children aged 3 through 9, or to a subset of that age range (e.g., ages 3 through 5).

(2) A State may not require an LEA to adopt and use the term developmental delay for any children within its jurisdiction.

(3) If an LEA uses the term developmental delay for children described in Sec. 300.7(b), the LEA must conform to both the State's definition of that term and to the age range that has been adopted by the State.

(4) If a State does not adopt the term developmental delay, an LEA may not independently use that term as a basis for establishing a child's eligibility under this part.

(b) Use of individual disability categories.

(1) Any State or LEA that elects to use the term developmental delay for children aged 3 through 9 may also use one or more of the disability categories described in Sec. 300.7 for any child within that age range if it is determined, through the evaluation conducted under Secs. 300.530-300.536, that the child has an impairment described in Sec. 300.7, and because of that impairment needs special education and related services.

(2) The State or LEA shall ensure that all of the child's special education and related services needs that have been identified through the evaluation described in paragraph (b)(1) of this section are appropriately addressed.

(c) Common definition of developmental delay. A State may adopt a common definition of developmental delay for use in programs under Parts B and C of the Act.

(Authority: 20 U.S.C. 1401(3)(A) and (B))

Evaluations and Reevaluations

Sec. 300.320 Initial evaluations.

(a) Each public agency shall ensure that a full and individual evaluation is conducted for each child being considered for special education and related services under Part B of the Act—

(1) To determine if the child is a "child with a disability" under Sec. 300.7; and

(2) To determine the educational needs of the child.

(b) In implementing the requirements of paragraph (a) of this section, the public agency shall ensure that—

(1) The evaluation is conducted in accordance with the procedures described in Secs. 300.530-300.535; and

(2) The results of the evaluation are used by the child's IEP team in meeting the requirements of Secs. 300.340-300.350.

(Authority: 20 U.S.C. 1414(a), (b), and (c))

Sec. 300.340 Definitions related to IEPs.

(a) Individualized education program. As used in this part, the term individualized education program or IEP means a written statement for a child with a disability that is developed, reviewed, and revised in a meeting in accordance with Secs. 300.341-300.350.

(b) Participating agency. As used in Sec. 300.348, participating agency means a State or local agency, other than the public agency responsible for a student's education, that is financially and legally responsible for providing transition services to the student.

(Authority: 20 U.S.C. 1401(11), 1412(a)(10)(B))

Sec. 300.341 Responsibility of SEA and other public agencies for IEPs.

(a) The SEA shall ensure that each public agency—

(1) Except as provided in Secs. 300.450-300.462, develops and implements an IEP for each child with a disability served by that agency; and

(2) Ensures that an IEP is developed and implemented for each eligible child placed in or referred to a private school or facility by the public agency.

(b) Paragraph (a) of this section applies to—

(1) The SEA, if it is involved in providing direct services to children with disabilities, in accordance with Sec. 300.370(a) and (b)(1); and

(2) Except as provided in Sec. 300.600(d), the other public agencies described in Sec. 300.2, including LEAs and other State agencies that provide special education and related services either directly, by contract, or through other arrangements.

(Authority: 20 U.S.C. 1412(a)(4), (a)(10)(B))

Sec. 300.342 When IEPs must be in effect.

(a) General. At the beginning of each school year, each public agency shall have an IEP in effect for each child with a disability within its jurisdiction.

(b) Implementation of IEPs. Each public agency shall ensure that—

(1) An IEP—

(i) Is in effect before special education and related services are provided to an eligible child under this part; and

(ii) Is implemented as soon as possible following the meetings described under Sec. 300.343;

(2) The child's IEP is accessible to each regular education teacher, special education teacher, related service provider, and other service provider who is responsible for its implementation; and

(3) Each teacher and provider described in paragraph (b)(2) of this section is informed of—

(i) His or her specific responsibilities related to implementing the child's IEP; and

(ii) The specific accommodations, modifications, and supports that must be provided for the child in accordance with the IEP.

(c) IEP or IFSP for children aged 3 through 5.

(1) In the case of a child with a disability aged 3 through 5 (or, at the discretion of the SEA a 2-year-old child with a disability who will turn age 3 during the school year), an IFSP that contains the material described in section 636 of the Act, and that is developed in accordance with Secs. 300.341-300.346 and Secs. 300.349-300.350, may serve as the IEP of the child if using that plan as the IEP is—

(i) Consistent with State policy; and

(ii) Agreed to by the agency and the child's parents.

(2) In implementing the requirements of paragraph (c)(1) of this section, the public agency shall—

(i) Provide to the child's parents a detailed explanation of the differences between an IFSP and an IEP; and

(ii) If the parents choose an IFSP, obtain written informed consent from the parents.

(d) Effective date for new requirements. All IEPs developed, reviewed, or revised on or after July 1, 1998 must meet the requirements of Secs. 300.340-300.350.

(Authority: 20 U.S.C. 1414(d)(2)(A) and (B), Pub. L. 105-17, sec. 201(a)(2)(A), (C)

Sec. 300.343 IEP meetings.

(a) General. Each public agency is responsible for initiating and conducting meetings for the purpose of developing, reviewing, and revising the IEP of a child with a disability (or, if consistent with Sec. 300.342(c), an IFSP).

(b) Initial IEPs; provision of services.

(1) Each public agency shall ensure that within a reasonable period of time following the agency's receipt of parent consent to an initial evaluation of a child—

(i) The child is evaluated; and

(ii) If determined eligible under this part, special education and related services are made available to the child in accordance with an IEP.

(2) In meeting the requirement in paragraph (b)(1) of this section, a meeting to develop an IEP for the child must be conducted within 30-days of a determination that the child needs special education and related services.

(c) Review and revision of IEPs. Each public agency shall ensure that the IEP team—

(1) Reviews the child's IEP periodically, but not less than annually, to determine whether the annual goals for the child are being achieved; and

(2) Revises the IEP as appropriate to address—

(i) Any lack of expected progress toward the annual goals described in Sec. 300.347(a), and in the general curriculum, if appropriate;

(ii) The results of any reevaluation conducted under Sec. 300.536;

(iii) Information about the child provided to, or by, the parents, as described in Sec. 300.533(a)(1);

(iv) The child's anticipated needs; or

(v) Other matters.

(Authority: 20 U.S.C. 1413(a)(1), 1414(d)(4)(A)

Sec. 300.344 IEP team.

(a) General. The public agency shall ensure that the IEP team for each child with a disability includes—

(1) The parents of the child;

(2) At least one regular education teacher of the child (if the child is, or may be, participating in the regular education environment);

(3) At least one special education teacher of the child, or if appropriate, at least one special education provider of the child;

(4) A representative of the public agency who—

(i) Is qualified to provide, or supervise the provision of, specially designed instruction to meet the unique needs of children with disabilities;

(ii) Is knowledgeable about the general curriculum; and

(iii) Is knowledgeable about the availability of resources of the public agency;

(5) An individual who can interpret the instructional implications of evaluation results, who may be a member of the team described in paragraphs (a)(2) through (6) of this section;

(6) At the discretion of the parent or the agency, other individuals who have knowledge or special expertise regarding the child, including related services personnel as appropriate; and

(7) If appropriate, the child.

(b) Transition services participants.

(1) Under paragraph (a)(7) of this section, the public agency shall invite a student with a disability of any age to attend his or her IEP meeting if a purpose of the meeting will be the consideration of—

(i) The student's transition services needs under Sec. 300.347(b)(1);

(ii) The needed transition services for the student under Sec. 300.347(b)(2); or

(iii) Both.

(2) If the student does not attend the IEP meeting, the public agency shall take other steps to ensure that the student's preferences and interests are considered.

(3)(i) In implementing the requirements of Sec. 300.347(b)(2), the public agency also shall invite a representative of any other agency that is likely to be responsible for providing or paying for transition services.

(ii) If an agency invited to send a representative to a meeting does not do so, the public agency shall take other steps to obtain participation of the other agency in the planning of any transition services.

(c) Determination of knowledge and special expertise. The determination of the knowledge or special expertise of any individual described in paragraph (a)(6) of this section shall be made by the party (parents or public agency) who invited the individual to be a member of the IEP.

(d) Designating a public agency representative. A public agency may designate another public agency member of the IEP team to also serve as the agency representative, if the criteria in paragraph (a)(4) of this section are satisfied.

(Authority: 20 U.S.C. 1401(30), 1414(d)(1)(A)(7), (B))

Sec. 300.345 Parent participation.

(a) Public agency responsibility—general. Each public agency shall take steps to ensure that one or both of the parents of a child with a disability are present at each IEP meeting or are afforded the opportunity to participate, including—

(1) Notifying parents of the meeting early enough to ensure that they will have an opportunity to attend; and

(2) Scheduling the meeting at a mutually agreed on time and place.

(b) Information provided to parents.

(1) The notice required under paragraph (a)(1) of this section must—

(i) Indicate the purpose, time, and location of the meeting and who will be in attendance; and

(ii) Inform the parents of the provisions in Sec. 300.344(a)(6) and (c) (relating to the participation of other individuals on the IEP team who have knowledge or special expertise about the child).

(2) For a student with a disability beginning at age 14, or younger, if appropriate, the notice must also—

(i) Indicate that a purpose of the meeting will be the development of a statement of the transition services needs of the student required in Sec. 300.347(b)(1); and

(ii) Indicate that the agency will invite the student.

(3) For a student with a disability beginning at age 16, or younger, if appropriate, the notice must—

(i) Indicate that a purpose of the meeting is the consideration of needed transition services for the student required in Sec. 300.347(b)(2);

(ii) Indicate that the agency will invite the student; and

(iii) Identify any other agency that will be invited to send a representative.

(c) Other methods to ensure parent participation. If neither parent can attend, the public agency shall use other methods to ensure parent participation, including individual or conference telephone calls.

(d) Conducting an IEP meeting without a parent in attendance. A meeting may be conducted without a parent in attendance if the public agency is unable to convince the parents that they should attend. In this case the public agency must have a record of its attempts to arrange a mutually agreed on time and place, such as—

(1) Detailed records of telephone calls made or attempted and the results of those calls;

(2) Copies of correspondence sent to the parents and any responses received; and

(3) Detailed records of visits made to the parent's home or place of employment and the results of those visits.

(e) Use of interpreters or other action, as appropriate. The public agency shall take whatever action is necessary to ensure that the parent understands the proceedings at the IEP meeting, including arranging for an interpreter for parents with deafness or whose native language is other than English.

(f) Parent copy of child's IEP. The public agency shall give the parent a copy of the child's IEP at no cost to the parent.

(Authority: 20 U.S.C. 1414(d)(1)(B)(i))

Sec. 300.346 Development, review, and revision of IEP.

(a) Development of IEP.

(1) General. In developing each child's IEP, the IEP team, shall consider—

(i) The strengths of the child and the concerns of the parents for enhancing the education of their child;

(ii) The results of the initial or most recent evaluation of the child; and

(iii) As appropriate, the results of the child's performance on any general State or district-wide assessment programs.

(2) Consideration of special factors. The IEP team also shall—

(i) In the case of a child whose behavior impedes his or her learning or that of others, consider, if appropriate, strategies, including positive behavioral interventions, strategies, and supports to address that behavior;

(ii) In the case of a child with limited English proficiency, consider the language needs of the child as those needs relate to the child's IEP;

(iii) In the case of a child who is blind or visually impaired, provide for instruction in Braille and the use of Braille unless the IEP team determines, after an evaluation of the child's reading and writing skills, needs, and appropriate reading and writing media (including an evaluation of the child's future needs for instruction in Braille or the use of Braille), that instruction in Braille or the use of Braille is not appropriate for the child;

(iv) Consider the communication needs of the child, and in the case of a child who is deaf or hard of hearing, consider the child's language and communication needs, opportunities for direct communications with peers and professional personnel in the child's language and communication mode, academic level, and full range of needs, including opportunities for direct instruction in the child's language and communication mode; and

(v) Consider whether the child requires assistive technology devices and services.

(b) Review and Revision of IEP. In conducting a meeting to review, and, if appropriate, revise a child's IEP, the IEP team shall consider the factors described in paragraph (a) of this section.

(c) Statement in IEP. If, in considering the special factors described in paragraphs (a)(1) and (2) of this section, the IEP team determines that a child needs a particular device or service (including an intervention, accommodation, or other program modification) in order for the child to receive FAPE, the IEP team must include a statement to that effect in the child's IEP.

(d) Requirement with respect to regular education teacher. The regular education teacher of a child with a disability, as a member of the IEP team, must, to the extent appropriate, participate in the development, review, and revision of the child's IEP, including assisting in the determination of—

(1) Appropriate positive behavioral interventions and strategies for the child; and

(2) Supplementary aids and services, program modifications or supports for school personnel that will be provided for the child, consistent with Sec. 300.347(a)(3).

(e) Construction. Nothing in this section shall be construed to require the IEP team to include information under one component of a child's IEP that is already contained under another component of the child's IEP.

(Authority: 20 U.S.C. 1414(d)(3) and (4)(B) and (e))

Sec. 300.347 Content of IEP.

(a) General. The IEP for each child with a disability must include—

(1) A statement of the child's present levels of educational performance, including—

(i) How the child's disability affects the child's involvement and progress in the general curriculum (i.e., the same curriculum as for nondisabled children); or

(ii) For preschool children, as appropriate, how the disability affects the child's participation in appropriate activities;

(2) A statement of measurable annual goals, including benchmarks or short-term objectives, related to—

(i) Meeting the child's needs that result from the child's disability to enable the child to be involved in and progress in the general curriculum (i.e., the same curriculum as for nondisabled children), or for preschool children, as appropriate, to participate in appropriate activities; and

(ii) Meeting each of the child's other educational needs that result from the child's disability;

(3) A statement of the special education and related services and supplementary aids and services to be provided to the child, or on behalf of the child, and a statement of the program modifications or supports for school personnel that will be provided for the child—

(i) To advance appropriately toward attaining the annual goals;

(ii) To be involved and progress in the general curriculum in accordance with paragraph (a)(1) of this section and to participate in extracurricular and other nonacademic activities; and

(iii) To be educated and participate with other children with disabilities and nondisabled children in the activities described in this section;

(4) An explanation of the extent, if any, to which the child will not participate with nondisabled children in the regular class and in the activities described in paragraph (a)(3) of this section;

(5)(i) A statement of any individual modifications in the administration of State or district-wide assessments of student achievement that are needed in order for the child to participate in the assessment; and

(ii) If the IEP team determines that the child will not participate in a particular State or district-wide assessment of student achievement (or part of an assessment), a statement of—

(A) Why that assessment is not appropriate for the child; and

(B) How the child will be assessed;

(6) The projected date for the beginning of the services and modifications described in paragraph (a)(3) of this section, and the anticipated frequency, location, and duration of those services and modifications; and

(7) A statement of—

(i) How the child's progress toward the annual goals described in paragraph (a)(2) of this section will be measured; and

(ii) How the child's parents will be regularly informed (through such means as periodic report cards), at least as often as parents are informed of their nondisabled children's progress, of—

(A) Their child's progress toward the annual goals; and

(B) The extent to which that progress is sufficient to enable the child to achieve the goals by the end of the year.

(b) Transition services. The IEP must include—

(1) For each student with a disability beginning at age 14 (or younger, if determined appropriate by the IEP team), and updated annually, a statement of the transition service needs of the student under the applicable components of the student's IEP that focuses on the student's courses of study (such as participation in advanced-placement courses or a vocational education program); and

(2) For each student beginning at age 16 (or younger, if determined appropriate by the IEP team), a statement of needed transition services for the student, including, if appropriate, a statement of the interagency responsibilities or any needed linkages.

(c) Transfer of rights. In a State that transfers rights at the age majority, beginning at least one year before a student reaches the age of majority under State law, the student's IEP must include a statement that the student has been informed of his or her rights under Part B of the Act, if any, that will transfer to the student on reaching the age of majority, consistent with Sec. 300.517.

(d) Students with disabilities convicted as adults and incarcerated in adult prisons. Special rules concerning the content of IEPs for students with disabilities convicted as adults and incarcerated in adult prisons are contained in Sec. 300.311(b) and (c).

(Authority: 20 U.S.C. 1414(d)(1)(A) and (d)(6)(A)(ii))

Sec. 300.348 Agency responsibilities for transition services.

(a) If a participating agency, other than the public agency, fails to provide the transition services described in the IEP in accordance with Sec. 300.347(b)(1), the public agency shall reconvene the IEP team to identify alternative strategies to meet the transition objectives for the student set out in the IEP.

(b) Nothing in this part relieves any participating agency, including a State vocational rehabilitation agency, of the responsibility to provide or pay for any transition service that the agency would otherwise provide to students with disabilities who meet the eligibility criteria of that agency.

(Authority: 20 U.S.C. 1414(d)(5); 1414(d)(1)(A)(vii))

Sec. 300.349 Private school placements by public agencies.

(a) Developing IEPs.

(1) Before a public agency places a child with a disability in, or refers a child to, a private school or facility, the agency shall initiate and conduct a meeting to develop an IEP for the child in accordance with Secs. 300.346 and 300.347.

(2) The agency shall ensure that a representative of the private school or facility attends the meeting. If the representative cannot attend, the agency shall use other methods to ensure participation by the private school or facility, including individual or conference telephone calls.

(b) Reviewing and revising IEPs.

(1) After a child with a disability enters a private school or facility, any meetings to review and revise the child's IEP may be initiated and conducted by the private school or facility at the discretion of the public agency.

(2) If the private school or facility initiates and conducts these meetings, the public agency shall ensure that the parents and an agency representative—

(i) Are involved in any decision about the child's IEP; and

(ii) Agree to any proposed changes in the IEP before those changes are implemented.

(c) Responsibility. Even if a private school or facility implements a child's IEP, responsibility for compliance with this part remains with the public agency and the SEA.

(Authority: 20 U.S.C. 1412(a)(10)(B))

Sec. 300.350 IEP—accountability.

(a) Provision of services. Subject to paragraph (b) of this section, each public agency must—

(1) Provide special education and related services to a child with a disability in accordance with the child's IEP; and

(2) Make a good faith effort to assist the child to achieve the goals and objectives or benchmarks listed in the IEP.

(b) Accountability. Part B of the Act does not require that any agency, teacher, or other person be held accountable if a child does not achieve the growth projected in the annual goals and benchmarks or objectives. However, the Act does not prohibit a State or public agency from establishing its own accountability systems regarding teacher, school, or agency performance.

(c) Construction—parent rights. Nothing in this section limits a parent's right to ask for revisions of the child's IEP or to invoke due process procedures if the parent feels that the efforts required in paragraph (a) of this section are not being made.

(Authority: 20 U.S.C. 1414(d))

Subpart D: Children in Private Schools

Sec. 300.400 Applicability of Secs. 300.400-300.402. Children With Disabilities in Private Schools Placed or Referred by Public Agencies

Sections 300.401-300.402 apply only to children with disabilities who are or have been placed in or referred to a private school or facility by a public agency as a means of providing special education and related services.

(Authority: 20 U.S.C. 1412(a)(10)(B))

Sec. 300.401 Responsibility of State educational agency.

Each SEA shall ensure that a child with a disability who is placed in or referred to a private school or facility by a public agency—

(a) Is provided special education and related services—

(1) In conformance with an IEP that meets the requirements of Secs. 300.340-300.350; and

(2) At no cost to the parents;

(b) Is provided an education that meets the standards that apply to education provided by the SEA and LEAs (including the requirements of this part); and

(c) Has all of the rights of a child with a disability who is served by a public agency.

(Authority: 20 U.S.C. 1412(a)(10)(B))

Sec. 300.402 Implementation by State educational agency.

In implementing Sec. 300.401, the SEA shall—

(a) Monitor compliance through procedures such as written reports, on-site visits, and parent questionnaires;

(b) Disseminate copies of applicable standards to each private school and facility to which a public agency has referred or placed a child with a disability; and

(c) Provide an opportunity for those private schools and facilities to participate in the development and revision of State standards that apply to them.

(Authority: 20 U.S.C. 1412(a)(10)(B))

Sec. 300.403 Placement of children by parents if FAPE is at issue.

(a) General. This part does not require an LEA to pay for the cost of education, including special education and related services, of a child with a disability at a private school or facility if that agency made FAPE available to the child and the parents elected to place the child in a private school or facility. However, the public agency shall include that child in the population whose needs are addressed consistent with Secs. 300.450-300.462.

(b) Disagreements about FAPE. Disagreements between a parent and a public agency regarding the availability of a program appropriate for the child, and the question of financial responsibility, are subject to the due process procedures of Secs. 300.500-300.517.

(c) Reimbursement for private school placement. If the parents of a child with a disability, who previously received special education and related services under the authority of a public agency, enroll the child in a private preschool, elementary, or secondary school without the consent of or referral by the public agency, a court or a hearing officer may require the agency to reimburse the parents for the cost of that enrollment if the court or hearing officer finds that the agency had not made FAPE available to the child in a timely manner prior to that enrollment and that the private placement is appropriate. A parental placement may be found to be appropriate by a hearing officer or a court even if it does not meet the State standards that apply to education provided by the SEA and LEAs.

(d) Limitation on reimbursement. The cost of reimbursement described in paragraph (c) of this section may be reduced or denied—

(1) If—

(i) At the most recent IEP meeting that the parents attended prior to removal of the child from the public school, the parents did not inform the IEP team that they were rejecting the placement proposed by the public agency to provide FAPE to their child, including stating their concerns and their intent to enroll their child in a private school at public expense; or

(ii) At least ten (10) business days (including any holidays that occur on a business day) prior to the removal of the child from the public school, the parents did not give written notice to the public agency of the information described in paragraph (d)(1)(i) of this section;

(2) If, prior to the parents' removal of the child from the public school, the public agency informed the parents, through the notice requirements described in Sec. 300.503(a)(1), of its intent to evaluate the child (including a statement of the purpose of the evaluation that was appropriate and reasonable), but the parents did not make the child available for the evaluation; or

(3) Upon a judicial finding of unreasonableness with respect to actions taken by the parents.

(e) Exception. Notwithstanding the notice requirement in paragraph (d)(1) of this section, the cost of reimbursement may not be reduced or denied for failure to provide the notice if—

(1) The parent is illiterate and cannot write in English;

(2) Compliance with paragraph (d)(1) of this section would likely result in physical or serious emotional harm to the child;

(3) The school prevented the parent from providing the notice; or

(4) The parents had not received notice, pursuant to section 615 of the Act, of the notice requirement in paragraph (d)(1) of this section.

(Authority: 20 U.S.C. 1412(a)(10)(C))

Sec. 300.450 Definition of "private school children with disabilities."

As used in this part, private school children with disabilities means children with disabilities enrolled by their parents in private schools or facilities other than children with disabilities covered under Secs. 300.400-300.402.

(Authority: 20 U.S.C. 1412(a)(10)(A))

Sec. 300.451 Child find for private school children with disabilities.

(a) Each LEA shall locate, identify, and evaluate all private school children with disabilities, including religious-school children residing in the jurisdiction of the LEA, in accordance with Secs. 300.125 and 300.220. The activities undertaken to carry out this responsibility for private school children with disabilities must be comparable to activities undertaken for children with disabilities in public schools.

(b) Each LEA shall consult with appropriate representatives of private school children with disabilities on how to carry out the activities described in paragraph (a) of this section.

(Authority: 20 U.S.C. 1412(a)(10)(A)(ii))

Sec. 300.452 Provision of services—basic requirement.

(a) General. To the extent consistent with their number and location in the State, provision must be made for the participation of private school children with disabilities in the program assisted or carried out under Part B of the Act by providing them with special education and related services in accordance with Secs. 300.453-300.462.

(b) SEA Responsibility—services plan. Each SEA shall ensure that, in accordance with paragraph (a) of this section and Secs. 300.454- 300.456, a services plan is developed and imple-

mented for each private school child with a disability who has been designated to receive special education and related services under this part.

(Authority: 20 U.S.C. 1412(a)(10)(A)(i))

Sec. 300.453 Expenditures.

(a) Formula. To meet the requirement of Sec. 300.452(a), each LEA must spend on providing special education and related services to private school children with disabilities—

(1) For children aged 3 through 21, an amount that is the same proportion of the LEA's total subgrant under section 611(g) of the Act as the number of private school children with disabilities aged 3 through 21 residing in its jurisdiction is to the total number of children with disabilities in its jurisdiction aged 3 through 21; and

(2) For children aged 3 through 5, an amount that is the same proportion of the LEA's total subgrant under section 619(g) of the Act as the number of private school children with disabilities aged 3 through 5 residing in its jurisdiction is to the total number of children with disabilities in its jurisdiction aged 3 through 5.

(b) Child count.

(1) Each LEA shall—

(i) Consult with representatives of private school children in deciding how to conduct the annual count of the number of private school children with disabilities; and

(ii) Ensure that the count is conducted on December 1 or the last Friday of October of each year.

(2) The child count must be used to determine the amount that the LEA must spend on providing special education and related services to private school children with disabilities in the next subsequent fiscal year.

(c) Expenditures for child find may not be considered. Expenditures for child find activities described in Sec. 300.451 may not be considered in determining whether the LEA has met the requirements of paragraph (a) of this section.

(d) Additional services permissible. State and local educational agencies are not prohibited from providing services to private school children with disabilities in excess of those required by this part, consistent with State law or local policy.

(Authority: 20 U.S.C. 1412(a)(10)(A))

Sec. 300.454 Services determined.

(a) No individual right to special education and related services.

(1) No private school child with a disability has an individual right to receive some or all of the special education and related services that the child would receive if enrolled in a public school.

(2) Decisions about the services that will be provided to private school children with disabilities under Secs. 300.452-300.462, must be made in accordance with paragraphs (b), and (c) of this section.

(b) Consultation with representatives of private school children with disabilities.

(1) General. Each LEA shall consult, in a timely and meaningful way, with appropriate representatives of private school children with disabilities in light of the funding under Sec.

300.453, the number of private school children with disabilities, the needs of private school children with disabilities, and their location to decide—

(i) Which children will receive services under Sec. 300.452;

(ii) What services will be provided;

(iii) How and where the services will be provided; and

(iv) How the services provided will be evaluated.

(2) Genuine opportunity. Each LEA shall give appropriate representatives of private school children with disabilities a genuine opportunity to express their views regarding each matter that is subject to the consultation requirements in this section.

(3) Timing. The consultation required by paragraph (b)(1) of this section must occur before the LEA makes any decision that affects the opportunities of private school children with disabilities to participate in services under Secs. 300.452-300.462.

(4) Decisions. The LEA shall make the final decisions with respect to the services to be provided to eligible private school children.

(c) Services plan for each child served under Secs. 300.450-300.462. If a child with a disability is enrolled in a religious or other private school and will receive special education or related services from an LEA, the LEA shall—

(1) Initiate and conduct meetings to develop, review, and revise a services plan for the child, in accordance with Sec. 300.455(b); and

(2) Ensure that a representative of the religious or other private school attends each meeting. If the representative cannot attend, the LEA shall use other methods to ensure participation by the private school, including individual or conference telephone calls.

(Authority: 1412(a)(10)(A))

Sec. 300.455 Services provided.

(a) General.

(1) The services provided to private school children with disabilities must be provided by personnel meeting the same standards as personnel providing services in the public schools.

(2) Private school children with disabilities may receive a different amount of services than children with disabilities in public schools.

(3) No private school child with a disability is entitled to any service or to any amount of a service the child would receive if enrolled in a public school.

(b) Services provided in accordance with a services plan.

(1) Each private school child with a disability who has been designated to receive services under Sec. 300.452 must have a services plan that describes the specific special education and related services that the LEA will provide to the child in light of the services that the LEA has determined, through the process described in Secs. 300.453-300.454, it will make available to private school children with disabilities.

(2) The services plan must, to the extent appropriate—

(i) Meet the requirements of Sec. 300.347, with respect to the services provided; and

(ii) Be developed, reviewed, and revised consistent with Secs. 300.342-300.346.

(Authority: 20 U.S.C. 1412(a)(10)(A))

Sec. 300.456 Location of services; transportation.

(a) On-site. Services provided to private school children with disabilities may be provided on-site at a child's private school, including a religious school, to the extent consistent with law.

(b) Transportation.

(1) General.

(i) If necessary for the child to benefit from or participate in the services provided under this part, a private school child with a disability must be provided transportation—

(A) From the child's school or the child's home to a site other than the private school; and

(B) From the service site to the private school, or to the child's home, depending on the timing of the services.

(ii) LEAs are not required to provide transportation from the child's home to the private school.

(2) Cost of transportation. The cost of the transportation described in paragraph (b)(1)(i) of this section may be included in calculating whether the LEA has met the requirement of Sec. 300.453.

(Authority: 20 U.S.C. 1412(a)(10)(A))

Sec. 300.457 Complaints.

(a) Due process inapplicable. The procedures in Secs. 300.504- 300.515 do not apply to complaints that an LEA has failed to meet the requirements of Secs. 300.452-300.462, including the provision of services indicated on the child's services plan.

(b) Due process applicable. The procedures in Secs. 300.504-300.515 do apply to complaints that an LEA has failed to meet the requirements of Sec. 300.451, including the requirements of Secs. 300.530-300.543.

(c) State complaints. Complaints that an SEA or LEA has failed to meet the requirements of Secs. 300.451-300.462 may be filed under the procedures in Secs. 300.660-300.662.

(Authority: 20 U.S.C. 1412(a)(10)(A))

Sec. 300.458 Separate classes prohibited.

An LEA may not use funds available under section 611 or 619 of the Act for classes that are organized separately on the basis of school enrollment or religion of the students if—

(a) The classes are at the same site; and

(b) The classes include students enrolled in public schools and students enrolled in private schools.

(Authority: 20 U.S.C. 1412(a)(10)(A))

Sec. 300.459 Requirement that funds not benefit a private school.

(a) An LEA may not use funds provided under section 611 or 619 of the Act to finance the existing level of instruction in a private school or to otherwise benefit the private school.

(b) The LEA shall use funds provided under Part B of the Act to meet the special education and related services needs of students enrolled in private schools, but not for—

(1) The needs of a private school; or

(2) The general needs of the students enrolled in the private school.

(Authority: 20 U.S.C. 1412(a)(10)(A))

Sec. 300.460 Use of public school personnel.

An LEA may use funds available under sections 611 and 619 of the Act to make public school personnel available in other than public facilities—

(a) To the extent necessary to provide services under Secs. 300.450- 300.462 for private school children with disabilities; and

(b) If those services are not normally provided by the private school.

(Authority: 20 U.S.C. 1412(a)(10)(A))

Sec. 300.461 Use of private school personnel.

An LEA may use funds available under section 611 or 619 of the Act to pay for the services of an employee of a private school to provide services under Secs. 300.450-300.462 if—

(a) The employee performs the services outside of his or her regular hours of duty; and

(b) The employee performs the services under public supervision and control.

(Authority: 20 U.S.C. 1412(a)(10)(A))

Sec. 300.462 Requirements concerning property, equipment, and supplies for the benefit of private school children with disabilities.

(a) A public agency must keep title to and exercise continuing administrative control of all property, equipment, and supplies that the public agency acquires with funds under section 611 or 619 of the Act for the benefit of private school children with disabilities.

(b) The public agency may place equipment and supplies in a private school for the period of time needed for the program.

(c) The public agency shall ensure that the equipment and supplies placed in a private school—

(1) Are used only for Part B purposes; and

(2) Can be removed from the private school without remodeling the private school facility.

(d) The public agency shall remove equipment and supplies from a private school if—

(1) The equipment and supplies are no longer needed for Part B purposes; or

(2) Removal is necessary to avoid unauthorized use of the equipment and supplies for other than Part B purposes.

(e) No funds under Part B of the Act may be used for repairs, minor remodeling, or construction of private school facilities.

(Authority: 20 U.S.C. 1412(a)(10)(A))

Subpart E: Procedural Safeguards

Sec. 300.500 General responsibility of public agencies; definitions.

Due Process Procedures for Parents and Children

(a) Responsibility of SEA and other public agencies. Each SEA shall ensure that each public agency establishes, main-

tains, and implements procedural safeguards that meet the requirements of Secs. 300.500- 300.529.

(b) Definitions of "consent," "evaluation," and "personally identifiable." As used in this part —

(1) Consent means that —

(i) The parent has been fully informed of all information relevant to the activity for which consent is sought, in his or her native language, or other mode of communication;

(ii) The parent understands and agrees in writing to the carrying out of the activity for which his or her consent is sought, and the consent describes that activity and lists the records (if any) that will be released and to whom; and

(iii)(A) The parent understands that the granting of consent is voluntary on the part of the parent and may be revoked at anytime.

(B) If a parent revokes consent, that revocation is not retroactive (i.e., it does not negate an action that has occurred after the consent was given and before the consent was revoked).

(2) Evaluation means procedures used in accordance with Secs. 300.530-300.536 to determine whether a child has a disability and the nature and extent of the special education and related services that the child needs; and

(3) Personally identifiable means that information includes—

(i) The name of the child, the child's parent, or other family member;

(ii) The address of the child;

(iii) A personal identifier, such as the child's social security number or student number; or

(iv) A list of personal characteristics or other information that would make it possible to identify the child with reasonable certainty.

(Authority: 20 U.S.C. 1415(a))

Sec. 300.501 Opportunity to examine records; parent participation in meetings.

(a) General. The parents of a child with a disability must be afforded, in accordance with the procedures of Secs. 300.562-300.569, an opportunity to—

(1) Inspect and review all education records with respect to—

(i) The identification, evaluation, and educational placement of the child; and

(ii) The provision of FAPE to the child; and

(2) Participate in meetings with respect to —

(i) The identification, evaluation, and educational placement of the child; and

(ii) The provision of FAPE to the child.

(b) Parent participation in meetings.

(1) Each public agency shall provide notice consistent with Sec. 300.345(a)(1) and (b)(1) to ensure that parents of children with disabilities have the opportunity to participate in meetings described in paragraph (a)(2) of this section.

(2) A meeting does not include informal or unscheduled conversations involving public agency personnel and conversations on issues such as teaching methodology, lesson plans, or coordination of service provision if those issues are not

addressed in the child's IEP. A meeting also does not include preparatory activities that public agency personnel engage in to develop a proposal or response to a parent proposal that will be discussed at a later meeting.

(c) Parent involvement in placement decisions.

(1) Each public agency shall ensure that the parents of each child with a disability are members of any group that makes decisions on the educational placement of their child.

(2) In implementing the requirements of paragraph (c)(1) of this section, the public agency shall use procedures consistent with the procedures described in Sec. 300.345(a) through (b)(1).

(3) If neither parent can participate in a meeting in which a decision is to be made relating to the educational placement of their child, the public agency shall use other methods to ensure their participation, including individual or conference telephone calls, or video conferencing.

(4) A placement decision may be made by a group without the involvement of the parents, if the public agency is unable to obtain the parents' participation in the decision. In this case, the public agency must have a record of its attempt to ensure their involvement, including information that is consistent with the requirements of Sec. 300.345(d).

(5) The public agency shall make reasonable efforts to ensure that the parents understand, and are able to participate in, any group discussions relating to the educational placement of their child, including arranging for an interpreter for parents with deafness, or whose native language is other than English.

(Authority: 20 U.S.C. 1414(f), 1415(b)(1))

Sec. 300.502 Independent educational evaluation.

(a) General.

(1) The parents of a child with a disability have the right under this part to obtain an independent educational evaluation of the child, subject to paragraphs (b) through (e) of this section.

(2) Each public agency shall provide to parents, upon request for an independent educational evaluation, information about where an independent educational evaluation may be obtained, and the agency criteria applicable for independent educational evaluations as set forth in paragraph (e) of this section.

(3) For the purposes of this part—

(i) Independent educational evaluation means an evaluation conducted by a qualified examiner who is not employed by the public agency responsible for the education of the child in question; and

(ii) Public expense means that the public agency either pays for the full cost of the evaluation or ensures that the evaluation is otherwise provided at no cost to the parent, consistent with Sec. 300.301.

(b) Parent right to evaluation at public expense.

(1) A parent has the right to an independent educational evaluation at

public expense if the parent disagrees with an evaluation obtained by the public agency.

(2) If a parent requests an independent educational evaluation at public expense, the public agency must, without unnecessary delay, either—

(i) Initiate a hearing under Sec. 300.507 to show that its evaluation is appropriate; or

(ii) Ensure that an independent educational evaluation is provided at public expense, unless the agency demonstrates in a hearing under Sec. 300.507 that the evaluation obtained by the parent did not meet agency criteria.

(3) If the public agency initiates a hearing and the final decision is that the agency's evaluation is appropriate, the parent still has the right to an independent educational evaluation, but not at public expense.

(4) If a parent requests an independent educational evaluation, the public agency may ask for the parent's reason why he or she objects to the public evaluation. However, the explanation by the parent may not be required and the public agency may not unreasonably delay either providing the independent educational evaluation at public expense or initiating a due process hearing to defend the public evaluation.

(c) Parent-initiated evaluations. If the parent obtains an independent educational evaluation at private expense, the results of the evaluation—

(1) Must be considered by the public agency, if it meets agency criteria, in any decision made with respect to the provision of FAPE to the child; and

(2) May be presented as evidence at a hearing under this subpart regarding that child.

(d) Requests for evaluations by hearing officers. If a hearing officer requests an independent educational evaluation as part of a hearing, the cost of the evaluation must be at public expense.

(e) Agency criteria.

(1) If an independent educational evaluation is at public expense, the criteria under which the evaluation is obtained, including the location of the evaluation and the qualifications of the examiner, must be the same as the criteria that the public agency uses when it initiates an evaluation, to the extent those criteria are consistent with the parent's right to an independent educational evaluation.

(2) Except for the criteria described in paragraph (e)(1) of this section, a public agency may not impose conditions or timelines related to obtaining an independent educational evaluation at public expense.

(Authority: 20 U.S.C. 1415(b)(1))

Sec. 300.503 Prior notice by the public agency; content of notice.

(a) Notice.

(1) Written notice that meets the requirements of paragraph (b) of this section must be given to the parents of a child with a disability a reasonable time before the public agency—

(i) Proposes to initiate or change the identification, evaluation, or educational placement of the child or the provision of FAPE to the child; or

(ii) Refuses to initiate or change the identification, evaluation, or educational placement of the child or the provision of FAPE to the child.

(2) If the notice described under paragraph (a)(1) of this section relates to an action proposed by the public agency that also requires parental consent under Sec. 300.505, the agency may give notice at the same time it requests parent consent.

(b) Content of notice. The notice required under paragraph (a) of this section must include—

(1) A description of the action proposed or refused by the agency;

(2) An explanation of why the agency proposes or refuses to take the action;

(3) A description of any other options that the agency considered and the reasons why those options were rejected;

(4) A description of each evaluation procedure, test, record, or report the agency used as a basis for the proposed or refused action;

(5) A description of any other factors that are relevant to the agency's proposal or refusal;

(6) A statement that the parents of a child with a disability have protection under the procedural safeguards of this part and, if this notice is not an initial referral for evaluation, the means by which a copy of a description of the procedural safeguards can be obtained; and

(7) Sources for parents to contact to obtain assistance in understanding the provisions of this part.

(c) Notice in understandable language.

(1) The notice required under paragraph (a) of this section must be—

(i) Written in language understandable to the general public; and

(ii) Provided in the native language of the parent or other mode of communication used by the parent, unless it is clearly not feasible to do so.

(2) If the native language or other mode of communication of the parent is not a written language, the public agency shall take steps to ensure—

(i) That the notice is translated orally or by other means to the parent in his or her native language or other mode of communication;

(ii) That the parent understands the content of the notice; and

(iii) That there is written evidence that the requirements in paragraphs (c)(2) (i) and (ii) of this section have been met.

(Authority: 20 U.S.C. 1415(b)(3), (4) and (c), 1414(b)(1))

Sec. 300.504 Procedural safeguards notice.

(a) General. A copy of the procedural safeguards available to the parents of a child with a disability must be given to the parents, at a minimum—

(1) Upon initial referral for evaluation;

(2) Upon each notification of an IEP meeting;

(3) Upon reevaluation of the child; and

(4) Upon receipt of a request for due process under Sec. 300.507.

(b) Contents. The procedural safeguards notice must include a full explanation of all of the procedural safeguards available under Secs. 300.403, 300.500-300.529, and 300.560-300.577, and the State complaint procedures available under Secs. 300.660-300.662 relating to—

(1) Independent educational evaluation;

(2) Prior written notice;

(3) Parental consent;

(4) Access to educational records;

(5) Opportunity to present complaints to initiate due process hearings;

(6) The child's placement during pendency of due process proceedings;

(7) Procedures for students who are subject to placement in an interim alternative educational setting;

(8) Requirements for unilateral placement by parents of children in private schools at public expense;

(9) Mediation;

(10) Due process hearings, including requirements for disclosure of evaluation results and recommendations;

(11) State-level appeals (if applicable in that State);

(12) Civil actions;

(13) Attorneys' fees; and

(14) The State complaint procedures under Secs. 300.660-300.662, including a description of how to file a complaint and the timelines under those procedures.

(c) Notice in understandable language. The notice required under paragraph (a) of this section must meet the requirements of Sec. 300.503(c).

(Authority: 20 U.S.C. 1415(d))

Sec. 300.505 Parental consent.

(a) General. (1) Subject to paragraphs (a)(3), (b) and (c) of this section, informed parent consent must be obtained before—

(i) Conducting an initial evaluation or reevaluation; and

(ii) Initial provision of special education and related services to a child with a disability.

(2) Consent for initial evaluation may not be construed as consent for initial placement described in paragraph (a)(1)(ii) of this section.

(3) Parental consent is not required before—

(i) Reviewing existing data as part of an evaluation or a reevaluation; or

(ii) Administering a test or other evaluation that is administered to all children unless, before administration of that test or evaluation, consent is required of parents of all children.

(b) Refusal. If the parents of a child with a disability refuse consent for initial evaluation or a reevaluation, the agency may continue to pursue those evaluations by using the due process procedures under Secs. 300.507-300.509, or the mediation procedures under Sec. 300.506 if appropriate, except to the extent inconsistent with State law relating to parental consent.

(c) Failure to respond to request for reevaluation.

(1) Informed parental consent need not be obtained for reevaluation if the public agency can demonstrate that it has taken reasonable measures to obtain that consent, and the child's parent has failed to respond.

(2) To meet the reasonable measures requirement in paragraph (c)(1) of this section, the public agency must use procedures consistent with those in Sec. 300.345(d).

(d) Additional State consent requirements. In addition to the parental consent requirements described in paragraph (a) of this section, a State may require parental consent for other services and activities under this part if it ensures that each public agency in the State establishes and implements effective procedures to ensure that a parent's refusal to consent does not result in a failure to provide the child with FAPE.

(e) Limitation. A public agency may not use a parent's refusal to consent to one service or activity under paragraphs (a) and (d) of this section to deny the parent or child any other service, benefit, or activity of the public agency, except as required by this part.

(Authority: 20 U.S.C. 1415(b)(3); 1414(a)(1)(C) and (c)(3))

Sec. 300.506 Mediation.

(a) General. Each public agency shall ensure that procedures are established and implemented to allow parties to disputes involving any matter described in Sec. 300.503(a)(1) to resolve the disputes through a mediation process that, at a minimum, must be available whenever a hearing is requested under Secs. 300.507 or 300.520-300.528.

(b) Requirements. The procedures must meet the following requirements:

(1) The procedures must ensure that the mediation process—

(i) Is voluntary on the part of the parties;

(ii) Is not used to deny or delay a parent's right to a due process hearing under Sec. 300.507, or to deny any other rights afforded under Part B of the Act; and

(iii) Is conducted by a qualified and impartial mediator who is trained in effective mediation techniques.

(2)(i) The State shall maintain a list of individuals who are qualified mediators and knowledgeable in laws and regulations relating to the provision of special education and related services.

(ii) If a mediator is not selected on a random (e.g., a rotation) basis from the list described in paragraph (b)(2)(i) of this section, both parties must be involved in selecting the mediator and agree with the selection of the individual who will mediate.

(3) The State shall bear the cost of the mediation process, including the costs of meetings described in paragraph (d) of this section.

(4) Each session in the mediation process must be scheduled in a timely manner and must be held in a location that is convenient to the parties to the dispute.

(5) An agreement reached by the parties to the dispute in the mediation process must be set forth in a written mediation agreement.

(6) Discussions that occur during the mediation process must be confidential and may not be used as evidence in any subsequent due process hearings or civil proceedings, and the parties to the mediation process may be required to sign a confidentiality pledge prior to the commencement of the process.

(c) Impartiality of mediator.

(1) An individual who serves as a mediator under this part—

(i) May not be an employee of—

(A) Any LEA or any State agency described under Sec. 300.194; or

(B) An SEA that is providing direct services to a child who is the subject of the mediation process; and

(ii) Must not have a personal or professional conflict of interest.

(2) A person who otherwise qualifies as a mediator is not an employee of an LEA or State agency described under Sec. 300.194 solely because he or she is paid by the agency to serve as a mediator.

(d) Meeting to encourage mediation. (1) A public agency may establish procedures to require parents who elect not to use the mediation process to meet, at a time and location convenient to the parents, with a disinterested party—

(i) Who is under contract with a parent training and information center or community parent resource center in the State established under section 682 or 683 of the Act, or an appropriate alternative dispute resolution entity; and

(ii) Who would explain the benefits of the mediation process, and encourage the parents to use the process.

(2) A public agency may not deny or delay a parent's right to a due process hearing under Sec. 300.507 if the parent fails to participate in the meeting described in paragraph (d)(1) of this section.

(Authority: 20 U.S.C. 1415(e))

Sec. 300.507 Impartial due process hearing; parent notice.

(a) General.

(1) A parent or a public agency may initiate a hearing on any of the matters described in Sec. 300.503(a)(1) and (2) (relating to the identification, evaluation or educational placement of a child with a disability, or the provision of FAPE to the child).

(2) When a hearing is initiated under paragraph (a)(1) of this section, the public agency shall inform the parents of the availability of mediation described in Sec. 300.506.

(3) The public agency shall inform the parent of any free or low- cost legal and other relevant services available in the area if—

(i) The parent requests the information; or

(ii) The parent or the agency initiates a hearing under this section.

(b) Agency responsible for conducting hearing. The hearing described in paragraph (a) of this section must be conducted by the SEA or the public agency directly responsible for the education of the child, as determined under State statute, State regulation, or a written policy of the SEA.

(c) Parent notice to the public agency. (1) General. The public agency must have procedures that require the parent of a child with a disability or the attorney representing the child, to provide notice (which must remain confidential) to the public agency in a request for a hearing under paragraph (a)(1) of this section.

(2) Content of parent notice. The notice required in paragraph (c)(1) of this section must include—

(i) The name of the child;

(ii) The address of the residence of the child;

(iii) The name of the school the child is attending;

(iv) A description of the nature of the problem of the child relating to the proposed or refused initiation or change, including facts relating to the problem; and

(v) A proposed resolution of the problem to the extent known and available to the parents at the time.

(3) Model form to assist parents. Each SEA shall develop a model form to assist parents in filing a request for due process that includes the information required in paragraphs (c)(1) and (2) of this section.

(4) Right to due process hearing. A public agency may not deny or delay a parent's right to a due process hearing for failure to provide the notice required in paragraphs (c)(1) and (2) of this section.

(Authority: 20 U.S.C. 1415(b)(5), (b)(6), (b)(7), (b)(8), (e)(1) and (f)(1))

Sec. 300.508 Impartial hearing officer.

(a) A hearing may not be conducted—

(1) By a person who is an employee of the State agency or the LEA that is involved in the education or care of the child; or

(2) By any person having a personal or professional interest that would conflict with his or her objectivity in the hearing.

(b) A person who otherwise qualifies to conduct a hearing under paragraph (a) of this section is not an employee of the agency solely because he or she is paid by the agency to serve as a hearing officer.

(c) Each public agency shall keep a list of the persons who serve as hearing officers. The list must include a statement of the qualifications of each of those persons.

(Authority: 20 U.S.C. 1415(f)(3))

Sec. 300.509 Hearing rights.

(a) General. Any party to a hearing conducted pursuant to Secs. 300.507 or 300.520-300.528, or an appeal conducted pursuant to Sec. 300.510, has the right to—

(1) Be accompanied and advised by counsel and by individuals with special knowledge or training with respect to the problems of children with disabilities;

(2) Present evidence and confront, cross-examine, and compel the attendance of witnesses;

(3) Prohibit the introduction of any evidence at the hearing that has not been disclosed to that party at least 5 business days before the hearing;

(4) Obtain a written, or, at the option of the parents, electronic, verbatim record of the hearing; and

(5) Obtain written, or, at the option of the parents, electronic findings of fact and decisions.

(b) Additional disclosure of information. (1) At least 5 business days prior to a hearing conducted pursuant to Sec. 300.507(a), each party shall disclose to all other parties all

evaluations completed by that date and recommendations based on the offering party's evaluations that the party intends to use at the hearing.

(2) A hearing officer may bar any party that fails to comply with paragraph (b)(1) of this section from introducing the relevant evaluation or recommendation at the hearing without the consent of the other party.

(c) Parental rights at hearings.

(1) Parents involved in hearings must be given the right to—

(i) Have the child who is the subject of the hearing present; and

(ii) Open the hearing to the public.

(2) The record of the hearing and the findings of fact and decisions described in paragraphs (a)(4) and (a)(5) of this section must be provided at no cost to parents.

(d) Findings and decision to advisory panel and general public. The public agency, after deleting any personally identifiable information, shall —

(1) Transmit the findings and decisions referred to in paragraph (a)(5) of this section to the State advisory panel established under Sec. 300.650; and

(2) Make those findings and decisions available to the public.

(Authority: 20 U.S.C. 1415(f)(2) and (h))

Sec. 300.510 Finality of decision; appeal; impartial review.

(a) Finality of decision. A decision made in a hearing conducted pursuant to Secs. 300.507 or 300.520-300.528 is final, except that any party involved in the hearing may appeal the decision under the provisions of paragraph (b) of this section and Sec. 300.512.

(Authority: 20 U.S.C. 1415(i)(1)(A))

(b) Appeal of decisions; impartial review.

(1) General. If the hearing required by Sec. 300.507 is conducted by a public agency other than the SEA, any party aggrieved by the findings and decision in the hearing may appeal to the SEA.

(2) SEA responsibility for review. If there is an appeal, the SEA shall conduct an impartial review of the hearing. The official conducting the review shall—

(i) Examine the entire hearing record;

(ii) Ensure that the procedures at the hearing were consistent with the requirements of due process;

(iii) Seek additional evidence if necessary. If a hearing is held to receive additional evidence, the rights in Sec. 300.509 apply;

(iv) Afford the parties an opportunity for oral or written argument, or both, at the discretion of the reviewing official;

(v) Make an independent decision on completion of the review; and

(vi) Give a copy of the written, or, at the option of the parents, electronic findings of fact and decisions to the parties.

(c) Findings and decision to advisory panel and general public. The SEA, after deleting any personally identifiable information, shall—

(1) Transmit the findings and decisions referred to in paragraph (b)(2)(vi) of this section to the State advisory panel established under Sec. 300.650; and

(2) Make those findings and decisions available to the public.

(d) Finality of review decision. The decision made by the reviewing official is final unless a party brings a civil action under Sec. 300.512.

(Authority: 20 U.S.C. 1415(g); H. R. Rep. No. 94-664, at p. 49 (1975))

Sec. 300.511 Timelines and convenience of hearings and reviews.

(a) The public agency shall ensure that not later than 45 days after the receipt of a request for a hearing—

(1) A final decision is reached in the hearing; and

(2) A copy of the decision is mailed to each of the parties.

(b) The SEA shall ensure that not later than 30 days after the receipt of a request for a review—

(1) A final decision is reached in the review; and

(2) A copy of the decision is mailed to each of the parties.

(c) A hearing or reviewing officer may grant specific extensions of time beyond the periods set out in paragraphs (a) and (b) of this section at the request of either party.

(d) Each hearing and each review involving oral arguments must be conducted at a time and place that is reasonably convenient to the parents and child involved.

(Authority: 20 U.S.C. 1415)

Sec. 300.512 Civil action.

(a) General. Any party aggrieved by the findings and decision made under Secs. 300.507 or 300.520-300.528 who does not have the right to an appeal under Sec. 300.510(b), and any party aggrieved by the findings and decision under Sec. 300.510(b), has the right to bring a civil action with respect to the complaint presented pursuant to Sec. 300.507. The action may be brought in any State court of competent jurisdiction or in a district court of the United States without regard to the amount in controversy.

(b) Additional requirements. In any action brought under paragraph (a) of this section, the court—

(1) Shall receive the records of the administrative proceedings;

(2) Shall hear additional evidence at the request of a party; and

(3) Basing its decision on the preponderance of the evidence, shall grant the relief that the court determines to be appropriate.

(c) Jurisdiction of district courts. The district courts of the United States have jurisdiction of actions brought under section 615 of the Act without regard to the amount in controversy.

(d) Rule of construction. Nothing in this part restricts or limits the rights, procedures, and remedies available under the Constitution, the Americans with Disabilities Act of 1990, title V of the Rehabilitation Act of 1973, or other Federal laws protecting the rights of children with disabilities, except that be-

fore the filing of a civil action under these laws seeking relief that is also available under section 615 of the Act, the procedures under Secs. 300.507 and 300.510 must be exhausted to the same extent as would be required had the action been brought under section 615 of the Act.

(Authority: 20 U.S.C. 1415(i)(2), (i)(3)(A), and 1415(l))

Sec. 300.513 Attorneys' fees.

(a) In any action or proceeding brought under section 615 of the Act, the court, in its discretion, may award reasonable attorneys' fees as part of the costs to the parents of a child with a disability who is the prevailing party.

(b)(1) Funds under Part B of the Act may not be used to pay attorneys' fees or costs of a party related to an action or proceeding under section 615 of the Act and subpart E of this part.

(2) Paragraph (b)(1) of this section does not preclude a public agency from using funds under Part B of the Act for conducting an action or proceeding under section 615 of the Act.

(c) A court awards reasonable attorney's fees under section 615(i)(3) of the Act consistent with the following:

(1) Determination of amount of attorneys' fees. Fees awarded under section 615(i)(3) of the Act must be based on rates prevailing in the community in which the action or proceeding arose for the kind and quality of services furnished. No bonus or multiplier may be used in calculating the fees awarded under this subsection.

(2) Prohibition of attorneys' fees and related costs for certain services. (i) Attorneys' fees may not be awarded and related costs may not be reimbursed in any action or proceeding under section 615 of the Act for services performed subsequent to the time of a written offer of settlement to a parent if—

(A) The offer is made within the time prescribed by Rule 68 of the Federal Rules of Civil Procedure or, in the case of an administrative proceeding, at any time more than 10 days before the proceeding begins;

(B) The offer is not accepted within 10 days; and

(C) The court or administrative hearing officer finds that the relief finally obtained by the parents is not more favorable to the parents than the offer of settlement.

(ii) Attorneys' fees may not be awarded relating to any meeting of the IEP team unless the meeting is convened as a result of an administrative proceeding or judicial action, or at the discretion of the State, for a mediation described in Sec. 300.506 that is conducted prior to the filing of a request for due process under Secs. 300.507 or 300.520-300.528.

(3) Exception to prohibition on attorneys' fees and related costs. Notwithstanding paragraph (c)(2) of this section, an award of attorneys' fees and related costs may be made to a parent who is the prevailing party and who was substantially justified in rejecting the settlement offer.

(4) Reduction of amount of attorneys' fees. Except as provided in paragraph (c)(5) of this section, the court reduces, accordingly, the amount of the attorneys' fees awarded under section 615 of the Act, if the court finds that—

(i) The parent, during the course of the action or proceeding, unreasonably protracted the final resolution of the controversy;

(ii) The amount of the attorneys' fees otherwise authorized to be awarded unreasonably exceeds the hourly rate prevailing in the community for similar services by attorneys of reasonably comparable skill, reputation, and experience;

(iii) The time spent and legal services furnished were excessive considering the nature of the action or proceeding; or

(iv) The attorney representing the parent did not provide to the school district the appropriate information in the due process complaint in accordance with Sec. 300.507(c).

(5) Exception to reduction in amount of attorneys' fees. The provisions of paragraph (c)(4) of this section do not apply in any action or proceeding if the court finds that the State or local agency unreasonably protracted the final resolution of the action or proceeding or there was a violation of section 615 of the Act.

(Authority: 20 U.S.C. 1415(i)(3)(B)-(G))

Sec. 300.514 Child's status during proceedings.

(a) Except as provided in Sec. 300.526, during the pendency of any administrative or judicial proceeding regarding a complaint under Sec. 300.507, unless the State or local agency and the parents of the child agree otherwise, the child involved in the complaint must remain in his or her current educational placement.

(b) If the complaint involves an application for initial admission to public school, the child, with the consent of the parents, must be placed in the public school until the completion of all the proceedings.

(c) If the decision of a hearing officer in a due process hearing conducted by the SEA or a State review official in an administrative appeal agrees with the child's parents that a change of placement is appropriate, that placement must be treated as an agreement between the State or local agency and the parents for purposes of paragraph (a) of this section.

(Authority: 20 U.S.C. 1415(j))

Sec. 300.515 Surrogate parents.

(a) General. Each public agency shall ensure that the rights of a child are protected if—

(1) No parent (as defined in Sec. 300.20) can be identified;

(2) The public agency, after reasonable efforts, cannot discover the whereabouts of a parent; or

(3) The child is a ward of the State under the laws of that State.

(b) Duty of public agency. The duty of a public agency under paragraph (a) of this section includes the assignment of an individual to act as a surrogate for the parents. This must include a method—

(1) For determining whether a child needs a surrogate parent; and

(2) For assigning a surrogate parent to the child.

(c) Criteria for selection of surrogates. (1) The public agency may select a surrogate parent in any way permitted under State law.

(2) Except as provided in paragraph (c)(3) of this section, public agencies shall ensure that a person selected as a surrogate—

(i) Is not an employee of the SEA, the LEA, or any other agency that is involved in the education or care of the child;

(ii) Has no interest that conflicts with the interest of the child he or she represents; and

(iii) Has knowledge and skills that ensure adequate representation of the child.

(3) A public agency may select as a surrogate a person who is an employee of a nonpublic agency that only provides non-educational care for the child and who meets the standards in paragraphs (c)(2)(ii) and (iii) of this section.

(d) Non-employee requirement; compensation. A person who otherwise qualifies to be a surrogate parent under paragraph (c) of this section is not an employee of the agency solely because he or she is paid by the agency to serve as a surrogate parent.

(e) Responsibilities. The surrogate parent may represent the child in all matters relating to—

(1) The identification, evaluation, and educational placement of the child; and

(2) The provision of FAPE to the child.

(Authority: 20 U.S.C. 1415(b)(2))

Sec. 300.517 Transfer of parental rights at age of majority.

(a) General. A State may provide that, when a student with a disability reaches the age of majority under State law that applies to all students (except for a student with a disability who has been determined to be incompetent under State law)—

(1)(i) The public agency shall provide any notice required by this part to both the individual and the parents; and

(ii) All other rights accorded to parents under Part B of the Act transfer to the student; and

(2) All rights accorded to parents under Part B of the Act transfer to students who are incarcerated in an adult or juvenile, State or local correctional institution.

(3) Whenever a State transfers rights under this part pursuant to paragraph (a)(1) or (a)(2) of this section, the agency shall notify the individual and the parents of the transfer of rights.

(b) Special rule. If, under State law, a State has a mechanism to determine that a student with a disability, who has reached the age of majority under State law that applies to all children and has not been determined incompetent under State law, does not have the ability to provide informed consent with respect to his or her educational program, the State shall establish procedures for appointing the parent, or, if the parent is not available another appropriate individual, to represent the educational interests of the student throughout the student's eligibility under Part B of the Act.

(Authority: 20 U.S.C. 1415(m))

Discipline Procedures

Sec. 300.519 Change of placement for disciplinary removals.

For purposes of removals of a child with a disability from the child's current educational placement under Secs. 300.520-300.529, a change of placement occurs if—

(a) The removal is for more than 10 consecutive school days; or

(b) The child is subjected to a series of removals that constitute a pattern because they cumulate to more than 10 school days in a school year, and because of factors such as the length of each removal, the total amount of time the child is removed, and the proximity of the removals to one another.

(Authority: 20 U.S.C. 1415(k))

Sec. 300.520 Authority of school personnel.

(a) School personnel may order—

(1)(i) To the extent removal would be applied to children without disabilities, the removal of a child with a disability from the child's current placement for not more than 10 consecutive school days for any violation of school rules, and additional removals of not more than 10 consecutive school days in that same school year for separate incidents of misconduct (as long as those removals do not constitute a change of placement under Sec. 300.519(b));

(ii) After a child with a disability has been removed from his or her current placement for more than 10 school days in the same school year, during any subsequent days of removal the public agency must provide services to the extent required under Sec. 300.121(d); and

(2) A change in placement of a child with a disability to an appropriate interim alternative educational setting for the same amount of time that a child without a disability would be subject to discipline, but for not more than 45 days, if—

(i) The child carries a weapon to school or to a school function under the jurisdiction of a State or a local educational agency; or

(ii) The child knowingly possesses or uses illegal drugs or sells or solicits the sale of a controlled substance while at school or a school function under the jurisdiction of a State or local educational agency.

(b)(1) Either before or not later than 10 business days after either first removing the child for more than 10 school days in a school year or commencing a removal that constitutes a change of placement under Sec. 300.519, including the action described in paragraph (a)(2) of this section—

(i) If the LEA did not conduct a functional behavioral assessment and implement a behavioral intervention plan for the child before the behavior that resulted in the removal described in paragraph (a) of this section, the agency shall convene an IEP meeting to develop an assessment plan.

(ii) If the child already has a behavioral intervention plan, the IEP team shall meet to review the plan and its implementation, and, modify the plan and its implementation as necessary, to address the behavior.

(2) As soon as practicable after developing the plan described in paragraph (b)(1)(i) of this section, and completing the assessments required by the plan, the LEA shall convene an IEP meeting to develop appropriate behavioral interventions to address that behavior and shall implement those interventions.

(c)(1) If subsequently, a child with a disability who has a behavioral intervention plan and who has been removed from the child's current educational placement for more than 10 school days in a school year is subjected to a removal that does not constitute a change of placement under Sec. 300.519, the IEP team members shall review the behavioral intervention plan and its implementation to determine if modifications are necessary.

(2) If one or more of the team members believe that modifications are needed, the team shall meet to modify the plan and its implementation, to the extent the team determines necessary.

(d) For purposes of this section, the following definitions apply:

(1) Controlled substance means a drug or other substance identified under schedules I, II, III, IV, or V in section 202(c) of the Controlled Substances Act (21 U.S.C. 812(c)).

(2) Illegal drug—

(i) Means a controlled substance; but

(ii) Does not include a substance that is legally possessed or used under the supervision of a licensed health-care professional or that is legally possessed or used under any other authority under that Act or under any other provision of Federal law.

(3) Weapon has the meaning given the term "dangerous weapon" under paragraph (2) of the first subsection (g) of section 930 of title 18, United States Code.

(Authority: 20 U.S.C. 1415(k)(1), (10))

Sec. 300.521 Authority of hearing officer.

A hearing officer under section 615 of the Act may order a change in the placement of a child with a disability to an appropriate interim alternative educational setting for not more than 45 days if the hearing officer, in an expedited due process hearing—

(a) Determines that the public agency has demonstrated by substantial evidence that maintaining the current placement of the child is substantially likely to result in injury to the child or to others;

(b) Considers the appropriateness of the child's current placement;

(c) Considers whether the public agency has made reasonable efforts to minimize the risk of harm in the child's current placement, including the use of supplementary aids and services; and

(d) Determines that the interim alternative educational setting that is proposed by school personnel who have consulted with the child's special education teacher, meets the requirements of Sec. 300.522(b).

(e) As used in this section, the term substantial evidence means beyond a preponderance of the evidence.

(Authority: 20 U.S.C. 1415(k)(2), (10))

Sec. 300.522 Determination of setting.

(a) General. The interim alternative educational setting referred to in Sec. 300.520(a)(2) must be determined by the IEP team.

(b) Additional requirements. Any interim alternative educational setting in which a child is placed under Secs. 300.520(a)(2) or 300.521 must—

(1) Be selected so as to enable the child to continue to progress in the general curriculum, although in another setting, and to continue to receive those services and modifications, including those described in the child's current IEP, that will enable the child to meet the goals set out in that IEP; and

(2) Include services and modifications to address the behavior described in Secs. 300.520(a)(2) or 300.521, that are designed to prevent the behavior from recurring.

(Authority: 20 U.S.C. 1415(k)(3))

Sec. 300.523 Manifestation determination review.

(a) General. If an action is contemplated regarding behavior described in Secs. 300.520(a)(2) or 300.521, or involving a removal that constitutes a change of placement under Sec. 300.519 for a child with a disability who has engaged in other behavior that violated any rule or code of conduct of the LEA that applies to all children—

(1) Not later than the date on which the decision to take that action is made, the parents must be notified of that decision and provided the procedural safeguards notice described in Sec. 300.504; and

(2) Immediately, if possible, but in no case later than 10 school days after the date on which the decision to take that action is made, a review must be conducted of the relationship between the child's disability and the behavior subject to the disciplinary action.

(b) Individuals to carry out review. A review described in paragraph (a) of this section must be conducted by the IEP team and other qualified personnel in a meeting.

(c) Conduct of review. In carrying out a review described in paragraph (a) of this section, the IEP team and other qualified personnel may determine that the behavior of the child was not a manifestation of the child's disability only if the IEP team and other qualified personnel—

(1) First consider, in terms of the behavior subject to disciplinary action, all relevant information, including —

(i) Evaluation and diagnostic results, including the results or other relevant information supplied by the parents of the child;

(ii) Observations of the child; and

(iii) The child's IEP and placement; and

(2) Then determine that—

(i) In relationship to the behavior subject to disciplinary action, the child's IEP and placement were appropriate and the special education services, supplementary aids and services, and behavior intervention strategies were provided consistent with the child's IEP and placement;

(ii) The child's disability did not impair the ability of the child to understand the impact and consequences of the behavior subject to disciplinary action; and

(iii) The child's disability did not impair the ability of the child to control the behavior subject to disciplinary action.

(d) Decision. If the IEP team and other qualified personnel determine that any of the standards in paragraph (c)(2) of this section were not met, the behavior must be considered a manifestation of the child's disability.

(e) Meeting. The review described in paragraph (a) of this section may be conducted at the same IEP meeting that is convened under Sec. 300.520(b).

(f) Deficiencies in IEP or placement. If, in the review in paragraphs (b) and (c) of this section, a public agency identifies deficiencies in the child's IEP or placement or in their implementation, it must take immediate steps to remedy those deficiencies.

(Authority: 20 U.S.C. 1415(k)(4))

Sec. 300.524 Determination that behavior was not manifestation of disability.

(a) General. If the result of the review described in Sec. 300.523 is a determination, consistent with Sec. 300.523(d), that the behavior of the child with a disability was not a manifestation of the child's disability, the relevant disciplinary procedures applicable to children without disabilities may be applied to the child in the same manner in which they would be applied to children without disabilities, except as provided in Sec. 300.121(d).

(b) Additional requirement. If the public agency initiates disciplinary procedures applicable to all children, the agency shall ensure that the special education and disciplinary records of the child with a disability are transmitted for consideration by the person or persons making the final determination regarding the disciplinary action.

(c) Child's status during due process proceedings. Except as provided in Sec. 300.526, Sec. 300.514 applies if a parent requests a hearing to challenge a determination, made through the review described in Sec. 300.523, that the behavior of the child was not a manifestation of the child's disability.

(Authority: 20 U.S.C. 1415(k)(5))

Sec. 300.525 Parent appeal.

(a) General.

(1) If the child's parent disagrees with a determination that the child's behavior was not a manifestation of the child's disability or with any decision regarding placement under Secs. 300.520-300.528, the parent may request a hearing.

(2) The State or local educational agency shall arrange for an expedited hearing in any case described in paragraph (a)(1) of this section if a hearing is requested by a parent.

(b) Review of decision. (1) In reviewing a decision with respect to the manifestation determination, the hearing officer shall determine whether the public agency has demonstrated that the child's behavior was not a manifestation of the child's disability consistent with the requirements of Sec. 300.523(d).

(2) In reviewing a decision under Sec. 300.520(a)(2) to place the child in an interim alternative educational setting, the hearing officer shall apply the standards in Sec. 300.521.

(Authority: 20 U.S.C. 1415(k)(6))

Sec. 300.526 Placement during appeals.

(a) General. If a parent requests a hearing or an appeal regarding a disciplinary action described in Sec. 300.520(a)(2) or 300.521 to challenge the interim alternative educational setting or the manifestation determination, the child must remain in the interim alternative educational setting pending the decision of the hearing officer or until the expiration of the time period provided for in Sec. 300.520(a)(2) or 300.521, whichever occurs first, unless the parent and the State agency or local educational agency agree otherwise.

(b) Current placement. If a child is placed in an interim alternative educational setting pursuant to Sec. 300.520(a)(2) or 300.521 and school personnel propose to change the child's placement after expiration of the interim alternative placement, during the pendency of any proceeding to challenge the proposed change in placement the child must remain in the current placement (the child's placement prior to the interim alternative educational setting), except as provided in paragraph (c) of this section.

(c) Expedited hearing.

(1) If school personnel maintain that it is dangerous for the child to be in the current placement (placement prior to removal to the interim alternative education setting) during the pendency of the due process proceedings, the LEA may request an expedited due process hearing.

(2) In determining whether the child may be placed in the alternative educational setting or in another appropriate placement ordered by the hearing officer, the hearing officer shall apply the standards in Sec. 300.521.

(3) A placement ordered pursuant to paragraph (c)(2) of this section may not be longer than 45 days.

(4) The procedure in paragraph (c) of this section may be repeated, as necessary.

(Authority: 20 U.S.C. 1415(k)(7))

Sec. 300.527 Protections for children not yet eligible for special education and related services.

(a) General. A child who has not been determined to be eligible for special education and related services under this part and who has engaged in behavior that violated any rule or code of conduct of the local educational agency, including any behavior described in Secs. 300.520 or 300.521, may assert any of the protections provided for in this part if the LEA had knowledge (as determined in accordance with paragraph (b) of this section) that the child was a child with a disability before the behavior that precipitated the disciplinary action occurred.

(b) Basis of knowledge. An LEA must be deemed to have knowledge that a child is a child with a disability if—

(1) The parent of the child has expressed concern in writing (or orally if the parent does not know how to write or has a disability that prevents a written statement) to personnel of the appropriate educational agency that the child is in need of special education and related services;

(2) The behavior or performance of the child demonstrates the need for these services, in accordance with Sec. 300.7;

(3) The parent of the child has requested an evaluation of the child pursuant to Secs. 300.530-300.536; or

(4) The teacher of the child, or other personnel of the local educational agency, has expressed concern about the behavior or performance of the child to the director of special education of the agency or to other personnel in accordance with the agency's established child find or special education referral system.

(c) Exception. A public agency would not be deemed to have knowledge under paragraph (b) of this section if, as a result of receiving the information specified in that paragraph, the agency—

(1) Either—

(i) Conducted an evaluation under Secs. 300.530-300.536, and determined that the child was not a child with a disability under this part; or

(ii) Determined that an evaluation was not necessary; and

(2) Provided notice to the child's parents of its determination under paragraph (c)(1) of this section, consistent with Sec. 300.503.

(d) Conditions that apply if no basis of knowledge.

(1) General. If an LEA does not have knowledge that a child is a child with a disability (in accordance with paragraphs (b) and (c) of this section) prior to taking disciplinary measures against the child, the child may be subjected to the same disciplinary measures as measures applied to children without disabilities who engaged in comparable behaviors consistent with paragraph (d)(2) of this section.

(2) Limitations.

(i) If a request is made for an evaluation of a child during the time period in which the child is subjected to disciplinary measures under Sec. 300.520 or 300.521, the evaluation must be conducted in an expedited manner.

(ii) Until the evaluation is completed, the child remains in the educational placement determined by school authorities, which can include suspension or expulsion without educational services.

(iii) If the child is determined to be a child with a disability, taking into consideration information from the evaluation conducted by the agency and information provided by the parents, the agency shall provide special education and related services in accordance with the provisions of this part, including the requirements of Secs. 300.520- 300.529 and section 612(a)(1)(A) of the Act.

(Authority: 20 U.S.C. 1415(k)(8))

Sec. 300.528 Expedited due process hearings.

(a) Expedited due process hearings under Secs. 300.521-300.526 must—

(1) Meet the requirements of Sec. 300.509, except that a State may provide that the time periods identified in Secs. 300.509(a)(3) and Sec. 300.509(b) for purposes of expedited due process hearings under Secs. 300.521-300.526 are not less than two business days; and

(2) Be conducted by a due process hearing officer who satisfies the requirements of Sec. 300.508.

(b)(1) Each State shall establish a timeline for expedited due process hearings that results in a written decision being mailed to the parties within 45 days of the public agency's receipt of the request for the hearing, without exceptions or extensions.

(2) The timeline established under paragraph (b)(1) of this section must be the same for hearings requested by parents or public agencies.

(c) A State may establish different procedural rules for expedited hearings under Secs. 300.521-300.526 than it has established for due process hearings under Sec. 300.507.

(d) The decisions on expedited due process hearings are appealable consistent with Sec. 300.510.

(Authority: 20 U.S.C. 1415(k)(2), (6), (7))

Sec. 300.529 Referral to and action by law enforcement and judicial authorities.

(a) Nothing in this part prohibits an agency from reporting a crime committed by a child with a disability to appropriate authorities or to prevent State law enforcement and judicial authorities from exercising their responsibilities with regard to the application of Federal and State law to crimes committed by a child with a disability.

(b)(1) An agency reporting a crime committed by a child with a disability shall ensure that copies of the special education and disciplinary records of the child are transmitted for consideration by the appropriate authorities to whom it reports the crime.

(2) An agency reporting a crime under this section may transmit copies of the child's special education and disciplinary records only to the extent that the transmission is permitted by the Family Educational Rights and Privacy Act.

(Authority: 20 U.S.C. 1415(k)(9))

Procedures for Evaluation and Determination of Eligibility

Sec. 300.530 General.

Each SEA shall ensure that each public agency establishes and implements procedures that meet the requirements of Secs. 300.531-300.536.

(Authority: 20 U.S.C. 1414(b)(3); 1412(a)(7))

Sec. 300.531 Initial evaluation.

Each public agency shall conduct a full and individual initial evaluation, in accordance with Secs. 300.532 and 300.533, before the initial provision of special education and related services to a child with a disability under Part B of the Act.

(Authority: 20 U.S.C. 1414(a)(1))

Sec. 300.532 Evaluation procedures.

Each public agency shall ensure, at a minimum, that the following requirements are met:

(a)(1) Tests and other evaluation materials used to assess a child under Part B of the Act—

(i) Are selected and administered so as not to be discriminatory on a racial or cultural basis; and

(ii) Are provided and administered in the child's native language or other mode of communication, unless it is clearly not feasible to do so; and

(2) Materials and procedures used to assess a child with limited English proficiency are selected and administered to ensure that they measure the extent to which the child has a disability and needs special education, rather than measuring the child's English language skills.

(b) A variety of assessment tools and strategies are used to gather relevant functional and developmental information about the child, including information provided by the parent, and information related to enabling the child to be involved in and progress in the general curriculum (or for a preschool child, to participate in appropriate activities), that may assist in determining—

(1) Whether the child is a child with a disability under Sec. 300.7; and

(2) The content of the child's IEP.

(c)(1) Any standardized tests that are given to a child—

(i) Have been validated for the specific purpose for which they are used; and

(ii) Are administered by trained and knowledgeable personnel in accordance with any instructions provided by the producer of the tests.

(2) If an assessment is not conducted under standard conditions, a description of the extent to which it varied from standard conditions (e.g., the qualifications of the person administering the test, or the method of test administration) must be included in the evaluation report.

(d) Tests and other evaluation materials include those tailored to assess specific areas of educational need and not merely those that are designed to provide a single general intelligence quotient.

(e) Tests are selected and administered so as best to ensure that if a test is administered to a child with impaired sensory, manual, or speaking skills, the test results accurately reflect the child's aptitude or achievement level or whatever other factors the test purports to measure, rather than reflecting the child's impaired sensory, manual, or speaking skills (unless those skills are the factors that the test purports to measure).

(f) No single procedure is used as the sole criterion for determining whether a child is a child with a disability and for determining an appropriate educational program for the child.

(g) The child is assessed in all areas related to the suspected disability, including, if appropriate, health, vision, hearing, social and emotional status, general intelligence, academic performance, communicative status, and motor abilities.

(h) In evaluating each child with a disability under Secs. 300.531-300.536, the evaluation is sufficiently comprehensive to identify all of the child's special education and related services needs, whether or not commonly linked to the disability category in which the child has been classified.

(i) The public agency uses technically sound instruments that may assess the relative contribution of cognitive and behavioral factors, in addition to physical or developmental factors.

(j) The public agency uses assessment tools and strategies that provide relevant information that directly assists persons in determining the educational needs of the child.

(Authority: 20 U.S.C. 1412(a)(6)(B), 1414(b)(2) and (3))

Sec. 300.533 Determination of needed evaluation data.

(a) Review of existing evaluation data.

As part of an initial evaluation (if appropriate) and as part of any reevaluation under Part B of the Act, a group that includes the individuals described in Sec. 300.344, and other qualified professionals, as appropriate, shall—

(1) Review existing evaluation data on the child, including—

(i) Evaluations and information provided by the parents of the child;

(ii) Current classroom-based assessments and observations; and

(iii) Observations by teachers and related services providers; and

(2) On the basis of that review, and input from the child's parents, identify what additional data, if any, are needed to determine—

(i) Whether the child has a particular category of disability, as described in Sec. 300.7, or, in case of a reevaluation of a child, whether the child continues to have such a disability;

(ii) The present levels of performance and educational needs of the child;

(iii) Whether the child needs special education and related services, or in the case of a reevaluation of a child, whether the child continues to need special education and related services; and

(iv) Whether any additions or modifications to the special education and related services are needed to enable the child to meet the measurable annual goals set out in the IEP of the child and to participate, as appropriate, in the general curriculum.

(b) Conduct of review. The group described in paragraph (a) of this section may conduct its review without a meeting.

(c) Need for additional data. The public agency shall administer tests and other evaluation materials as may be needed to produce the data identified under paragraph (a) of this section.

(d) Requirements if additional data are not needed.

(1) If the determination under paragraph (a) of this section is that no additional data are needed to determine whether the child continues to be a child with a disability, the public agency shall notify the child's parents—

(i) Of that determination and the reasons for it; and

(ii) Of the right of the parents to request an assessment to determine whether, for purposes of services under this part, the child continues to be a child with a disability.

(2) The public agency is not required to conduct the assessment described in paragraph (d)(1)(ii) of this section unless requested to do so by the child's parents.

(Authority: 20 U.S.C. 1414(c)(1), (2) and (4))

Sec. 300.534 Determination of eligibility.

(a) Upon completing the administration of tests and other evaluation materials—

(1) A group of qualified professionals and the parent of the child must determine whether the child is a child with a disability, as defined in Sec. 300.7; and

(2) The public agency must provide a copy of the evaluation report and the documentation of determination of eligibility to the parent.

(b) A child may not be determined to be eligible under this part if—

(1) The determinant factor for that eligibility determination is—

(i) Lack of instruction in reading or math; or

(ii) Limited English proficiency; and

(2) The child does not otherwise meet the eligibility criteria under Sec. 300.7(a).

(c)(1) A public agency must evaluate a child with a disability in accordance with Secs. 300.532 and 300.533 before determining that the child is no longer a child with a disability.

(2) The evaluation described in paragraph (c)(1) of this section is not required before the termination of a student's eligibility under Part B of the Act due to graduation with a regular high school diploma, or exceeding the age eligibility for FAPE under State law.

(Authority: 20 U.S.C. 1414(b)(4) and (5), (c)(5))

Sec. 300.535 Procedures for determining eligibility and placement.

(a) In interpreting evaluation data for the purpose of determining if a child is a child with a disability under Sec. 300.7, and the educational needs of the child, each public agency shall—

(1) Draw upon information from a variety of sources, including aptitude and achievement tests, parent input, teacher recommendations, physical condition, social or cultural background, and adaptive behavior; and

(2) Ensure that information obtained from all of these sources is documented and carefully considered.

(b) If a determination is made that a child has a disability and needs special education and related services, an IEP must be developed for the child in accordance with Secs. 300.340-300.350.

(Authority: 20 U.S.C. 1412(a)(6), 1414(b)(4))

Sec. 300.536 Reevaluation.

Each public agency shall ensure—

(a) That the IEP of each child with a disability is reviewed in accordance with Secs. 300.340-300.350; and

(b) That a reevaluation of each child, in accordance with Secs. 300.532-300.535, is conducted if conditions warrant an evaluation, or if the child's parent or teacher requests an evaluation, but at least once every three years.

(Authority: 20 U.S.C. 1414(a)(2))

Additional Procedures for Evaluating Children With Specific Learning Disabilities

Sec. 300.540 Additional team members.

The determination of whether a child suspected of having a specific learning disability is a child with a disability as defined in Sec. 300.7, must be made by the child's parents and a team of qualified professionals which must include—

(a)(1) The child's regular teacher; or

(2) If the child does not have a regular teacher, a regular classroom teacher qualified to teach a child of his or her age; or

(3) For a child of less than school age, an individual qualified by the SEA to teach a child of his or her age; and

(b) At least one person qualified to conduct individual diagnostic examinations of children, such as a school psychologist, speech-language pathologist, or remedial reading teacher.

(Authority: Sec. 5(b), Pub. L. 94-142)

Sec. 300.541 Criteria for determining the existence of a specific learning disability.

(a) A team may determine that a child has a specific learning disability if—

(1) The child does not achieve commensurate with his or her age and ability levels in one or more of the areas listed in paragraph (a)(2) of this section, if provided with learning experiences appropriate for the child's age and ability levels; and

(2) The team finds that a child has a severe discrepancy between achievement and intellectual ability in one or more of the following areas:

(i) Oral expression.

(ii) Listening comprehension.

(iii) Written expression.

(iv) Basic reading skill.

(v) Reading comprehension.

(vi) Mathematics calculation.

(vii) Mathematics reasoning.

(b) The team may not identify a child as having a specific learning disability if the severe discrepancy between ability and achievement is primarily the result of—

(1) A visual, hearing, or motor impairment;

(2) Mental retardation;

(3) Emotional disturbance; or

(4) Environmental, cultural or economic disadvantage.

(Authority: Sec. 5(b), Pub. L. 94-142)

Sec. 300.542 Observation.

(a) At least one team member other than the child's regular teacher shall observe the child's academic performance in the regular classroom setting.

(b) In the case of a child of less than school age or out of school, a team member shall observe the child in an environment appropriate for a child of that age.

(Authority: Sec. 5(b), Pub. L. 94-142)

Sec. 300.543 Written report.

(a) For a child suspected of having a specific learning disability, the documentation of the team's determination of eligibility, as required by Sec. 300.534(a)(2), must include a statement of—

(1) Whether the child has a specific learning disability;

(2) The basis for making the determination;

(3) The relevant behavior noted during the observation of the child;

(4) The relationship of that behavior to the child's academic functioning;

(5) The educationally relevant medical findings, if any;

(6) Whether there is a severe discrepancy between achievement and ability that is not correctable without special education and related services; and

(7) The determination of the team concerning the effects of environmental, cultural, or economic disadvantage.

(b) Each team member shall certify in writing whether the report reflects his or her conclusion. If it does not reflect his or her conclusion, the team member must submit a separate statement presenting his or her conclusions.

(Authority: Sec. 5(b), Pub. L. 94-142))

Least Restrictive Environment (LRE)

Sec. 300.550 General LRE requirements.

(a) Except as provided in Sec. 300.311(b) and (c), a State shall demonstrate to the satisfaction of the Secretary that the State has in effect policies and procedures to ensure that it meets the requirements of Secs. 300.550-300.556.

(b) Each public agency shall ensure—

(1) That to the maximum extent appropriate, children with disabilities, including children in public or private institutions or other care facilities, are educated with children who are non disabled; and

(2) That special classes, separate schooling or other removal of children with disabilities from the regular educational environment occurs only if the nature or severity of the disability is such that education in regular classes with the use of supplementary aids and services cannot be achieved satisfactorily.

(Authority: 20 U.S.C. 1412(a)(5))

Sec. 300.551 Continuum of alternative placements.

(a) Each public agency shall ensure that a continuum of alternative placements is available to meet the needs of children with disabilities for special education and related services.

(b) The continuum required in paragraph (a) of this section must—

(1) Include the alternative placements listed in the definition of special education under Sec. 300.26 (instruction in regular classes, special classes, special schools, home instruction, and instruction in hospitals and institutions); and

(2) Make provision for supplementary services (such as resource room or itinerant instruction) to be provided in conjunction with regular class placement.

(Authority: 20 U.S.C. 1412(a)(5))

Sec. 300.552 Placements.

In determining the educational placement of a child with a disability, including a preschool child with a disability, each public agency shall ensure that—

(a) The placement decision—

(1) Is made by a group of persons, including the parents, and other persons knowledgeable about the child, the meaning of the evaluation data, and the placement options; and

(2) Is made in conformity with the LRE provisions of this subpart, including Secs. 300.550-300.554;

(b) The child's placement—

(1) Is determined at least annually;

(2) Is based on the child's IEP; and

(3) Is as close as possible to the child's home;

(c) Unless the IEP of a child with a disability requires some other arrangement, the child is educated in the school that he or she would attend if nondisabled;

(d) In selecting the LRE, consideration is given to any potential harmful effect on the child or on the quality of services that he or she needs; and

(e) A child with a disability is not removed from education in age-appropriate regular classrooms solely because of needed modifications in the general curriculum.

(Authority: 20 U.S.C. 1412(a)(5))

Sec. 300.553 Nonacademic settings.

In providing or arranging for the provision of nonacademic and extracurricular services and activities, including meals, recess periods, and the services and activities set forth in Sec. 300.306, each public agency shall ensure that each child with a disability participates with nondisabled children in those services and activities to the maximum extent appropriate to the needs of that child.

(Authority: 20 U.S.C. 1412(a)(5))

Sec. 300.554 Children in public or private institutions.

Except as provided in Sec. 300.600(d), an SEA must ensure that Sec. 300.550 is effectively implemented, including, if necessary, making arrangements with public and private institutions (such as a memorandum of agreement or special implementation procedures).

(Authority: 20 U.S.C. 1412(a)(5))

Sec. 300.555 Technical assistance and training activities.

Each SEA shall carry out activities to ensure that teachers and administrators in all public agencies—

(a) Are fully informed about their responsibilities for implementing Sec. 300.550; and

(b) Are provided with technical assistance and training necessary to assist them in this effort.

(Authority: 20 U.S.C. 1412(a)(5))

Sec. 300.556 Monitoring activities.

(a) The SEA shall carry out activities to ensure that Sec. 300.550 is implemented by each public agency.

(b) If there is evidence that a public agency makes placements that are inconsistent with Sec. 300.550, the SEA shall—

(1) Review the public agency's justification for its actions; and

(2) Assist in planning and implementing any necessary corrective action.

(Authority: 20 U.S.C. 1412(a)(5))

Confidentiality of Information

Sec. 300.560 Definitions.

As used in Secs. 300.560-300.577—

(a) Destruction means physical destruction or removal of personal identifiers from information so that the information is no longer personally identifiable.

(b) Education records means the type of records covered under the definition of "education records" in 34 CFR part 99 (the regulations implementing the Family Educational Rights and Privacy Act of 1974).

(c) Participating agency means any agency or institution that collects, maintains, or uses personally identifiable information, or from which information is obtained, under Part B of the Act.

(Authority: 20 U.S.C. 1221e-3, 1412(a)(8), 1417(c))

Sec. 300.561 Notice to parents.

(a) The SEA shall give notice that is adequate to fully inform parents about the requirements of Sec. 300.127, including—

(1) A description of the extent that the notice is given in the native languages of the various population groups in the State;

(2) A description of the children on whom personally identifiable information is maintained, the types of information sought, the methods the State intends to use in gathering the information (including the sources from whom information is gathered), and the uses to be made of the information;

(3) A summary of the policies and procedures that participating agencies must follow regarding storage, disclosure to third parties, retention, and destruction of personally identifiable information; and

(4) A description of all of the rights of parents and children regarding this information, including the rights under the Family Educational Rights and Privacy Act of 1974 and implementing regulations in 34 CFR part 99.

(b) Before any major identification, location, or evaluation activity, the notice must be published or announced in newspapers or other media, or both, with circulation adequate to notify parents throughout the State of the activity.

(Authority: 20 U.S.C. 1412(a)(8), 1417(c))

Sec. 300.562 Access rights.

(a) Each participating agency shall permit parents to inspect and review any education records relating to their children that are collected, maintained, or used by the agency under this part. The agency shall comply with a request without unnecessary delay and before any meeting regarding an IEP, or any hearing pursuant to Secs. 300.507 and 300.521-300.528, and in no case more than 45 days after the request has been made.

(b) The right to inspect and review education records under this section includes—

(1) The right to a response from the participating agency to reasonable requests for explanations and interpretations of the records;

(2) The right to request that the agency provide copies of the records containing the information if failure to provide those copies would effectively prevent the parent from exercising the right to inspect and review the records; and

(3) The right to have a representative of the parent inspect and review the records.

(c) An agency may presume that the parent has authority to inspect and review records relating to his or her child unless the agency has been advised that the parent does not have the authority under applicable State law governing such matters as guardianship, separation, and divorce.

(Authority: 20 U.S.C. 1412(a)(8), 1417(c))

Sec. 300.563 Record of access.

Each participating agency shall keep a record of parties obtaining access to education records collected, maintained, or used under Part B of the Act (except access by parents and authorized employees of the participating agency), including the name of the party, the date access was given, and the purpose for which the party is authorized to use the records.

(Authority: 20 U.S.C. 1412(a)(8), 1417(c))

Sec. 300.564 Records on more than one child.

If any education record includes information on more than one child, the parents of those children have the right to inspect and review only the information relating to their child or to be informed of that specific information.

(Authority: 20 U.S.C. 1412(a)(8), 1417(c))

Sec. 300.565 List of types and locations of information.

Each participating agency shall provide parents on request a list of the types and locations of education records collected, maintained, or used by the agency.

(Authority: 20 U.S.C. 1412(a)(8), 1417(c))

Sec. 300.566 Fees.

(a) Each participating agency may charge a fee for copies of records that are made for parents under this part if the fee does not effectively prevent the parents from exercising their right to inspect and review those records.

(b) A participating agency may not charge a fee to search for or to retrieve information under this part.

(Authority: 20 U.S.C. 1412(a)(8), 1417(c))

Sec. 300.567 Amendment of records at parent's request.

(a) A parent who believes that information in the education records collected, maintained, or used under this part is inaccurate or misleading or violates the privacy or other rights of the child may request the participating agency that maintains the information to amend the information.

(b) The agency shall decide whether to amend the information in accordance with the request within a reasonable period of time of receipt of the request.

(c) If the agency decides to refuse to amend the information in accordance with the request, it shall inform the parent of the refusal and advise the parent of the right to a hearing under Sec. 300.568.

(Authority: 20 U.S.C. 1412(a)(8); 1417(c))

Sec. 300.568 Opportunity for a hearing.

The agency shall, on request, provide an opportunity for a hearing to challenge information in education records to ensure that it is not inaccurate, misleading, or otherwise in violation of the privacy or other rights of the child.

(Authority: 20 U.S.C. 1412(a)(8), 1417(c))

Sec. 300.569 Result of hearing.

(a) If, as a result of the hearing, the agency decides that the information is inaccurate, misleading or otherwise in violation of the privacy or other rights of the child, it shall amend the information accordingly and so inform the parent in writing.

(b) If, as a result of the hearing, the agency decides that the information is not inaccurate, misleading, or otherwise in violation of the privacy or other rights of the child, it shall inform the parent of the right to place in the records it maintains on the child a statement commenting on the information or setting forth any reasons for disagreeing with the decision of the agency.

(c) Any explanation placed in the records of the child under this section must—

(1) Be maintained by the agency as part of the records of the child as long as the record or contested portion is maintained by the agency; and

(2) If the records of the child or the contested portion is disclosed by the agency to any party, the explanation must also be disclosed to the party.

(Authority: 20 U.S.C. 1412(a)(8), 1417(c))

Sec. 300.570 Hearing procedures.

A hearing held under Sec. 300.568 must be conducted according to the procedures under 34 CFR 99.22.

(Authority: 20 U.S.C. 1412(a)(8), 1417(c))

Sec. 300.571 Consent.

(a) Except as to disclosures addressed in Sec. 300.529(b) for which parental consent is not required by Part 99, parental consent must be obtained before personally identifiable information is—

(1) Disclosed to anyone other than officials of participating agencies collecting or using the information under this part, subject to paragraph (b) of this section; or

(2) Used for any purpose other than meeting a requirement of this part.

(b) An educational agency or institution subject to 34 CFR part 99 may not release information from education records to participating agencies without parental consent unless authorized to do so under part 99.

(c) The SEA shall provide policies and procedures that are used in the event that a parent refuses to provide consent under this section.

(Authority: 20 U.S.C. 1412(a)(8), 1417(c))

Sec. 300.572 Safeguards.

(a) Each participating agency shall protect the confidentiality of personally identifiable information at collection, storage, disclosure, and destruction stages.

(b) One official at each participating agency shall assume responsibility for ensuring the confidentiality of any personally identifiable information.

(c) All persons collecting or using personally identifiable information must receive training or instruction regarding the State's policies and procedures under Sec. 300.127 and 34 CFR part 99.

(d) Each participating agency shall maintain, for public inspection, a current listing of the names and positions of those employees within the agency who may have access to personally identifiable information.

(Authority: 20 U.S.C. 1412(a)(8), 1417(c))

Sec. 300.573 Destruction of information.

(a) The public agency shall inform parents when personally identifiable information collected, maintained, or used under this part is no longer needed to provide educational services to the child.

(b) The information must be destroyed at the request of the parents. However, a permanent record of a student's name, address, and phone number, his or her grades, attendance record, classes attended, grade level completed, and year completed may be maintained without time limitation.

(Authority: 20 U.S.C. 1412(a)(8), 1417(c))

Sec. 300.574 Children's rights.

(a) The SEA shall provide policies and procedures regarding the extent to which children are afforded rights of privacy similar to those afforded to parents, taking into consideration the age of the child and type or severity of disability.

(b) Under the regulations for the Family Educational Rights and Privacy Act of 1974 (34 CFR 99.5(a)), the rights of parents regarding education records are transferred to the student at age 18.

(c) If the rights accorded to parents under Part B of the Act are transferred to a student who reaches the age of majority, consistent with Sec. 300.517, the rights regarding educational records in Secs. 300.562-300.573 must also be transferred to the student. However, the public agency must provide any notice required under section 615 of the Act to the student and the parents.

(Authority: 20 U.S.C. 1412(a)(8), 1417(c))

Sec. 300.575 Enforcement.

The SEA shall provide the policies and procedures, including sanctions, that the State uses to ensure that its policies and procedures are followed and that the requirements of the Act and the regulations in this part are met.

(Authority: 20 U.S.C. 1412(a)(8), 1417(c))

Sec. 300.576 Disciplinary information.

(a) The State may require that a public agency include in the records of a child with a disability a statement of any current or previous disciplinary action that has been taken against the child and transmit the statement to the same extent that the disciplinary information is included in, and transmitted with, the student records of nondisabled children.

(b) The statement may include a description of any behavior engaged in by the child that required disciplinary action, a description of the disciplinary action taken, and any other information that is relevant to the safety of the child and other individuals involved with the child.

(c) If the State adopts such a policy, and the child transfers from one school to another, the transmission of any of the child's records must include both the child's current individualized education program and any statement of current or previous disciplinary action that has been taken against the child.

(Authority: 20 U.S.C. 1413(j))

Sec. 300.577 Department use of personally identifiable information.

If the Department or its authorized representatives collect any personally identifiable information regarding children with disabilities that is not subject to 5 U.S.C. 552a (the Privacy Act of 1974), the Secretary applies the requirements of 5 U.S.C. 552a (b)(1)-(2), (4)-(11); (c); (d); (e)(1), (2), (3)(A), (B), and (D),(5)-(10); (h); (m); and (n); and the regulations implementing those provisions in 34 CFR part 5b.

(Authority: 20 U.S.C. 1412(a)(8), 1417(c))

Department Procedures

Subpart F: State Administration

Sec. 300.650 Establishment of advisory panels.

(a) Each State shall establish and maintain, in accordance with Secs. 300.650-300.653, a State advisory panel on the education of children with disabilities.

(b) The advisory panel must be appointed by the Governor or any other official authorized under State law to make those appointments.

(c) If a State has an existing advisory panel that can perform the functions in Sec. 300.652, the State may modify the existing panel so that it fulfills all of the requirements of Secs. 300.650-300.653, instead of establishing a new advisory panel.

(Authority: 20 U.S.C. 1412(a)(21)(A))

Sec. 300.651 Membership.

(a) General. The membership of the State advisory panel must consist of members appointed by the Governor, or any other official authorized under State law to make these appointments, that is representative of the State population and that is composed of individuals involved in, or concerned with the education of children with disabilities, including—

(1) Parents of children with disabilities;

(2) Individuals with disabilities;

(3) Teachers;

(4) Representatives of institutions of higher education that prepare special education and related services personnel;

(5) State and local education officials;

(6) Administrators of programs for children with disabilities;

(7) Representatives of other State agencies involved in the financing or delivery of related services to children with disabilities;

(8) Representatives of private schools and public charter schools;

(9) At least one representative of a vocational, community, or business organization concerned with the provision of transition services to children with disabilities; and

(10) Representatives from the State juvenile and adult corrections agencies.

(b) Special rule. A majority of the members of the panel must be individuals with disabilities or parents of children with disabilities.

(Authority: 20 U.S.C. 1412(a)(21)(B) and (C))

Sec. 300.652 Advisory panel functions.

(a) General. The State advisory panel shall—

(1) Advise the SEA of unmet needs within the State in the education of children with disabilities;

(2) Comment publicly on any rules or regulations proposed by the State regarding the education of children with disabilities;

(3) Advise the SEA in developing evaluations and reporting on data to the Secretary under section 618 of the Act;

(4) Advise the SEA in developing corrective action plans to address findings identified in Federal monitoring reports under Part B of the Act; and

(5) Advise the SEA in developing and implementing policies relating to the coordination of services for children with disabilities.

(b) Advising on eligible students with disabilities in adult prisons. The advisory panel also shall advise on the education of eligible students with disabilities who have been convicted as adults and incarcerated in adult prisons, even if, consistent with Sec. 300.600(d), a State assigns general supervision responsibility for those students to a public agency other than an SEA.

(Authority: 20 U.S.C. 1412(a)(21)(D))

Sec. 300.653 Advisory panel procedures.

(a) The advisory panel shall meet as often as necessary to conduct its business.

(b) By July 1 of each year, the advisory panel shall submit an annual report of panel activities and suggestions to the SEA. This report must be made available to the public in a manner consistent with other public reporting requirements of Part B of the Act.

(c) Official minutes must be kept on all panel meetings and must be made available to the public on request.

(d) All advisory panel meetings and agenda items must be announced enough in advance of the meeting to afford interested parties a reasonable opportunity to attend. Meetings must be open to the public.

(e) Interpreters and other necessary services must be provided at panel meetings for panel members or participants. The State may pay for these services from funds under Sec. 300.620.

(f) The advisory panel shall serve without compensation but the State must reimburse the panel for reasonable and necessary expenses for attending meetings and performing duties. The State may use funds under Sec. 300.620 for this purpose.

(Authority: 20 U.S.C. 1412(a)(21))

State Complaint Procedures

Sec. 300.660 Adoption of State complaint procedures.

(a) General. Each SEA shall adopt written procedures for—

(1) Resolving any complaint, including a complaint filed by an organization or individual from another State, that meets the requirements of Sec. 300.662 by—

(i) Providing for the filing of a complaint with the SEA; and

(ii) At the SEA's discretion, providing for the filing of a complaint with a public agency and the right to have the SEA review the public agency's decision on the complaint; and

(2) Widely disseminating to parents and other interested individuals, including parent training and information centers, protection and advocacy agencies, independent living centers, and other appropriate entities, the State's procedures under Secs. 300.660-300.662.

(b) Remedies for denial of appropriate services. In resolving a complaint in which it has found a failure to provide appropriate services, an SEA, pursuant to its general supervisory authority under Part B of the Act, must address:

(1) How to remediate the denial of those services, including, as appropriate, the awarding of monetary reimbursement or other corrective action appropriate to the needs of the child; and

(2) Appropriate future provision of services for all children with disabilities.

(Authority: 20 U.S.C. 1221e-3)

Sec. 300.661 Minimum State complaint procedures.

(a) Time limit; minimum procedures. Each SEA shall include in its complaint procedures a time limit of 60 days after a complaint is filed under Sec. 300.660(a) to—

(1) Carry out an independent on-site investigation, if the SEA determines that an investigation is necessary;

(2) Give the complainant the opportunity to submit additional information, either orally or in writing, about the allegations in the complaint;

(3) Review all relevant information and make an independent determination as to whether the public agency is violating a requirement of Part B of the Act or of this part; and

(4) Issue a written decision to the complainant that addresses each allegation in the complaint and contains—

(i) Findings of fact and conclusions; and

(ii) The reasons for the SEA's final decision.

(b) Time extension; final decision; implementation. The SEA's procedures described in paragraph (a) of this section also must—

(1) Permit an extension of the time limit under paragraph (a) of this section only if exceptional circumstances exist with respect to a particular complaint; and

(2) Include procedures for effective implementation of the SEA's final decision, if needed, including—

(i) Technical assistance activities;

(ii) Negotiations; and

(iii) Corrective actions to achieve compliance.

(c) Complaints filed under this section, and due process hearings under Secs. 300.507 and 300.520-300.528.

(1) If a written complaint is received that is also the subject of a due process hearing under Sec. 300.507 or Secs. 300.520-300.528, or contains multiple issues, of which one or more are part of that hearing, the State must set aside any part of the complaint that is being addressed in the due process hearing, until the conclusion of the hearing. However, any issue in the complaint that is not a part of the due process action must be resolved using the time limit and procedures described in paragraphs (a) and (b) of this section.

(2) If an issue is raised in a complaint filed under this section that has previously been decided in a due process hearing involving the same parties—

(i) The hearing decision is binding; and

(ii) The SEA must inform the complainant to that effect.

(3) A complaint alleging a public agency's failure to implement a due process decision must be resolved by the SEA.

(Authority: 20 U.S.C. 1221e-3)

Sec. 300.662 Filing a complaint.

(a) An organization or individual may file a signed written complaint under the procedures described in Secs. 300.660-300.661.

(b) The complaint must include—

(1) A statement that a public agency has violated a requirement of Part B of the Act or of this part; and

(2) The facts on which the statement is based.

(c) The complaint must allege a violation that occurred not more than one year prior to the date that the complaint is received in accordance with Sec. 300.660(a) unless a longer period is reasonable because the violation is continuing, or the complainant is requesting compensatory services for a violation that occurred not more than three years prior to the date the complaint is received under Sec. 300.660(a).

(Authority: 20 U.S.C. 1221e-3)

Section 504 of the Rehabilitation Act of 1973 (Key Regulations)

Part 104—Nondiscrimination on the Basis of Handicap in Programs and Activities Receiving Federal Financial Assistance

Sec. 104.1 Purpose

The purpose of this part is to effectuate section 504 of the Rehabilitation Act of 1973, which is designed to eliminate discrimination on the basis of handicap in any program or activity receiving Federal financial assistance.

Sec. 104.2 Application

This part applies to each recipient of Federal financial assistance from the Department of Education and to each program or activity that receives or benefits from such assistance.

Sec. 104.3 Definitions

As used in this part, the term:

(a) The Act means the Rehabilitation Act of 1973, Pub. L. 93-112, as amended by the Rehabilitation Act Amendments of 1974, Pub. L. 93-516, 29 U.S.C. 794.

(b) Section 504 means section 504 of the Act.

(c) Education of the Handicapped Act means that statute as amended by the Education for all Handicapped Children Act of 1975, Pub. L. 94-142, 20 U.S.C. 1401 et seq.

(d) Department means the Department of Education.

(e) Assistant Secretary means the Assistant Secretary for Civil Rights of the Department of Education.

(f) Recipient means any state or its political subdivision, any instrumentality of a state or its political subdivision, any public or private agency, institution, organization, or other entity, or any person to which Federal financial assistance is extended directly or through another recipient, including any successor, assignee, or transferee of a recipient, but excluding the ultimate beneficiary of the assistance.

(g) Applicant for assistance means one who submits an application, request, or plan required to be approved by a Department official or by a recipient as a condition to becoming a recipient.

(h) Federal financial assistance means any grant, loan, contract (other than a procurement contract or a contract of insurance or guaranty), or any other arrangement by which the Department provides or otherwise makes available assistance in the form of:

(1) Funds;

(2) Services of Federal personnel; or

(3) Real and personal property or any interest in or use of such property, including:

(i) Transfers or leases of such property for less than fair market value or for reduced consideration; and

(ii) Proceeds from a subsequent transfer or lease of such property if the Federal share of its fair market value is not returned to the Federal Government.

(i) Facility means all or any portion of buildings, structures, equipment, roads, walks, parking lots, or other real or personal property or interest in such property.

(j) Handicapped person—

(1) Handicapped persons means any person who (i) has a physical or mental impairment which substantially limits one or more major life activities, (ii) has a record of such an impairment, or (iii) is regarded as having such an impairment.

(2) As used in paragraph (j)(1) of this section, the phrase:

(i) Physical or mental impairment means (A) any physiological disorder or condition, cosmetic disfigurement, or anatomical loss affecting one or more of the following body systems: neurological; musculoskeletal; special sense organs; respiratory, including speech organs; cardiovascular; reproductive, digestive, genito-urinary; hemic and lymphatic; skin; and endocrine; or (B) any mental or psychological disorder, such as mental retardation, organic brain syndrome, emotional or mental illness, and specific learning disabilities.

(ii) Major life activities means functions such as caring for one's self, performing manual tasks, walking, seeing, hearing, speaking, breathing, learning, and working.

(iii) Has a record of such an impairment means has a history of, or has been misclassified as having, a mental or physical impairment that substantially limits one or more major life activities.

(iv) Is regarded as having an impairment means (A) has a physical or mental impairment that does not substantially limit major life activities but that is treated by a recipient as constituting such a limitation; (B) has a physical or mental impairment that substantially limits major life activities only as a result of the attitudes of others toward such impairment; or (C) has none of the impairments defined in paragraph (j)(2)(i) of this section but is treated by a recipient as having such an impairment.

(k) Qualified handicapped person means:

(1) With respect to employment, a handicapped person who, with reasonable accommodation, can perform the essential functions of the job in question;

(2) With respect to public preschool elementary, secondary, or adult educational services, a handicappped person (i) of an age during which nonhandicapped persons are provided such services, (ii) of any age during which it is mandatory under state law to provide such services to handicapped persons, or (iii) to whom a state is required to provide a free appropriate public education under section 612 of the Education of the Handicapped Act; and

(3) With respect to postsecondary and vocational education services, a handicapped person who meets the academic and technical standards requisite to admission or participation in the recipient's education program or activity;

(4) With respect to other services, a handicapped person who meets the essential eligibility requirements for the receipt of such services.

(l) Handicap means any condition or characteristic that renders a person a handicapped person as defined in paragraph (j) of this section.

Sec. 104.4 Discrimination prohibited

(a) **General.** No qualified handicapped person shall, on the basis of handicap, be excluded from participation in, be denied the benefits of, or otherwise be subjected to discrimination under any program or activitiy which receives or benefits from Federal financial assistance.

(b) **Discriminatory actions prohibited.** (1) A recipient, in providing any aid, benefit, or service, may not, directly or through contractual, licensing, or other arrangements, on the basis of handicap:

(i) Deny a qualified handicapped person the opportunity to participate in or benefit from the aid, benefit, or service;

(ii) Afford a qualified handicapped person an opportunity to participate in or benefit from the aid, benefit, or service that is not equal to that afforded others;

(iii) Provide a qualified handicapped person with an aid, benefit, or service that is not as effective as that provided to others;

(iv) Provide different or separate aid, benefits, or services to handicapped persons or to any class of handicapped persons unless such action is necessary to provide qualified handicapped persons with aid, benefits, or services that are as effective as those provided to others;

(v) Aid or perpetuate discrimination against a qualified handicapped person by providing significant assistance to an agency, organization, or person that discriminates on the basis of handicap in providing any aid, benefit, or service to beneficiaries of the recipients program;

(vi) Deny a qualified handicapped person the opportunity to participate as a member of planning or advisory boards; or

(vii) Otherwise limit a qualified handicapped person in the enjoyment of any right, privilege, advantage, or opportunity enjoyed by others receiving an aid, benefit, or service.

(2) For purposes of this part, aids, benefits, and services, to be equally effective, are not required to produce the identical result or level of achievement for handicapped and nonhandicapped persons, but must afford handicapped persons equal opportunity to obtain the same result, to gain the same benefit, or to reach the same level of achievement, in the most integrated setting appropriate to the person's needs.

(3) Despite the existence of separate or different programs or activities provided in accordance with this part, a recipient may not deny a qualified handicapped person the opportunity to participate in such programs or activities that are not separate or different.

(4) A recipient may not, directly or through contractual or other arrangements, utilize criteria or methods of administration (i) that have the effect of subjecting qualified handicapped persons to discrimination on the basis of handicap, (ii) that have the purpose or effect of defeating or substantially impairing accomplishment of the objectives of the recipient's program with respect to handicapped persons, or (iii) that perpetuate the discrimination of another recipient if both recipients are subject to common administrative control or are agencies of the same State.

(5) In determining the site or location of a facility, an applicant for assistance or a recipient may not make selections (i)

that have the effect of excluding handicapped persons from, denying them the benefits of, or otherwise subjecting them to discrimination under any program or activity that receives or benefits from Federal financial assistance or (ii) that have the purpose or effect of defeating or substantially impairing the accomplishment of the objectives of the program or activity with respect to handicapped persons.

(6) As used in this section, the aid, benefit, or service provided under a program or activity receiving or benefiting from Federal financial assistance includes any aid, benefit, or service provided in or through a facility that has been constructed, expanded, altered, leased or rented, or otherwise acquired, in whole or in part, with Federal financial assistance.

(c) Programs limited by Federal law. The exclusion of nonhandicapped persons from the benefits of a program limited by Federal statute or executive order to handicapped persons or the exclusion of a specific class of handicapped persons from a program limited by Federal statute or executive order to a different class of handicapped persons is not prohibited by this part.

Sec.104.5 Assurances required

(a) Assurances. An applicant for Federal financial assistance for a program or activity to which this part applies shall submit an assurance, on a form specified by the Assistant Secretary, that the program will be operated in compliance with this part. An applicant may incorporate these assurances by reference in subsequent applications to the Department.

(b) Duration of obligation

(1) In the case of Federal financial assistance extended in the form of real property or to provide real property or structures on the property, the assurance will obligate the recipient or, in the case of a subsequent transfer, the transferee, for the period during which the real property or structures are used for the purpose for which Federal financial assistance is extended or for another purpose involving the provision of similar services or benefits.

(2) In the case of Federal financial assistance extended to provide personal property, the assurance will obligate the recipient for the period during which it retains ownership or possession of the property.

(3) In all other cases the assurance will obligate the recipient for the period during which Federal financial assistance is extended.

(c) Covenants

(1) Where Federal financial assistance is provided in the form of real property or interest in the property from the Department, the instrument effecting or recording this transfer shall contain a covenant running with the land to assure nondiscrimination for the period during which the real property is used for a purpose for which the Federal financial assistance is extended or for another purpose involving the provision of similar services or benefits.

(2) Where no transfer of property is involved but property is purchased or improved with Federal financial assistance, the recipient shall agree to include the covenant described in

paragraph (b)(2) of this section in the instrument effecting or recording any subsequent transfer of the property.

(3) Where Federal financial assistance is provided in the form of real property or interest in the property from the Department, the covenant shall also include a condition coupled with a right to be reserved by the Department to revert title to the property in the event of a breach of the covenant. If a transferee of real property proposes to mortgage or otherwise encumber the real property as security for financing construction of new, or improvement of existing, facilities on the property for the purposes for which the property was transferred, the Assistant Secretary may, upon request of the transferee and if necessary to accomplish such financing and upon such conditions as he or she deems appropriate, agree to forbear the exercise of such right to revert title for so long as the lien of such mortgage or other encumbrance remains effective.

Sec.104.21 Discrimination prohibited

No qualified handicapped person shall, because a recipient's facilities are inaccessible to or unusable by handicapped persons, be denied the benefits of, be excluded from participation in, or otherwise be subjected to discrimination under any program or activity to which this part applies.

Sec.104.22 Existing facilities

(a) Program accessibility. A recipient shall operate each program or activity to which this part applies so that the program or activity, when viewed in its entirety, is readily accessible to handicapped persons. This paragraph does not require a recipient to make each of its existing facilities or every part of a facility accessible to and usable by handicapped persons.

(b) Methods. A recipient may comply with the requirements of paragraph (a) of this section through such means as redesign of equipment, reassignment of classes or other services to accessible buildings, assignment of aides to beneficiaries, home visits, delivery of health, welfare, or other social services at alternate accessible sites, alteration of existing facilities and construction of new facilities in conformance with the requirements of Sec. 104.23, or any other methods that result in making its program or activity accessible to handicapped persons. A recipient is not required to make structural changes in existing facilities where other methods are effective in achieving compliance with paragraph (a) of this section. In choosing among available methods for meeting the requirement of paragraph (a) of this section, a recipient shall give priority to those methods that offer programs and activities to handicapped persons in the most integrated setting appropriate.

(c) Small health, welfare, or other social service providers. If a recipient with fewer than fifteen employees that provides health, welfare, or other social services finds, after consultation with a handicapped person seeking its services, that there is no method of complying with paragraph (a) of this section other than making a significant alteration in its existing facilities, the recipient may, as an alternative, refer the handicapped person to other providers of those services that are accessible.

(d) Time period. A recipient shall comply with the requirement of paragraph (a) of this section within sixty days of the effective date of this part except that where structural changes in facilities are necessary, such changes shall be made within three years of the effective date of this part, but in any event as expeditiously as possible.

(e) Transition plan. In the event that structural changes to facilities are necessary to meet the requirement of paragraph (a) of this section, a recipient shall develop, within six months of the effective date of this part, a transition plan setting forth the steps necessary to complete such changes. The plan shall be developed with the assistance of interested persons, including handicapped persons or organizations representing handicapped persons. A copy of the transition plan shall be made available for public inspection. The plan shall, at a minimum:

(1) Identify physical obstacles in the recipient's facilities that limit the accessibility of its program or activity to handicappped persons;

(2) Describe in detail the methods that will be used to make the facilities accessible;

(3) Specify the schedule for taking the steps necessary to achieve full program accessibility and, if the time period of the transition plan is longer than one year, identify the steps of that will be taken during each year of the transition period; and

(4) Indicate the person responsible for implementation of the plan.

(f) Notice. The recipient shall adopt and implement procedures to ensure that interested persons, including persons with impaired vision or hearing, can obtain information as to the existence and location of services, activities, and facilities that are accessible to and usuable by handicapped persons.

Sec.104.23 New construction

(a) Design and construction. Each facility or part of a facility constructed by, on behalf of, or for the use of a recipient shall be designed and constructed in such manner that the facility or part of the facility is readily accessible to and usable by handicapped persons, if the construction was commenced after the effective date of this part.

(b) Alteration. Each facility or part of a facility which is altered by, on behalf of, or for the use of a recipient after the effective date of this part in a manner that affects or could affect the usability of the facility or part of the facility shall, to the maximum extent feasible, be altered in such manner that the altered portion of the facility is readily accessible to and usable by handicapped persons.

(c) Conformance with Uniform Federal Accessibility Standards

(1) Effective as of January 18, 1991, design, construction, or alteration of buildings in conformance with sections 3-8 of the Uniform Federal Accessibility Standards (UFAS) (Appendix A to 41 CFR subpart 101-19.6) shall be deemed to comply with the requirements of this section with respect to those buildings. Departures from particular technical and scoping requirements of UFAS by the use of other methods are permit-

ted where substantially equivalent or greater access to and usability of the building is provided.

(2) For purposes of this section, section 4.1.6(1)(g) of UFAS shall be interpreted to exempt from the requirements of UFAS only mechanical rooms and other spaces that, because of their intended use, will not require accessibility to the public or beneficiaries or result in the employment or residence therein of persons with physical handicaps.

(3) This section does not require recipients to make building alterations that have little likelihood of being accomplished without removing or altering a load-bearing structural member. [45 FR 30936, May 9, 1980; 45 FR 37426, June 3, 1980, as amended at 55 FR 52138, 52141, Dec. 19, 1990]

Subpart D—Preschool, Elementary, and Secondary Education

Sec.104.31 Application of this subpart

Subpart D applies to preschool, elementary, secondary, and adult education programs and activities that receive or benefit from Federal financial assistance and to recipients that operate, or that receive or benefit from Federal financial assistance for the operation of, such programs or activities.

Sec.104.32 Location and notification

A recipient that operates a public elementary or secondary education program shall annually:

(a) Undertake to identify and locate every qualified handicapped person residing in the recipient's jurisdiction who is not receiving a public education; and

(b) Take appropriate steps to notify handicapped persons and their parents or guardians of the recipient's duty under this subpart.

Sec.104.33 Free appropriate public education

(a) General. A recipient that operates a public elementary or secondary education program shall provide a free appropriate public education to each qualified handicapped person who is in the recipient's jurisdiction, regardless of the nature or severity of the person's handicap.

(b) Appropriate education

(1) For the purpose of this subpart, the provision of an appropriate education is the provision of regular or special education and related aids and services that (i) are designed to meet individual educational needs of handicapped persons as adequately as the needs of nonhandicapped persons are met and (ii) are based upon adherence to procedures that satisfy the requirements of Secs. 104.34, 104.35, and 104.36.

(2) Implementation of an individualized education program developed in accordance with the Education of the Handicapped Act is one means of meeting the standard established in paragraph (b)(1)(i) of this section.

(3) A recipient may place a handicapped person in or refer such person to a program other than the one that it operates as its means of carrying out the requirements of this subpart. If so, the recipient remains responsible for ensuring that the

requirements of this subpart are met with respect to any handicapped person so placed or referred.

(c) Free education—

(1) *General.* For the purpose of this section, the provision of a free education is the provision of educational and related services without cost to the handicapped person or to his or her parents or guardian, except for those fees that are imposed on non-handicapped persons or their parents or guardian. It may consist either of the provision of free services or, if a recipient places a handicapped person in or refers such person to a program not operated by the recipient as its means of carrying out the requirements of this subpart, of payment for the costs of the program. Funds available from any public or private agency may be used to meet the requirements of this subpart. Nothing in this section shall be construed to relieve an insurer or similar third party from an otherwise valid obligation to provide or pay for services provided to a handicapped person.

(2) *Transportation.* If a recipient places a handicapped person in or refers such person to a program not operated by the recipient as its means of carrying out the requirements of this subpart, the recipient shall ensure that adequate transportation to and from the program is provided at no greater cost than would be incurred by the person or his or her parents or guardian if the person were placed in the program operated by the recipient.

(3) *Residential placement.* If placement in a public or private residential program is necessary to provide a free appropriate public education to a handicapped person because of his or her handicap, the program, including non-medical care and room and board, shall be provided at no cost to the person or his or her parents or guardian.

(4) *Placement of handicapped persons by parents.* If a recipient has made available, in conformance with the requirements of this section and Sec. 104.34, a free appropriate public education to a handicapped person and the person's parents or guardian choose to place the person in a private school, the recipient is not required to pay for the person's education in the private school. Disagreements between a parent or guardian and a recipient regarding whether the recipient has made such a program available or otherwise regarding the question of financial responsibility are subject to the due process procedures of Sec. 104.36

(d) Compliance. A recipient may not exclude any qualified handicapped person from a public elementary or secondary education after the effective date of this part. A recipient that is not, on the effective date of this regulation, in full compliance with the other requirements of the preceding paragraphs of this section shall meet such requirements at the earliest practicable time and in no event later than September 1, 1978.

Sec. 104.34 Educational setting

(a) Academic setting. A recipient to which this subpart applies shall educate, or shall provide for the education of, each qualified handicapped person in its jurisdiction with persons who are not handicapped to the maximum extent appropriate to the needs of the handicapped person. A recipi-

ent shall place a handicapped person in the regular educational environment operated by the recipient unless it is demonstrated by the recipient that the education of the person in the regular environment with the use of supplementary aids and services cannot be achieved satisfactorily. Whenever a recipient places a person in a setting other than the regular educational environment pursuant to this paragraph, it shall take into account the proximity of the alternate setting to the person's home.

(b) Nonacademic settings. In providing or arranging for the provision of nonacademic and extracurricular services and activities, including meals, recess periods, and the services and activities set forth in Sec. 104.37(a)(2), a recipient shall ensure that handicapped persons participate with nonhandicapped persons in such activities and services to the maximum extent appropriate to the needs of the handicapped person in question.

(c) Comparable facilities. If a recipient, in compliance with paragraph (a) of this section, operates a facility that is identifiable as being for handicapped persons, the recipient shall ensure that the facility and the services and activities provided therein are comparable to the other facilities, services, and activities of the recipient.

Sec. 104.35 Evaluation and placement

(a) Preplacement evaluation. A recipient that operates a public elementary or secondary education program shall conduct an evaluation in accordance with the requirements of paragraph (b) of this section of any person who, because of handicap, needs or is believed to need special education or related services before taking any action with respect to the initial placement of the person in a regular or special education program and any subsequent significant change in placement.

(b) Evaluation procedures. A recipient to which this subpart applies shall establish standards and procedures for the evaluation and placement of persons who, because of handicap, need or are believed to need special education or related services which ensure that:

(1) Tests and other evaluation materials have been validated for the specific purpose for which they are used and are administered by trained personnel in conformance with the instructions provided by their producer;

(2) Tests and other evaluation materials include those tailored to assess specific areas of educational need and not merely those which are designed to provide a single general intelligence quotient; and

(3) Tests are selected and administered so as best to ensure that, when a test is administered to a student with impaired sensory, manual, or speaking skills, the test results accurately reflect the student's aptitude or achievement level or whatever other factor the test purports to measure, rather than reflecting the student's impaired sensory, manual, or speaking skills (except where those skills are the factors that the test purports to measure).

(c) Placement procedures. In interpreting evaluation data and in making placement decisions, a recipient shall (1) draw upon information from a variety of sources, including aptitude and achievement tests, teacher recommendations, physical condition, social or cultural background, and adaptive behavior, (2) establish procedures to ensure that information obtained from all such sources is documented and carefully considered, (3) ensure that the placement decision is made by a group of persons, including persons knowledgeable about the child, the meaning of the evaluation data, and the placement options, and (4) ensure that the placement decision is made in conformity with Sec. 104.34.

(d) Reevaluation. A recipient to which this section applies shall establish procedures, in accordance with paragraph (b) of this section, for periodic reevaluation of students who have been provided special education and related services. A reevaluation procedure consistent with the Education for the Handicapped Act is one means of meeting this requirement.

Sec. 104.36 Procedural safeguards

A recipient that operates a public elementary or secondary education program shall establish and implement, with respect to actions regarding the identification, evaluation, or educational placement of persons who, because of handicap, need or are believed to need special instruction or related services, a system of procedural safeguards that includes notice, an opportunity for the parents or guardian of the person to examine relevant records, an impartial hearing with opportunity for participation by the person's parents or guardian and representation by counsel, and a review procedure. Compliance with the procedural safeguards of section 615 of the Education of the Handicapped Act is one means of meeting this requirement.

Sec. 104.37 Nonacademic services

(a) General

(1) A recipient to which this subpart applies shall provide nonacademic and extracurricular services and activities in such manner as is necessary to afford handicapped students an equal opportunity for participation in such services and activities.

(2) Nonacademic and extracurricular services and activities may include counseling services, physical recreational athletics, transportation, health services, recreational activities, special interest groups or clubs sponsored by the recipients, referrals to agencies which provide assistance to handicapped persons, and employment of students, including both employment by the recipient and assistance in making available outside employment.

(b) Counseling services. A recipient to which this subpart applies that provides personal, academic, or vocational counseling, guidance, or placement services to its students shall

provide these services without discrimination on the basis of handicap. The recipient shall ensure that qualified handicapped students are not counseled toward more restrictive career objectives than are nonhandicapped students with similar interests and abilities.

(c) Physical education and athletics

(1) In providing physical education courses and athletics and similar programs and activities to any of its students, a recipient to which this subpart applies may not discriminate on the basis of handicap. A recipient that offers physical education courses or that operates or sponsors interscholastic, club, or intramural athletics shall provide to qualified handicapped students an equal opportunity for participation in these activities.

(2) A recipient may offer to handicapped students physical education and athletic activities that are separate or different from those offered to nonhandicapped students only if separation or differentiation is consistent with the requirements of Sec. 104.34 and only if no qualified handicapped student is denied the opportunity to compete for teams or to participate in courses that are not separate or different.

Sec. 104.38 Preschool and adult education programs

A recipient to which this subpart applies that operates a preschool education or day care program or activity or an adult education program or activity may not, on the basis of handicap, exclude qualified handicapped persons from the program or activity and shall take into account the needs of such persons in determining the aid, benefits, or services to be provided under the program or activity.

Sec.104.39 Private education programs

(a) A recipient that operates a private elementary or secondary education program may not, on the basis of handicap, exclude a qualified handicapped person from such program if the person can, with minor adjustments, be provided an appropriate education, as defined in Sec. 104.33(b)(1), within the recipient's program

(b) A recipient to which this section applies may not charge more for the provision of an appropriate education to handicapped persons than to nonhandicapped persons except to the extent that any additional charge is justified by a substantial increase in cost to the recipient.

(c) A recipient to which this section applies that operates special education programs shall operate such programs in accordance with the provisions of Secs. 104.35 and 104.36. Each recipient to which this section applies is subject to the provisions of Secs. 104.34, 104.37, and 104.38. ■

Appendix 2

Federal and State Departments of Education

Federal Department of Education Offices

The federal Department of Education, Office of Special Education, has the responsibility to ensure that all states meet the requirements of IDEA. For information on IDEA, contact the DOE at:

U.S. Department of Education
Office of Special Education and Rehabilitation
  Services
400 Maryland Avenue, SW
Washington, DC 20202
202-205-5465 (voice)
www.ed.gov/about/offices/list/osers/osep/
  index.html?src=mr

The federal Department of Education, Office for Civil Rights, is one place to file a complaint for IDEA violations. You can contact any of the following OCR offices.

Main Office

U.S. Department of Education
Office for Civil Rights
Mary E. Switzer Building
330 C Street, SW
Washington, DC 20202
800-421-3481 (voice)
877-521-2172 (TDD)
202-205-9862 (fax)
ocr@ed.gov (email)
www.ed.gov/about/offices/list/ocr/index.html

Connecticut, Maine, Massachusetts, New Hampshire, Rhode Island, Vermont

U.S. Department of Education
Office for Civil Rights
J. W. McCormack Post Office and Courthouse
Room 701, 01-0061
Boston, MA 02109-4557
617-223-9662 (voice)
617-223-9695 (TDD)
617-223-9669 (fax)
ocr_boston@ed.gov (email)

New Jersey, New York

U.S. Department of Education
Office for Civil Rights
75 Park Place
New York, NY 10007-2146
212-637-6466 (voice)
212-637-0478 (TDD)
212-264-3803 (fax)
ocr_newyork@ed.gov (email)

Delaware, Kentucky, Maryland, Pennsylvania, West Virginia

U.S. Department of Education
Office for Civil Rights
100 Penn Square East, Suite 515
Philadelphia, PA 19107
215-656-8541 (voice)
215-656-8604 (TDD)
215-656-8605 (fax)
ocr_philadelphia@ed.gov (email)

Alabama, Florida, Georgia, South Carolina, Tennessee

Office for Civil Rights, Atlanta Office
U.S. Department of Education
61 Forsyth Street SW, Suite 19T70
Atlanta, GA 30303-3104
404-562-6350 (voice)
404-331-7236 (TDD)
404-562-6455 (fax)
ocr_atlanta@ed.gov (email)

Arkansas, Louisiana, Mississippi, Oklahoma, Texas

U.S. Department of Education
Office for Civil Rights
1999 Bryan Street, Suite 2600
Dallas, TX 75201
214-880-2459 (voice)
214-880-2456 (TDD)
214-880-3082 (fax)
ocr_dallas@ed.gov (email)

District of Columbia, North Carolina, Virginia

U.S. Department of Education
Office for Civil Rights
1100 Pennsylvania Avenue, NW, Rm. 316
P.O. Box 14620
Washington, DC 20044-4620
202-208-2545 (voice)
202-208-7741 (TDD)
202-208-7797 (fax)
ocr_dc@ed.gov (email)

Illinois, Indiana, Minnesota, Wisconsin

U.S. Department of Education
Office for Civil Rights
111 N. Canal Street, Suite 1053
Chicago, IL 60606-7204
312-886-8434 (voice)
312-353-2540 (TDD)
312-353-4888 (fax)
ocr_chicago@ed.gov (email)

Michigan, Ohio

U.S. Department of Education
Office for Civil Rights
600 Superior Avenue East
Bank One Center, Room 750
Cleveland, OH 44114-2611
216-522-4970 (voice)
216-522-4944 (TDD)
216-522-2573 (fax)
ocr_cleveland@ed.gov (email)

Iowa, Kansas, Missouri, Nebraska, North Dakota, South Dakota

U.S. Department of Education
Office for Civil Rights
8930 Ward Parkway, Suite 2037
Kansas City, MO 64114
816-268-0550 (voice)
800-437-0833 (TDD)
816-823-1404 (fax)
ocr_kansascity@ed.gov (email)

Arizona, Colorado, Montana, New Mexico, Utah, Wyoming

U.S. Department of Education
Office for Civil Rights
Federal Building, Suite 310
1244 Speer Boulevard
Denver, CO 80204-3582
303-844-5695 (voice)
303-844-3417 (TDD)
303-844-4303 (fax)
ocr_denver@ed.gov (email)

California

U.S. Department of Education
Office for Civil Rights
Old Federal Building
50 United Nations Plaza, Room 239
San Francisco, CA 94102-4102
415-556-4275 (voice)
415-437-7786 (TDD)
415-437-7783 (fax)
ocr_sanfrancisco@ed.gov (email)

Alaska, Hawaii, Idaho, Nevada, Oregon, Washington

U.S. Department of Education
Office for Civil Rights
915 Second Avenue, Room 3310
Seattle, WA 98174-1099
206-220-7900 (voice)
206-220-7907 (TDD)
206-220-7887 (fax)
ocr_seattle@ed.gov (email)

State Department of Education Offices

Your state department of education is the place to go to find legislation, curriculum material, or information on state special education programs as well as information about the IDEA and its requirements.

Alabama

Alabama Department of Education
Division of Special Education Services
(Gordon Persons Building)
P.O. Box 302101
Montgomery, AL 36130-2101
334-242-8114 (voice)
334-242-9192 (fax)
www.alsde.edu/html/home.asp

Alaska

Alaska Department of Education
Teaching and Learning Support
801 W. 10th Street, Suite 200
Juneau, AK 99801-1894
907-465-8693 (voice)
907-465-2806 (fax)
www.eed.state.ak.us

Arizona

Arizona Department of Education
Exceptional Student Services
1535 W. Jefferson Street
Phoenix, AZ 85007
602-364-4000 (voice)
602-542-5404 (fax)
www.ade.state.az.us

Arkansas

Arkansas Department of Education
Special Education
Victory Building
1401 W. Capitol, Suite 450
Little Rock, AR 72201-2936
501-682-4221 (voice)
501-682-5159 (fax)
http://arkedu.state.ar.us

California

California Department of Education
Special Education Division
Room 530, 428 J Street
Sacramento, CA 95812-1738
916-445-4602 (voice)
916-327-3706 (fax)
www.cde.ca.gov

Colorado

Colorado Department of Education
Special Education Services Unit
201 E. Colfax Avenue
Denver, CO 80203
303-866-6694 (voice)
303-866-6811 (fax)
www.cde.state.co.us

Connecticut

Connecticut Department of Education
Bureau of Special Education and Pupil Services
25 Industrial Park Road
Middletown, CT 06457
860-807-2025 (voice)
860-807-2047 (fax)
www.state.ct.us/sde

Delaware

Delaware Department of Education
Exceptional Children and Early Childhood
   Education
Townsend Building
P.O. Box 1402
Dover, DE 19903-1402
302-739-5471 (voice)
302-739-2388 (fax)
www.doe.state.de.us

District of Columbia

District of Columbia
Division of Special Education
825 North Capitol Street, NE
Washington, DC 20002
202-442-4800 (voice)
202-442-5117 (fax)
www.K12.dc.us

Florida

Florida Department of Education
Bureau of Instructional Support and Community
  Services
325 W. Gaines Street
Tallahassee, FL 32399-0400
850-488-1570 (voice)
850-921-8246 (fax)
www.firn.edu/doe

Georgia

Georgia Department of Education
Division for Exceptional Students
1870 Twin Towers East
Atlanta, GA 30334
404-656-3963 (voice)
404-651-6457 (fax)
www.doe.k12.ga.us

Hawaii

Hawaii Department of Education
Special Education Section
Building C, Room 102
637 18th Avenue
Honolulu, HI 96816
808-733-4400 (voice)
808-733-4841 (fax)
www.doe.k12.hi.us

Idaho

Idaho Department of Education
Bureau of Special Education
P.O. Box 83720
Boise, ID 83720-0027
208-332-6910 (voice)
208-334-4664 (fax)
www.sde.state.id.us

Illinois

Illinois State Board of Education
Office of Special Education
Mail Code N-253, 100 North First Street
Springfield, IL 62777-0001
217-782-5589 (voice)
217-782-0372 (fax)
www.isbe.state.il.us

Indiana

Indiana Department of Education
Division of Exceptional Learners
Room 229, State House
Indianapolis, IN 46204-2798
317-232-0570 (voice)
317-232-0589 (fax)
http://ideanet.doe.state.in.us

Iowa

Iowa Department of Education
Bureau of Children, Family and Community
  Services
Grimes State Office Building
Des Moines, IA 50319-0146
515-281-3176 (voice)
515-242-6019 (fax)
www.state.ia.us/educate

Kansas

Kansas State Board of Education
Student Support Services
120 SE Tenth Avenue
Topeka, KS 66612-1182
785-291-3097 (voice)
785-296-6715 (fax)
www.ksde.org

Kentucky

Kentucky Department of Education
Division of Exceptional Children Services
500 Mero Street, Eighth Floor
Frankfort, KY 40601
502-564-4970 (voice)
502-564-6721 (fax)
www.kde.state.ky.us

Louisiana

Louisiana Department of Education
Division of Special Populations
P.O. Box 94064
Baton Rouge, LA 70804-9064
225-342-3633 (voice)
225-342-6965 (fax)
www.doe.state.la.us

Maine

Maine Department of Education
Office of Special Services
23 State House Station
Augusta, ME 04333-0023
207-624-6650 (voice)
207-624-6651 (fax)
www.state.me.us/education/homepage.htm

Maryland

Maryland State Department of Education
Division of Special Education
200 W. Baltimore Street, 4th Floor
Baltimore, MD 21201
410-767-0238 (voice)
410-333-8165 (fax)
www.msde.state.md.us

Massachusetts

Massachusetts Department of Education
Director of Special Education
350 Main Street
Malden, MA 02148-5023
338-388-3388 (voice)
338-388-3396 (fax)
www.doe.mass.edu

Michigan

Michigan Department of Education
Office of Special Education
608 West Allegan
Lansing, MI 48933
517-373-9433 (voice)
517-373-7504 (fax)
www.michigan.gov/mde

Minnesota

Minnesota Department of Education
Department of Children, Families and Learning
1500 Highway 36 West
Roseville, MN 55113-4266
651-582-8289 (voice)
651-582-8729 (fax)
http://cfl.state.mn.us

Mississippi

Mississippi Department of Education
Office of Special Education
P.O. Box 771
359 North West Street, Suite 335
Jackson, MS 39205-0771
601-359-3498 (voice)
601-359-2198 (fax)
www.mde.k12.ms.us

Missouri

Missouri Department of Elementary and Secondary
  Education
Division of Special Education
P.O. Box 480
Jefferson City, MO 65102
573-751-5739 (voice)
573-526-4404 (fax)
www.dese.state.mo.us

Montana

Montana Office of Public Instruction
Division of Special Education
P.O. Box 202501
Helena, MT 59620-2501
406-444-4429 (voice)
406-444-3924 (fax)
www.opi.state.mt.us

Nebraska

Nebraska Department of Education
Special Populations Office
P.O. Box 94987
301 Centennial Mall South
Lincoln, NE 68509-4987
402-471-2295 (voice)
402-471-5022 (fax)
www.nde.state.ne.us

Nevada

Nevada Department of Education
Office of Special Education
700 E. 5th Street, Suite 113
Carson City, NV 89701
775-687-9171 (voice)
775-687-9123 (fax)
www.nde.state.nv.us

New Hampshire

New Hampshire Department of Education
Bureau for Special Education Services
101 Pleasant Street
Concord, NH 03301-3860
603-271-3741 (voice)
603-271-1953 (fax)
www.ed.state.nh.us

New Jersey

New Jersey Department of Education
Office of Special Education Programs
P.O. Box 500
Trenton, NJ 08625-0500
609-633-6833 (voice)
609-984-8422 (fax)
www.state.nj.us/education

New Mexico

New Mexico Department of Special Education
300 Don Gaspar Avenue
Sante Fe, NM 87501
505-827-6541 (voice)
505-827-6791 (fax)
http://sde.state.nm.us

New York

New York State Education Department
Office of Vocational and Educational Services for
    Individuals With Disabilities
One Commerce Plaza, Room 1606
Albany, NY 12234
518-474-2714 (voice)
518-474-8802 (fax)
www.vesid.nysed.gov

North Carolina

North Carolina Department of Public Instruction
Division of Exceptional Children
6356 Mail Service Center
Raleigh, NC 27699-6356
919-807-3969 (voice)
919-807-3243 (fax)
www.ncpublicschools.org

North Dakota

North Dakota Department of Public Instruction
Office of Special Education
600 E. Boulevard Avenue, Dept. 201
Bismarck, ND 58505-0440
701-328-2277 (voice)
701-328-4149 (fax)
www.dpi.state.nd.us

Ohio

Ohio Department of Education
Office for Exceptional Children
Second Floor, Mail Stop 202
25 S. Front Street
Columbus, OH 43215-4183
614-466-2650 (voice)
614-728-1097 (fax)
www.ode.state.oh.us

Oklahoma

Oklahoma Department of Education
Special Education Services
2500 N. Lincoln Blvd., Suite 411
Oklahoma City, OK 73105-4599
405-521-3351 (voice)
405-522-3503 (fax)
http://sde.state.ok.us

Oregon

Oregon Department of Education
Office of Special Education
255 Capitol Street, NE
Salem, OR 97310-0203
503-378-3600 (voice)
503-378-5156 (fax)
www.ode.state.or.us

Pennsylvania

Pennsylvania Department of Education
Bureau of Special Education
333 Market Street, 7th Floor
Harrisburg, PA 17126-0333
717-783-6913 (voice)
717-783-6139 (fax)
www.pde.state.pa.us

Rhode Island

Rhode Island Department of Education
Office of Special Needs
Shepard Building, Fourth Floor
255 Westminster Street
Providence, RI 02903
401-222-4600 (voice)
401-222-6030 (fax)
www.ridoe.net

South Carolina

South Carolina Department of Education
Office of Exceptional Children
1429 Senate Street, Room 808
Columbia, SC 29201-3799
803-734-8806 (voice)
803-734-4824 (fax)
www.myscschools.com

South Dakota

South Dakota Department of Education
Office of Special Education
700 Governors Drive
Pierre, SD 57501-2291
605-773-3678 (voice)
605-773-3782 (fax)
www.state.sd.us/deca

Tennessee

Tennessee Department of Education
Division of Special Education
710 James Robertson Parkway, 5th Floor
Nashville, TN 37243-0380
615-741-2851 (voice)
615-532-9412 (fax)
www.state.tn.us/education

Texas

Texas Education Agency
Division of Special Education
1701 N. Congress Avenue
Austin, TX 78701
512-463-9414 (voice)
512-463-9560 (fax)
www.tea.state.tx.us

Utah

Utah State Office of Education
Services for At-Risk Students
P.O. Box 144200
250 E. 500 South
Salt Lake City, UT 84114-4200
801-538-7711 (voice)
801-538-7991 (fax)
www.usoe.k12.ut.us

Vermont

Vermont Department of Education
Student Support Services Team
State Office Building
120 State Street
Montpelier, VT 05620-2501
802-828-5118 (voice)
802-828-0573 (fax)
www.state.vt.us/educ

Virginia

Virginia Department of Education
Office of Special Education
P.O. Box 2120
Richmond, VA 23218-2120
804-225-2402 (voice)
804-371-8796 (fax)
www.pen.k12.va.us

Washington

Washington Department of Public Instruction
Special Education Section
P.O. Box 47200
600 S. Washington Street
Olympia, WA 98504-7200
360-725-6075 (voice)
360-586-0247 (fax)
www.k12.wa.us

West Virginia

West Virginia Department of Education
Office of Special Education
Building #6
1900 Kanawha Boulevard East, Room 304
Charleston, WV 25305
304-558-2696 (voice)
304-558-3741 (fax)
http://wvde.state.wv.us

Wisconsin

Wisconsin Department of Public Instruction
Division for Learning Support
P.O. Box 7841
125 S. Webster Street
Madison, WI 53707-7841
608-266-1781 (voice)
608-267-3746 (fax)
www.dpi.state.wi.us

Wyoming

Wyoming Department of Education
Special Programs Unit
Hathaway Building
2300 Capitol Avenue, 2nd Floor
Cheyenne, WY 82002-0050
307-777-7417 (voice)
307-777-6221 (fax)
www.k12.wy.us

Appendix 3

Support Groups, Advocacy Organizations, and Other Resources

General Resources on Special Education

Adapted Physical Education National Standards

SUNY Cortland
E224 Park Center
P.O. Box 2000
Cortland, NY 13045
888-APENS-EXAM (voice)
www.cortland.edu/APENS

Ensures that physical education instruction is provided for students with disabilities by qualified physical education instructors. The project has developed national standards for the profession and a national certification examination to measure knowledge of these standards.

American Council on Rural Special Education

Utah State University
2865 Old Main Hill
Logan, UT 84322-2865
435-797-3911 (voice)
acres@cc.usu.edu (email)
http://extension.usu.edu/acres

Provides support and information to families of special education children living in rural America. ACRES publishes a national journal called the Rural Special Education Quarterly, and maintains an archive of article abstracts on its website. ACRES also publishes a bimonthly newsletter called RuraLink.

Disability Resources, Inc.

Four Glatter Lane
Centereach, NY 11720-1032
631-585-0290 (voice/fax)
www.disabilityresources.org

Offers a monthly newsletter and many articles on disabilities. Provides numerous links to other Internet resources.

Education Development Center, Inc.

55 Chapel Street
Newton, MA 02458-1060
617-969-7100 (voice)
617-969-5979 (fax)
617-964-5448 (TTY)
www.edc.org

Promotes the effective use of technology to enhance education for students with sensory, cognitive, physical, and social/emotional disabilities, and offers articles and information on assistive technologies. The Center also has offices in New York and the District of Columbia—check their website for more information.

ERIC Clearinghouse on Disabilities and Gifted Education

1110 North Glebe Road
Arlington, VA 22201-5704
800-328-0272 (voice)
ericec@cec.sped.org (email)
www.ericec.org

Provides a variety of services, research, articles, and products on a broad range of education-related issues. The AskERIC forum is a personalized Internet-based service providing education information to teachers, librarians, counselors, administrators, parents, and others. You can also search ERIC's extensive article database.

Family.com

http://family.go.com

An Internet site affiliated with Disney. Among other things, you can find articles on special education and children with disabilities.

Family Education Network

20 Park Plaza, 12th Floor
Boston, MA 02116
617-542-6500
http://familyeducation.com

Includes information on learning disabilities and children with special needs. Website features include a monthly column by a special education lawyer, "Ask the Expert"—what their expert has to say about learning issues, resources, and special education news.

Federal Resource Center for Special Education

1825 Connecticut Avenue, NW
Washington, DC 20009
202-884-8215 (voice)
202-884-8443 (fax)
202-884-8200 (TTY)
joppenhe@aed.org (email)
www.dssc.org/frc

Supports a nationwide special education technical assistance network (funded by the U.S. Department of Education's Office of Special Education and Rehabilitative Services), plans national meetings of education professionals, and links Regional Resource and Federal Centers with each other and with other technical assistance providers. The website includes the text of certain federal regulations, a list of links to disability organizations, publications (including the RRFC Links Online Newsletter), and proceedings of certain government conferences.

Internet Resources for Special Children

julioc@one.net (email)
www.irsc.org

An Internet site that provides lists of links relating to the needs of children with disabilities for parents, family members, caregivers, friends, educators, and medical professionals. Categories are extensive, including almost every possible disability affecting children.

National Early Childhood Technical Assistance Center

Campus Box 8040,UNC-CH
Chapel Hill, NC 27599-8040
919-962-2001 (voice)
919-843-3269 (TDD)
919-966-7463 (fax)
nectac@unc.edu (email)
www.nectac.org

A program of the Child Development Center at the University of North Carolina at Chapel Hill, geared towards younger children (through age five). NECTAC has resources on childhood disabilities, the text of IDEA, and descriptions of programs developed under IDEA.

National Information Center for Children and Youth With Disabilities

P.O. Box 1492
Washington, DC 20013
800-695-0285 (voice/TTY)
202-884-8441 (fax)
nichy@aed.org (email)
www.nichcy.org

Provides information on disabilities and disability-related issues for families, educators, and other professionals. The website contains contact information for local disability organizations, lists of disability organizations and government agencies by state, publications, and information on various disability topics, including how to prepare children with disabilities to make the transition from high school to the adult world.

Parent Soup

www.parentsoup.com

An Internet resource that includes an Education Central area. Topics include mainstreaming, ADD, ADHD, dyslexia, and IEPs. The site sponsors an expert message board and chat rooms for parents.

School Psychology Resources Online

www.schoolpsychology.net

An Internet site with information on learning disabilities, ADHD, gifted children, autism, adolescence, parenting, psychological assessment, classroom management, and more. You can download handouts aimed at parents and teachers.

Special Education Resources From the Curry School of Education at University of Virginia

P.O. Box 400260
Charlottesville, VA 22904-4260
434-924-3334 (voice)
434-924-0747 (fax)
http://curry.edschool.virginia.edu/sped/projects/ose/
   home.html

This site offers information for parents and teachers on special education, including articles on learning disabilities and links to special education organizations and websites.

Special Education Resources on the Internet

www.seriweb.com

A collection of Internet-accessible information in the field of special education, including material on disabilities (including learning disabilities and ADD), transition resources, technology, and more.

The Association for Persons With Severe Handicaps (TASH)

29 West Susquehanna Avenue, Suite 210
Baltimore, MD 21204
410-828-8274 (voice)
info@tash.org (email)
www.tash.org

Provides information on current trends and issues in the field of disabilities, organizes conferences and workshops, advocates for legislative changes, distributes publications and videos, and disseminates information through electronic media.

Technical Perspectives, Inc.

1411 East Campbell Road, Suite 1900
Richardson, TX 75081
800-594-3779 (voice)
sales@classplus.com (email)
www.classplus.com/classplus

Publishes a software program called Classplus, which you can use to create an Individual Education Plan (IEP). Classplus allows you to develop comprehensive curricula, goals, and objectives for every subject and functional assessments.

On the website, you can see sample reports containing goals and objectives, sample progress reports, and IEP forms.

Parent Training and Information Centers (PTI)

The U.S. Department of Education, Office of Special Education Programs, funds organized parent-to-parent programs. The work is done locally through programs known as Parent Training and Information (PTI) Centers. PTI Centers enable parents to participate more effectively with professionals in meeting the educational needs of children with disabilities. You can contact a local PTI for information; PTI online information is available through the Department of Education's website.

Alabama

Special Education Action Committee, Inc.
600 Bel Air Boulevard, Suite 210
P.O. Box 161274
Mobile, AL 36616-2274
334-478-1208 (voice/TTY)
800-222-7322 (voice—Alabama only)
334-473-7877 (fax)
seacofmobile@zebra.net (email)

Alaska

PARENTS, Inc.
4743 E. Northerns Lights Boulevard
Anchorage, AK 99508
907-337-7678 (voice)
800-478-7678 (voice—Alaska only)
907-337-7629 (TTY)
907-337-7671 (fax)
parents@parentsinc.org (email)
www.parentsinc.org

Arizona

Pilot Parents of Southern Arizona
2600 N. Wyatt Drive
Tucson, AZ 85712
520-324-3150 (voice)
877-365-7220 (voice)
520-324-3152 (fax)
ppsa@pilotparents.org (email)
www.pilotparents.org

Raising Special Kids
2400 N. Central Avenue, Suite 200
Phoenix, AZ 85004-9802
602-242-4366 (voice/TTY)
800-237-3007 (voice—Arizona only)
602-242-4306 (fax)
info@raisingspecialkids.org (email)
www.raisingspecialkids.org

Arkansas

Arkansas Disability Coalition
1123 S. University Drive, Suite 225
Little Rock, AR 72204
501-614-7020 (voice/TTY)
800-223-1330 (voice—Arkansas only)
501-614-9082 (fax)
adc@alltel.net (email)
www.adcpti.org

FOCUS, Inc.
305 W. Jefferson Avenue
Jonesboro, AR 72401
870-935-2750 (voice)
877-247-3843 (voice)
870-931-3755 (fax)
focusin_inc2@hotmail.com (email)

California

Central California PTI Center
4440 North First Street
Fresno, CA 93726
559-229-2000 (voice)
559-225-6059 (TTY)
559-229-2956 (fax)
epu1@exceptionalparents.org (email)
www.exceptionalparents.org

Exceptional Family Support, Education, and Advocacy Center of Northern California, Inc.
6402 Skyway
Paradise, CA 95969
530-876-8321 (voice)
888-263-1311 (voice)
530-876-0346 (fax)
sea@sea-center.org (email)
www.sea-center.org

Matrix: A Parent Network and Resource Center
94 Galli Drive, Suite C
Novato, CA 94949
415-884-3535 (voice)
415-884-3554 (TTY)
415-884-3555 (fax)
matrix@matrixparents.org (email)
www.matrixparents.org

Parents Helping Parents, Inc.
3041 Olcott Street
Santa Clara, CA 95054-3222
408-727-5775 (voice)
866-747-4040 (voice)
408-727-0182 (fax)
general@php.com (email)
www.php.com

Support for Families of Children With Disabilities
2601 Mission Street, Suite 606
San Francisco, CA 94110
415-282-7494 (voice)
415-282-1226 (fax)
info@supportforfamilies.org (email)
www.supportforfamilies.org

Teams of Advocates for Special Kids, Inc. (TASK)
3750 Convoy Street, Suite 303
San Diego, CA 92111-3741
858-874-2386 (voice)
858-874-0123 (fax)
taskca@yahoo.com (email)
www.taskca.org

Teams of Advocates for Special Kids, Inc. (TASK)
100 West Cerritos Avenue
Anaheim, CA 92805
714-533-8275 (voice)
866-828-8275 (voice)
714-533-2533 (fax)
taskca@yahoo.com (email)
www.taskca.org

Colorado

PEAK Parent Center, Inc.
611 North Weber, Suite 200
Colorado Springs, CO 80903
719-531-9400 (voice)
800-284-0251 (voice—Colorado only)
719-531-9403 (TTY)
719-531-9452 (fax)
info@peakparent.org (email)
www.peakparent.org

Connecticut

Connecticut Parent Advocacy Center, Inc.
338 Main Street
Niantic, CT 06357
860-739-3089 (voice)
800-445-2722 (voice—Connecticut only)
860-739-7460 (fax/TTY)
cpac@cpacinc.org (email)
www.cpacinc.org

Delaware

Parent Information Center
700 Barksdale Road, Suite 16
Newark, DE 19711
302-366-0152 (voice)
888-547-4412 (voice—Delaware only)
302-366-0276 (fax)
picofdel@picofdel.org (email)
www.picofdel.org

District of Columbia

Advocates for Justice and Education, Inc.
2041 MLK Avenue, SE, Suite 301
Washington, DC 20020
202-678-8060 (voice)
888-327-8060 (voice)
202-678-8062 (fax)
information@aje-dc.org (email)
www.aje-dc.org

Florida

Family Network on Disabilities
2735 Whitney Road
Clearwater, FL 33760-1610
727-523-1130 (voice)
800-825-5736 (voice—Florida only)
727-523-8687 (fax)
fnd@fndfl.org (email)
http://fndfl.org

Parent to Parent of Miami, Inc.
9040 Sunset Drive, Suite G
Miami, FL 33173
305-271-9797 (voice)
305-271-6628 (fax)
info@ptopmiami.org (email)
www.ptopmiami.org

Georgia

Parent Educating Parents and Professionals
5727 Palazzo Way, Suite B
Douglasville, GA 30134
770-577-7771 (voice)
800-322-7065 (voice—Georgia only)
770-577-7774 (fax)
peppac@peppac.org (email)
www.peppac.org

Hawaii

AWARE (Assisting With Appropriate Rights in Education)
200 North Vineyard Boulevard, Suite 310
Honolulu, HI 96817
808-536-9684 (voice)
800-533-9684 (voice—Hawaii only)
808-536-2280 (TTY)
808-537-6780 (fax)
ldah@ldahawaii.org (email)
www.ldahawaii.org

Idaho

Idaho Parents Unlimited, Inc.
Parent Education Resource Project Center
600 North Curtis, Suite 100
Boise, ID 83706
208-342-5884 (voice/TTY)
800-242-4785 (voice—Idaho only)
208-342-1408 (fax)
parents@ipulidaho.org (email)
www.ipulidaho.org

Illinois

Family Matters
2505 S. Veterans Drive
Effingham, IL 62401
217-347-0880 (voice)
866-436-7842 (voice—Illinois only/TTY)
217-347-5119 (fax)
info@fmptic.org
www.fmptic.org

Family Resource Center on Disabilities
20 East Jackson Boulevard, Room 300
Chicago, IL 60604
312-939-3513 (voice)
800-952-4199 (voice—Illinois only)
312-939-3519 (TDD/TTY)
312-939-7297 (fax)
frcdptiil@ameritech.net (email)
http://frcd.org

Indiana

Indiana Resource Center for Families With Special
    Needs
809 N. Michigan Street
South Bend, IN 46601-1036
219-234-7101 (voice)
800-322-4433 (voice—Indiana only)
219-234-7279 (fax)
insource@insource.org (email)
www.insource.org

Iowa

Access for Special Kids
321 East Sixth Street
Des Moines, IA 50309
515-243-1713 (voice)
800-450-8667 (voice)
515-243-1902 (fax)
PTIIowa@aol.com (email)
www.iowapti.com

Kansas

Families ACT
555 North Woodlawn, Suite #3105
Wichita, KS 67208
316-685-1821 (voice)
316-685-0768 (fax)
nina@mhasck.org (email)
www.mhasck.org

Families Together, Inc.
3340 W. Douglas, Suite 102
Wichita, KS 67203
316-945-7747 (voice)
888-815-6364 (voice—Kansas only)
316-945-7795 (fax)
wichita@familiestogetherinc.org (email)
www.familiestogetherinc.org

Kentucky

Special Parent Involvement Network
10301-B Deering Road
Louisville, KY 40272
502-937-6894 (voice)
800-525-7746 (voice)
502-937-6464 (fax)
spininc@aol.com (email)
www.kyspin.com

Louisiana

Program of Families Helping Families of Greater
    New Orleans: Project PROMPT
4323 Division Street, Suite 110
Metairie, LA 70002-3179
504-888-9111 (voice)
800-766-7736 (voice—Louisiana only)
504-888-0246 (fax)
fhfgno@ix.netcom.com (email)
www.projectprompt.org

Maine

Maine Parent Federation
P.O. Box 2067
Augusta, ME 04338
207-623-2144 (voice/TTY)
800-870-7746 (voice—Maine only)
207-623-2148 (fax)
parentconnect@mpf.org (email)
www.mpf.org

Maryland

Parents Place of Maryland, Inc.
7484 Candlewood Road, Suite S
Hanover, MD 21076-1306
410-859-5300 (voice/TTY)
410-859-5301 (fax)
info@ppmd.org (email)
www.ppmd.org

Massachusetts

Federation for Children With Special Needs
1135 Tremont Street, Suite 420
Boston, MA 02120-2140
617-236-7210 (voice/TTY)
800-331-0688 (voice—Massachusetts only)
617-572-2094 (fax)
fcsninfo@fcsn.org (email)
www.fcsn.org

Michigan

Citizens Alliance to Uphold Special Education
    (CAUSE)
2365 Woodlake Drive, Suite 100
Okemos, MI 48864
517-706-2287 (voice)
800-221-9105 (voice—Michigan only)
517-347-1004 (fax)
info@causeonline.org (email)
www.causeonline.org

Minnesota

PACER Center, Inc.
8161 Normandale Boulevard
Minneapolis, MN 55437
952-838-9000 (voice)
888-248-0822 (voice)
952-838-0190 (TTY)
952-838-0199 (fax)
pacer@pacer.org (email)
www.pacer.org

Mississippi

Parent Partners
Five Old River Place, Suite 101
Jackson, MS 39202
601-354-3302 (voice)
800-366-5707 (voice—Mississippi only)
601-354-2426 (fax)
info@parentpartners.org (email)
www.parentpartners.org

Project Empower
P.O. Box 1733
136 South Poplar Street
Greenville, MS 38701
662-332-4852 (voice)
800-337-4852 (voice)
662-332-1622 (fax)
empower@tecinfo.com (email)

Missouri

Missouri Parents Act (MPACT)
One West Armour, Suite 302
Kansas City, MO 64111
816-531-7070 (voice)
800-743-7634 (voice—Missouri only)
816-531-4777 (fax)
mpact@ptimpact.com (email)
www.ptimpact.com

Montana

Parents Let's Unite for Kids (PLUK)
516 N. 32nd Street
Billings, MT 59101
406-255-0540 (voice)
800-222-7585 (voice—Montana only)
406-255-0540 (TTY)
406-255-0523 (fax)
plukinfo@pluk.org (email)
www.pluk.org

Nebraska

PTI Nebraska
3135 North 93rd Street
Omaha, NE 68134
402-346-0525 (voice)
800-284-8520 (voice—Nebraska only)
402-934-1479 (fax)
info@pti-nebraska.org (email)
www.pti-nebraska.org

Nevada

Nevada PEP
2810 West Charleston, Suite G68
Las Vegas, NV 89102
702-388-8899 (voice)
800-216-5188 (voice)
702-388-2966 (fax)
pepinfo@nvpep.org (email)
www.nvpep.org

New Hampshire

Parent Information Center
P.O. Box 2405
Concord, NH 03302-2405
603-224-7005 (voice/TTY)
800-232-0986 (voice—New Hampshire only)
603-224-4365 (fax)
picnh@aol.com (email)

New Jersey

Statewide Parent Advocacy Network, Inc. (SPAN)
35 Halsey Street, 4th Floor
Newark, NJ 07102
973-642-8100 (voice)
800-654-SPAN (voice—New Jersey only)
973-642-8080 (fax)
SPAN@bellatlantic.net (email)
www.spannj.org

New Mexico

Parents Reaching Out (PRO)
1920B Columbia Drive, SE
Albuquerque, NM 87106
505-247-0192 (voice)
800-524-5176 (voice—New Mexico only)
505-247-1345 (fax)
nmproth@aol.com (email)
www.parentsreachingout.org

New York

Advocacy Center
590 South Avenue
Rochester, NY 14620
585-546-1700 (voice)
800-650-4967 (voice—New York only)
585-546-7069 (fax)
info@advocacycenter.com (email)
www.advocacycenter.com

Advocates for Children of New York
151 W. 30th Street, 5th Floor
New York, NY 10001
212-947-9779 (voice)
212-947-9790 (fax)
info@advocatesforchildren.org (email)
www.advocatesforchildren.org

Resources for Children With Special Needs
116 E. 16th Street, 5th Floor
New York, NY 10003
212-677-4650 (voice)
212-254-4070 (fax)
info@resourcesnyc.org (email)
www.resourcesnyc.org/rcsn.htm

Sinergia/Metropolitan Parent Center
15 W. 65th Street, 6th Floor
New York, NY 10023
212-496-1300 (voice)
212-496-5608 (fax)
sinergia@panix.com (email)
www.sinergiany.org

United We Stand of New York
202 Union Avenue, Suite L
Brooklyn, NY 11211
(718) 302-4313 (voice)
(718) 302-4315 (fax)
uwsofny@aol.com (email)

North Carolina

Exceptional Children's Assistance Center
907 Barra Row, Suites 102 & 103
Davidson, NC 28036
704-892-1321 (voice/TTY)
800-962-6817 (voice—North Carolina only)
704-892-5028 (fax)
ecac@ecacmail.org (email)
www.ECAC-parentcenter.org

North Dakota

Pathfinder Services
1600 Second Avenue, SW, Suite 19
Minot, ND 58701-3459
701-837-7500 (voice)
701-837-7501 (TTY)
701-837-7548 (fax)
ndpath01@minot.ndak.net (email)
www.pathfinder.minot.com

Ohio

Child Advocacy Center
1821 Summit Road, Suite 110
Cincinnati, OH 45237
513-821-2400 (voice/TTY)
888-540-3924 (voice)
513-821-2442 (fax)
cadcenter@aol.com (email)

Ohio Coalition for the Education of Children With
   Disabilities
Bank One Building
165 West Center Street, Suite 302
Marion, OH 43302-3741
740-382-5452 (voice/TTY)
800-374-2806 (voice)
740-383-6421 (fax)
ocecd@gte.net (email)

Oklahoma

Parents Reaching Out in Oklahoma
1917 South Harvard Avenue
Oklahoma City, OK 73128-3049
405-681-9710 (voice)
800-759-4142 (voice)
prook1@aol.com (email)

Oregon

Oregon COPE Project
1745 State Street
Salem, OR 97301
503-581-8156 (voice/TTY)
888-505-COPE (voice—Oregon only)
503-391-0429 (fax)
orcope@open.org (email)
www.open.org/~orpti

Pennsylvania

Hispanics United for Special Needs Children
Buena Vista Plaza
166 West Lehigh Avenue, Suite 400
Philadelphia, PA 19133-3838
215-425-6203 (voice)
215-425-6204 (fax)
huneinc@aol.com (email)

Mentor Parent Program, Inc.
P.O. Box 47
Cole Hill Road
Pittsfield, PA 16340
814-563-3470 (voice)
888-447-1431 (voice—Pennsylvania only)
814-563-3445 (fax)
gwalker@westpa.net (email)
www.mentorparent.org

Parent Education Network
2107 Industrial Highway
York, PA 17402
717-600-0100 (voice)
800-522-5827 (voice—Pennsylvania only/TTY)
717-600-8101 (fax)
pen@parentednet.org (email)

Rhode Island

Rhode Island Parent Information Network
175 Main Street, 1st Floor
Pawtucket, RI 02860
401-727-4144 (voice)
800-464-3399 (voice—Rhode Island only)
401-727-4040 (fax)
ripin@ripin.org (email)
www.ripin.org

South Carolina

Parent Training and Resource Center
    MUSC—College of Health Professions, Research
19 Hagood Avenue, Suite 910
P.O. Box 250882
Charleston, SC 29425
843-792-3025 (voice)
843-792-1107 (fax)
mccartyb@musc.edu (email)

PRO Parents
652 Bush River Road, Suite 218
Columbia, SC 29210
803-772-5688 (voice)
800-759-4776 (voice)
803-772-5341 (fax)
proparents@aol.com (email)

South Dakota

South Dakota Parent Connection
3701 W. 49th Street, Suite 200B
Sioux Falls, SD 57106
605-361-3171 (voice)
800-640-4553 (voice—South Dakota only/TTY)
605-361-2928 (fax)
sdpc@sdparent.org (email)

Tennessee

Support & Training for Exceptional Parents (STEP)
712 Professional Plaza
Greenville, TN 37745
423-639-0125 (voice)
800-280-7837 (voice—Tennessee only)
423-639-8802 (TTY)
423-636-8217 (fax)
tnstep@aol.com (email)
www.tnstep.org

Texas

Arc of Texas in the Rio Grande Valley
    Parents Supporting Parents Network
601 North Texas Boulevard
Weslaco, TX 78596
956-447-8408 (voice)
888-857-8688 (voice)
956-973-9503 (fax)
padillal@earthlink.net (email)
www.thearcoftexas.org

Grassroots Consortium
5055 Bellfort
P.O. Box 266958
Houston, TX 77207-6958
713-734-5355 (voice)
713-643-6291 (fax)
speckids@aol.com (email)

Partners Resource Network, Inc./PATH
1090 Longfellow Drive, Suite B
Beaumont, TX 77706-4819
409-898-4684 (voice)
800-866-4726 (voice—Texas only)
409-898-4816 (TTY)
409-898-4869 (fax)
path@partnerstx.org (email)
www.partnerstx.org

Project PODER
1017 North Main Avenue, Suite 207
San Antonio, TX 78212
210-222-2637 (voice)
800-682-9747 (voice—Texas only)
210-475-9283 (fax)
poder@tfepoder.org (email)
www.tfepoder.org

Utah

Utah Parent Center (UPC)
2290 East, 4500 South, Suite 110
Salt Lake City, UT 84117-4428
801-272-1051 (voice/TTY)
800-468-1160 (voice—Utah only)
801-272-8907 (fax)
helenpo@utahparentcenter.org (email)

Vermont

Vermont Parent Information Center (VPIC)
1 Mill Street, Suite 310
Burlington, VT 05401
802-658-5315 (voice/TTY)
800-639-7170 (voice—Vermont only)
802-658-5395 (fax)
vpic@vtpic.com (email)
www.vtpic.com

Virginia

PADDA, Inc.
813 Forrest Drive, Suite 3
Newport News, VA 23606
757-591-9119 (voice)
888-337-2332 (voice)
757-591-8990 (fax)
webmaster@padda.org (email)
www.padda.org

Parent Educational Advocacy Training Center
6320 Augusta Drive, Suite 1200
Springfield, VA 22150
703-932-0010 (voice/TTY)
800-869-6782 (voice—Virginia only)
703-923-0030 (fax)
partners@peatc.org (email)
www.peatc.org

Washington

Infant Toddler Early Intervention Program
P.O. Box 45201
Olympia, WA 98504-5201
360-902-8488 (voice)
800-322-2588 (voice—Washington only)
360-902-8497 (fax)
360-902-7864 (TTY)
LoercSK@dshs.wa.gov (email)
www.wa.gov/dshs/iteip/iteip.html

Parent to Parent Power (Washington)
1118 South 142nd Street, Suite B
Tacoma, WA 98444
253-531-2022 (voice)
253-538-1126 (fax)
p2ppower@yahoo.com (email)

Washington PAVE
6316 South 12th Street
Tacoma, WA 98465
253-565-2266 (voice/TTY)
800-572-7368 (voice)
253-566-8052 (fax)
wapave9@washingtonpave.com (email)
www.washingtonpave.com

West Virginia

West Virginia PTI
371 Broaddus Avenue
Clarksburg, WV 26301
304-624-1436 (voice/TTY)
800-281-1436 (voice—West Virginia only)
304-624-1438 (fax)
wvpti@aol.com (email)
www.wvpti.org

Wisconsin

Family Assistance Center for Education, Training, and Support
2714 North Martin Luther King Drive
Milwaukee, WI 53212
414-374-4645 (voice)
877-374-4677 (voice)
414-374-4655 (fax)
414-374-4635 (TTY)
wifacets@execpc.com
www.wifacets.org

Native American Family Empowerment Center
Great Lakes Inter-Tribal Council, Inc.
2932 Highway 47 North
P.O. Box 9
Lac du Flambeau, WI 54538
715-588-3324 (voice)
800-472-7207 (voice—Wisconsin only)
715-588-7900 (fax)
drosin@glitc.org (email)
www.glitc.org

Parent Education Project of Wisconsin, Inc. (PEP WI)
2192 South 60th Street
West Allis, WI 53219-1568
414-328-5520 (voice)
414-328-5525 (TTY)
414-328-5530 (fax)
pmcoletti@aol.com (email)

Wyoming

Wyoming PIC
5 North Lobban
Buffalo, WY 82834
307-684-2277 (voice)
800-660-9742 (voice—Wyoming only)
307-684-5314 (fax)
tdawson@wpic.org (email)
www.wpic.org

Legal Resources on Special Education

American Bar Association Commission on Mental and Physical Disability Law

740 15th Street, NW
Washington, DC 20005
202-662-1000 (voice)
www.abanet.org/disability/home.html

Puts out books, reporters, news updates, and other publications to assist lawyers who advocate for the rights of the disabled. The Commission also maintains a library of research materials and provides seminars and workshops.

Bazelon Center

1101 15th Street, NW, Suite 1212
Washington, DC 20005
202-467-5730 (voice)
202-467-4232 (TDD)
202-223-0409 (fax)
webmaster@bazelon.org (email)
www.bazelon.org

A public interest law firm that conducts test case litigation to defend the rights of people with mental disabilities. The Bazelon Center provides legal support to protection and advocacy agencies, legal services offices, and private attorneys, and monitors legislation and regulations.

Center for Law and Education

1875 Connecticut Avenue, NW, Suite 510
Washington, DC 20009
202-986-3000 (voice)
202-986-6648 (fax)
www.cleweb.org

Assists local legal services programs and litigates certain cases in matters concerning education of low-income people. As a national support center, CLE has developed enormous expertise about the legal rights and responsibilities of students and school personnel as well as about key education programs and initiatives, including vocational education programs and special education for students with disabilities.

Children's Defense Fund

25 E Street, NW
Washington, DC 20001
202-628-8787 (voice)
cdfinfo@childrensdefense.org (email)
www.childrensdefense.org

Assesses the adequacy of the screening, diagnosis and treatment programs for Medicaid-eligible children.

Disability Rights Education and Defense Fund, Inc.

2212 Sixth Street
Berkeley, CA 94710
510-644-2555 (voice/TTY)
510-841-8645 (fax)
dredf@dredf.org (email)
www.dredf.org

Dedicated to protecting and advancing the civil rights of people with disabilities through legislation, litigation, advocacy, technical assistance, and education and training of lawyers, people with disabilities, and parents of children with disabilities.

EDLAW, Inc.

1310 Minor Avenue #207
Seattle, WA 98101
edlaw@edlaw.net (email)
www.edlaw.net

The website includes information on newsletters, books, and conferences; a list of attorneys who specialize in special education; and full texts of special education statutes, regulations, and administrative interpretations. EDLAW also maintains a database of attorneys and advocates through COPAA (the Council of Parent Attorneys and Advocates).

LRP Publications

747 Dresher Road, Suite 500
P.O. Box 980
Horsham, PA 19044
800-341-7874 (voice)
215-784-0860 (voice)
215-784-9639 (fax)
www.lrp.com

Has an extensive library of legal materials, including special education publications. The website includes access to over 65 special education documents, covering assessments, behavior, IDEA, IEPs, Section 504, and much more. LRP also publishes the Individuals With Disabilities Education Law Reporter.

Wrightslaw

webmaster@wrightslaw.com (email)
www.wrightslaw.com

A website maintained by Pete and Pam Wright. Pete is an attorney who has represented special education children for more than 20 years. Pam is a psychotherapist who has worked with children and families in mental health centers, psychiatric clinics, schools, juvenile detention facilities, hospitals, and homes. Their website includes articles about special education advocacy; statutes, regulations, and cases; information on ordering their advocacy package; information about books, conferences, and other projects; and links to other useful information on the Internet.

Resources on Learning Disabilities and ADD/ADHD

Here you'll find listed some of the many organizations, websites, and advocacy groups dedicated to learning disabilities. There are many additional resources available on the Web. If you don't find what you're looking for in this list, simply type key words (such as "visual processing disorder" or "aphasia") into your favorite search engine to pull up organizations, articles, and much more.

Academic Therapy Publications

20 Commercial Boulevarda
Novato, CA 94949
800-422-7249
888-287-9975
www.academictherapy.com

A company that creates tests and assessments tools. The website offers lots of articles, assessment materials, reading aids, and other resources.

American Speech-Language Hearing Association

10801 Rockville Pike
Rockville, MD 20852
800-638-8255
actioncenter@asha.org (email)
www.asha.org

A scientific and credentialing association for speech-language pathologists and other professionals for speech, language, and hearing disorders. Offers materials on assessment and fact sheets. The website allows you to look up professionals in your area.

Association of Educational Therapists

1804 West Burbank Boulevard
Burbank, CA 91506
800-286-4267 (voice)
818-843-7423 (fax)
aet@aetonline.org (email)
www.aetonline.org

A national professional association for educational therapists, which offers training and certification and sets standards for professionals in the field. The website includes links to other organizations that specialize in learning disabilities, as well as a search feature you can use to find an educational therapist in your area.

Attention Deficit Disorder Association

P.O. Box 543
Pottstown, PA 19464
484-945-2101 (voice)
610-970-7520 (fax)
www.add.org

This website was under construction as this book went to press, but it promises articles and information on ADD/ADHD, as well as links to professionals, news, and information about conferences.

Attention Deficit Information Network, Inc.

58 Prince Street
Needham, MA 02492
781-455-9895 (voice)
adin@gis.net (email)
www.addinfonetwork.com

Offers support and information to families of children with ADD and provides training programs, conferences, and workshops for parents and professionals who work with individuals with ADD.

Center for Effective Collaboration and Practice

1000 Thomas Jefferson Street, NW, Suite 400
Washington, DC 20007
202-944-5300 (voice)
888-457-1551 (voice)
877-334-3499 (TTY)
202-944-5454 (fax)
http://cecp.air.org

This organization, dedicated to helping students, teachers, and parents address emotional and behavioral concerns, provides extensive information and strategies for dealing with disciplinary and behavior problems in school. The site offers detailed materials on functional behavioral assessments, with examples.

Child Development Institute

3528 E. Ridgeway Rd.
Orange, CA 92867
714-998-8617
www.cdipage.com

This site offers articles and research on child development and learning disabilities, as well as links to other sites on learning disabilities.

Children and Adults With Attention Deficit Disorder (CHADD)

8181 Professional Place, Suite 150
Landover, MD 20785
800-233-4050
www.chadd.org

Provides a network for parents of children with ADD and a forum of education for parents and professionals who work with people who have ADD, and works to provide positive educational experiences for children with ADD. CHADD publishes a quarterly newsletter and educators' manual. The site offers fact sheets, information on IDEA, and scientific research and studies of ADD.

Community Alliance for Special Education (CASE)

1500 Howard Street
San Francisco, CA 94103
415-431-2285

Provides low-cost support and advocacy services for children with learning disabilities.

Council for Exceptional Children, Division for Learning Disabilities

1110 N. Glebe Road, Suite 300
Arlington, VA 22201
888-CEC-SPED (voice)
703-264-9494 (fax)
703-264-9446 (TDD)
service@cec.sped.org (email)
www.cec.sped.org

Information and resources for teaching students with learning disabilities. The website includes information on the DLD's publications (Learning Disabilities Research and Practice Journal, Thinking About Inclusion & Learning Disabilities, Research on Classroom Ecologies, and DLD Times Newsletter), information on upcoming conferences, links to other organizations and government agencies, fact sheets, and detailed articles on particular learning disabilities and instruction techniques.

Council for Learning Disabilities

P.O. Box 4014
Leesburg, VA 20177
571-258-1010 (voice)
571-258-1011 (fax)
www.cldinternational.org

An organization of and for professionals who represent diverse disciplines and who are committed to enhancing the education and lifespan development of individuals with learning disabilities. The site offers fact sheets, information on research on learning disabilities, and legislative updates.

Dyslexia, Learning Disabilities & Literacy Resource Site

Greenwood Institute
14 Greenwood Lane
Putney, VT 05346
802-387-4545 (voice)
802-387-5396 (fax)

A website maintained by the Greenwood School, a boarding school for boys with dyslexia and language disorders. The site offers articles and information for parents, teachers, and home schoolers.

Dyspraxia Foundation

8 West Alley
Hitchin
Hertfordshire SG5 1EG
United Kingdom
www.dyspraxiafoundation.org.uk

A British organization that offers fact sheets on dyspraxia and links to other websites on learning disabilities.

ERIC Clearinghouse on Assessment and Evaluation

1131 Shriver Laboratory, Building 075
University of Maryland
College Park, MD 20742
800-464-3742 (voice)
301-405-7449 (voice)
301-405-8134 (fax)
feedback3@ericae.net (email)
http://ericae.net

Run by the U.S. Department of Education, this site offers detailed information and research on assessments. Use the "Test Locator" to find a list of assessment tools, descriptions of each, how they are administered, the purpose of the test, and much more.

International Dyslexia Association

The Chester Building, Suite 382
8600 LaSalle Road
Baltimore, MD 21286-2044
410-296-0232 (voice)
410-321-5069 (fax)
info@interdys.org (email)
www.interdys.org

Promotes effective teaching approaches and related clinical educational intervention strategies for people with dyslexia; supports and disseminates research through conferences, publications, and local and regional offices. The site offers research, fact sheets, and legislative updates.

International Reading Association

800 Barksdale Road
Newark, DE 19711
302-731-1600 (voice)
302-731-1057 (fax)
www.reading.org

A group for parents and teachers. The site includes articles on reading, reading disorders, and literacy.

Internet Special Education Resources

301-230-9010 (voice)
301-649-6207 (voice)
www.iser.com

This site offers fact sheets and information on assessments, as well as a directory of professionals, including therapists and independent assessors.

Learning Disabilities Association of America

4156 Library Road
Pittsburgh, PA 15234-1349
412-341-1515 (voice)
412-344-0224 (fax)
info@ldaamerica.org (email)
www.ldaamerica.org

A nonprofit membership organization with state and local affiliates. Members receive a national newsletter along with state and local chapter newsletters and information on advocating for their children, state and federal laws, and support groups. The site offers fact sheets, news, and other resources. Click "State LDA Pages" for links to state and local chapters.

LD Online

www.ldonline.com

One of my favorites, this site offers lots of detailed articles for parents, teachers, and kids on learning disabilities, assessments, methodologies, IEPs, IDEA, and much more. There's a special area of the site just for kids, as well as bulletin boards and lots of state-by-state links.

LD Resources

www.ldresources.com

A website with articles, a newsletter, and links to other sites that specialize in learning disabilities.

National Aphasia Association

351 Butternut Court
Millersville, MD 21108
800-922-4622 (voice)
naa@aphasia.org (email)
www.aphasia.org

Promotes public education, research, rehabilitation, and support services to assist people with aphasia and their families. The site offers information, research, fact sheets, and access to support groups.

National Association for the Education of African American Children With Learning Disabilities

P.O. Box 09521
Columbus, OH 43209
614-237-6021 (voice)
614-238-0928 (fax)
info@aacld.org (email)
www.charityadvantage.com/aacld/HomePage.asp

An organization that focuses on the specific issues facing African-American children with learning disabilities, including appropriate assessments, research, teaching methodologies, and the problem of over-identification of African-American students for special education. The site includes articles, information for teachers and parents, and a parent network.

National Center for Learning Disabilities

381 Park Avenue South, Suite 1401
New York, NY 10016
212-545-7510 (voice)
888-575-7373 (voice)
212-545-9665 (fax)
www.ncld.org

Provides information on learning disabilities and resources available in communities nationwide to parents, professionals, and adults with learning disabilities. One of NCLD's areas of primary concern is early identification and intervention, as well as teacher preparation. The website includes links to other LD organizations and school testing organizations, and information on legal issues, gifted/learning disabilities, ADD/ADHD, and home schooling. The site includes special information for older kids and adults with learning disabilities, as well as an "LD InfoZone" with fact sheets and remediation ideas.

National Coalition on Auditory Processing Disorders

4303 Ivey Glen Avenue
Orlando, FL 32826
info@nacpd.org (email)
www.ncapd.org

This site offers a newsletter and message boards, as well as information for and about professionals who specialize in auditory processing disorders.

National Institute of Neurological Disorders and Stroke

NIH Neurological Institute
P.O. Box 5801
Bethesda, MD 20824
800-352-9424 (voice)
301-496-5751 (voice)
301-468-5981 (TTY)
www.ninds.nih.gov

This federal government site provides information on various learning disabilities (and other neurological disorders), including aphasia, dyslexia, and dyspraxia.

Nonverbal Learning Disorders Association

2446 Albany Avenue
West Hartford, CT 06117
860-570-0217 (voice)
nlda@nlda.org
www.nlda.org

This site offers articles and resources on nonverbal learning disorders.

NLD Line

831-624-3542 (voice)
NLDline@aol.com (email)
www.nldline.com

This site offers lots of articles, resources, links, and other information on nonverbal learning disorders (including materials on auditory processing disorders). The site has information on assessments, appropriate teaching methods, diagnosis, IEPs, and much more.

Nonverbal Learning Disorders on the Web

www.ldontheweb.org

This site has articles and information on nonverbal learning disorders, including lists of local resources for parents and teachers.

Schwab Learning

1650 South Amphlett Boulevard, Suite 300
San Mateo, CA 94402
650-655-2410 (voice)
650-655-2411 (fax)
infodesk@schwablearning.org (email)
www.schwablearning.org

The Schwab Foundation provides parents and educators in the San Francisco area quarterly educational programs, information and referrals, and guidance counseling. The website includes extensive resources about ADD, assessments, dyslexia, homework, IEPs, learning disabilities, tutors, teaching methods, family issues, and much more.

University of Kansas Center for Research on Learning

Joseph R. Pearson Hall
1122 W. Campus Road, Room 521
Lawrence, KS 66045-3101
785-864-4780 (voice)
crl@du.edu (email)
www.ku-crl.org

The Center provides information and research for educators on teaching, including teaching students with learning disabilities.

World Dyslexia Network Foundation

http://web.ukonline.co.uk/wdnf

This British site provides fact sheets and resources on dyslexia, as well as links to other websites.

Bibliography

If you can, pay a visit to a large public library or bookstore to see the array of materials for parents and teachers of children with learning disabilities. You could also browse online booksellers. Here is just a small sample of the many available titles:

- Compton, Carolyn, *A Guide to 100 Tests for Special Education* (Simon and Schuster Education Group).
- Davies, Dorothy, and Johnson, M.D., *I Can't Sit Still: Educating and Affirming Inattentive and Hyperactive Children* (ETR Association).
- Fisher, Gary, Cummings, Rhoda et al., *The Survival Guide for Kids With LD*, *The Survival Guide for Teenagers With LD*, and *When Your Child Has LD: A Survival Guide for Parents* (all by Free Spirit Publishing).
- Flanagan, Dawn et al., *The Achievement Test Desk Reference: Comprehensive Assessment and Learning Disabilities* (Pearson Allyn & Bacon).
- Kaufman, Alan and Nadeen, *Specific Learning Disabilities and Difficulties in Children and Adolescents: Psychological Assessment and Evaluation* (Cambridge U. Press).
- Levine, Dr. Mel, *A Mind at a Time*, *The Myth of Laziness*, *All Kinds of Minds*, *Keeping a Head in School*, and more (various publishers).
- Rief, Sandra, *How to Reach and Teach ADD/ADHD Children* (Jossey-Bass).
- Stowe, Cynthia, *How to Reach and Teach Children and Teens with Dyslexia* (Jossey-Bass).
- Wehman, Paul, *Life Beyond the Classroom: Transition Strategies for Young People with Learning Disabilities* (Paul H. Brooks Pub. Co.).

Appendix 4

Sample IEP Form

Every school district, in every state, has its own IEP form. While the forms vary, they must include the same information. I strongly recommend that you request a copy of your school's IEP form early in the process.

To get you familiar with IEP forms, we have included a sample here, reprinted with permission of the Marin County (California) Office of Education. Note the section on Learning Disabilities at pages 3–4. The section on California tests (pages 18–20a) won't apply if you live in another state, but you may find it useful. You can also access this form at www.marinschools.org/selpa.htm.

Individualized Education Program

**MARIN
SELPA**
IEP
Page 1
7/02

Date _____

> Shaded boxes are situational.
> All other areas must be addressed.

IDENTIFYING INFORMATION

Student:_____ Birthdate _____ Age _____ Grade _____ ❏ M ❏ F

Parent/Guardian _____
❏ LCI
❏ Foster Home _____

Address _____ City _____ Zip _____

Home Phone _____ Work Phone(s) _____ Home Language _____

District of Residence _____ School _____

Student's Language Proficiency ❏ English Only ❏ Fluent English Proficient ❏ Limited English Proficient ❏ Non English Proficient

Determined by _____ Date _____ Primary Language Level _____

Name of Test

DATES OF ANTICIPATED MEETINGS

Annual Review _____ AB 3632 6 Month Review _____ 3-yr. Reevaluation _____ Add'l Review _____

Month/Day/Year   Month/Day/Year   Month/Day/Year   Month/Day/Year

IEP MEETING INFORMATION

Purpose of the meeting: (*Check all that apply*)
❏ Initial ❏ Annual Review ❏ Review Based on 3-yr. Reevaluation ❏ AB3632 6 Month Review ❏ Promotion/Retention
❏ Manifestation Determination   ❏ Transition ❏ Parent Request   ❏ Amend IEP dated _____
❏ Review assessments   ❏ Determine eligibility   ❏ Develop goals and objectives   ❏ Develop/review behavioral plan
❏ Recommend placement/service(s)   ❏ _____

WHAT CONCERN(S) DOES THE PARENT WANT TO SEE ADDRESSED IN THIS IEP TO ENHANCE THE STUDENT'S EDUCATION?

THE FOLLOWING ASSESSMENT REPORT(S) WERE REVIEWED. REPORT(S) INCLUDE DESCRIPTION(S) OF THE CHILD'S STRENGTHS, GENERAL EDUCATION PERFORMANCE INCLUDING STAR TESTING RESULTS AND REPORT CARDS, AND ACHIEVEMENT TOWARDS GOALS AND OBJECTIVES (*Please list name of report, examiner(s), and date of report*)

Student _____   Date of Meeting _____

MARIN SELPA
IEP
Page 2
10/02

ELIGIBILITY AS AN INDIVIDUAL WITH EXCEPTIONAL NEEDS - Circle primary handicapping condition

1. Meets eligibility criteria as indicated: IEP team previously determined eligibility on _____

❑ Mentally Retarded   ❑ Hard of Hearing   ❑ Visually Impaired   ❑ Orthopedically Impaired
❑ Language or Speech Disorder   ❑ Emotionally Disturbed ❑ Traumatic Brain Injury ❑ Deaf/Blind
❑ Autistic-Like Behaviors   ❑ Deaf   ❑ Multi-Handicapped _____
❑ Specific Learning Disability   ❑ Other Health Impaired *Specific Impairment* _____

2. Specific eligibility was unable to be determined. Recommend: _____
3. Does not meet eligibility for handicaps considered: _____

REQUIRED IEP TEAM CONSIDERATIONS - If "yes", indicate where the need is addressed in the IEP

Does the child's behavior impede his or her learning or that of others?	❑ Yes ❑ No	IEP Page _____
Does the child have limited English proficiency?	❑ Yes ❑ No	IEP Page _____
Does the child have any special communication needs?	❑ Yes ❑ No	IEP Page _____
Does the child require any assistive technology devices or services in order to be involved, and to progress in the general curriculum or to be educated in a less restrictive environment?	❑ Yes ❑ No	IEP Page _____
If the child is blind or visually impaired, does the evaluation of the child's reading and writing skills, needs and appropriate reading and writing media (including an evaluation of the child's future need for instruction in Braille or the use of Braille), indicate the instruction in Braille or the use of Braille is appropriate for the child?	❑ Yes ❑ No ❑ NA	IEP Page _____
If the child is deaf or hard of hearing, does the child have any special language or communication needs that affect their education needs?	❑ Yes ❑ No ❑ NA	IEP Page _____

GOALS AND OBJECTIVES

❑ Draft IEP goals and objectives were reviewed, revised, and are recommended.
❑ IEP goals and objectives were recommended on _____ and are continued.*
❑ In addition to IEP goals and objectives continued from the meeting on _____,* additional goals and
   objectives were reviewed, reivised and are recommended.
  *At or after the Annual Review

PUPIL PROMOTION AND RETENTION (GRADES 2-8)

Promotion from grade _____ to grade _____ shall be based on the following criteria:
❑ District adopted criteria for general education students
❑ IEP Individualized Promotion Standards (specify standards below or on page _____. These promotion standards may
   include grades and achievement of IEP objectives, and level of achievement required for promotion. Grades 2-4
   require reading standards only; grades 5-8 require reading, language arts, and math.)
_____
_____

Is the student at risk of retention? ❑ Yes ❑ No If "yes", the following must be considered by the IEP team:
❑ Yes ❑ No Is the current IEP for the student's academic, linguistic, social and emotional, and behavioral needs appropriate?
❑ Yes ❑ No Is the manner of assessment, including any accommodations and modifications, identified in the IEP appropriate?
❑ Yes ❑ No Were all the services required by the student to make progress in the general education curriculum appropriately identified
                    in the student's IEP?
❑ Yes ❑ No Did the student receive all the services identified in the IEP?
❑ Yes ❑ No Was the assessment conducted consistent with the IEP?
❑ Yes ❑ No Was the student's promotion standard appropriate and clarified in the IEP?

See page _____ for IEP Team recommendations

Distribution: White-Permanent File   Canary-Parent   Copies may be made for other team members

Student _____   Date of Meeting _____

ELIGIBILITY FOR A SPECIFIC LEARNING DISABILITY

I. Presence of a Severe Discrepancy (Select either A or B and then complete items II through IV)

❑ A. The IEP Team finds a severe discrepancy (18.5 points or more) between measures of intellectual ability and one or more of the following areas of achievement:

❑ Oral Expression   ❑ Written Expression   ❑ Listening Comprehension
❑ Mathematics Calculation ❑ Mathematics Reasoning   ❑ Basic Reading Skills
❑ Reading Comprehension

Measure of Intellectual Ability_____ Score(s) _____

Test(s) of Academic Achievement/Scores(s) _____
_____

Discrepancy between Intellectual Ability and Academic Achievement _____

❑ B. Standard measures do not reveal a severe discrepancy, but the IEP team finds a severe discrepancy does exist based upon the additional documentation provided in the attached report. (Complete and attach "Specific Learning Disability Discrepancy" documentation-See page 4)

II. The discrepancy identified in Item 1 (above) is directly related to a processing disorder. ❑ Yes ❑ No
Check the appropriate area(s):
❑ Sensory Motor Skills   ❑ Visual Processing   ❑ Auditory Processing   ❑ Attention
❑ Cognitive Abilities (including asssociation, conceptualization, and expression)
Name of Test _____ Score _____

III. If any of the items below (A-E) are checked "Yes", the student may not be identified as having a specific learning disability.

A. The discrepancy is due primarily to limited school experience or poor school attendance.   ❑ Yes ❑ No
B. The discrepancy is a result of environmental, cultural difference or economic disadvantage.   ❑ Yes ❑ No
C. The discrepancy is due primarily to mental retardation or emotional disturbance.   ❑ Yes ❑ No
D. The discrepany is due primarily to a visual, hearing or motor disability   ❑ Yes ❑ No
E. This discrepancy can be corrected through other regular or categorical services offered within the regular instructional program.   ❑ Yes ❑ No

IV. The student has a specific learning disability. ❑ Yes ❑ No

I agree with the conclusions stated above:

_____   _____
Credentialed School Psychologist/Date   Special Ed. Admin./Designee/Date

_____   _____
Resource Specialist/Date   Teacher/Date

_____   _____
Language Speech Specialist/Date   Nurse/Date

_____   _____
Parent/Guardian/Date   Other/Date

_____   _____
Other/Date   Other/Date

My assessment of this student differs from the above report as follows: Statement (attach additional pages as necessary)

_____
Signature and Title/Date
Distribution: White-Permanent File   Canary-Parent   Copies may be made for other team members

Student _____   Date of Meeting _____

SPECIFIC LEARNING DISABILITY DISCREPANCY DOCUMENTATION REPORT

This form is to be completed in order to document the presence of a Specific Learning Disability in instances when the student does not exhibit a severe discrepancy between ability and achievement as measured by standardized tests. (Ed. Code 3030 (j)(C))

1. Data from assessment instruments (ability and achievement): _____
   _____
   _____
   _____
   _____

2. Information provided by parent: _____
   _____
   _____
   _____
   _____

3. Information provided by the pupil's present teacher: _____
   _____
   _____
   _____
   _____

4. Summary of the pupil's classroom performance:
   a. Observations: _____
   _____
   _____

   b. Work Samples: _____
   _____
   _____

   c. Group Test Scores: _____
   _____
   _____

5. Consideration of the pupil's age: _____
   _____
   _____
   _____
   _____

6. Additional Relevant Information _____
   _____
   _____
   _____
   _____

Student _____ Date of Meeting _____

**MARIN
SELPA**
IEP
Page 5
6/01

ELIGIBILITY FOR LANGUAGE OR SPEECH DISORDER

Must Meet One or More of Criteria 1-5 and Criteria 6 and 7.

❏ 1. **Articulation Disorder -** Such that the pupil's production of speech significantly interferes with communication and attracts adverse attention. Significant interference in communication occurs when the pupil's production of single or multiple speech sounds on a developmental scale of articulation competency is below that expected for his or her chronological age or developmental level.
Chronological Age or Developmetal Level _____
Articulation Test _____ Age Equivalent, Standard Score or %ile _____

❏ 2. **Abnormal Voice -** A pupil has an abnormal voice which is characterized by persistent, defective voice quality, pitch or loudness. (Student must have medical clearance for voice therapy.)

❏ 3. **Fluency Disorders -** A pupil has a fluency disorder when the flow of verbal expression including rate and rhythm adversely affects communication between the pupil and listener.

❏ 4. **Language or Speech Disorder** - Which is the result of a hearing loss.

❏ 5. **Language Disorder** - *The pupil has an expressive or receptive language disorder when he or she meets one of the following criteria:*

    ❏ A. The pupil scores at least 1.5 standard deviations (22.5 points) below the mean or below the 7th percentile, for his or her chronological age or developmental level on *two or more* standardized tests in one or more of the following areas of language development. *Check appropriate area(s):*
        ❏ Morphology   ❏ Syntax   ❏ Semantics   ❏ Pragmatics
        Chronological Age or Developmental Level _____
        Standardized Test _____ Discrepancy _____ %ile _____
        Standardized Test _____ Discrepancy _____ %ile _____

    ❏ B. The pupil scores at least 1.5 standard deviations below the mean or the score is below the 7%ile for his or her chronological age or developmental level on one or more standardized tests in one of the areas listed above *AND* displays inappropriate or inadequate usage of expressive or receptive language as measured by a representative spontaneous or elicited language sample of fifty utterances. *Check appropriate area(s):*
        ❏ Morphology   ❏ Syntax   ❏ Semantics   ❏ Pragmatics
        Chronological Age or Developmental Level _____
        Standardized Test: _____ Discrepancy _____ %ile _____
        Language Sample Results _____

❏ 6. **Adversely affects educational performance.**

❏ 7. **Cannot be corrected without special education and related services.**

ELIGIBILITY FOR CHILDREN BETWEEN THE AGES OF THREE AND FIVE YEARS

Must Meet Criteria I and II

I. **Meets eligibility criteria as indicated:**

    ❏ Mentally Retarded   ❏ Hard of Hearing   ❏ Multi-Handicapped   ❏ Visually Impaired
    ❏ Orthopedically Impaired   ❏ Other Health Impaired *Specific Impairment* _____
    ❏ Deaf/Blind   ❏ Autistic-Like Behaviors   ❏ Traumatic Brain Injury   ❏ Deaf
    ❏ Specific Learning Disability   ❏ Language or Speech Disorder   ❏ Emotionally Disturbed
    or
    ❏ Has an established medical disability, which is defined as a disabling medical condition or congenital syndrome which the IEP team determines has a high predictability of requiring intensive special education and services.
    Specify: _____

II. **If any of the items below (A-D) are checked "Yes", The student may not be eligible for special education and services if his or her educational needs are due primarily to:**
    A. Unfamiliarity with the English Language   ❏ Yes ❏ No
    B. Temporary physical disabilities   ❏ Yes ❏ No
    C. Social maladjustment   ❏ Yes ❏ No
    D. Environmental, cultural or economic factors   ❏ Yes ❏ No
III. **Needs cannot be met with modification of regular environment**   ❏ Yes ❏ No

Distribution: White-Permanent File   Canary-Parent   Copies may be made for other team members

Transition Service Needs

Beginning at age 14

MARIN SELPA

IEP
Page 6
1/03

Student _____   Date of Meeting _____

Anticipated Date of Graduation or Completion _____

DESIRED POST-SCHOOL OUTCOME STATEMENT - Long-Range Goals

Employment/ Post-Secondary Education Outcomes	Domestic	Community Functioning	Transportation	Recreation
Employment ❑ Competitive employment without support ❑ Competitve employment with time-limited support ❑ Competitive employment with long-term support ❑ Supported employment ❑ Sheltered employment ❑ Military ❑ _____ **Education** ❑ Apprenticeship program ❑ Vocational college ❑ Technical institute ❑ Community College ❑ 4-year College ❑ GED Program ❑ _____	**Housing** ❑ Live alone without supports ❑ Live alone with support ❑ Live with family/relative ❑ Live with roommate(s) ❑ Group home-specialized training ❑ Supervised apartment ❑ Residential/nursing facility ❑ Individual services coordinator ❑ Lifetime support/planning ❑ _____ **Income/Resources** ❑ Earned wages ❑ Social Security benefits ❑ Unearned income ❑ Trust/will ❑ Food stamps ❑ _____ **Medicaid Services** ❑ Personal assistive devices ❑ Group insurance ❑ Independent in monitoring medical needs ❑ Requires medical vision/ scheduling ❑ Special therapies and treatments	**Adult Responsibilities** ❑ Voter registration ❑ Registration for selective service ❑ Social Security registration ❑ Self-consumer advocacy ❑ Parenting ❑ Voluteerism ❑ _____ **Support Services** ❑ Guardianship ❑ Family planning ❑ Counseling services ❑ Respite services ❑ Day Activities ❑ _____	**Mode of Transportation** ❑ Self (Driver's License) ❑ Public transportation ❑ Specialized transportation ❑ Family transports ❑ Car pool ❑ _____	**Social and Leisure** ❑ Independent recreation and leisure ❑ Family supported recreation and leisure ❑ Specialized recreation ❑ Community-supported recreation program ❑ Local clubs ❑ Day programs ❑ _____

PROPOSED COURSES RELATED TO DESIRED POST SCHOOL OUTCOMES				
8th Grade	**9th Grade**	**10th Grade**	**11th Grade**	**12th Grade**

Distribution: White-Permanent File   Canary-Parent   Copies may be made for other team members

MARIN SELPA
IEP
Page 7
1/03

Transition Services

BEGINNING AT AGE 16 OR YOUNGER, IF DETERMINED APPROPRIATE BY THE IEP TEAM

Student _____   Date of Meeting _____

❏ If 17 years old, student received a copy of the Procedural Rights _____

Student's Signature

SUMMARY OF STUDENT'S NEEDS, INTERESTS, AND PREFERENCES

_____
_____
_____
_____

STATEMENT OF NEEDED SERVICES

Development of Employment/Post-Secondary Education Outcomes

Provide justification if services not needed:

_____
_____
_____

Indicate Outcomes for the Current Year	Semesters	Person or Agency Responsible
❏ Locate sources of occupational and training information		
❏ Classify jobs into occupational categories		
❏ Investigate local occupational and training opportunities		
❏ Submit referral to Department of Rehabilitation		
❏ Make realistic occupational choices		
❏ Identify requirements of appropriate and available jobs		
❏ Identify occupational aptitudes		
❏ Identify major occupational interests		
❏ Plan and make realistic training and job placement decisions		
❏ Develop training plan for occupational choice		
❏ Identify local apprenticeship programs		
❏ Explore enrollment in GED program		
❏ Identify entrance requirements for military services		
❏ Identify entrance requirements for vocational college, technical institute, community college, and/or four year college		
❏ Take the SAT Exam		
❏ Follow directions and observe regulations		
❏ Recognize importance of attendance and punctuality		
❏ Recognize the importance of supervision		
❏ Work with others		
❏ Meet demands for quality and quantity work standards		
❏ Work at a satisfactory rate		
❏ Search for a job		
❏ Apply for a job		
❏ Interview for a job		
❏ _____		

Distribution: White-Permanent File   Canary-Parent   Copies may be made for other team members

Transition Services

BEGINNING AT AGE 16 OR YOUNGER, IF DETERMINED APPROPRIATE BY THE IEP TEAM

**MARIN
SELPA**
IEP
Page 8
1/03

Student _____   Date of Meeting _____

Domestic Skills Outcome for the Current Year

Provide justification if service not needed _____

Indicate Outcomes for the Current Year	Semesters	Person or Agency Responsible
❑ Count money and make correct change		
❑ Keep basic financial records		
❑ Calculate and pay taxes		
❑ Use banking services		
❑ Maintain living environment exterior/interior		
❑ Use basic appliances and tools		
❑ Select adequate housing/personal living space		
❑ Set up household/personal living space		
❑ Exhibit proper grooming and hygiene		
❑ Dress appropriately		
❑ Demonstrate knowledge of common illness, prevention, and treatment		
❑ Practice personal safety and/or basic first aid		
❑ Purchase food		
❑ Demonstrate cleaning food prep area, meal clean-up, and food storage		
❑ Prepare food		
❑ Demonstrate appropriate eating habits		
❑ Plan/eat well balanced meals		
❑ Wash/clean clothing		
❑ Purchase clothing		
❑ Iron, mend, and store clothing		
❑ _____		

Community Functioning Outcomes for the Current Year

Provide justification if services not needed _____

Indicate Outcomes for the Current Year	Semesters	Person or Agency Responsible
❑ Demonstrate knowledge of civil rights and responsibilities		
❑ Identify physical and psychological needs		
❑ Identify interests and abilities		
❑ Express feelings of self-worth and self-confidence		
❑ Accept and give praise/criticism		
❑ Demonstrate listening and responding skills		
❑ Make and maintain friendships		
❑ Demonstrate self-organization		
❑ _____		

Distribution: White-Permanent File   Canary-Parent   Copies may be made for other team members

Transition Services

BEGINNING AT AGE 16 OR YOUNGER, IF DETERMINED APPROPRIATE BY THE IEP TEAM

**MARIN
SELPA**
IEP
Page 9
6/02

Student _____ Date of Meeting _____

Post-Secondary Transportation Outcomes for the Current Year

Provide justification if service not needed _____

_____

_____

_____

Indicate Outcomes for the Current Year	Semesters	Person or Agency Responsible
❏ Demonstrate knowledge of traffic rules and safety		
❏ Demonstrate knowledge and use of various means of transportation		
❏ Find way around community		
❏ Access available transportation		
❏ Study for and take driving test		
❏ Obtain a California Driver's License or ID		
❏ Demonstrate knowledge of car insurance		
❏ _____		

Recreation Outcomes for the Current Year

Provide justification if service not needed

_____

_____

_____

Indicate Outcomes for the Current Year	Semesters	Person or Agency Responsible
❏ Demonstrate knowledge of community leisure/recreational resources		
❏ Choose and plan leisure/recreational activities		
❏ Engage in group and individual leisure/recreational activities		
❏ _____		

DOCUMENTATION OF AGENCY CONTACTS AND LINKAGES

Date	Agency Contacted/ To Be Contacted	Needed Services	Team Member Who Will Make Contact and Follow-Up	Comments
	Department of Rehabilitation	Client? ❏ Yes ❏ No		
	Golden Gate Regional Center	Client? ❏ Yes ❏ No		
	Social Security Administration	Client? ❏ Yes ❏ No		
	Employment Development	Client? ❏ Yes ❏ No		
	Community Mental Health	Client? ❏ Yes ❏ No		
	Social Services	Client? ❏ Yes ❏ No		
		Client? ❏ Yes ❏ No		

Distribution: White-Permanent File   Canary-Parent   Copies may be made for other team members

Behavioral Intervention Plan

Student _____   Date of Meeting _____

TARGET BEHAVIOR

Describe the behavior that impedes learning. What does it look like?

How often does the behavior occur? With what intensity? How long does it last?

What happens before the behavior occurs? With whom? Where? When? (Most and least likely)

The IEP team believes the behavior occurs because (function/communicative intent):

What is in or missing from the environment, curriculum, or instruction that contributes to this behavior?

TARGET BEHAVIOR PREVENTION PLAN - Based upon antecedent/predictor analysis

What environmental structures and supports need to be changed or introduced to prevent the behavior from occurring?

Distribution: White-Permanent File   Canary-Parent   Copies may be made for other team members

Behavioral Intervention Plan

MARIN SELPA
IEP
Page 11
6/02

Student _____   Date of Meeting _____

REPLACEMENT BEHAVIOR

What strengths does the student have that will help him/her to be successful in using/learning the replacement behaviors?

What should the student do instead of this behavior? (This should serve the same function/communicatve intent of the target behavior)

Does the student currently have the skills to use the behavior? If "yes", when is it most likey to occur?

Are there goals and objectives related to this plan? ❏ Yes ❏ No If "yes", please indicate page number(s) of goal(s).

REPLACEMENT BEHAVIOR PLAN

Does the replacement behavior identified need reinforcement only?   ❏ Yes   ❏ No

Does the replacement behavior need to be taught and reinforced?   ❏ Yes   ❏ No
If "yes", describe the teaching strategies needed to help the student master the new behavior:

Are accommodations in curriculum and instruction needed?   ❏ Yes   ❏ No
If "yes", see page 18 of the IEP for needed accommodations.

What is the plan for reinforcing the desired replacement behavior when it occurs?

What will the response of staff be if the target behavior occurs?

Distribution: White-Permanent File   Canary-Parent   Copies may be made for other team members

Proposed Behavior Intervention Plan (Hughes Bill)

Student _____   Date of Meeting _____

SUMMARY OF FUNCTIONAL ANALYSIS ASSESSMENT

OBJECTIVE AND MEASURABLE DESCRIPTION OF TARGETED MALADAPTIVE AND REPLACEMENT BEHAVIORS

Targeted maladaptive behavior(s)

Replacement positive behavior(s)

STUDENT'S GOALS AND OBJECTIVES SPECIFIC TO THE BEHAVIORAL INTERVENTION PLAN

DESCRIPTION OF INTERVENTIONS TO BE USED AND CIRCUMSTANCES FOR USE

Distribution: White-Permanent File   Canary-Parent   Copies may be made for other team members

Student _____ Date of Meeting _____

**MARIN
SELPA**
IEP
Page 13
6/01

RECORDING SCHEDULES

Frequency of use of interventions

Frequency of data collection (targeted and replacement behavior(s)

Criteria for discontinuing use of interventions due to lack of effectiveness

Criteria for phasing out or less intense/frequent schedules or techniques

EXTENT TO WHICH INTERVENTIONS WILL BE CARRIED OUT IN OTHER SETTINGS (WORK, COMMUNITY, HOME, ETC.)

DATES FOR PERIODIC REVIEW BY IEP TEAM TO DETERMINE EFFICACY OF PROGRAM

Distribution: White-Permanent File   Canary-Parent   Copies may be made for other team members

Manifestation Determination

**MARIN
SELPA**
IEP
Page 14
2/03

Student _____   Date of Present Meeting _____

DESCRIPTION OF BEHAVIOR SUBJECT TO DISCIPLINARY ACTION

THE IEP TEAM CONSIDERED ALL THE RELEVANT INFORMATION INCLUDING:

Evaluation and Diagnostic Results

Information Supplied by the Parents

Observation of the Student

The Student's IEP and Placement

Distribution: White-Permanent File   Canary-Parent   Copies may be made for other team members

**MARIN
SELPA
IEP**
Page 15
2/03

Student _____ Date of Meeting _____

THE IEP TEAM HAS DETERMINED

In relationship to the behavior subject to the disciplinary action:

❏ Yes ❏ No   Were the student's IEP and placement appropriate?
If "no", specify why the IEP and placement were not appropriate:

❏ Yes ❏ No   Were the special education services, supplementary aids and services, and behavior intervention strategies provided consistent with the student's IEP and placement?

If "no", specify: 1) why the IEP was not implemented and 2) whether the failure to implement the IEP impacted the student's behavior. It may be necessary to review and revise the IEP and placement.

❏ Yes ❏ No   Did the student's disability impair his/her ability to understand the impact and consequences of the behavior subject to disciplinary action.
If "yes", the behavior must be considered a manifestation of the student's disability.

❏ Yes ❏ No   Did the student's disability impair his/her disability to control the behavior subject to disciplinary action.
If "yes", the behavior must be considered a manifestation of the student's disability.

Check the appropriate box:

❏   The student's behavior WAS NOT a manifestation of his/her disability. The relevant disciplinary procedures applicable to students without disabilities may be applied to the student in the same manner in which they are applied to students without disabiilities. However, the district must continue to make FAPE available to the student.

❏   The student's behavior WAS a manifestation of his/her disability. The IEP team must review and revise the student's IEP as appropriate, including development or review of a behavioral intervention plan.

Student _____   Date of Meeting _____

MARIN
SELPA
IEP
Page 16
6/02

DISTRICT JUSTIFICATION FOR EDUCATIONAL PLACEMENT

RECOMMENDED EDUCATIONAL PLACEMENT	CORRESPONDING PLACEMENT
IEP services can be provided solely in the general education classroom	❑ General Education Classroom
Some IEP services should be provided outside the general education classroom	❑ Some services outside the General Education classroom
All IEP services should be provided outside the general education classroom.	❑ Special Day Class
All IEP services should be provided outside the general education classroom and separately from a school that also serves students without disabilities.	❑ Special Day Class on an isolated site ❑ Non Public School - Day Program
IEP services require a 24-hour educational program.	❑ AB 3632 Residential Placement
Home-based IEP services for a student who is 3 to 5 years of age.	❑ Home-based Early Childhood Program
IEP services provided in a program outside of the home for a student who is 3 to 5 years of age.	❑ Center-based Early Childhood Program
A mix of IEP services that are not provided in primarily school-based settings.	❑ Other

JUSTIFICATION FOR NON PARTICIPATION IN GENERAL EDUCATION

Is the student removed from the general education classroom at any time? ❑ Yes ❑ No
Percent of time out of general education classroom? _____%
If "yes", why is removal considered critical to the student's program?

1. ❑ Small group instruction is necessary for this student to acquire skills specified in the IEP.
2. ❑ Behavioral intervention plan and/or behavioral goals and objectives recommended in the student's IEP require a degree of structure which cannot be implemented in a large group setting.
3. ❑ The student's needs as addressed in IEP goals and objectives cannot be satisfactorily achieved in the general educational/preschool environment even with the provision of supplemental aids and services.
4. ❑ Student's behavior significantly impairs his/her ability to learn in a large group setting, as well as impairing the learning of other students in a large group setting.
5. ❑ Based upon individual needs and goals and objectives in the student's IEP,
   ❑ the general curriculum/appropriate preschool activities would need to be completely restructured.
   ❑ additional individualized instruction is required to facilitate his/her learning.
   ❑ an intensive behavior management program is required.
6. ❑ A more structured environment is needed than can be provided in the general education classroom.
7. ❑ Student requires utilization of the Severely Handicapped Alternative Curriculum Guide in a highly structured environment to acquire skills specified in their IEP.
8. ❑ _____
   _____

TYPE OF PHYSICAL EDUCATION

❑ Regular Physical Education   ❑ Adapted Physical Education   ❑ Modified Physical Education
❑ Specially Designed Physical Education   ❑ Not Applicable

Distribution: White-Permanent File   Canary-Parent   Copies may be made for other team members

Student _____ Date of Meeting _____

MARIN SELPA
IEP
Page 17
8/02

PLACEMENT, SERVICES, AND EQUIPMENT CONSIDERED AND RECOMMENDED

Considered / IEP Team Recommends

	Dates Unless otherwise specified, services will be for the regular school year.	**Location** Please check appropriate box(es) and specify location

❏ Special Day Class   From_____ To _____   ❏ Public-Home School _____

    ❏ Day ❏ Residential ❏ Pursuant to AB 3632   ❏ Public-Other Than Home School*_____
    ❏ Certified Non Public School* _____
    ❏ _____ *

*If not home school, rationale: ❏ Public Preschool ❏ Student would benefit from program available on an isolated site.
❏ Needs cannot be met at home school ❏ Student would benefit from program available at site other than home school

Considered / IEP Team Recommends

Dates (Month/Day/Year) Services checked below will be provided until the next annual review excluding holidays, non-student days, and all vacations unless otherwise specified.	**Frequency**	**Location** Please identify the specific location(s) of the program(s)/service(s) and indicate C = Classroom OR R = Room Other Than Gen. Ed. or SDC

❏ Resource Specialist From_____ To _____ _____ _____ ❏ C ❏ R
                    ❏ Direct   ❏ Consult

❏ Language/Speech From_____ To _____ _____ _____ ❏ C ❏ R
                    ❏ Direct   ❏ Consult

❏ Occupational Tx From_____ To _____ _____ _____ ❏ C ❏ R
                    ❏ Direct   ❏ Consult

❏ CCS Services From_____ To _____ _____ _____
                ❏ Direct   ❏ Consult   ❏ Monitor ❏ Occupational Therapy   ❏ Physical Therapy

❏ Home/Hospital From_____ To _____ _____ _____ ❏ C ❏ R
                ❏ Direct   ❏ Consult

❏ Add. Classroom From_____ To _____ _____ _____ ❏ C ❏ R
Support

❏ Community Mental From_____ To _____ _____ _____ ❏ C ❏ R
Health

❏ _____ From_____ To _____ _____ _____ ❏ C ❏ R
                ❏ Direct   ❏ Consult

❏ _____ From_____ To _____ _____ _____ ❏ C ❏ R
                ❏ Direct   ❏ Consult

❏ Transportation _____

❏ Specialized equipment/services _____
_____

EXTENDED SCHOOL YEAR

❏ Does not require special education and related services in excess of the regular academic year.
❏ Recommended based upon unique or severe needs.

Program/DIS Service	**Dates (Month/Day/Year)**	**Frequency**	**Location**
❏ Special Day Class	From_____ To _____		
_____	From_____ To _____	_____	_____ ❏ C ❏ R
_____	From_____ To _____	_____	_____ ❏ C ❏ R
_____	From_____ To _____	_____	_____ ❏ C ❏ R
_____	From_____ To _____	_____	_____ ❏ C ❏ R
Transportation	From_____ To _____	_____	

Distribution: White-Permanent File   Canary-Parent   Copies may be made for other team members

Student _____   Date of Meeting _____

ACCOMMODATIONS, MODIFICATIONS, AND GRADING

These are to assist the student in attaining the annual goals stated on the IEP as well as increasing the student's involvement and progress in the general curriculum.

Accommodations are adjustments for students with disabilities in instruction or student output that minimize the impact of the disability but do not fundamentally alter or lower course standards or expectations.

Modifications are adjustments for students with disabilities in instruction or student output that minimize the impact of the disability but fundamentally alter or lower course standards or expectations. **Grades** may be modified or a course description may be modified to reflect modified curriculum.

ACCOMMODATION	List specific COURSES	ACCOMMODATION	List specific COURSES
1. Highlighted Texts		13. Preferential Seating	
2. Taped Texts		14. Reduced Paper/Pencil Tasks	
3. Note-Taking Assistance		15. Repeated Review/Drill	
4. Taped Lectures		16. Alternative Materials/Assignments	
5. Peer Buddy		17. Assistive Technology	
6. Peer Tutor		18. Reader Services	
7. Assignment Notebooks		19. Calculator	
8. Extended Time for Completing Assignments		20. Study Sheets	
9. Shortened Assignments		21. Braille	
10. Frequent Breaks		22. Large Type	
11. Directions Given in a Variety of Ways		23. _____	
12. Increased Verbal Response		24. _____	

ACCOMMODATIONS FOR CLASSROOM OR DISTRICT TESTS OTHER THAN STATEWIDE - Specify Course(s)/Tests

1. Extended Time		4. Alternative Tests	
2. Oral Tests		5. Short-Answer Tests	
3. Alternative Setting		6.	

SUPPORTS FOR SCHOOL PERSONNEL

❏ Yes ❏ No   Are supports for school personnel needed for the student to advance appropriately toward attaining the annual goals, participate in the general curriculum, and be educated and participate with others in educational activities? If yes, specify what supports are needed. _____

Distribution: White-Permanent File   Canary-Parent   Copies may be made for other team members

Student _____ Date of Meeting _____

MARIN SELPA
IEP
Page 19
7/03

MODIFICATIONS - Use the codes below or use an additional page to describe modifications per course or content area		
CONTENT AREAS	**CODE**	**DESCRIPTION OF MODIFICATION OF CURRICULUM**
Reading		
Math		
Social Studies/History		
Science		
Language Arts		
Spelling		
Classroom or District Tests Other Than Statewide		

CODES
1. Out of Level Curriculum
2. Partial Curriculum (specify which concepts and standards are covered and which are omitted).
3. Individualized Curriculum, adapting standards to student's ability (attach description of curriculum concepts/ standards to be covered and expectations of student).

GRADES - Required if grade/course are to be modified

Which of the courses will result in a modified grade?

How does a modified grade show on the student's report card? On the student's transcript?

Does it affect honor roll or academic awards? ❏ Yes ❏ No   Does it affect class ranking? ❏ Yes ❏ No

Elementary and Middle School Students	**Middle School and High School Students**
Does the modified grade/course affect STAR testing? ❏ Yes ❏ No If "yes", what is the result? ❏ Student participates in STAR Testing with modifications ❏ Student participate in the CAPA	Does the modified grade/course affect credits towards high school graduation? ❏ Yes ❏ No If "yes", what is the result?
Does the modified grade/course affect Promotion/Retention? ❏ Yes ❏ No If "yes", what is the result? ❏ IEP Individualized Promotion Standards ❏	Does the modified grade/course affect ability to pass High School Exit Exam? ❏ Yes ❏ No If "yes", what is the result?

Reason for Modified Curriculum/Grade:
❏ Student requires utilization of SH Modified Alternative Curriculum Guide in a highly structured environment to acquire skills specified in their IEP.
❏ _____

I understand that my son/daughter will receive a modified grade in the subjects/courses listed above and I consent to the modification.
Parent/Guardian Signature _____ Date _____

Distribution: White-Permanent File   Canary-Parent   Copies may be made for other team members

Student _____ Date of Meeting _____

MARIN SELPA
IEP
Page 20a
7/03

PARTICIPATION IN STATEWIDE ASSESSMENT OF STUDENT ACHIEVEMENT - STAR TESTING

STAR Testing - Required for grades 2-11

❏ Student can participate in the statewide achievement testing program without accommodations/modifications.

Eligibility for the CAPA is based on a student's Individualized Education Program (IEP), which reflects an emphasis on functional life skills. To be eligible for participation in alternate assessment, the response to each of the statements below must be "Agree". If the answer to any of these questions is "Disagree", then the IEP team should consider including the student in the state's large-scale assessment.

Circle "Agree" or "Disagree" for each item:

Agree   Disagree   The student requires extensive instruction in multiple settings to acquire, maintain, and generalize skills necessary for application in school, work, home and community environments.

Agree   Disagree   The student demonstrates academic/cognitive ability and adaptive behavior that require substantial adjustments to the general curriculum. That student may participate in many of the same activities as their non-disabled peers; however, their learning objectives and expected outcomes focus on the functional applications of the general curriculum.

Agree   Disagree   The student cannot address the performance level assessed in the statewide assessment, even with extensive accommodations.

Agree   Disagree   The decision to participate in the alternate assessment is not primarily based on excessive or extended absences.

Agree   Disagree   The decision to participate in the alternate assessment is not primarily based on language, cultural or economic differences.

Agree   Disagree   The decision to participate in the alternate assessment is not primarily based deafness, blindness, visual, auditory, and/or motor disabilities.

Agree   Disagree   The decision to participate in the alternate assessment is not primarily based on achievement significantly lower than his or her same age peers.

Agree   Disagree   The decision to participate in the alternate assessment is not primarily based on a specific categorical label.

Agree   Disagree   The decision for alternate assessment is an IEP team decision, rather than an administrative decision.

❏ Student will participate in the California Alternate Performance Assessment (CAPA) at the level corresponding to his/ her grade level placement.

❏ Student will participate in the California Alternate Performance Assessment (CAPA) Level 1 because he/she:
  • is between the ages of seven and sixteen (grades 2-11) as of December 2
  • has severe, pervasive disabilities
  • functions at the sensorimotor developmental stage, approximately 24 months or less.

Distribution: White-Permanent File   Canary-Parent   Copies may be made for other team members

Student _____   Date of Meeting _____

MARIN SELPA
IEP
Page 20b
12/02

ACCOMMODATIONS/MODIFICATIONS FOR CALIFORNIA STATEWIDE ASSESSMENTS

❏ Student can participate in the statewide achievement testing program with the following ❏ accommodations ❏ modifications.

Accommodation/Modification	CAT/6	CST	SABE/2	CAHSEE	GSE	CELDT	Physical Fitness
Presentation							
Braille	2	2	2*	2	2	2*	Not Applicable
Large Print	2	2	2	2	2	2	Not Applicable
Use visual magnifying equipment	1	1	1	1	1	1	Not Applicable
Use audio amplication equipment	1	1	1	1	1	1	1
Simplify or clarify test directions	1	1	1	1	1	Not allowed on listening/speaking portion 2 Reading and writing portion	1
Use sign language to translate directions	2	2	2	2	2	2	2
Questions or items read aloud to student/audio presentation.	2 Except reading test 3 Reading test	2 Except ELA Test 3 ELA Test	2	2 Math portion 3** ELA Portion	2 Except reading, writing, and Spanish tests 3 Reading, writing, and Spanish tests	2 Writing portion only	Not Applicable
Use sign language to translate questions or items to student	2 Except reading test 3 Reading test	2 Except ELA Test 3 ELA Test		2 Math portion 3** ELA Portion	2 Except reading, writing, and Spanish tests 3 Reading, writing, and Spanish tests	2 Writing portion only	Not Applicable
Student highlights key words in test booklet	2	2	2	2	2	2	Not Applicable
On task reminders/verbal encouragement	1	1	1	1	1	1	1
Noise buffers	1	1	1	1	1	1	1
Turn pages for student	1	1	1	1	1	1	Not Applicable
Timing/Scheduling							
Extra time within a testing day	2	1	2	1	2	1	1
Test over more than one day (for test expected to be completed within one session)	2	2	2	2 Contact test contractor	2	2	2
Breaks within a subtest (supervised)	2	2	2	2	2	2	2
Administer at time most beneficial to student	2	2	2	2 Contact test contractor	2	2	2
Setting							
Test individually (supervised)	1	1	1	1	1	1	1
Test in small group	1	1	1	1	1	1	1
Provide special lighting	1	1	1	1	1	1	Not Applicable
Use adaptive furniture	1	1	1	1	1	1	Not Applicable
Test in study carrel/study enclosure	1	1	1	1	1	1	Not Applicable
Test at home or in hospital	2	2	2	2	2	2	2

Distribution: White-Permanent File   Canary-Parent   Copies may be made for other team members

Student _____   Date of Meeting _____

MARIN SELPA
IEP
Page 20c
12/02

ACCOMMODATIONS/MODIFICATIONS FOR CALIFORNIA STATEWIDE ASSESSMENTS - CONTINUED

Accommodation/Modification	CAT/6	CST	SABE/2	CAHSEE	GSE	CELDT	Physical Fitness
Response							
Student marks response in test booklet (adult transfers to answer document)	2	2	2	2	2	2	Not Applicable
Indicate responses to a scribe for selected response items	Not Applicable	2	2	2	2	2	Not Applicable
Indicate responses to a scribe for a writing test (student indicates all spelling and language conventions)	Not Applicable	2	Not Applicable	2	2	2	Not Applicable
Indicate responses to a scribe for a writing test (scribe provides spelling, grammar, and language conventions)	3	3	Not Applicable	3**	3	3	Not Applicable
Use of Aids or Tools							
Use dictionary	3	3	3	3**	3	3	Not Applicable
Use word processing software with spell and grammar check tools turned off	2	2	Not Applicable	2	2	2	Not Applicable
Use spellchecker, grammar checker, or word processing software that checks spelling and grammar	3	3	Not Applicable	3**	3	3	Not Applicable
Use assistive device that does not interfere with the independent work of the student	2	2	2	2	2	2	Not Applicable
Use assistive device that interferes with the independent work of the student	3	3	3	3**	3	3	Not Applicable
Use calculator (program disabled)	3	3	3	3**	3	3	Not Applicable
Use an arithmetic table	3	3	3	3**	3	3	Not Applicable
Use a marker or mask to maintain place	1	1	1	1	1	1	Not Applicable
Use colored overlay	1	1	1	1	1	1	Not Applicable
Other							
Out of Level Testing	Not allowed for grades 2-4 Limited to no more than two grade levels for grades 5 through 11	Not allowed for grades 2-4 Limited to no more than two grade levels for grades 5 through 11	Not allowed for grades 2-4 Limited to no more than two grade levels for grades 5 through 11	Not Applicable	Not Applicable	Not Applicable	Not Applicable
Unlisted accommodation or modification	Check with CDE	Check with CDE	Check with CDE	Check with CDE	Check with CDE	Check with CDE	Check with CDE

*Contact the California Department of Education to find out when a Braille version will be available.

**See waiver policy for the California High School Exit Exam

Category 1 - Testing condition available to students who regularly use it in the classroom

Category 2 - Accommodation available only to students with documentation in IEP or 504 plan

Category 3 - Modification (fundamentally alters what the test measures) available only to students with documentation in IEP or 504 plan

Distribution: White-Permanent File   Canary-Parent   Copies may be made for other team members

Student _____   Date _____

**MARIN
SELPA**
IEP
Page 21
7/03

CULMINATION GOAL (FOR SECONDARY STUDENTS)

A student's right to FAPE is terminated upon graduation with a regular high school diploma
Working toward: ❑ Diploma ❑ Certificate of Completion
Anticipated Date of Graduation/Culmination_____
Student has completed _____ units towards graduation.

For students with anticipated dates of graduation before 2003-2004 school year:
1. The District requires proficiency standards ❑ Yes ❑ No

For students with anticipated dates of graduation beginning with the 2003-2004 school year:
1. The High School Exit Exam has been passed: ❑ Math ❑ Reading and Writing
2. The District's prescribed course of study has been completed? ❑ Yes ❑ No
3. The student has demonstrated satisfactory attendance ❑ Yes ❑ No

---

PLAN TO TRANSITION FROM NPS OR SDC TO GENERAL CLASS PROGRAM

❑ Training for regular ed. teacher and/or other staff.
    Topic:_____
❑ Conference with parents and service providers to talk
    about the special needs of student.
❑ Discussion with students in the regular class.
        Topic:_____
❑ Behavior Plan for use in regular class (See page _____).
❑ Provide regular education assignments to student while
    still in special education class.

❑ Special education teacher, parent, and/or student visit
    the general education/special day class.
❑ General education class routine reviewed with student.
❑ Peer monitor from general education class assigned.
❑ Gradual transition into general education/special day
    class beginning on _____.
❑ _____
    _____

REFERRALS AND ACTIONS REQUIRED FOLLOWING THE IEP

Action	*Responsible Personnel and Position*	*By When*
❑ Transportation		
❑ Additional Assessment for _____		
❑ Additional Assessment for _____		
❑ Referral for AB 3632 Assessment		
❑ Copy of IEP to All Service Providers		
❑		
❑		
❑		
❑		
❑		
❑		

Distribution: White-Permanent File   Canary-Parent   Copies may be made for other team members

Student: _____ Date of Meeting _____

MARIN SELPA
IEP
Page 22___
6/01

REFERRALS AND/OR ADDITIONAL RECOMMENDATIONS/COMMENTS

Distribution: White-Permanent File   Canary-Parent   Copies may be made for other team members

Student _____ Date of Meeting _____

MARIN
SELPA
IEP
Page 23
7/03

This IEP document contains the following pages:
1❏ 2❏ 3❏ 4❏ 5❏ 6❏ 7❏ 8❏ 9❏ 10❏ 11❏ 12❏ 13❏ 14❏ 15❏ 16❏ 17❏ 18❏ 19❏
20a❏ 20b❏ 20c❏ 21❏ 22 ____ to ____ ❏ 23❏ and Goals and Objectives pages _____ through _____.

TEAM MEMBERS - The following persons affirm that they were in attendance at the IEP Meeeting

Administrator _____	Parent _____
Administrator _____	Parent _____
Administrator _____	Physical Therapist _____
Agency Rep. _____	Resource Specialist _____
Community Mental Health _____	SDC Teacher _____
CCS _____	Social Worker _____
District Representative _____	Speech/Language Specialist _____
Guidance Counselor _____	Student _____
Hearing Impaired Specialist _____	Teacher for the Visually Impaired _____
Nurse _____	Teacher _____
Psychologist _____	Teacher _____
Occupational Therapist _____	Translator/Interpreter _____
Orientation/Mobility Instructor _____	_____

❏   A copy of Procedural Safeguards was provided to the parent(s) with the notice of the IEP team meeting.
❏   Parent(s) given a copy of the IEP at no cost.
❏   Parent(s) given a copy of the ❏ evaluation report(s) and ❏ eligibility determination, if appropriate, at no cost.

PARENT DECISION/SIGNATURE

❏ I was notified of the IEP meeting and was able to attend; I have reviewed the IEP and consent to it.
❏ I was notified of the IEP meeting and was able to attend; I choose not to make a decision at this time. I have received a
    copy of the IEP and a copy of "Notification of IEP Recommendations".
❏ I agree and give my consent for the above recommendations to be implemented with the exception of:
        ❏ assessment   ❏ eligibility   ❏ goals and objectives   ❏ services   ❏ placement
_____
❏ I acknowledge that my child is not an individual with exceptional needs and thus not eligible for Special Ed. services.
❏ I disagree and wish to schedule: ❏ an IEP meeting ❏ informal meeting ❏ local mediation
                            ❏ prehearing mediation conference   ❏ state due process hearing
❏ I decline the services offered.
❏ I agree that the District has offered my child a free appropriate public education. However, I am voluntarily placing my
    child in a private school.
❏ I request a copy of the IEP to be provided in my primary language or alternative format (braille or tape recording).

_____   _____
Signature of Parent/Guardian Signature/Authorized Representative   Date

_____   _____
Signature of Parent/Guardian Signature/Authorized Representative   Date
Distribution: White-Permanent File   Canary-Parent   Copies may be made for other team members

Appendix 5

Tear-Out Forms

Request for Information on Special Education

Request to Begin Special Education Process and Assessment

Request for Child's School File

Request to Amend Child's School File

Special Education Contacts

IEP Journal

Monthly IEP Calendar

IEP Blueprint

Letter Requesting Assessment Report

Request for Joint IEP Eligibility/Program Meeting

Progress Chart

Program Visitation Request Letter

Class Visitation Checklist

Goals and Objectives Chart

IEP Material Organizer Form

IEP Meeting Participants

IEP Meeting Attendance Objection Letter

IEP Preparation Checklist

Letter Confirming Informal Negotiation

Letter Requesting Due Process

Request for Information on Special Education

Date: _____

To: _____

_____

_____

_____

Re: _____

I am writing to you because my child is experiencing difficulties in school. I understand there is a special process for evaluating a child and determining eligibility for special education programs and services. Please send me any written information you have about that process. Please also send me information about how I can contact other parents and local support groups involved in special education.

Thank you very much for your kind assistance. I look forward to talking with you further about special education.

Sincerely,

_____

_____

_____

_____

_____

NOLO
www.nolo.com
Request for Information on Special Education

Request to Begin Special Education Process and Assessment

Date: _____

To: _____

_____

_____

_____

Re: _____

I am writing to you because my child is experiencing difficulties in school. _____

_____

_____

_____

_____

_____ .

I am formally requesting that the school immediately begin its special education process, including initial assessment for eligibility. I understand that you will send me an assessment plan explaining the tests that may be given to my child. Because I realize the assessment can take some time, I would appreciate receiving the assessment plan within ten days. Once you receive my approval for the assessment, would you please let me know when the assessment will be scheduled?

I would also appreciate any other information you have regarding the assessment, how eligibility is determined, and the general IEP process.

Thank you very much for your kind assistance. I look forward to working with you and your staff.

Sincerely,

_____

_____

_____

_____

_____

Request for Child's School File

Date: _____

To: _____

_____

_____

_____

Re: _____

I would like a copy of my child's records, including all tests, reports, assessments, grades, notes by teachers or other staff members, memoranda, photographs—in short, *everything* in my child's school file. I understand I have a right to these files under _____

_____

_____

_____

_____ .

I would greatly appreciate having these files within the next five days. I would be happy to pick them up. I will call you to discuss how and when I will get copies.

Thank you for your kind assistance.

Sincerely,

_____

_____

_____

_____

_____

Request to Amend Child's School File

Date: _____

To: _____

_____

_____

_____

Re: _____

I recently reviewed a copy of my child's file and would like to have a portion of the file amended, specifically:

_____

_____

_____

_____

_____

_____ .

IDEA provides that I have the right to request that all information that is "inaccurate or misleading, or violates the privacy of [my] child" be amended. (34 C.F.R. § 300.567.) I feel that this is just such a case. Therefore, I request that you immediately rectify the situation.

Please notify me in writing as soon as possible of your decision regarding this matter. Thank you.

Sincerely,

_____

_____

_____ .

_____

Special Education Contacts

School Staff

_____

_____

_____

_____

_____

_____

Outside Professionals

_____

_____

_____

_____

_____

_____

Other Parents

_____

_____

_____

_____

_____

Support Groups

_____

_____

State Department of Education

_____

_____

_____

Other

_____

_____

_____

_____

IEP Journal

Date: _____ **Time:** _____ a.m./p.m.

Action: ☐ Phone Call _____ ☐ Meeting _____

☐ Other: _____

Person(s) Contacted: _____

Notes: _____

_____

_____

_____

_____

_____

_____

_____

_____

_____

_____

IEP Journal

Date: _____ **Time:** _____ a.m./p.m.

Action: ☐ Phone Call _____ ☐ Meeting _____

☐ Other: _____

Person(s) Contacted: _____

Notes: _____

_____

_____

_____

_____

_____

_____

_____

_____

_____

_____

Monthly IEP Calendar

Month and Year: _____

1	2	3	4	5	6	7
8	9	10	11	12	13	14
15	16	17	18	19	20	21
22	23	24	25	26	27	28
29	30	31				

NOLO
www.nolo.com

IEP Blueprint

The IEP Blueprint represents the ideal IEP for your child. Use it as a guide to make and record the educational desires you have for your child.

Areas of the IEP	Preferred Situation for Your Child

1. Classroom Setting and Peer Needs— issues to consider:

☐ regular versus special education class

☐ partially or fully mainstreamed

☐ type of special education class

☐ number of children in the classroom

☐ ages and cognitive ranges of children in class

☐ kinds of students and behaviors that might or might not be appropriate for your child, and

☐ language similarities.

2. Teacher and Staff Needs—issues to consider:

☐ number of teachers and aides

☐ teacher-pupil ratio

☐ experience, training, and expertise of the teacher, and

☐ training and expertise of aides.

3. Curricula and Teaching Methodology— be specific. If you don't know what you *do* want, specify what you *don't* want.

Areas of the IEP	Ideal Situation for Your Child

4. Related Services—issues to consider:

☐ specific needed services

_____

_____

☐ type of services

_____

_____

☐ frequency of services, and

_____

_____

☐ length of services.

_____

_____

5. Identified Programs—specify known programs that you think would work for your child and the school that offers them.

_____

_____

_____

_____

_____

_____

6. Goals and Objectives—goals are long range in nature, while objectives are more short term.

_____

_____

_____

_____

_____

_____

_____

_____

7. Classroom Environment and Other Features—issues to consider:

☐ distance from home

_____

_____

☐ transition plans for mainstreaming

_____

_____

☐ vocational needs

_____

_____

☐ extracurricular and social needs, and

_____

_____

☐ environmental needs.

_____

_____

Letter Requesting Assessment Report

Date: _____

To: _____

_____

_____

_____

Re: _____

I appreciate your involvement in my child's assessment and look forward to your report. Would you please:

1. Send me a copy of a draft of your report before you finalize it. As you can imagine, the process can be overwhelming for parents. It would be most helpful to me to see your report, because the proposed tests are complicated and I need time to evaluate the results.

2. Send me your final report at least four weeks before the IEP meeting.

Again, thank you for your kind assistance.

Sincerely,

_____

_____

_____

_____

_____

Request for Joint IEP Eligibility/Program Meeting

Date: _____

To: _____

_____

_____

_____

Re: _____

I believe there is sufficient information for us to discuss both my child's eligibility for special education and the specifics of my child's IEP at the same meeting. I would appreciate it if you would plan enough time to discuss both those important items at the _____ IEP meeting. I would also like to see any and all reports and other written material that you will be introducing at the IEP meeting, at least two weeks before the meeting.

Thanks in advance for your help. I hope to hear from you soon.

Sincerely,

_____

_____

_____

_____

_____

Progress Chart

Student: _____

Class: _____

Date: _____

Key Goals and Objectives	Current Status	Comments
Math	Progressing appropriately? ☐ yes ☐ no	_____ _____ _____
Reading	Progressing appropriately? ☐ yes ☐ no	_____ _____ _____
Writing	Progressing appropriately? ☐ yes ☐ no	_____ _____ _____
Spelling	Progressing appropriately? ☐ yes ☐ no	_____ _____ _____
Social-Behavioral	Progressing appropriately? ☐ yes ☐ no	_____ _____ _____
Language development	Progressing appropriately? ☐ yes ☐ no	_____ _____ _____
Motor development	Progressing appropriately? ☐ yes ☐ no	_____ _____ _____
Other	Progressing appropriately? ☐ yes ☐ no	_____ _____ _____

Program Visitation Request Letter

Date: _____

To: _____

_____

_____

_____

Re: _____

I appreciate the concerns you have and realize that you can't know which programs are appropriate for my child until after the IEP meeting. Nonetheless, I think it would be very helpful for me to see existing programs so I can be a more effective member of the IEP team. I do not feel I can make an informed IEP decision without seeing, first-hand, all possible options. I want to assure you that I understand that by giving me the names of existing programs, you are not stating an opinion as to their appropriateness for my child.

I assure you that I will abide by all rules and regulations for parental visits. If those rules and regulations are in writing, please send me a copy.

Thanks in advance for your help. I hope to hear from you soon.

Sincerely,

_____

_____

_____

_____

_____

Class Visitation Checklist

Date: _____ Time: _____ a.m./p.m.

School: _____

Class: _____

Student Description:

Total students: _____ Gender range: _____

Age range: _____

Cognitive range: _____

_____

_____

Language/communication range: _____

_____

_____

_____

Disability range: _____

_____

_____

_____

Behavioral range: _____

_____

_____

_____

Other observations: _____

_____

_____

_____

Staff Description:

Teachers: _____

_____

_____

_____

Aides: _____

_____

_____

_____

Other observations: _____

_____

_____

_____

Curricula/Classroom Strategies:

Curricula: _____

_____

_____

_____

Strategies: _____

_____

_____

_____

_____

Classroom Environment:

Description: _____

_____

_____

_____

_____

_____

Related Services:

_____

_____

_____

Other Comments:

_____

_____

_____

_____

_____

How This Program Relates to IEP Blueprint:

_____

_____

_____

_____

_____

_____

Goals and Objectives Chart

Skill Area	Annual Goal	Short-Term Objective (or Benchmark)	Present Performance Level	How Progress Measured	Date of Completion
Reading					
Math					
Emotional and psychological					

Goals and Objectives Chart

Skill Area	Annual Goal	Short-Term Objective (or Benchmark)	Present Performance Level	How Progress Measured	Date of Completion
Social-behavioral					
Linguistic and communication					
Self-help and independent living skills (transition services)					

Goals and Objectives Chart

NOLO
△ www.nolo.com

IEP Material Organizer Form

Use this form to track documents and persons that provide support for or opposition to your goals.

Issue: _____

Document or Witness* Name(s):	Binder Location (if applicable)	Helps You	Hurts You	Key Supportive or Oppositional Information	Rebuttal Document or Witness Name(s) (If hurts) (If none, what will you say at meeting?)

* A "witness" is someone (teacher, doctor, assessor, tutor, psychologist) who gives an oral or written opinion regarding your child's needs at the IEP meeting.

www.nolo.com

IEP Material Organizer Form

IEP Meeting Participants

Name	Position/Employer	Purpose for Attending	Point of View

 www.nolo.com

IEP Meeting Attendance Objection Letter

Date: _____

To: _____

_____

_____

_____

Re: _____

I understand that _____,

will be at _____ IEP meeting. _____

knows nothing about _____ and appears to have no knowledge that

might be of use to the IEP team. I am formally requesting that _____

not attend, unless there is some clear reason that makes _____

attendance appropriate and necessary for the development of _____

IEP plan. As you know, IEP meetings can be particularly difficult for parents. We are already anxious about ours and would prefer that you not take action that will heighten our stress level.

If you insist on _____ attending without any reason, then we will file a complaint with the state and federal departments of education.

I will call you in a few days to find out your decision on this issue. Thank you for considering my request.

Sincerely,

_____

_____

_____

_____

_____

IEP Preparation Checklist

☐ Find out the date, time, and location.

☐ Get a copy of the school's agenda.

☐ Make your own agenda.

☐ Prepare your IEP Material Organizer.

☐ Draft IEP plan.

☐ Find out who is attending on behalf of school district.

☐ Invite and prepare your own IEP participants.

☐ Give the school a copy of the following:

    ☐ independent assessments

    ☐ documents such as reports and work samples

    ☐ names and titles of people attending IEP, and

    ☐ notice of intent to tape record IEP meeting (if applicable)

☐ Create a meeting reminder list of items you want to be sure to remember.

Letter Confirming Informal Negotiation

Date: _____

To: _____

_____

_____

_____

Re: _____

I appreciated the chance to meet on _____ and discuss
_____. I also appreciated your
point of view and the manner in which we solved the problem.

I want to confirm our agreement that _____
_____
_____
_____ .

I greatly appreciate the manner in which you helped solve this problem. _____
_____
_____
_____ .

Thank you.

Sincerely,

_____

_____

_____

_____

_____

Letter Requesting Due Process

Date: _____

To: _____

      _____

      _____

      _____

Re: _____

_____

_____

We are formally requesting due process, beginning with mediation. We believe _____

_____

_____

_____ .

We believe an appropriate solution would include, but should not be limited to, the following:

_____

_____

_____

_____

_____ .

We understand IDEA (34 C.F.R. § 300.511) requires that a fair hearing decision be rendered within 45 days after you receive this request. We would appreciate it if you would contact us at once to schedule the mediation.

Sincerely,

_____

_____

_____

_____

_____

Index